THE STAUFFER SYMPOSIUM
ON APPLIED PSYCHOLOGY
AT THE CLAREMENT COLLEGES

ries of volumes highlight important new developments on the lead-
e of applied psychology. Each volume focuses on one area in which
logical knowledge is being applied to the resolution of social prob-
ithin that area, a distinguished group of authorities present chap-
mmarizing recent theoretical views or empirical findings, including
lts of their own research and applied activities. An introductory
frames the material, pointing out common themes and varied areas
ical applications. Thus, each volume brings together trenchant new
search results, and fruitful applications bearing on an area of cur-
ial interest. The volumes will be of value not only to practitioners
archers, but also to students and lay people interested in this vital
anding area of psychology.

ries books published by Lawrence Erlbaum Associates:

uating Social Programs and Problems: Visions for the New Millennium,
d by Stewart I. Donaldson and Michael Scriven (2002).

ied Psychology: New Frontiers and Rewarding Careers, edited by Stew-
Donaldson, Dale E. Berger, and Kath Pezdek (2006).

D1116935

This se
ing edg
psycho
lems. W
ters su
the res
chapter
of pract
ideas, re
rent soc
and rese
and exp

APPLIED PSYCHO

*New Frontiers
and Rewarding Care*

S

- *Eval
  edite
- *Appl
  art l.

APPLIED PSYCHOLOGY

*New Frontiers
and Rewarding Careers*

Edited by

**Stewart I. Donaldson
Dale E. Berger
Kathy Pezdek**
Claremont Graduate University

LEA LAWRENCE ERLBAUM ASSOCIATES, PUBLISHERS
2006 Mahwah, New Jersey   London

Lawrence Erlbaum Associates, Inc., Publishers
10 Industrial Avenue
Mahwah, New Jersey 07430
www.erlbaum.com

Cover design by Kathryn Houghtaling Lacey

Library of Congress Cataloging-in-Publication Data

Applied psychology : new frontiers and rewarding careers / edited by Stewart I.
  Donaldson, Dale E. Berger, Kathy Pezdek.
     p. cm.
  Includes bibliographical references and index.
  ISBN: 0-8058-5348-0 (alk. paper)
  ISBN: 0-8058-5349-9 (pbk. : alk. paper)
  1. Psychology, Applied 2. Psychology, Applied—Vocational guidance. I. Donaldson,
Stewart I. (Stewart Ian). II. Berger, Dale E. III. Pezdek, Kathy.

BF636.A63 2006
158—dc22   2005055499
                                                                     CIP

Printed in the United States of America
10 9 8 7 6 5 4 3 2 1

Dedicated to Agents of Social Change

This volume is dedicated to our passionate students and colleagues
—past, present, and future—
who devote their talents and careers
to educating and improving the lives of others.

Contents

Preface

The image on the cover is intended to express our enthusiasm and understanding about the rise and promise of applied psychology. A growing global network with many intersecting connections enhanced by rapidly evolving information technologies is facilitating a quantum leap in opportunities for positive applications of psychological science worldwide.

The power of applied psychological science is no longer in question. Unfortunately, principles and methods of psychological science can and have been used to manipulate, persuade, and coerce for purposes of greed, corruption, and personal and political gain. We feel it is our responsibility to caution and remind you that applied psychology without humane values can be dangerous and destructive, as we have witnessed at times throughout history.

However, this volume aspires to demonstrate how psychologists have harnessed the power of applied psychology to promote human welfare and optimal human functioning, and to prevent and ameliorate a wide range of human and social problems. We strongly believe that after you read this volume you will agree that psychology indeed does matter, and it will continue to grow in its contribution to improving the way we work and live across the global landscape well into the 21st century.

In this volume you will discover an amazing range of recent positive applications and achievements of the discipline and profession of psychology. One purpose of this work was to provide an outlet for some of the most prominent psychologists responsible for advancing scientific psychology and promoting its growth, to share with us their views about pathways for using scientific psychology to promote human welfare and social betterment. This journey, guided by intellectual giants who are concerned about using scientific psychology to improve the human condition around the world, is intended to be inspirational, and promises to illuminate for you that a future has never been brighter for undergraduate psychology majors interested in careers applying the science of psychology.

This book is intended as a supplementary reader for introductory psychology courses, as well as one of the main readers for a range of intermediate and advanced undergraduate and graduate courses. This book can be used to illustrate for students the relevance of psychology as a discipline, and to demonstrate the opportunities that now exist to use their psychology education to promote human welfare across a wide range of settings.

We also believe this book will be of value to psychologists interested in state-of-the-art applications of psychological theory and research. For example, psychologists considering new career options, or mentoring others interested in nonacademic scientific careers are likely to rely on this resource. Finally, we expect that graduate programs in applied psychology and campus career centers will use this volume to inform prospective graduate students of the opportunities that now exist within the discipline and profession of psychology.

The editors of this volume express their sincere thanks to The John Stauffer Charitable Trust for providing the resources that made this symposium and volume possible, and to symposium presenters and chapter authors for their outstanding work and unwavering commitment to using psychological science to improve the plight of humankind.

Special thanks go to Paul Thomas and his impressive team of Claremont Graduate University students for making the 2nd Stauffer Symposium on Applied Psychology a smashing success. They skillfully assisted more than 465 participants and helped them enjoy and become engaged in the day-long symposium focused on *"The Rise of Applied Psychology: Rewarding Careers and New Frontiers for Improving the Human Condition."* We owe a sincere debt of gratitude to our graduate assistant, Shanelle Boyle, for her endless devotion to helping us edit and finalize the production of this manuscript. Finally, we are grateful for the helpful reviews and suggestions for improvement provided by Thomas F. Pettigrew, University of California at Santa Cruz, P. Wesley Schultz, California State University at San Marcos, and Debra Riegert of Lawrence Erlbaum Associates, Inc.

Please allow your imagination to help you engage the ideas contained in this book. We hope they inspire you to dream about ways you can apply the science of psychology in your career for the purposes of human and social betterment, becoming an agent of positive social change.

—*Stewart I. Donaldson*
—*Dale E. Berger*
—*Kathy Pezdek*

INTRODUCTION

1

The Rise and Promise of Applied Psychology in the 21st Century

Stewart I. Donaldson
Dale E. Berger
Claremont Graduate University

Profound changes are occurring throughout the world in the new age of rapidly advancing information technology and globalization. The need for theory and research-based applications of the social sciences has never been greater, and is likely to grow even stronger as the 21st century unfolds. At least on the surface, applications of the social science discipline of psychology seem to be far outpacing other social sciences in terms of growth and impact on human welfare and social betterment. This volume will take you beneath the surface to discover important ways that psychology is growing as it continues to mature as a discipline and profession.

PSYCHOLOGY COMES OF AGE

Psychology has been extraordinarily successful at attracting the next generation of social scientists into the discipline. The growth of interest in psychology during the past three decades is most striking when we compare psychology to our sister social science disciplines of sociology, political science, and economics. Figure 1.1 shows the number of bachelor's degrees granted by year from 1970 to 2000 by discipline. Although there were fluctuations over this 30-year period, in 2000 psychology's sister disciplines conferred about the same number of bachelor's degrees as they did in 1970.

The growth in psychology as an undergraduate major is striking. In sharp contrast to the other social science disciplines, the number of bachelor's degrees conferred in psychology more than doubled, from 33,679 in 1970 to 74,060 in 2000 (U.S. Department of Education, 2005). Furthermore,

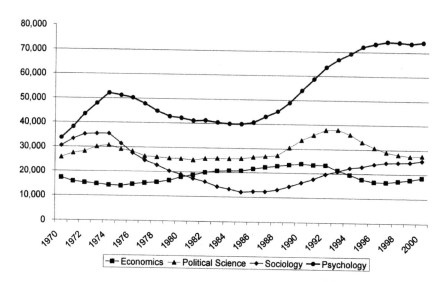

FIG. 1.1. Bachelor's degrees by year by discipline (USA).

the most recent data available show there were 76,671 bachelor's degrees awarded in psychology in 2002, the most ever, while the sister disciplines remained stable. This growth represents a remarkable achievement for the discipline of psychology, and it presents the discipline with an imposing opportunity. Each year in the past decade has produced 70,000 or more new college graduates with psychology degrees in the United States alone.

The success of psychology is even more remarkable when we consider graduate training. Again, our sister disciplines have no more than held their own over the past 30 years, with only modest fluctuations. In sharp contrast, Fig. 1.2 shows that the number of master's degrees each year in psychology has nearly tripled, rising from 5,158 in 1970 to 14,465 in 2000. In 2002, this number rose to 14,888 (U.S. Department of Education, 2005).

A similar pattern is seen in Fig. 1.3, which shows the number of doctorates granted per year (U.S. Department of Education, 2005). While our sister disciplines have not grown over the past 30 years, psychology has more than doubled the number of people entering the profession at the doctorate level each year. In recent years, more than 4,000 people earned doctoral degrees in psychology each year.

EMPLOYMENT TRENDS

Where do all these new psychology graduates find employment? Is the old stereotype true, that education in psychology is not practical, and typically leads to low-paying jobs and career paths? Does a degree in psychology

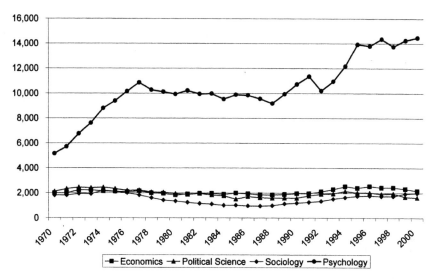

FIG. 1.2. Master's degrees by year by discipline (USA).

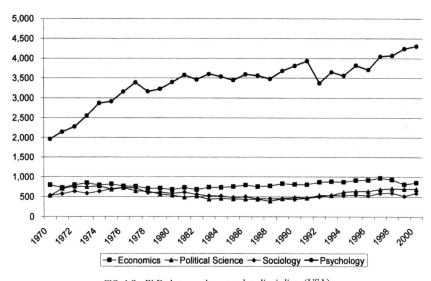

FIG. 1.3. PhD degrees by year by discipline (USA).

limit you to working in traditional counseling and mental health care service jobs and settings? Do PhD-level psychologists trained in the research areas only teach, write, and conduct research? The chapters in this volume provide compelling evidence that these old stereotypes of psychology are outdated and highly inaccurate. You will read about numerous ways that psychology majors now apply their education.

One special focus of this volume is identifying and describing personally rewarding and lucrative career opportunities that involve applying
the science of psychology. Approximately 60,000 new psychology graduates, or about 80% of those who earn bachelor's degrees in psychology in
the United States, enter the workforce each year (Fennell, 2002). Only 25%
of these new graduates report that they are working in psychology or a
closely related field. This fact suggests that every year approximately
45,000 new psychology graduates apply their education and skills across a
wide range of occupational settings outside of jobs traditionally associated with psychology:

- 41% in for-profit organizations
- 18% in federal government
- 11% in nonprofit organizations
- 10% in state and local government
- 7% in universities
- 13% in other educational organizations (Fennell, 2002).

There is also a trend toward more diverse careers applying the science
of psychology at the graduate level. Although it remains true that the majority (60%) of PhD-level psychologists are trained and work in the traditional mental health service areas of clinical, counseling, and school psychology, many more of the other 40% who are trained in the research areas
(e.g., social, personality, developmental, organizational) choose careers in
applied settings rather than university faculty positions (Fennell, 2002). For
example, in 1970 only 30% or approximately 600 new PhD-level research psychologists reported working outside the university in applied positions. By
2000, these numbers swelled to more than 2,100 as approximately 50% of
new PhDs in research psychology obtained applied positions over faculty
positions.

In summary, as psychology has blossomed as a discipline and profession
over the past three decades, far outpacing our closest sister disciplines,
students trained in psychology have found opportunities to apply their
skills in many new ways toward the betterment of society and human welfare. Opportunities for students entering the field of psychology have never
been greater than today.

APPLIED PSYCHOLOGY

It is clear that the field of psychology has grown and changed markedly
over the past generation. The field is now in the position of enjoying a powerful flow of undergraduates who are eager to develop careers where they

can use their training and follow their interests in psychology. The extraordinary growth of applied psychology, especially in applied areas of business, government, law, health, prevention, social change, and education, signals a momentous change in the role of psychology in society. The most prominent professional associations of psychologists have taken note of this change, and now commit significant time and resources to further the development of applied psychology.

The oldest international association of psychologists, the International Association of Applied Psychology (IAAP) continues to grow and now boasts more than 1,500 members from more than 80 countries. IAAP continues to be a global leader in sponsoring events and activities to fulfill its mission of promoting the science and practice of applied psychology, and facilitating interaction and communication about applied psychology around the world (see http://www.iaapsy.org). Additionally, the largest American psychological professional organizations have developed key initiatives aimed at elevating the profile and impact of scientific psychology in society. For example, the Human Capital Initiative and the Decade of Behavior are two notable initiatives that illustrate this new energy and value that has been placed on applying psychology to promote human welfare and achievement in society (American Psychological Association, 2005c; American Psychological Society, 2004).

In 1990 the American Psychological Society (APS) convened a Behavioral Science Summit with representatives from 65 psychological science associations, a group that eventually grew to include more than 100 organizations. These organizations unanimously endorsed the development of a national research agenda that would help policymakers set funding priorities for psychology and related sciences. The result was 'The Human Capital Initiative,' which outlined six areas of broad concern where psychological science could make substantial contributions:

- Productivity in the work place
- Schooling and literacy
- The aging society
- Drug and alcohol abuse
- Health
- Violence

Each of these areas presents issues that are fundamentally problems of human behavior. The Human Capital Initiative embraced the goal of coordinating efforts to apply social science to address these fundamental problems that transcend boundaries. A premise is that to achieve the goal of maximizing human potential, we need to know in scientific terms how people interact with their environment and each other—how we learn, remember, and express ourselves as individuals and in groups—and we need to know and understand the factors that influence and modify these behaviors. This effort has motivated an agenda for basic research and funding policies, and it has supported applications of psychological science outside of the university.

More recently, the years of 2000–2010 have been designated as the Decade of Behavior. Virtually all of the same organizations plus many international organizations are participating in this enterprise. The Decade of Behavior is a multidisciplinary initiative to focus the talents, energy, and creativity of the behavioral and social sciences on meeting many of society's most significant challenges. Behavioral and social scientists are encouraged to bring their research results forward to help inform the public and the public policy process about the Decade's five major themes:

- Improving health
- Increasing safety
- Improving education
- Increasing prosperity
- Promoting democracy

The goals of this initiative are to educate the public about the importance and relevance of behavioral and social science research, to translate research findings into public policy, to generate new knowledge relevant to current problems, and to recruit the next generation of scholars into the behavioral and social sciences (APA, 2005c).

In recent years, the American Psychological Association (APA) and American Psychological Society (APS) have also developed activities and initiatives to help students understand the diverse opportunities that now exist within psychology (APA, 2005b; Romero, 2003). APA regularly features articles and information about applied psychology graduate training at both the master's and doctoral level on their Web site (APA, 2005a). Table 1.1 displays APA's growing list of graduate programs that specifically train scientific psychologists for nonacademic careers.

Students considering a career in applied psychology often report that it is very difficult to identify and understand the specific career and job opportunities that exist in applied psychology. After all, unlike most professions, there are very few job ads with the obvious title of "Looking for an Applied Scientific Psychologist." APA has recently engaged in a project to help address this problem. The Interesting Careers in Psychology for Non-

TABLE 1.1

Nonacademic Careers for Scientific Psychologists:
Graduate Programs in Applied Psychology

Applied Cognition

Claremont Graduate University
George Mason University
Georgia, The University of
Maryland–College Park, University of
Missouri–Columbia, University of
Oklahoma, University of

Applied Developmental Psychology

Boston College
Bryn Mawr College
Claremont Graduate University
Connecticut, University of
Fordham University
George Mason University
Georgia State University
Guelph, University of
Illinois–Urbana-Champaign, University of
Houston, University of
Maryland–Baltimore County, University of
Memphis, University of
Miami, University of
Nebraska–Omaha, University of
New Orleans, University of
Notre Dame, University of
Peabody College, Vanderbilt University
Portland State University
Stanford University
Tennessee, University of
Tufts University
York University

Applied Experimental Psychology

New Orleans, University of
Nevada–Las Vegas, University of
Portland State University
Southern Illinois University at Carbondale

Applied Industrial/Organizational Psychology

Claremont Graduate University
George Mason University
Georgia, The University of
Portland State University
San Diego State University
Oklahoma, University of

(Continued)

TABLE 1.1
(Continued)

Applied Social Psychology

Brigham Young University
British Columbia, University of
City University of New York Graduate School
Claremont Graduate University
Colorado State University
Connecticut, University of
George Washington University
Guelph, University of
Iowa State University
Kentucky, University of
Loyola University, Chicago
Miami University of Ohio
Missouri–Columbia, University of
New Mexico State University
Northern Illinois University
Oklahoma, University of
Peabody College, Vanderbilt University
Portland State University
St. Louis University
Southern California Medical School, University of
Syracuse University
Wayne State University
Windsor, University of
York University

Program Evaluation

Claremont Graduate University
San Diego State University

Academic Scientific Psychologists project begins with the following question:

> True or False? The only career option for a scientifically trained psychologist is a faculty position in a college or university.
> The answer is a resounding False!

In this project, APA project members have produced an *Interesting Careers in Psychology* series to illustrate the various skill-sets and expertise that scientifically trained psychologists possess which are also highly valued by employers outside of academe (APA, 2005b). "The non-traditional career paths represented by these personal success stories illustrate the different types of unique contributions made by scientific psychologists in many different employment settings" (APA, 2005b). Table 1.2 presents occupations

TABLE 1.2
Nonacademic Careers for Scientific Psychologists:
Interesting Careers in Psychology

- Acquisitions Editor
- Research Psychologist in a Medical School
- Research Director for a Non-Profit Organization
- An Experimental Psychologist in a Behavioral Science Research Firm
- Medical Error Consultant
- A Social Psychologist in Rehabilitation Technology
- Psychology Emerges in a Multimedia World
- Engineering Psychology in Research and Development
- Becoming a Science Writer
- Technology Consultant in the Telecom Industry
- Social Science Analyst in the Public Sector
- Research Psychology at Microsoft
- Human–Computer Interface Designer
- Cognitive and I/O Psychologists in the Technology Industry
- Highway Safety Research Analyst
- Policy Scientist as an Independent Consultant
- International Market Research Consultant
- Human Factors Expert
- Statistical and Methodological Consultant
- A Psychologist in the White House
- Police Psychology in the Federal Government
- Clinical Neuropsycho-pharmacologist
- Market Research Consultant
- Human Factors Psychologist in Aviation
- Academic Research Administrator
- Science Museum Education and Research Specialist
- Chemical Senses Scientist
- NASA Research Scientist
- University Provost
- NASA Research Psychologist
- Animal Programs Psychologist
- Design Psychologist
- Foundation Executive
- A Forensic Psychologist in the FBI
- Federal Regulatory Officer for Protection of Human Subjects
- Human Resources Research Organization
- Corporate Investment Strategist for the Military
- Federal Drug Science Specialist
- Executive Search Consultant
- Organizational Development Consultant
- A Neuropsychologist Prospers in Pharmaceuticals
- Trial Consultant
- Policy Scientist for a Federal Agency
- Aviation Human Factors Practitioner
- Expert Witness in Employment Discrimination Cases
- Psychology Meets Philanthropy

and interviews that are posted on the APA applied psychology Web pages as part of this project (see http://www.apa.org/science/nonacad_careers .html). These interviews provide excellent examples and information about how to develop a career in applied psychology.

Claremont Graduate University (CGU) recently completed a project along these same lines to get even more specific about job titles and organizations that employ graduates trained specifically for careers applying the science of psychology (see http://www.cgu.edu/pages/675.asp). CGU is known as one of the pioneer institutions with more than three decades of experience in providing applied psychology graduate programs across a range of domains (e.g., social, organizational, cognitive, developmental, human resources, and program evaluation). The Claremont Alumni Project involved identifying alumni Web pages to determine their current job title and employer. Again, the purpose of this project was to provide specific examples of job and career possibilities for those trained in applied psychology. A sample of jobs held by Claremont Graduate University alumni is presented in Table 1.3. This project and the various projects described above represent just a few examples of exciting developments that are leading to a better understanding of the growing opportunities for careers for psychologists outside of clinical and traditional academic settings.

DEEPENING OUR UNDERSTANDING OF APPLIED PSYCHOLOGY

The trends and developments described earlier set the context for the main event. The purpose of this project and volume is to hear directly from some of the individuals responsible for advancing scientific psychology and promoting its growth, to learn their views about the progress and promise of using scientific psychology to promote human welfare and social betterment throughout the 21st century.

To accomplish this goal, the editors of this volume invited a wide range of psychologists to Claremont to participate in a symposium on *"The Rise of Applied Psychology: Rewarding Careers and New Frontiers for Improving the Human Condition."* The 2nd Stauffer Symposium on Applied Psychology at Claremont Graduate University was a smashing success, with more than 465 participants gathering on a beautiful Southern California day in the newly renovated Garrison Theater. Guests from San Diego to Seattle and from Santa Barbara to New York came to hear about how psychological science is now being used to improve many aspects of American society, as well as to prevent the spread of HIV and other social problems in many other parts of the world. Participants learned about classic and cutting-edge work in areas such as self-efficacy-based programming via the mass

TABLE 1.3

A Sample of Job Titles of Claremont Graduate
University Psychology Alumni Working in Nonacademic Settings

Leadership Positions

- President (former), University of New Hampshire
- Associate Vice Chancellor, University of North Carolina, Chapel Hill
- Provost, Chief Academic Officer, Azusa Pacific University
- Dean & Chair of Psychology, Claremont Graduate University
- Vice President, Ethan C. Eldon Associates, Inc.
- President & Co-founder, Oregon Center for Applied Science
- Senior Vice President, Moore & Associates, Bellevue, WA
- Regional Director, Providence Health System, Portland, Oregon
- Chair & Professor of Psychology, Whittier College
- Director of Care Management, Kaiser Permanente
- Associate Vice President, C.H. Dean & Associates
- CEO and Owner, The Advocacy and Learning Associates
- President, Freedom Adult Foster Care
- Vice President, Organizational Development, Banco Santiago
- Senior Principal and Head Regional Health Care, William M. Mercer, Inc.
- President, Coffin, DeLao & Associates
- Senior Vice President of Human Resources, Associated Securities Corp.
- Founder & Director, Health Horizon
- President, Foundation for Behavioral Health
- Director of Institutional Research, University of La Verne
- Owner, Sun Publishers
- Director, Pacific Institute for Research and Evaluation
- President, Lilian Abrams, Ph.D. & Associates, Passaic, NJ
- CEO, Metro Dynamics, Inc.
- Director, Neurobehavioral Outpatient Clinic, John Hopkins University
- Director of Research Operations, Maritz Marketing Research
- President, Justice Policy Research Corporation
- President, Human Resource Software
- Owner, Visual Realization Consulting
- Director of Consulting Services, Lodestar Management/Research
- CEO and Founder, Naseehah Associates
- Executive Director, Claremont Information and Technology Institute
- Director of Outcome Research/Professor, Kessler Institute for Rehabilitation Research
- Principal and Managing Director, Applied Research-West, Inc.
- Executive Director, Information Technology, Loyola Marymount University
- Chief Technical Officer, Catenas, Inc.
- Executive Director, Los Angeles County Mental Health
- Chairperson & President, Development, Legacy Interactive, Inc.
- Director of Psychotherapy Program, VA Medical Center
- Chair, Department of Psychology, Vanguard
- Director, OCC Transport
- President, MGP Enterprises, Inc.
- President & Founder, Momentum Market Intelligence (MMI), Portland, Oregon
- Executive Director, Creative Alternative Learning
- Director, North West Government
- President, McCoy Productions
- Interim President, Earlham College

(Continued)

TABLE 1.3
(Continued)

Leadership Positions (cont.)

- Co-Owner, Profile Associates
- Chief Executive Officer, Media Integration, Inc.
- President, St. Croix Consulting Services
- Distinguished Chair of Psychology & Professor, Grossmont College
- President, Nofsinger Strayer Consulting, Seattle, WA
- Chair & Professor of Psychology, Santa Barbara City College
- Owner, Network Personnel Service, Hermosa Beach
- Executive Director, Lanterman Developmental Center, Pomona, California
- Associate Dean of Administration & Professor, Rosemead School of Psychology
- Director of Human Resources, the Clorox Company, Oakland, CA
- Chief Executive Officer, Chess Kings International
- Owner, Pool Service Technicians
- Chief Operating Officer, Rose Hills Company
- Director, Development Research & Programs, Inc.
- President & Owner, Frantz Cleaners
- Chief Information Officer, Franklin University
- Director of Human Resources, Summa Industries
- Program Director, Small Business Innovation Research, NIH
- Senior Vice President, Leiberman Research Worldwide
- Chief People Officer, Harmonic Communications Corp.
- President, Labor Temps, Inc.
- Director of Administrative Computing, Harvey Mudd College
- Executive Vice President, Mental Health Resource Center
- Founder & Senior Principal, Learning in Action Technologies, Inc.
- Co-owner, Cenpro Consulting
- President, G.H. Smart & Company Management Consulting Firm
- Director, Health Outcomes Management Group, Reimbursement Dynamics, Inc.
- Department Chair, Management & Human Resources, College of Business, California State Polytechnic University, Pomona
- Department Head, House Ear Institute: Advance Hearing Science
- Project Manager, Rockwell International Corporation, Paradise, CA
- Assistant Director, Senior Meals and Services Inc.
- Manager, Health Research, Health Net
- President/Partner, Nofsinger Strayer Consulting, Seattle, WA
- CEO, Squire Consulting
- President, Travis Research Associates, Inc., Westlake Village, CA
- Director, PsyberMetrics, Langhorne, PA
- Project Manager, University of Washington
- Chair of Privilege and Tenure Committee/Professor, University of Colorado
- Special Project Manager, Premier Designs, Inc.
- Chief Executive Officer, Context Machines
- Vice President of Marketing, Dynaptics
- Manager, Orange County Office of the District Attorney
- Project Manager, American Marketing Services, Irvine Valley College
- Manager, KPMG Peat Marwick Foundation, Inc.
- P.O.S., Training Manager, Robinsons-May
- Manager, Human Resources, Red Herring Communication

(Continued)

TABLE 1.3
(Continued)

Leadership Positions (cont.)

- Manager, Participation/Analysis, National Broadcasting Company
- Training & Recruitment Manager, Nabisco Biscuit Company
- Program Manager, Office of Juvenile Justice and Delinquency Prevention, U.S. Department Justice, Washington DC
- Associate Director, National Asian Pacific Center of Aging
- Managing Director, RHR International Management Consulting, Los Angeles, CA
- Program Director, Sonoma State University
- Managing Director, Northern California, Applied Research-West, Inc.
- Manager of Training & Development, Babson College
- Deputy Director, Delaware Drug and Alcohol Abuse Division
- Program Manager, HR, Southern California Edison
- Associate Director of Health Sciences, California State University, Long Beach
- Assistant Project Director, Scripps College
- Project Manager, Riverside County Sheriff's Department
- Program Manager, South Central Los Angeles Regional Center for Persons with Developmental Disabilities, Inc.
- Deputy Director, J. Paul Getty Museum
- Business Line Analysis Manager, Kaiser Permanente
- Information Systems Manager, Stanford University
- Senior Project Director, Market Probe, Inc.

Applied Research

- Research Social Scientist, Pacific Northwest Research Station, Anchorage, Alaska
- Human Factors and Ergonomics Specialist, IAC Industries
- Research Psychologist, Stanford University
- Research Psychologist, Behavioral Health Department Mental Health Service, Ventura County, California
- Researcher, Towers Perrin Global Management Consulting
- Senior Research Planning Analyst, Pasadena City College
- Research Technician, California State University, Northridge
- Research Psychologist, LA County Department of Mental Health
- Assistant Research Psychiatrist, University of California, Los Angeles
- Research Consultant, Data Recognition Corporation
- Research Psychologist, Navy Personnel R&D Center
- Research Psychologist, House Ear Institute
- Senior Research Associate, University of California, Berkeley
- Research Assistant, UCLA Harbor Medical Center
- Statistician, U.S. Food and Drug Administration
- Measurement Research Evaluation Specialist, National Endowment for Financial Education
- Senior Research Associate, Westat Research Corporation
- Research Psychologist, National Institute of Health
- Senior Research Assistant, University of California, Los Angeles
- Lab Assistant, University of California, Los Angeles
- Research Psychologist, Ventura County Behavioral Health
- Research Associate, DecisionQuest
- Research Assistant, Pitzer College
- Investigator, Los Amigos Research & Education Institute

TABLE 1.3
(Continued)

Applied Research (cont.)

- Senior Scientist, Mead Johnson Nutritionals, Procter & Gamble
- Research Associate, RMC Research Corporation
- Research Analyst, Los Angeles Unified School District
- Research Assistant, Institute for Research and Learning
- Research Psychologist, University of Michigan, Poverty Research & Training Center
- Research Analyst, Orange County Transit District
- Organizational Behavior Specialist, Haworth, Inc.
- Senior Statistician, J.D. Power and Associates
- Senior Research Analyst, Los Angeles Unified School District
- Research Psychologist, Pipeline Software, Inc., Newport Beach, CA
- Research Associate, Center for Mental Health Services
- Research & Evaluation Manager, California Department of Education
- Research Analyst, University of Washington
- Social Psychologist, RAND
- Research Psychologist, UCLA Integrated Substance Abuse Program
- Research Fellow, Pacific Island Development Program
- Research Psychologist, Navy Research & Development
- Senior Research Associate, Wayne Howard & Associates
- Research Associate, California State University
- Research Psychologist/Analyst, Riverside County Department of Mental Health
- Research Psychologist, San Bernardino County Office of Alcohol & Drug Programs
- Senior Research Analyst, Los Angeles Unified School District
- Senior Research Associate, UCLA Neuropsychiatry Institute
- Research Associate, Vanderbilt University
- Research Associate, Amplica, Inc.
- Research Psychologist, Parent Care
- Management & Budget Analyst, LA County Metropolitan Transport Authority
- Socio Economic Analysis, RDN, Inc.
- Health Service Research, Self-Employed
- Associate for Clinical Research, House Ear Institute
- Senior Associate, Northwest Regional Educational Lab, Oregon
- Research Psychologist, Research and Treatment Institute
- Research Psychologist, Hillview Mental Health Center

Consulting Positions

- Market Research & Consulting, Harris Interactive Corporate Headquarters
- Relocation Consultant, HR, ARCO-Atlantic Richfield Co.
- Management Consultant, Spencer Stuart Management Consulting
- Senior Consultant, Catalyst Consulting Team
- Organization Development Consultant, Palitz-Elliot and Associates
- Consultant, Custom Performance Solutions
- Consultant, Human Factors and Training
- Consultant, Accenture
- Consultant, Jorgenson HR
- Consultant, Lanterman Developmental Center, Pomona, California
- Consultant/Owner, WG Clark Company

(Continued)

TABLE 1.3
(Continued)

Consulting Positions (cont.)

- Consultant, Westbrook Health Services
- Research Consultant, Data Recognition Corporation
- Associate Consultant & Ergonomic Engineer, Humantech
- Paralegal/Workers Comp Consultant, Self-Employed
- Independent Consultant, ECCHO Consulting
- Consulting Psychologist, Behavioral Associates
- Trial Consultant, Self-Employed
- Consultant, California Department of Education

Human Resource Positions

- Human Resource Manager, CBC Industries, California
- Chief Recruiter, Viking Components
- Personnel Analyst, California Department of Justice
- Human Resources, Northrop Grumman Integrated Systems
- Employee Relations Manager, Chiron Vision
- Payroll Administrator, CA Commerce Bank
- HR Placement Counselor, Kaiser Permanente
- Personnel Manager, Toyota Motor Credit
- Employee Services Manager, Human Resources, Glendale Community College
- Human Resources Administrator, Unisource Worldwide
- Staff Specialist, Jet Propulsion Laboratory (JPL)
- Personnel Administrator, Alvarado Manufacturing Co.
- Assistant Director, Human Resources, Citrus Valley Health Partners
- Compensation Analyst, The Boeing Co.
- Human Resources, PALL Medical
- Human Resource Coordinator, R.R. Donnelley & Sons Co.
- Human Resource Coordinator, Simulation Sciences
- Human Resource Manager, CPC International
- Personnel Analyst, L.A. County Sanitation
- Senior Employee Relations Representative, Countrywide Funding Corporation
- Research Psychologist, PERSEREC

---

media, health promotion and disease prevention, work and family balance, law and psychology, career and organizational development, the science of learning and education, child development and parenting, racial and ethnic disparities in mental health, and the power of expectations in classrooms, clinics, corporations, and courtrooms. A range of rewarding and exciting new career opportunities for those with bachelor's, master's, or doctorate degrees in psychology were also presented and discussed.

This volume aspires to share with you, and to add to, some of the lively discourse and insights about the accomplishments and prospects for the future of applied psychology. All of the symposium speakers were asked to provide a chapter for this volume that shares some of their views about new frontiers and/or careers in applied psychology. The editors invited additional chapters from prominent psychologists working in some of the applied areas not represented at the symposium. Because there is great diversity in how psychologists approach applied psychology in their subdomains, we encouraged authors to express that diversity in how they structured and selected topics related to our theme.

FOUNDATIONS AND FRONTIERS

Philip G. Zimbardo provided us with a wonderful overview chapter (chap. 2) illustrating many ways that psychology is making a significant difference in our lives. He describes a sampling of tangible evidence that demonstrates how and why psychology matters. This chapter builds on and refers readers to the newly developed APA Web site that documents current operational uses of psychological research, theory, and methodology (its creation was Zimbardo's APA presidential initiative in 2003): www.Psychology Matters.org.

Next, in chapter 3, Albert Bandura illustrates how one of the most well researched and supported theories in psychology today, Social Cognitive Theory, is used to address urgent global health and social problems. The foundations of social cognitive theory are described in some detail, as well as their applications to psychology-based interventions that promote society-wide changes that better the lives of millions of people in Africa, Asia, and Latin America. This chapter exemplifies the power and potential of applied psychology to improve lives on a national and global scale. Bandura presents data that demonstrate effective interventions to promote national literacy, to prevent the spread of HIV, to improve the status and quality of life of women, and to promote environment sustainability by stemming population growth.

In chapter 4, Stuart Oskamp and P. Wesley Schultz show how psychological science can be applied to prevent looming ecological disaster. They have articulated a disturbing list of current threats to global ecological sustainability. More importantly, they describe how an accumulation of sound theory and research from psychology can be used to guide important steps toward sustainability. For example, you will learn how applied behavior analysis, social marketing programs, techniques of feedback and persuasion, and capitalizing on social norms and the Theory of Planned Behavior can be used to design effective interventions, and to influence public policy in proenvironmental directions.

Robert Rosenthal examines the history and diversity of research on interpersonal expectancy effects in chapter 5. He shows how one person's expectation for another person's behavior comes to serve as a self-fulfilling prophecy, which can dramatically affect learning in the classroom, health care services, research participants, corporate performance, and verdicts in the courtroom. This chapter illustrates how psychological science can uncover psychological principles that affect people and processes across a wide range of settings in modern society.

In chapter 6, Stanley Sue reports that racial and ethnic disparities and inequities in mental health services undermine the quality of care for African Americans, American Indians and Alaska Natives, Asian Americans and Pacific Islanders, and Hispanic Americans. After describing psychological research findings that uncover the nature of these disparities, he shows how applied psychological science can be used to provide more culturally sensitive, appropriate, and compatible mental health services. This chapter provides tangible examples of how psychological science can be used to uncover and address racial and ethnic bias and discrimination in our current health care system, overcoming methodological and conceptual problems inherent in this domain of applied psychological research.

Patricia M. Greenfield provides a useful example of how basic developmental psychology research has been used to provide cross-cultural training programs for educators (chap. 7). A major goal of the Bridging Cultures program she describes in some detail was to reduce cultural conflict between home and school. In chapter 7, you will find many grounded examples of how developmental psychological science is used to promote the well-being of students from diverse cultural backgrounds in the U.S. educational system. Finally, the chapter does an excellent job of showing the interplay between basic and applied research, and how basic developmental psychological science can be applied toward social betterment.

In chapter 8, Sherylle J. Tan and Diane F. Halpern discuss some of the challenges involved with using findings from psychological research to influence the public and public policy. In general, they argue that the public distrusts science and scientists, preferring to rely on their own personal experiences and anecdotes. The new frontier they explore in this chapter involves methods, strategies, and techniques for improving the acceptance and impact of psychological research in the public domain. The applied psychologist of the 21st century is challenged to better disseminate research findings, to build stronger partnerships with the media, to take a much stronger role in educating the public about psychological research, and to improve communication and collaboration with communities.

CAREERS

As we talk about the rise and promise of applied psychology with undergraduate students, prospective graduate students, and the next generation psychological scientists, students often wonder what kind of career options and opportunities might exist for them in applied psychology. Therefore, in the next set of chapters, we explicitly asked the authors to help the readers understand some of the career opportunities in their domain of applied psychology. Most of the chapters begin with an overview of the research and applications in an important subarea of psychology, and then provide a discussion of ways to get involved and to develop personally rewarding careers in applied psychology.

In chapter 9, Deborah Davis and Elizabeth F. Loftus demonstrate the rapid expansion of the involvement of psychologists at all levels of legal systems in America and across the world. They show how psychologists contribute at the very fundamental level of providing research evidence to courts and legislatures to help them choose wise social policies and effective laws to facilitate the common good. They describe a wide range of activities that applied psychologists are involved in, and show rather convincingly how our legal system provides a variety of interesting, challenging, and exciting careers for young psychologists interested in applying psychology to real-life issues. This chapter reviews activities and careers that are sure to inspire others to pursue careers in psychology and law.

Howard S. Friedman, in chapter 10, shows how psychological science is used to promote health and well-being across a wide range of settings in modern societies. He emphasizes three domains where psychological science is responsible for promoting health: establishing connections between mental and physical health; changing habits and behaviors to promote health or avoid risk; and using psychological science to improve health care delivery. After exploring a wide range of research literatures and applications in these areas, career opportunities for applied health psychologists are provided. This chapter clearly illustrates many applications of health psychology, and reveals many career settings such as government organizations, medical facilities and universities, public health agencies, and businesses and private companies.

In chapter 11, Kathy Pezdek, Kenneth A. Deffenbacher, Shirley Lam, and Robert R. Hoffman dispel the common myth that cognitive psychology is concerned only with basic research that has very few links to real-world problems. In this chapter, you learn that cognitive psychology has a rich history of application, and that many cognitive psychologists work in industry, educational settings, and the private sector. For example, a significant number of cognitive psychologists are now working in the domains of forensic psychology, marketing and advertising, education, the military, and human factors. The authors do an outstanding job of illuminating career opportunities in applied settings for those interested in cognitive psychology.

Stewart I. Donaldson and Christine A. Christie discuss why the transdisciplinary profession of evaluation science offers an exciting, socially meaningful, and potentially lucrative career niche for those interested in applying the science of psychology (chap. 12). Societies all around the globe embrace the values of accountability and professionalism, and increasingly rely on applied psychologists and other social scientists to provide professional evaluations of efforts to promote human welfare and achievement. Although the most common application of evaluation science for psychologists has been program evaluation, applied psychologists with evaluation skills have rapidly expanding opportunities to conduct policy, project, community, organizational, product, proposal, and technology evaluations. One of the unique features of this chapter is that you will learn how evaluation science can enhance the various subdomains of applied psychology (e.g., social, organizational, developmental, cognitive, health, and educational), by connecting applied psychologists more closely to a wide range of "real-world" settings.

William D. Crano discusses the value of conducting rigorous and methodologically sophisticated research on important basic and applied social issues in chapter 13. He illustrates why training in the foundations of social psychological theory and contemporary research prepares students to pursue successful careers in the academy or in applied research settings, including federal, state, and local governments and the private sector. He concludes the chapter by showing the advantages of careers that facilitate moving between basic theory and applications of social psychological principles to important societal problems.

Psychologists have a long history and impressive track record of using psychological science to improve quality of work life, human performance and productivity, and organizational effectiveness. In chapter 14, Stewart I. Donaldson and Michelle C. Bligh review some of the major theoretical, research, and practical contributions of psychological science toward improving the world of work. They also explore a range of traditional and emerging career opportunities for psychologists interested in building human strengths and promoting optimal functioning. These careers often involve applying psychological science to improve person–organization fit, teamwork, conflict resolution skills, leadership development, mentoring and executive coaching, job enrichment, career planning and development, strengths of cross-cultural and diverse workforces, work and family balance, organizational learning, and organizational development and strategic change. They conclude by emphasizing that career opportunities in these areas are likely to remain among the most intellectually challenging, personally rewarding, and financial lucrative in the evolving global and virtual workplaces of tomorrow.

Finally, Dale E. Berger has provided a chapter devoted to teaching the next generation of psychologists how to prepare for a rewarding career applying the science of psychology. In chapter 15, you learn about the career paths and reflections of psychologists who have entered a dazzling array of careers in applied psychology. Drawing on these accounts and his personal experiences as a faculty member and administrator for an applied psychology graduate program, he summarizes implications for students and for graduate programs in psychology. He ends by arguing that it is now clear that no one is better qualified for many new and rewarding careers than someone trained to apply the science of psychology.

CONCLUDING REMARK

We believe you will come away from this volume with a new understanding of the value and opportunities that now exist for applying psychological science toward social and human betterment in the 21st century. We must acknowledge that many other chapters could have been invited and many additional important applications of applied psychology could have been included. As you read the volume, we hope you develop an appreciation that applied psychology is rapidly evolving, and has become so vast that striving for a comprehensive volume on this subject was beyond our reach. Therefore, the main goals we set for this project were to illustrate how the value of applied psychology has grown across many domains, and to facilitate a process that would allow readers to hear directly from a diverse group of distinguished psychologists who have been instrumental in promoting the growth of applied psychological science. We hope you will conclude that we have accomplished these goals, and have inspired the next generation of psychologists to at least consider joining the professional world of applied psychology, and using their psychology education, talents, and energy toward efforts to improve the human condition.

REFERENCES

American Psychological Association. (2005a). *Non-academic careers for scientific psychologists: Graduate program in applied psychology.* Retrieved March 8, 2005, from http://www.apa.org/science/nonacad-grad.html

American Psychological Association. (2005b). *Non-academic careers for scientific psychologists: Interesting careers in psychology.* Retrieved March 8, 2005, from http://www.apa.org/science/nonacad_careers.html

American Psychological Association. (2005c). *Psychological science agenda.* Retrieved March 8, 2005, from http://www.apa.org/science/psa/psacover.html

American Psychological Society. (2004). Why study psychology? *Observer, 17*(4), 31–35.

Fennell, K. (2002, May). *Where are new psychologists going? Employment, debt, and salary data.* Presentation at the Annual Convention of the Midwestern Psychological Association, Chicago, Illinois.

Romero, V. L. (2003). The changing image of psychology: The rise of applied psychology. *Observer, 16*(7), 27–30.

U.S. Department of Education. (2005). National Center for Educational Statistics, Higher Education General Information Survey. Retrieved March 8, 2005, from http://nces.ed.gov/programs/digest/d03/tables/xls/tab293.xls and http://nces.ed.gov/programs/digest/d03/tables/xls/tab296.xls

FOUNDATIONS AND FRONTIERS IN APPLIED PSYCHOLOGICAL SCIENCE

CHAPTER

2

Does Psychology Make a Significant Difference in Our Lives?*

Philip G. Zimbardo
Stanford University

Does psychology matter? Does what we do, and have done for 100 years or more, really make a significant difference in the lives of individuals or the functioning of communities and nations? Can we demonstrate that our theories, our research, our professional practice, our methodologies, our way of thinking about mind, brain, and behavior, make life better in any measurable way? Has what we have to show for our discipline been applied in the "real world" beyond academia and practitioners' offices to improve health, education, welfare, safety, organizational effectiveness, and more?

Such questions, and finding their answers, have always been my major personal and professional concern. First, as an introductory psychology teacher for nearly six decades, I have always worked to prove relevance as well as essence of psychology to my students. Next, as an author of the now classic basic text, *Psychology and Life* (Ruch & Zimbardo, 1971) that claimed to wed psychology to life applications, I constantly sought to put more psychology in our lives and more life in our psychology (Gerrig & Zimbardo, 2004; Zimbardo, 1992). To reach an even broader student audience, I have coauthored *Core Concepts in Psychology* (Zimbardo, Weber, & Johnson, 2002) that strives to bring the excitement of scientific and applied psychology to students in state and community colleges.

In order to further expand the audience for what is best in psychology, I accepted an invitation to help create, be scientific advisor for, and narrator

*This chapter is reprinted from "Does Psychology Make a Difference in Our Lives?" by P. G. Zimbardo, 2004, *American Psychologist, 59*, pp. 339–351. Copyright 2004 by the American Psychological Association. Reprinted with permission.

27

of the 26-program PBS-TV series, *Discovering Psychology* (1989; updated 2001). For this general public audience we have provided answers—as viewable instances—to their "so what?" questions. This award-winning series is shown both nationally and internationally (in at least 10 nations), and has been the foundation for the most popular telecourse among all the Annenberg CPB Foundation's many academic programs (see www.learner.org). Finally, as president of the American Psychological Association (2002), my major initiative became developing a compendium of exemplars of how psychology has made a significant difference in our lives. This web-based summary of 'psychology in applied action' has been designed as a continually modifiable and updatable repository of demonstrable evidence of psychological knowledge in meaningful applications. In a later section of this chapter, the compendium is described more fully and some of its examples highlighted.

I was fortunate in my graduate training at Yale University (1954–1960) to be inspired by three exceptional mentors each of whom modeled a different aspect of the relevance and applicability of basic psychology to vital issues facing individuals and our society. Carl Hovland developed the Yale Communication and Attitude Change Program after coming out of his military assignment in WWII of analyzing the effectiveness of propaganda and training programs (Hovland, Lumsdaine, & Sheffield, 1949). He went on to transform what was at that time a complex, global and vague study of communication and persuasion into identifiable processes, discrete variables and integrative hypotheses that made possible both experimental research and applications (Hovland, Janis, & Kelley, 1953). Neal Miller always straddled the fence between basic and applied research, despite being known for his classic experimental and theoretical formulations of motivation and reward in learning and conditioning. His WWII experience of training pilots to overcome fears so that they could return to combat was an applied precursor of his later role in developing biofeedback through his laboratory investigations of conditioning autonomic nervous system responses (Miller, 1978, 1985, 1992). The last of my Yale mentors, Seymour Sarason, moved out from his research program on test anxiety in children into the community as one of the founders of Community Psychology (Sarason, 1974). It was a daring move at that time in a field that honored only the scientific study of *individual* behavior.

Psychology of the 1950s was also a field that honored basic research well above applied research, which was typically accorded second-class status, if not denigrated by the "experimentalists," a popular brand name in that era. Psychology at many major universities aspired to be "soft physics," as in the heady days of our Germanic forebears, Wundt, Fechner, Ebbinghaus, Titchner, et al. (see Green, Shore, & Teo, 2001). Anything applied was seen at best as crude social engineering by tinkerers, not real thinkers. Moreover, behaviorism was still rampant, with animal models that stripped away from learning what nonsense syllable memory researchers had deleted from memory—merely the context, the content, the human meaning, and the culture of behavior. The most prominent psychologist from the 1950s through the 1980s, B. F. Skinner, was an anomaly in this regard. Half of him remained a Watsonian radical behaviorist who refused to admit the existence of either motivation or cognition into his psychology (Skinner, 1938, 1966, 1974). Meanwhile, the other Skinner side applied operant conditioning principles to train pigeons for military duties and outlined a behaviorist utopia in *Walden Two* (Skinner, 1948).

GIVING PSYCHOLOGY AWAY: THE CALL FOR SOCIETAL ACCOUNTABILITY

And then along came George Miller whose APA presidential address in 1969 stunned the psychological establishment because one of its own first-born sons committed the heresy of exhorting them to go public, get real, get down, give it up and be relevant. Well, that is the way I think I heard it back then when Miller told his audience that it was time to begin "to give psychology away to the public." It was time to stop talking only to other psychologists. It was time to stop writing only for professional journals hidden away in library stacks. It was time to go beyond the endless quest for experimental rigor in the perfectly designed study to test a theoretically derived hypothesis. Maybe it was time to begin finding answers to the kinds of questions your mother asked about why people acted the way they did. Perhaps it was acceptable to start considering how best to translate what we knew into a language that most ordinary citizens could understand and even come to appreciate.

I for one applauded George Miller's stirring call to action for all these reasons. It was heady for me because I believed that coming from such a distinguished serious theorist and researcher, not some do-gooder, liberal communitarian whom the establishment could readily dismiss; his message would have a big impact in our field. Sadly, the banner raised by Miller's inspirational speech did not fly very high over most psychology departments for many years to come. Why not? I think for four reasons: excessive modesty about *What* psychology really had of value to offer the public; ignorance about *Who* was "The Public"; clueless about *How* to go about the mission of giving psychology away; and lack of sufficient concern about *Why* psychology needed to be accountable to the public.

How shall we counter-argue against such reasoning? First, scanning the breadth and depth of our field makes apparent that there is no need for such professional modesty. Rather, the time has come to be overtly proud of our past and current accomplishments, as I try to demonstrate here. We have much to be proud of in our heritage and in our current accomplishments. Second, "the Public" starts with our students, our clients, and our patients, and extends to our funding agencies, national and local politicians, all nonpsychologists and the media. And it also means your mother whose "bubba psychology" sometimes needs reality checks based on solid evidence we have gathered. Third, it is essential to recognize that "The Media" are the gatekeepers between the best, relevant psychology we want to give away and that elusive public we hope will value what we have to offer. We need to learn how best to utilize the different kinds of media that are most appropriate for delivering specific messages to particular target audiences that we want to reach. Psychologists need to learn how to write effective brief press releases, timely Op-Ed newspaper essays, interesting articles for popular magazines, valuable trade books based on empirical evidence, and how best to give radio, TV, and print interviews. Simple awareness of media needs makes evident, for example, that TV requires visual images, therefore, we should be able to provide video records of research, of our interventions, or other aspects of the research or therapeutic process that will form a story's core.

"Media smarts" also means realizing that to reach adolescents with a helpful message (that is empirically validated) a brief public service announcement on MTV, or an article in a teen magazine will have a broader impact than detailed journal articles or even popular books on the subject.[1] Thus it becomes essential to our mission of making the public wiser consumers of psychological knowledge to learn how to communicate effectively to the media and to work with the media.

Finally, we can challenge the fourth consideration regarding societal accountability with the awareness that taxpayers fund much of our research as well as some of the education of our graduate students. It is imperative that we convey the sense to the citizens of our states and nation that we are responsive to society's needs, and further, that we feel responsible for finding solutions to some of its problems (Zimbardo, 1975). It has become standard operating procedure for most granting agencies now to require a statement about the potential societal value of any proposed research. That does not mean that all research must be applied to dealing with current social or individual problems, because there is considerable evidence

---

[1]Recognizing the importance of bringing psychology's understanding that violence is a learned behavior to the public, APA has joined with the National Association for the Education of Young Children and the Advertising Council to create a national multimedia public service advertising campaign designed to remind adults of the role they play in teaching children to use or avoid violence and then empower these adults to model and teach the right lessons. The campaign, first launched in 2000, has reached more than 50 million households. At the community level, the campaign includes collaborations with local groups in a train the trainer model to bring early childhood violence prevention awareness and know-how to parents, teachers and other caregivers.

that research that originally seemed esoterically "basic" has in time found valuable applications (see Swazey, 1974). It does mean that while some of our colleagues begin with a focus on a problem in an applied domain, the others who start with an eye on theory testing or understanding some basic phenomena should feel obligated to stretch their imaginations by considering potential applications of their knowledge.

THE PROFOUND AND PERVASIVE IMPACT OF PAST PSYCHOLOGICAL KNOWLEDGE

Before I outline some recent, specific instances of how psychological research, theory, and methodology have been applied in various settings, I first highlight some of the fundamental contributions psychology has already made in our lives. Many of them have become so pervasive and their impact so unobtrusively profound, that they are taken for granted. They have come to be incorporated into the way we think about certain domains, have influenced our attitudes and values, and so changed the way individuals and agencies behave that they now seem like the natural, obvious way the world should be run. Psychology often gets little or no credit for these contributions—when we should be deservedly proud of them.

Psychological Testing and Assessment

One of psychology's major achievements has been the development and the extensive reliance on objective, quantifiable means of assessing human talents, abilities, strengths, and weaknesses. In the 100 years since Alfred Binet first measured intellectual performance, systematic assessment has replaced the subjective, often biased judgments of teachers, employers, clinicians, and others in positions of authority by objective, valid, reliable, quantifiable, and normed tests (Binet, 1911; Binet & Simon, 1915). It is hard to imagine a test-free world. Modern testing stretches from assessments of intelligence, achievement, personality and pathology to domains of vocational and values assessment, personnel selection and more. Vocational interest measures are the backbone of guidance counseling and career advising. The largest single application of classified testing in the world is the Armed Services Vocational Aptitude Battery that is given to as many as 2 million enlisted personnel annually. Personnel selection testing has more than 90 years of validity research and proven utility.

We are more familiar with the SAT and GRE standardized testing, currently being revised in response to various critiques, but they are still the yardstick for admission to many colleges and universities (Sternberg, 2000). Workplace job skills assessment and training involves huge numbers of workers and managers in many countries around the world (DuBois, 1970). Little wonder then that such pervasive use of assessments has spawned a multibillion dollar industry. (Because I am serving here in this chapter in the capacity as cheerleader for our discipline, I will not raise questions about the political misuse or overuse of testing, nor indeed be critical of some of the other contributions that follow; see Cronbach [1975].)

Positive Reinforcement

The earlier emphasis in schools and in child rearing on punishment for errors and inappropriate behavior has been gradually displaced by a fundamentally divergent focus on the utility of positive reinforcement for correct, appropriate responding (Straus & Kantor, 1994). Punishing the "undesirable person" has been replaced by punishing only "undesirable behavioral acts." Time-outs for negative behavior have proven remarkably effective as a behavior-modification strategy (Wolfe, Risley, & Mees, 1965). It has become so effective that it has become a favorite technique for managing child behavior by parents in the United States. "Half the parents and teachers in the United States use this nonviolent practice and call it 'time-out,' which makes it a social intervention unmatched in modern psychology," according to the American Academy of Pediatrics publication (1998).

Animal training has benefited enormously from procedures of shaping complex behavioral repertoires and the use of conditioned reinforcers (such as clickers' soundings paired with food rewards). An unexpected value of such training, as reported by animal caregivers, is that they enhance the mental health of many animal species through the stimulation provided by learning new behaviors. Skinner and his behaviorist colleagues deserve the credit for this transformation in how we think about and go about changing behavior by means of response-contingent reinforcement. Their contributions have moved out of animal laboratories into schools, sports, clinics, and hospitals (see Axelrod & Apsche, 1983; Druckman & Bjork, 1991; Kazdin, 1994; Skinner, 1974).

Psychological Therapies

The mission of our psychological practitioners of relieving the suffering of those with various forms of mental illness by means of appropriately delivered types of psychological therapy has proven successful. Since Freud's (1923, 1965) early cases documenting the efficacy of "talk therapy" for neurotic disorders, psychotherapy has taken many forms. Cognitive behavior modification, systematic desensitization, and exposure therapies have proven especially effective in treating phobias, anxiety disorders, and panic attacks, thanks to the application of Pavlovian principles of classical conditioning (Pavlov, 1902, 1927), first developed by Joseph Wolpe (1958). Even clinical depression is best treated with a combination of psychotherapy and medication, and psychotherapy has been shown to be as effective as the drugs alone (Hollon, Thase, & Markowitz, 2002). At a more general level, psychology has helped to demystify "madness," to bring humanity into the treatment of those with emotional and behavioral disorders, and to give people hope that such disorders can be changed (Beck, 1976). Our practitioners and clinical theorists have also developed a range of treatments designed especially for couples, families, groups, for those in rehabilitation from drugs or physical disabilities, as well as for many specific types of problems such as, addictions, divorce, or shyness.

Self-Directed Change

The shelves of most bookstores in the United States are now as likely to be filled with "self-help" books as they are with cooking and dieting books. Although many of them can be dismissed as bad forms of "pop psych" which offer guidance and salvation without any solid empirical footing to back their claims, others provide a valuable service to the general public. At best, they empower people to engage in self-directed change processes for optimal personal adjustment (see Maas, 1998; Myers, 1993; Zimbardo, 1977). In part, their success comes from providing wise advice and counsel based on a combination of extensive expert experience and relevant research packaged in narratives that ordinary people find personally meaningful.

Dynamic Development Across the Life Span

Earlier conceptions of children as small adults, as property, and later as valuable property were changed in part by the theories and research of developmental psychologists (see McCoy, 1988; Pappas, 1983). In recent times, the emerging status of "the child as person" has afforded children legal rights, due process, and self-determination, along with the recognition that they should be regarded as competent persons worthy of considerable freedom (Horowitz, 1984). Psychology has been a human service profession whose knowledge base has been translated into support for a positive ideology of children (Hart, 1991). The human organism is continually changing, ever modifying itself to engage its environments more effectively, from birth through old age. This fundamental conception has made evident that babies need stimulation of many kinds for optimal development, just as do their grandparents. There is now widespread psychological recognition that: Infants do experience pain; learning often depends on critical age-related developmental periods; nature and nurture typically interact in synergistic ways to influence our intelligence and many attributes; mental growth follows orderly progressions, as does language acquisition and production, and that the elderly don't lose their mental agility and competence if they continue to exercise their cognitive skills throughout life (see Baltes & Staudinger, 2000; Bee, 1994; Erikson, 1963; Piaget, 1954, 1993; Pinker, 1994; Plomin & McClearn, 1993; Scarr, 1998). These are but a few of the fundamental contributions of psychology to the way our society now thinks about human development over the course of a lifetime because of decades of research by our developmentalist colleagues.

Parenting

Advice by psychologists on best parental practices has varied in quality and value over time. However, there now seems to be agreement that children need to develop secure attachments to parents or caregivers, and that the most beneficial parenting style for generating an effective child–parent bond is "authoritative." Authoritative parents make age-appropriate demands on children while being responsive to their needs, autonomy, and freedom (see Baumrind, 1973; Collins, Maccoby, Steinberg, Hetherington, & Bornstein, 2000; Darling & Steinberg, 1993; Maccoby, 1980, 1992, 2000).

Psychological Stress

Is there any day in our modern lives that stress does not seem to be omnipresent? We are stressed by time pressures on us, by our jobs (Maslach, 1982), by our marriages, by our friends or by our lack of them. Back when I was a graduate student, stress was such a novel concept that it was surprising when our professor, Irving Janis (1958) wrote one of the first books on the subject of psychological stress. The concept of psychological stress was virtually unrecognized in medical care in the 1950s and 1960s. Psychosomatic disorders baffled physicians who never recognized stress as a causal factor in illness and disease. Since then, psychological research and theorizing has helped to move the notion of stress to the center of the biopsycho-social health model that is revolutionizing medical treatments (Ader & Cohen, 1993; Cohen & Herbert, 1996). Psychologists have shown that our appraisals of stress and our lifestyle habits have a major impact on many of the major causes of illness and death (see Lazarus, 1993; Lazarus & Folkman, 1984). We have made commonplace the ideas of coping with stress, reducing lifestyle risk factors, and building social support networks to enable people to live healthier and longer lives (see Coe, 1999; Cohen & Syme, 1985; Taylor & Clark, 1986).

Unconscious Motivation

Psychology brought into the public mind, as did dramatists such as Edward Albee, Arthur Miller, and Tennessee Williams, that what we think and do is not always based on conscious decisions. Rather, human behavior may be triggered by unconscious motivations of which we have no awareness. Another nod of thanks goes out to the wisdom of Sigmund Freud and Carl Jung (Jung, 1959) for helping to illuminate this previously hidden side of human nature. In a similar vein, slips of the tongue and pen are now generally interpreted as potentially meaningful symptoms of suppressed intentions. It is relatively common in many levels of U.S. society for people to believe that accidents may not be accidental but motivated, that dreams might convey important messages, and also that we use various defense mechanisms, such as projection, to protect fragile egos from awareness of negative information.

Prejudice and Discrimination

Racial prejudice motivates a range of emotions and behaviors among both those targeted and those who are its agents of hatred. Discrimination is the overt behavioral sequela of prejudiced beliefs. It enforces inequalities and injustices based on categorical assignments to presumed racial groups. Stereotypes embody a biased conception of the attributes people presumably possess or lack. The 1954 decision by the Supreme Court of the United States (*Brown v. Board of Education of Topeka, KS*) that formally desegregated public schools was based on some critical social psychological research. The body of empirical research by Kenneth and Mamie Clark (1939a, 1939b, 1940, 1950) effectively demonstrated for the Court that the segregated educational conditions of that era had a negative impact on the sense of self-worth of Negro school children (the then preferred term). The Court, and the thoughtful public since then, accepted the psychological premise that segregated education which separates the races can never be really equal for those being stigmatized by that system of discrimination. Imposed segregation not only is the consequence of prejudice, it contributes further to maintaining and intensifying prejudice, negative stereotypes, and discrimination. In the classic analysis of the psychology of prejudice by Gordon Allport (1954), the importance of equal status contact between the races was advanced as a dynamic hypothesis that has since been widely validated in a host of different contexts (Pettigrew, 1997).

Humanizing Factory Work

Dehumanizing factory assembly lines in which workers were forced to do the same repetitive, mindless task, as if they were robots, initially gave Detroit automakers a production advantage. However, Japanese automakers replaced such routinized assembly lines with harmonious, small work teams operating under conditions of participatory management and in-group democratic principles. The remarkable success of the Japanese auto-makers in overtaking their American counterparts in a relatively short time is due in part to their adaptation of the principles of group dynamics developed by Kurt Lewin, his colleagues, and students at the Massachusetts Institute of Technology and the University of Michigan (Lewin, 1947a, 1947b, 1948). Paradoxically, U.S. auto manufacturers are now incorporating this "Japanese" work model into their factories, decades after they should have done so. This is one way in which psychological theory can be credited with a humanizing impact on industrial work. But psychologists working in the industrial/organizational framework have done even more to help businesses appreciate and promote the importance of goal setting, worker–job fit, job satisfaction, and personnel selection and training.

Political Polling

It is hard to imagine elections without systematic polling of various segments of the electorate using sampling techniques as predictors of election outcomes. Polling for many other purposes by Gallup, Roper, and other opinion polling agencies has become big business. Readers might be surprised to learn that psychologist Hadley Cantril (1991) pioneered in conducting research into the methodology of polling in the 1940s. Throughout World War II, Cantril provided President Roosevelt with valuable information on American public opinion. He also established The Office of Public Opinion Research, which became a central archive for polling data.

HOW AND WHY PSYCHOLOGY MATTERS IN OUR LIVES

I am proud to be a psychologist. As APA president (2002), one of my goals was to spread that pride far and wide among my colleagues, as well as among all students of psychology. For starters, we can all be proud of the many contributions we have made collectively to enrich the way people think about the human condition, a bit of which was outlined earlier. I am also proud of the fact that our scientific approach to understanding the behavior of individuals has guided some policy and improved some operating procedures in our society. We have always been one of the most vigilant and outspoken proponents of the use of the scientific method for bringing reliable evidence to bear on a range of issues. Given any intervention or new policy, psychologists insist on raising the question, "but does it really work?" and utilizing evaluative methodologies and meta-analyses to help make that decision. Psychologists have modeled the approach to reducing errors in advancing behavior-based conclusions through random assignment, double-blind tests, and sensitivity to the many biases present in uncontrolled observations and research procedures. Many of us have also been leaders in advancing a variety of innovations in education through our awareness of principles of attention, learning, memory, individual differences, and classroom dynamics. In addition, I am proud of our discipline's dedication to relieving all forms of human suffering through effective therapeutic interventions along with promoting prevention strategies and appropriate environmental change. As psychologists, we should also be pleased by discovering that our theories, research, and methodologies are serving to influence individual and societal actions, as will be shown next.

PsychologyMatters.Org

The scaffolding for such pride in psychology might best be manifest in a newly developed compendium, which shows society what we have done, and are doing, to improve the quality of life. I wanted to have available in one easily accessible and indexed source a listing of the research and theories that have been translated into practice. Such a resource would indicate how each item is being applied in various settings, such as schools, clinics, hospitals, businesses, and community services, legal and governmental agencies. It would establish the fact that psychology makes a significant difference in our lives by means of these concrete exemplars of its relevant applications. Ideally, this compendium would indicate how psychological contributions have saved lives, reduced or prevented suffering, saved money, made money, enhanced educational goals, improved security and safety, promoted justice and fairness, made organizations operate more effectively, and more. By designing this compendium as a web-based open file, it can be continually updated, modified, and expanded as promising research meets the criterion of acceptability as having made a practically significant difference.

This effort to devise a compendium began with the help of APA's Science Directorate, by issuing a call for submissions to many e-mail lists serving APA members, and through requests in the APA *Monitor* and on the APA.org Web site. The initial set of items was vetted independently by Len Mitnick (formerly of the National Institute of Mental Health) and me. A "blue-ribbon" task force of journal editors, textbook authors, and senior scientists was formed to further vet these final items, help revise them, and then to work at expanding our base.[2]

---

[2]The task force selected to identify and evaluate the research, theory and methodology in psychology that qualified for inclusion in the Psychology Matters compendium has been ably

Because this compendium offers the opportunity to portray an attractive, intelligent face of psychology to the public, final drafts have been edited or rewritten by science writers in APA's Communication and Public Interest Office, ably directed by Rhea Farberman. Ideally, the submissions appear in a jargon-free, readable style appealing to the nonpsychologist public, as well as to our professional colleagues. In addition to having the individual items categorized into many general topical domains, readily searchable by key words or phrases, we have expanded the value of this site by adding an extensive glossary of psychological terms, an historical time-line of major psychological events and contributors, and basic information on "how to be a wiser consumer of research." We will include other extensions as appropriate based on feedback from colleagues and the public we are serving.

The criteria for inclusion are that each submission be presented: (a) in sufficient detail to allow an independent assessment; (b) with evidence of significant statistical effects obtained within the study; (c) with reported application or extension of the submitted research, methodology, or theory in some specific domain of relevance; and (d) with evidence of where and how it has made a significant difference, such as citation of a new law, policy, standardized procedure, or operating system that was based on the submitted item. Items with *promise* of such applicability in the future (because they were too new to have been subject to any evaluation of outcome effectiveness) are being held in a "Wait-and-check-back-later" file. I should mention in passing that many submitted items described research that was interesting, including some classic studies, but they have never met the test of societal applicability.

I welcome the feedback of *American Psychologist* readers on this first phase of our efforts, while also issuing a cordial invitation to add your voice to this compendium with additional worthy submissions. The reach of these initial efforts will hopefully be extended by having this compendium serve as a model to the psychological associations of countries around the world, adding to psychology's global relevance.

Please visit us at: http://www.PsychologyMatters.org. But do wait a moment before booting up your computer, until you finish reading the next section of this chapter, which highlights a sampling of what you will find there.

---

co-chaired by David Myers and Robert Bjork. Other members have included: Alan Boneau, Gordon Bower, Nancy Eisenberg, Sam Glucksberg, Philip Kendall, Kevin Murphy, Scott Plous, Peter Salovey, Alana Conner-Snibbe, Beth Sulzer-Azanoff, Chris Wickens and Alice Young. They have been assisted by the addition of Brett Pelham and David Partenheimer. Rhea Farberman and her staff in APA's Office of Public Communications have played a vital role in the development and continuing evolution of this project. The staff of the Science Directorate aided in the early development of the survey that was circulated to initiate electronic input of candidate items from APA constituent groups.

HIGHLIGHTS OF PSYCHOLOGY'S
REAL-WORLD RELEVANCE

I want to conclude with a dozen or so examples taken from our compendium that illustrate a range of its different topics and domains of applicability. This presentation will end with one extended instance of what I consider a model collaboration of theory, research, media applicability, and global dissemination of psychological knowledge conveyed in a unique format—soap operas! It is the ingenious application of the theory of social modeling by Albert Bandura (1965, 1977) in the design of scenarios used in soap operas to encourage literacy, birth control, education of woman, environmental sustainability, and more.

Human Factors

Traffic safety has been improved by researchers in the area of human factors and ergonomics through a better understanding of visual perception. We now know that changing the standard color of red emergency trucks to a lime-green color reduces accidents because that greenish hue is better perceived in dim light. Similarly, changing traffic sign fonts to increase their recognition at night is another safety improvement resulting from psychological research by Allen (1970), Solomon and King (1985), and by Garvey, Pietrucha, and Meeker (1997).

Scott Geller's (2001, 2003) research program applies Skinnerian behavior analysis to increase safe behaviors, reduce at-risk behaviors, and prevent unintentional injuries at work and on the road. Such unintentional injury is the leading cause of death to people ages 44 and under. The behavior-based safety (BBS) approach for increasing safety identifies critical behaviors that are targeted for change, establishes baselines, applies change interventions, and evaluates workers' change away from specific risky behaviors to more beneficial directions. This approach has been applied in thousands of organizations with great success, such as in having people wear seat belts and in occupational safety programs. The rate of reported injuries after 5 years of implementation of this behavioral approach decreased by as much as an average 72% across a number of organizations. For a summary of the evidence for the extent of injury reduction please see the report by Beth Sulzer-Azanoff and John Austin (2000). One indicator of the social significance of applying behavior analysis is apparent in the *Clinical Practice Guidelines* of New York State's Department of Health, Early Intervention Program. "It is recommended that principles of applied behavior analysis (ABA) and behavior intervention strategies be included as important elements in any intervention program for young children with autism" (p. 13).

Navigational aids for blind and visually impaired people have been developed by psychologists Roberta Klatsky and Jack Loomis, working with geographer Reginald Golledge (Loomis, Klatsky, & Golledge, 2001) over several decades. They utilize principles of spatial cognition along with those of space and auditory perception to guide locomotion. Their new technology is now in development funded by the National Institute for Disability and Rehabilitation Research.

Criminal Justice

Cognitive and social psychologists have shown that eyewitness testimony is surprisingly unreliable. Their research reveals the ease with which recall of criminal events is biased by external influences in interrogations and police line-ups. The seminal work of Beth Loftus (1975, 1979, 1992) and Gary Wells (Wells & Olson, 2003), among others, has been recognized by the U.S. Attorney General's office in drawing up national guidelines for the collection of accurate and unbiased eyewitness identification (see Malpass & Devine, 1981; Stebley, 1997).

The Stanford Prison Experiment has become a classic demonstration of the power of social situational forces to negatively impact upon the behavior of normal, healthy participants who began to act in pathological or evil ways in a matter of a few days (Zimbardo, Haney, Banks, & Jaffe, 1973). It added a new awareness of institutional power to the authority power of Stanley Milgram's (1974) blind obedience studies (see Zimbardo, Maslach, & Haney, 1999). The lessons of this research have gone well beyond the classroom. In part as a consequence of my testimony before a Senate Judiciary Committee on crime and prisons (Zimbardo, 1974), its committee chair, Senator Birch Bayh, prepared a new law for federal prisons requiring juveniles in pretrial detention to be housed separately from adult inmates (to prevent their being abused). Our participants were juveniles in the pretrial detention facility of the Stanford jail. A video documentary of the study, *Quiet Rage: The Stanford Prison Experiment,* has been used extensively by many agencies within the civilian and military criminal justice system, as well as in shelters for abused women. I recently discovered that it is even used to educate role-playing military interrogators in the Navy SEAR program (Search, Evasion and Resistance) about the dangers of abusing their power against others role-playing spies and terrorists (Annapolis Naval College psychology staff, personal communication, September 18, 2003). The Web site for the Stanford Prison Experiment gets more than 800 visitors daily, and has had more than 13 million unique page views in the past 4 years (www.prisonexp.org). Those surprising figures should be telling us that we must focus new efforts on utilizing the power of the Web as a major new medium for disseminating psychology's messages directly to a worldwide audience.

Education

Among the many examples of psychology at work in the field of education, two of my favorites naturally have a social psychological twist. Elliot Aronson and his research team in Austin, Texas, dealt with the negative consequences of desegregated schools by creating "Jigsaw classrooms." Prejudice against minority children was rampant, those children were not performing well, and elementary school classes were marked by high degrees of tension. But when all students were taught to share a set of materials in small learning teams where each child has one set of information indispensable to the rest of the team, and on which tests and grades depend, remarkable things happened. All kids started to listen to the other kids, especially minority kids who they used to ignore or disparage, because such attention and cooperation became essential to getting a good grade. Not only did the self-esteem of the minority children escalate, but so did their academic performance, as prejudice and discrimination declined. The techniques of the Jigsaw classroom are inexpensive for teachers to learn and to operationalize, so it is no wonder that Aronson's simple concept is now being incorporated into the curricula of hundreds of schools in many states, with similarly impressive results (Aronson, 1990; Aronson, Blaney, Stephan, Sikes, & Snapp, 1978; Aronson & Gonzalez, 1988; Aronson & Patnoe, 1997).

Teaching young children interpersonal cognitive problem-solving skills (ICPS) reduces physical and verbal aggression, increases coping with frustrations, and promotes positive peer relationships. This research program developed by Myrna Shure and George Spivak (Shure & Spivak, 1982) over the past several decades is a major violence prevention approach being applied in schools and family agencies in programs called "Raising a Thinking Child" and by the U.S. Department of Education's "I Can Problem Solve" program.

Health

Environmental health is threatened by a host of toxic substances, such as lead, mercury, solvents, and pesticides. Experimental psychologists, behavioral analysts, and psychometricians have helped create the field of behavioral toxicology that recognizes the nervous system as the target for many toxins, with defects in behavior and mental processes as the symptomatic consequences. Pioneering work by psychologist Bernard Weiss (1999) and others has had a significant impact on writing behavioral tests into federal legislation, thereby better regulating the use of a wide range of neurotoxins in our environment. That research documents the vulnerability of children's developing brains to chemicals in the environment.

Among the many negative consequences of America's involvement in the Vietnam War was the explosion of the phenomenon of Post-Traumatic Stress Disorder (PTSD). A large number of veterans suffer this debilitating disorder as uncovered in their psychological treatment. The more we discovered about this delayed, persistent, intense stress reaction to violence and trauma, the more we realized that veterans of earlier wars had also experienced PTSD, but it was unlabeled. That was also the case with many civilian victims of trauma, among them rape victims and those who had experienced child abuse. PTSD has become a well-recognized and publicly acknowledged phenomenon today because it was one of the mental health consequences of the monumental trauma from the terrorist attacks on September 11, 2001, in New York City and Washington, DC. Credit for the early recognition, identification, measurement, and treatment of PTSD goes to the programs of research funded by the Veterans Administration, and pioneered by the research team of clinical psychologist Terry Keane (Keane, Malloy, & Fairbank, 1984; Weathers, Keane, & Davidson, 2001).

The Magic of Touch

One of the consequences of a host of amazing medical advances is saving the lives of many premature infants who would have died even just a decade ago. With modern intensive care preemies weighing only a few pounds now survive, but the essential hospital costs are staggering, up to $10,000 a day for weeks or months! The simple solution for sending these babies home sooner depends on accelerating their growth by means of touch therapy. Psychologist Tiffany Field extended earlier research she had done with biologist Saul Schanberg (Field, 1998; Field & Schanberg, 1990; Field, Schanberg, et al., 1986) on massaging infant rat pups that were motherless. Just as the infant rats rapidly grew in response to that vigorous touch, so did the human preemies. Massaging them several times a day for only 15 minutes was sufficient to stimulate growth hormones. On average, such massaged infants are able to go home 6 days sooner than comparison preemies treated in the conventional way. Given that 470,000 premature infants are born each year in the U.S. alone, it is evident that billions of dollars in health care costs could be saved if this simple inexpensive treatment was made standard procedure in more hospital intensive care units (see also Meltz, 2000).

To establish the societal value of any intervention designed to save lives or enhance health and well-being, its cost-effectiveness must be systematically evaluated. That means establishing a ratio of the benefits compared to various cost estimates of putting the intervention into operation and sustaining it over time. Such a ratio was developed for dollar costs per year of life saved and applied to more than 500 life-saving interventions (Tengs et al., 1995). Across all these interventions the median cost was $42,000 per year life saved. Although some programs save more resources than they cost, others cost millions of dollars for each year of life they save and thus become of questionable social value. Using this standard measure, we discover that new neonatal intensive care for low birth-weight infants (preemies) costs a whooping $270,000 for each year of their lives saved. By that yardstick, the inexpensive touch therapy intervention would dramatically reduce that cost-effectiveness ratio.

The puzzling issue then is why such a simple procedure is not now standard operating procedure in every such intensive care unit in the nation or the world? One goal of our compendium development team is to investigate why some potentially useful interventions have not been applied in the venues where they could make a significant difference. For instance, social psychologists have shown convincingly that elderly patients in a home for the aged who were given a sense of control and responsibility over even minor events, became healthier and lived significantly longer than comparison patients (Langer & Rodin, 1976; Rodin & Langer, 1977). Amazingly, this simple, powerful intervention has not ever been utilized—even in the institution where the research was conducted.

Undoing Dyslexia via Video Games

Treatment for dyslexia by speech therapists and counselors is a slow, long, expensive, and frustrating experience for professionals, parents, and children. Cognitive neuroscientist, Paula Tallal, is using new fMRI techniques to identify the source of reading dyslexia in brain regions that do not adequately process fast appearing sound–sight phonemic combinations. She then worked with a computer-programming agency to develop special video games that systematically shape these children's ever-faster responses to various sights and sounds in the games. With this new technology, children treat themselves in an atmosphere of entertainment and adventure, rely only on intrinsic motivation of game playing, get personalized feedback, and need minimal supervision by highly skilled professionals.

The special computerized video game is called "Fast ForWord." It provides intensive, highly individualized adaptive training across a large number of cognitive, linguistic and reading skills that are vital for academic success. By adapting trial by trial to each child's performance, progress in aural and written language skills of children with dyslexia is reduced to but a few weeks from what had been typically years of intervention efforts. Approximately 375,000 individuals have completed such training across 2,200 public schools nationwide, and more than 2,000 private practice professionals use Fast ForWord programs in their clinics. (For more information, visit: www.scientificlearning.com and www.brainconnection.com)

This sensitive application of psychological knowledge and new methods blended with high technology has resulted in enhanced quality of life for these children as well as their families and teachers, not to mention much money and resources saved (see Holly Fitch & Tallal, 2003; Tallal & Benasich, 2002; Tallal, Galaburda, Llinas, & Von Euler, 1993).

AN IDEALIZED EXAMPLE OF PSYCHOLOGY APPLIED GLOBALLY

The use of intrinsically interesting media, such as video games and Tele-Health dynamic systems, is being used to enable adults as well as children to play central roles in individualized health-management programs. The power of the media also has been extended to television as a far-reaching medium to convey vital persuasive messages about behavior changes that are essential to cope with many of the social-economic-political-health problems facing individuals around the globe. Can psychology contribute to effectively dealing with the population explosion in many countries, increase the status and education of women, and minimize or prevent AIDS? A tall order, for sure. However, it is now happening through a remarkable collaboration of a wise TV producer, a brilliant psychologist, and an international agency that distributes their unusual messages worldwide (Bandura, 2002; Smith, 2002).

Promoting Family Planning

The population explosion around the world is one of our most urgent global problems. Ecologically sustainable development and growth is being challenged by a variety of entwined phenomena, such as high fertility rates in many countries coupled with suboptimal birth rates in others, dramatically increased longevity in some nations along with the spread of deadly communicable diseases in others. One means of population control in over-populated countries involves women and men actively engaged in their own family planning. However, the question is how to do so effectively and efficiently since most previous efforts have met with minimal success?

A TV producer in Mexico, Miguel Sabido, created soap operas that were serialized daily dramas, with prosocial messages about practicing family planning, and also others that promote literacy and education of women. Woven into the narrative of his commercial dramas were elements taken from Albert Bandura's sociocognitive theory of the importance of social models in shaping desired behaviors (Bandura, 1965, 1977, 1986). In many Spanish-speaking countries, most family members watch soap operas fervently each day as their plots unfold over many weeks or months. Viewers identify with attractive, desirable models and dis-identify with those whose actions seem repulsive or create unwanted problems for the "good" guys. In some scenarios there are also actors who represent "transitional models," starting off engaging in high risk or undesirable behaviors but then changing in socially appropriate directions. After some programs there is informational or community support for the cause being projected, by celebrities, government officials, or members of the clergy. This secondary influence path for behavior change adds the key element of making connections to the viewers' personal social networks and community settings in addition to the direct path from the media message to desired changes in target behaviors.

Does it really work? After watching the Mexican programs promoting family planning many women enrolled in family planning clinics. The 32-percentage increase of woman starting to use this service was similar to the increase in contraceptive users. This was true even though there was never an explicit message about contraception for family planning (in deference to the negative position on this birth control issue by Catholic Church). Another key result was that the greater the level of media exposure to these family-oriented TV soap operas, the greater was the percentage of women using contraceptives and also discussing family planning with spouses "many times."

Preventing the Spread of AIDS

These dramas were shown in one region of Tanzania, Africa, and their effects compared to a control region where TV viewers were not exposed to the dramas (later on they got to see the same soap operas). One of the many prosocial effects was an increase in new family planning adopters following the viewing of these dramatic serials compared to no change in the control region. Seventeen segments were included in dramas in Tanzania to prevent the spread of the AIDS virus, a special problem among truck drivers who have unprotected sex with hundreds of prostitutes working at truck stop hubs. Actors portrayed positive models that adopt safe sex practices or negative ones who do not—and then they die of AIDS! Condom distribution soared following viewing this series while it remained low in the control, no soap opera region. Along with this critical change in behavior were also reports of reduced number of sexual partners, more talk about HIV infection, and changed beliefs in personal risk of HIV infection from unprotected sex. Such attitudinal and behavioral changes are vital to slowing the spread of AIDS, which is estimated to make orphans of up to 25 million children worldwide in the next half dozen years (14th International AIDS Conference, Barcelona, Spain, 2002; Naik, 2002; The Straits Times, 2002).

Female Literacy

Education of women is one of the most powerful prophylaxes for limiting population growth, so these soap opera programs in many countries show stories that endorse women continuing with their education as one way of liberating young women from male and matriarchal dominance. In one village in India there was an immediate 30% increase in women going to school after the airing of these soap operas.

A POTENT BLENDING OF TALENTS, WISDOM, AND RESOURCES FOR SOCIAL GOOD

So here we have the unique case of a wise person in the media borrowing ideas from a psychologist, and then extending the scope of influence by pairing up with a nonprofit agency, Population Communications International (PCI), to disseminate these dramas worldwide. PCI's "mission is to work creatively with the media and other organizations to motivate individuals and communities to make choices that influence population trends encouraging development and environmental protection" (PCI, 2002). PCI's efforts at social diffusion span more than 17 countries worldwide with radio and television serial dramas, comic books, and videos for classroom use. Finally, there is a fourth essential component, of systematic evaluation of outcomes by an independent organization of all these entertainment-educational change programs (see www.population.org).

It is evident that these serial dramatizations use the power of narrative storytelling over an extended time, that the public views voluntarily, to motivate specific behavior change in directions guided by the information conveyed in the drama, which in turn has its origins in sound psychological theory and research. What also becomes evident is that when psychologists want to give psychology away to the public, we need to collaborate with those who understand best *how* to reach "The Public," namely those intimately involved with the mass media. They are our gatekeepers to the audiences we want to reach and influence. We have to find ways of inviting and intriguing media with the utility of psychological knowledge for crafting entertaining stories that can make a significant difference in the quality of lives of individuals and society.

ACCENTUATING PSYCHOLOGY'S POSITIVE MESSAGES

The collaboration between psychologist Albert Bandura, media master Miguel Sabido, and the resourcefulness of the PCI agency is an ideal model for us to emulate and extend in spreading more of our positive messages.

Among those new messages are the two exciting directions that psychology can be expected to take in the next decade. The emergence of Martin Seligman's revolutionary "Positive Psychology" enterprise (Seligman, 2002) is creating a new vital force for recognizing and enriching the talents, strengths and virtues of even ordinary people (see Diener, 2000; Myers, 2002; Snyder & Lopez, 2002). It is shifting attention away from deficits, disabilities, and disorders toward a focus on what is special about human nature like our resilience in the face of trauma, our joys, sense of wonder, curiosity, and capacity for goodness and love.

The fertile field of "behavioral economics" integrates psychology with economics and neuroscience to understand the economically irrational human element in judgments under uncertainty (see Simon, 1955; Kahneman & Tversky, 1979; Tversky & Kahneman, 1974, 1986). We can anticipate that Daniel Kahneman's winning the 2003 Nobel Prize in economics has made him a role model for the next generation of professional psychologists to emulate and to enter this exciting domain of relevant inquiry.

In conclusion, I repeat the questions that got me to this point and the simple answer that I now feel is justified—and I hope readers of this chapter agree with its positive bias.

Does psychology matter? Can psychological research, theory, methods, and practice make a significant difference in the lives of individuals, communities, and nations? Do we psychologists have a legacy of which we can be proud? Can we do more and better research that has significant applied effects in the real world? Are we ready now "to give psychology away to the public" in useful, accessible ways? And finally, can we learn how better to collaborate with the media, with technology experts, with community leaders, and with other medical and behavioral scientists for psychology to make an even more significant difference in the coming decade?

My final answer is simply: YES, YES indeed! May the positive forces of psychology be with you.

Author Note

This chapter is an expanded revision of my APA 2002 presidential address delivered at APA's Toronto Convention, August 2003. Both this address and that of Robert Sternberg, 2003 APA president, were presented at this convention to catch up on the year lag that had developed in the last decade of giving presidential addresses.

REFERENCES

Ader, R., & Cohen, N. (1993). Psychoneuroimmunology: Conditioning and stress. *Annual Review of Psychology, 44*, 53–85.

Allen, M. J. (1970). *Vision and highway safety*. Philadelphia: Chilton.

Allport, G. (1954). *The nature of prejudice.* Reading, MA: Addison-Wesley.

American Academy of Pediatrics. (1968). Guidance for effective discipline. *Pediatrics, 101,* 723–728. [Prepared by the Committee on Psychosocial Aspect of Child and Family Health]

Aronson, E. (1990). Applying social psychology to desegregation and energy conservation. *Personality and Social Psychology Bulletin, 16,* 118–132.

Aronson, E., Blaney, N., Stephan, C., Sikes, J., & Snapp, M. (1978). *The jigsaw classroom.* Beverly Hills, CA: Sage.

Aronson, E., & Gonzalez, A. (1988). Desegregation jigsaw, and the Mexican-American experience. In P. A. Katz & D. Taylor (Eds.), *Towards the elimination of racism: Profiles in controversy.* New York: Plenum Press.

Aronson, E., & Patnoe, S. (1997). *The jigsaw classroom: Building cooperation in the classroom* (2nd ed.). New York: Addison Wesley Longman.

Axelrod, S., & Apsche, H. (1983). *Effects of punishment on human behavior.* New York: Academic Press.

Baltes, P. B., & Staudinger, U. M. (2000). Wisdom: A metaheuristic (pragmatic) to orchestrate mind and virtue toward excellence. *American Psychologist, 55,* 122–136.

Bandura, A. (1965). Influence of models' reinforcement contingencies on the acquisition of imitated responses. *Journal of Personality and Social Psychology, 1,* 589–595.

Bandura, A. (1977). *Social learning theory.* Englewood Cliffs, NJ: Prentice-Hall.

Bandura, A. (1986). *Social foundations of thought and action: A social cognitive theory.* Englewood Cliffs, NJ: Prentice-Hall.

Bandura, A. (2002). Environmental sustainability by sociocognitive deceleration of population growth. In P. Schmuck & W. Schultz (Eds.), *The psychology of sustainable development* (pp. 209–238). Dordrecht, Netherlands: Kluwer.

Baumrind, D. (1973). The development of instrumental competence through socialization. In A. Pick (Ed.), *Self-processes and development. The Minnesota symposia in child development* (Vol. 6). Minneapolis: University of Minnesota Press.

Beck, A. T. (1976). *Cognitive therapy and emotional disorders.* New York: International Universities Press.

Bee, H. (1944). *Lifespan development.* New York: HarperCollins.

Binet, A. (1911). *Les idées modernes sur les enfants* [Modern ideas about children]. Paris: Flammarion.

Binet, A., & Simon, T. (1915). *A method of measuring the development of intelligence of young children.* Chicago: Chicago Medical Books.

Campbell, D. T. (1969). Reforms as experiments. *American Psychologist, 24,* 409–429.

Cantril, A. H. (1991). *The opinion connection: Polling, politics, and the press.* Washington, DC: CQ Press.

Clark, K. B., & Clark, M. K. (1939a). The development of consciousness of self and the emergence of racial identification in Negro preschool children. *Journal of Social Psychology, 10,* 591–599.

Clark, K. B., & Clark, M. K. (1939b). Segregation as a factor in the racial identification of Negro preschool children: A preliminary report. *Journal of Experimental Education, 8,* 161–163.

Clark, K. B., & Clark, M. K. (1940). Skin color as a factor in racial identification of Negro preschool children. *Journal of Social Psychology, 11,* 159–169.

Clark, K. B., & Clark, M. K. (1950). Emotional factors in racial identification and preference in Negro children. *Journal of Negro Education, 19,* 341–350.

Coe, C. L. (1999). Psychosocial factors and psychoneuroimmunology within a lifespan perspective. In D. P. Keating & C. Hertzman (Eds.), *Developmental health and the wealth of nations: Social, biological, and educational dynamics* (pp. 201–219). New York: Guilford Press.

Cohen, S., & Herbert, T. B. (1996). Health psychology: Psychological factors and physical disease from the perspective of human psychoneuroimmunology. *Annual Review of Psychology, 47,* 113–142.

Cohen, S., & Syme, S. L. (Eds.). (1985). *Social support and health*. Orlando, FL: Academic Press.

Collins, W. A., Maccoby, E. E., Steinberg, L., Hetherington, E. M., & Bornstein, M. H. (2000). Contemporary research on parenting: The case for nature and nurture. *American Psychologist, 55*, 218–232.

Cronbach, L. J. (1975). Five decades of public controversy over mental testing. *American Psychologist, 30*, 1–14.

Darling, N., & Steinberg, L. (1993). Parenting style as context: An integrative model. *Psychological Bulletin, 113*, 487–496.

Diener, E. (2000). Subjective well-being: The science of happiness, and a proposal for a national index. *American Psychologist, 55*, 34–43.

Discovering psychology [Television series]. (1990; updated 2001). Boston: WGBH, with the American Psychological Association. (Funded and distributed by the Annenberg CPB Foundation, Washington, DC)

Druckman, D., & Bjork, R. A. (1991). *In the mind's eye: Enhancing human performance*. Washington, DC: National Academy Press.

DuBois, P. H. (1970). *A history of psychological testing*. Boston: Allyn & Bacon.

Erikson, E. H. (1963). *Childhood and society* (2nd ed.). New York: Norton.

Field, T. (1989). Massage therapy effects. *American Psychologist, 53*, 1270–1281.

Field, T. F., & Schanberg, S. M. (1990). Massage alters growth and catecholamine production in preterm newborns. In N. Gunzenhauser (Ed.), *Advances in touch* (pp. 96–104). Skillman, NJ: Johnson & Johnson.

Field, T., Schanberg, S. M., Scafidi, F., Bauer, C. R., Vega-Lahr, N., Garcia, R., et al. (1986). Tactile/kinesthetic stimulation effects on preform neonates. *Pediatrics, 77*, 654–658.

Freud, S. (1923). *Introductory lectures on psycho-analysis* (J. Riviera, Trans.). London: Allen & Unwin.

Freud, S. (1965). *The interpretation of dreams*. New York: Avon. (Original work published 1900)

Garvey, P. M., Pietrucha, M. T., & Meeker, D. (1997). *Effects of font and capitalization on legibility of guide signs*. Transportation Research Record No. 1605, 73–79.

Geller, E. S. (2001). *The psychology of safety handbook*. Boca Raton, FL: CRC Press.

Geller, E. S. (2003). Behavior-base safety in industry: Realizing the large-scale potential of behavior analysis to promote human welfare. *Applied & Preventive Psychology, 10*, 87–105.

Gerrig, R., & Zimbardo, P. G. (2004). *Psychology and life* (17th ed.). Boston: Allyn & Bacon.

Green, C. D., Shore, M., & Teo, T. (2001). *The transformation of psychology: Influences of 19th century philosophy, technology, and natural science*. Washington, DC: APA Books.

Hart, S. N. (1991). From property to person status: Historical perspective on children's rights. *American Psychologist, 46*, 53–59.

Hollon, S. D., Thase, M. E., & Markowitz, J. C. (2002). Treatment and prevention of depression. *Psychological Science in the Public Interest, 3*, 39–77.

Holly Fitch, R., & Tallal, P. (2003). Neural mechanisms of language-based learning impairments: Insights from human populations and animal models. *Behavior and Cognitive Neuroscience Reviews, 2*, 155–178.

Horowitz, R. M. (1984). Children's rights: A look backward and a glance ahead. In R. M. Horowitz & J. B. Lazar (Eds.), *Legal rights of children* (pp. 1–9). New York: McGraw-Hill.

Hovland, C. I., Janis, I. L., & Kelley, H. H. (1953). *Communication and persuasion*. New Haven, CT: Yale University Press.

Hovland, C. I., Lumsdaine, A. A., & Sheffield, F. D. (1949). *Experiments on mass communication*. Princeton, NJ: Princeton University Press.

Janis, I. L. (1958). *Psychological stress: Psychoanalytical and behavioral studies of surgical patients*. New York: Wiley.

Jung, C. G. (1959). The concept of the collective unconscious. In *The archetypes and the collective unconscious, collected works* (Vol. 9, Part 1, pp. 54–74). Princeton, NJ: Princeton University Press. (Original work published 1936)

Kahneman, D., & Tversky, A. (1979). Prospect theory: An analysis of decision under risk. *Econometrica, 47*, 263–291.

Kazdin, A. E. (1994). *Behavior modification in applied settings* (5th ed.). Pacific Grove, CA: Brooks/Cole.

Keane, T. M., Malloy, P. F., & Fairbank, J. A. (1984). Empirical development of an MMPI subscale for the assessment of PTSD. *Journal of Consulting and Clinical Psychology, 52*, 138–140.

Langer, E. F., & Rodin, J. (1976). The effects of choice and enhanced personal responsibility for the aged: A field experiment in an institutionalized setting. *Journal of Personality and Social Psychology, 34*, 191–198.

Lazarus, R. S. (1993). From psychological stress to the emotions: A history of changing outlooks. *Annual Review of Psychology, 44*, 1–21.

Lazarus, R. S., & Folkman, S. (1984). *Stress, appraisal, and coping.* New York: Springer.

Lewin, K. (1947a). Frontiers in group dynamics: Concept, method and reality in social science; social equilibria and social change. *Human Relations, 1*, 5–41.

Lewin, K. (1947b). Frontiers in group dynamics. II. Channels of group life; social planning and action research. *Human Relations, 1*, 143–153.

Lewin, K. (1948). *Resolving social conflicts.* New York: Harper.

Loftus, E. F. (1975). Leading questions and the eyewitness report. *Cognitive Psychology, 7*, 560–572.

Loftus, E. F. (1979). *Eyewitness testimony.* Cambridge, MA: Harvard University Press.

Loftus, E. F. (1992). When a lie becomes memory's truth: Memory distortion after exposure to misinformation. *Current Directions in Psychological Science, 1*, 121–123.

Loomis, J. M., Klatsky, R. L., & Golledge, R. G. (2001). Navigating without vision: Basic and applied research. *Optometry and Vision Science, 78*, 282–289.

Maas, J. (1998). *Power sleep: The revolutionary program that prepares your mind for peak performance.* New York: Villard.

Maccoby, E. E. (1980). *Social development: Psychological growth and the parent–child relationship.* San Diego: Harcourt Brace Jovanovich.

Maccoby, E. E. (1992). The role of parents in the socialization of children: An historical overview. *Developmental Psychology, 28*, 1006–1017.

Maccoby, E. E. (2000). Parenting and its effects on children: On reading and misreading behavior genetics. *Annual Review of Psychology, 51*, 1–27.

Malpass, R. S., & Devine, P. G. (1981). Eyewitness identification: Lineup instructions and the absence of the offender. *Journal of Applied Psychology, 66*, 482–489.

Maslach, C. (1982). *Burnout: The cost of caring.* Englewood Cliffs, NJ: Prentice Hall. (Reprinted 2003, Malor Books, Cambridge, MA)

McCoy, E. (1988). Childhood through the ages. In K. Finsterbush (Ed.), *Sociology 88/89* (pp. 44–47). Guilford, CT: Duskin.

Meltz, B. F. (2000, November 20). Do you touch your baby enough? *Boston Globe*, p. H1.

Milgram, S. (1974). *Obedience to authority.* New York: Harper & Row.

Miller, G. (1969). Psychology as a means of promoting human welfare. *American Psychologist, 24*, 1063–1075.

Miller, N. E. (1978). Biofeedback and visceral learning. *Annual Review of Psychology, 29*, 373–404.

Miller, N. E. (1985). The value of behavioral research on animals. *American Psychologist, 40*, 423–440.

Miller, N. E. (1992). Introducing and teaching much-needed understanding of the scientific process. *American Psychologist, 47*, 848–850.

Myers, D. G. (1993). *The pursuit of happiness.* New York: Avon.

Myers, D. G. (2002). *Intuition: Its powers and perils.* New Haven, CT: Yale University Press.

Naik, G. (2002, July 5). Uganda AIDS study suggests education stems spread of HIV. *Wall Street Journal*, p. A14.

New York State. (1999). *Clinical practice guidelines.* New York: Department of Health, Early Intervention Program.

Pappas, A. M. (1983). Introduction. In A. M. Pappas (Ed.), *Law and the status of the child* (pp. xxvii–lv). New York: United Nations Institute for Training and Research.

Pavlov, I. P. (1902). *The work of the digestive glands* (W. H. Thompson, Trans.). London: Griffin. (Original work published 1897)

Pavlov, I. P. (1927). *Conditioned reflexes* (G. V. Anrep, Trans.). London: Oxford University Press.

Pettigrew, T. F. (1997). Generalized intergroup contact effects on prejudice. *Personality and Social Psychology Bulletin, 23*, 173–185.

Piaget, J. (1954). *The construction of reality in the child.* New York: Basic Books.

Pinker, S. (1994). *The language instinct: How the mind creates language.* New York: Morrow.

Plomin, R., & McClearn, G. E. (1993). *Nature, nurture, and psychology.* Washington, DC: American Psychological Association.

Population Communications International. (2002). *15th anniversary: Keeping pace with change.* New York: Author.

Rodin, J., & Langer, E. F. (1977). Long-term effects of a control relevant intervention among the institutionalized aged. *Journal of Personality and Social Psychology, 35*, 897–902.

Ruch, F. L., & Zimbardo, P. G. (1971). *Psychology and life* (8th ed.). Glenview, IL: Scott, Foresman.

Sarason, S. B. (1974). *The psychological sense of community: Prospects for a community psychology.* Oxford, England: Jossey-Bass.

Scarr, S. (1998). American child care today. *American Psychologist, 53*, 95–108.

Seligman, M. (2002). *Authentic happiness: Using the new positive psychology to realize your potential for lasting fulfillment.* New York: Free Press.

Shure, M. B., & Spivak, G. (1982). Interpersonal problem solving in children: A cognitive approach to prevention. *American Journal of Community Psychology, 10*, 341–356.

Simon, H. (1955). A behavioral model of rational choice. *Quarterly Journal of Economics, 69*, 99–118.

Skinner, B. F. (1938). *The behavior of organisms: An experimental analysis.* New York: Appleton-Century.

Skinner, B. F. (1948). *Walden two.* New York: Macmillan.

Skinner, B. F. (1966). What is the experimental analysis of behavior? *Journal of the Experimental Analysis of Behavior, 9*, 213–218.

Skinner, B. F. (1974). *About behaviorism.* New York: Knopf.

Smith, D. (2002). The theory heard "round the world." *Monitor on Psychology, 33*, 30–32.

Snyder, C. R., & Lopez, S. J. (2002). *Handbook of positive psychology.* New York: Oxford University Press.

Solomon, S. S., & King, J. G. (1985). Influence of color on fire vehicle accidents. *Journal of Safety Research, 26*, 47.

Stebley, N. M. (1997). Social influence in eyewitness recall: A meta-analytic review of line-up instruction effects. *Law and Human Behavior, 21*, 283–298.

Sternberg, R. J. (Ed.). (2000). *Handbook of intelligence.* Cambridge, England: Cambridge University Press.

The Straits Times. (2002, July 12). *The HIV orphan mega-crisis.* 14th International AIDS Conference, Hong Kong.

Straus, M. A., & Kantor, G. K. (1994). Corporal punishment of adolescents by parents: A risk factor in the epidemiology of depression, suicide, alcohol abuse, child abuse, and wife beating. *Adolescence, 29*, 543–561.

Sulzer-Azanoff, B., & Austin, J. (2000). Does BBS work? Behavior-based safety & injury reduction: A survey of the evidence. *Professional Safety*, July, 19–24.

Swazey, J. P. (1974). *Chlorpromazine in psychiatry: A study of therapeutic innovation.* Cambridge, MA: MIT Press.

Tallal, P., & Benasich, A. A. (2002). Developmental language learning impairments. *Development and Psychopathology, 14,* 559–579.

Tallal, P., Galaburda, A. M., Llinas, R. R., & Von Euler, C. (Eds.). (1993). *Temporal information processing in the nervous system: Special reference to dyslexia and dysphasia* (Vol. 682). New York: New York Academy of Sciences.

Taylor, S. E., & Clark, L. F. (1986). Does information improve adjustments to noxious events? In M. J. Saks & L. Saxe (Eds.), *Advances in applied social psychology* (Vol. 3, pp. 1–28). Hillsdale, NJ: Lawrence Erlbaum Associates.

Tengs, T. O., Adams, M. E., Pliskin, J. S., Safan, D. G., Siegel, J. E., Weinstein, M. C., & Graham, J. D. (1995). Five-hundred life-saving interventions and their cost effectiveness. *Risk Analysis, 15,* 369–390.

Tversky, A., & Kahneman, D. (1974). Judgment under uncertainty: Heuristics and biases. *Science, 185,* 1124–1131.

Tversky, A., & Kahneman, D. (1986). The framing of decisions and the psychology of choice. *Science, 211,* 453–458.

Weathers, F. W., Keane, T. M., & Davidson, J. R. T. (2001). Clinicians' administered PTSD scale: A review of the first ten years of research. *Depression & Anxiety, 13,* 132–156.

Weiss, B. (1992). Behavioral toxicology: A new agenda for assessing the risks of environmental pollution. In J. Grabowski & G. VandenBos (Eds.), *Psychopharmacology: Basic mechanisms and applied interventions. Master lectures in psychology* (pp. 167–207). Washington, DC: American Psychological Association.

Weiss, B. (1999, May). *The vulnerability of the developing brain to chemicals in the environment.* Paper presented at the New York Academy of Medicine conference on Environmental Toxins and Neurological Disorders, New York.

Wells, G. L., & Olson, E. A. (2003). Eyewitness testimony. *Annual Review of Psychology, 54,* 277–295.

Wolfe, M. M., Risley, T. R., & Mees, H. L. (1965). Application of operant conditioning procedures to behavior problems of an autistic child. *Research and Therapy, 1,* 302–312.

Wolpe, J. (1958). *Psychotherapy by reciprocal inhibition.* Stanford, CA: Stanford University Press.

Zimbardo, P. G. (1974). The detention and jailing of juveniles (Hearings before U.S. Senate Committee on the Judiciary Subcommittee to Investigate Juvenile Delinquency, 10, 11, 17, September, 1973). Washington, DC: U.S. Government Printing Office, 141–161.

Zimbardo, P. G. (1975). On transforming experimental research into advocacy for social change. In M. Deutsch & H. Hornstein (Eds.), *Applying social psychology: Implications for research, practice and training* (pp. 33–66). Hillsdale, NJ: Lawrence Erlbaum Associates.

Zimbardo, P. G. (1977). *Shyness: What it is, what to do about it.* Reading, MA: Addison-Wesley.

Zimbardo, P. G. (1992). *Psychology and life* (13th ed.). New York: HarperCollins.

Zimbardo, P. G. (2004). Does psychology make a difference in our lives? *American Psychologist, 59,* 339–351.

Zimbardo, P. G., Haney, C., Banks, W. C., & Jaffe, D. (1973, April 8). The mind is a formidable jailer: A Pirandellian prison. *The New York Times Magazine,* Section 6, pp. 38, ff.

Zimbardo, P. G., Maslach, C., & Haney, C. (1999). Reflections on the Stanford Prison Experiment: Genesis, transformations, consequences. In T. Blass (Ed.), *Obedience to authority: Current perspectives on the Milgram paradigm* (pp. 193–237). Mahwah, NJ: Lawrence Erlbaum Associates.

Zimbardo, P. G., Weber, A. L., & Johnson, R. L. (2002). *Psychology: Core concepts* (4th ed.). Boston, MA: Allyn & Bacon.

Going Global With Social Cognitive Theory: From Prospect to Paydirt

Albert Bandura
Stanford University

The present chapter addresses the applications of social cognitive theory to some of the most urgent global problems. These macrosocial applications are rooted in the agentic perspective of social cognitive theory (Bandura, 1986, 2001a). To be an agent, is to influence intentionally one's own functioning and life circumstances. In this view, people are producers of their life circumstances, not just products of them. Social cognitive theory rejects the duality of personal agency and social structure. People create social systems and their lives are, in turn, influenced by them. Human self-development, adaptation, and change thus involve a dynamic interplay between personal and social structural influences within the larger societal context.

Soaring population growth is the most urgent global problem. It is destroying the ecosystems that sustain life, degrading the quality of life, and draining resources needed for national development. The problem is especially severe in less developed nations which are doubling their populations at an accelerating rate. Impoverished populations struggle to survive under scarcities of food, fresh water, medical services, and other necessities of life. Another widespread problem is the pernicious gender inequality in familial, educational, health, occupational, and social life. In these societies women are subjugated and denied their liberty, dignity, and opportunities to develop their talents. The demands of this new information era favor intelligence over brawn. Given that women constitute approximately half the population, societies that marginalize or subjugate women undermine their nation's social, technological, and economic viability. Fostering the talents and social rights of women provides nations with powerful leverage for national development and renewal. The same is true for ethnic minorities. The spreading AIDS epidemic is another mounting global problem with devastating societal consequences.

Long running serial dramas serve as the principal vehicle for addressing these life conditions. Storytelling, structured along enabling social cognitive lines, is an especially influential vehicle for effecting personal and social changes. It brings life to people's everyday struggles and the consequences of different social practices. It speaks ardently to people's fears, hopes, and aspirations for a better life.

These macrosocial applications inform, enable, motivate, and guide viewers for personal and social changes that can alter the course of their lives. The dramatic productions are not just fanciful stories. They dramatize people's own everyday lives and the problems they have to manage. The enabling dramas help viewers to see a better life and provide the strategies and incentives that enable them to take the steps to achieve it. The story lines model family planning, women's equality, degrading dowry systems, spouse abuse, environmental conservation, AIDS prevention, and a variety of life skills. Some societies present unique problems that require special social themes tailored to their cultural practices. Approximately 130 million women are subjected to the brutal genital mutilation procedure. In Mali, child traffickers trick impoverished parents with large families to give up children under the promise that they will receive good care and send money home. They are then sold for slave labor under inhumane conditions. Orphans of parents who died of AIDS are also sold for slave labor.

To change deeply held beliefs requires strong emotional bonding to enabling models who inspire viewers and provide them with a vision of a better future. Hundreds of episodes get people emotionally engaged in the evolving lives of the models and identify with them. A formerly illiterate college-bound teenager, who was inspired by a lead character to pursue her school, describes the depth and power of emotional bonding, *"There are moments when I feel that Taru is directly talking to me, usually at night. She is telling me, 'Usha, you can follow your dreams.' I feel she is like my elder sister . . . and giving me encouragement."*

SOCIAL COGNITIVE THEORY

A comprehensive theory of human behavior must explain how people acquire competencies, attitudes, values, styles of behavior, and how they motivate and regulate their level of functioning. The major principles of social cognitive theory (Bandura, 1986, 1997) provide guidelines for constructing effective media productions. The theoretical principles that are especially relevant for this purpose are discussed briefly in this section.

Social Modeling

There are two basic modes of learning. People learn through the direct experience of rewarding and punishing effects of actions, and through the power of social modeling. Modeling enables people to shortcut the tedious and sometimes costly trial-and-error learning by profiting from the successes and mistakes of others. Another major advantage of modeling, especially through the media, is that it can reach vast populations simultaneously in widely dispersed locales. Symbolic modeling has, therefore, become the dominant vehicle for disseminating new ideas, values, and styles of conduct. Modeling influences serve diverse functions in promoting personal and social change. They include instructive, motivational, social prompting, and social construction functions. With regard to the instructive function, models serve as transmitters of knowledge, competencies, values, cognitive skills, and new styles of behavior. Observers also acquire emotional proclivities toward people, places, and things through modeled emotional experiences. Observers learn to fear what frightened or injured models; to dislike what repulsed them; and to like what gratified them. Self-debilitating fears and inhibitions can be eliminated by modeling that depicts effective coping strategies and instills a sense of coping efficacy.

The motivational function operates through the depicted benefits and detriments of modeled courses of action. Seeing others gain desired outcomes by their actions can create outcome expectancies that serve as positive motivators. Observed punishing outcomes can create negative outcome expectancies that function as disincentives for similar courses of action. The behavior of others also serves as social prompts that activate, channel, and support modeled styles of behavior. The types of models who predominate in a social milieu determine which human qualities are promoted from among many alternatives.

Televised portrayals of human nature, social roles, power relations, and the norms and structure of society shape the public consciousness (Gerbner, Gross, Morgan, Signorielli, & Shanahan, 2002) and people's social construction of their reality. It is one thing to learn new styles of behavior. It is another to put them into practice, especially in the face of impediments. Several motivators provide support for adopting new forms of behavior.

Perceived Self-Efficacy

Among the mechanisms of human agency, none is more central or pervasive than beliefs of personal efficacy (Bandura, 1997, 2000). This core belief is the foundation of human agency. Unless people believe they can produce desired effects by their actions, they have little incentive to act or to persevere in the face of difficulties. Whatever other factors serve as guides and motivators, they are rooted in the core belief that one has the power to effect changes by personal and collective action.

Human well-being and attainments require an optimistic and resilient sense of efficacy. This is because the usual daily realities are strewn with difficulties. They are full of frustrations, conflicts, impediments, inequities, adversities, failures, and setbacks. These are the price of progress. People must have a strong belief in their efficacy to sustain the perseverant effort needed to succeed. The functional belief system combines realism about tough odds, but optimism that one can beat those odds through self-development and perseverant effort.

Efficacy beliefs regulate human functioning through four major processes: cognitive, motivational, emotional, and decisional. Such beliefs influence whether people think pessimistically or optimistically, self-enhancingly or self-hinderingly. Efficacy beliefs play a central role in the self-regulation of motivation through goal challenges and outcome expectations. It is partly on the basis of efficacy beliefs that people choose what challenges to undertake, how much effort to expend in the endeavor, how long to persevere in the face of obstacles and failures, and whether failures are motivating or demoralizing. The likelihood that people will act on the outcomes they expect prospective behaviors to produce depends on their beliefs about whether or not they can produce the required performances. A strong sense of coping efficacy reduces vulnerability to stress and depression in taxing situations and strengthens resiliency to adversity.

Efficacy beliefs also play a key role in shaping the courses lives take by influencing the types of activities and environments people choose. Social influences operating in the chosen environments continue to promote certain competencies, values, and interests. Thus, by choosing and shaping their environments, people can have a hand in what they become.

People's beliefs in their efficacy can be developed in four ways. The most effective way of instilling a strong sense of efficacy is through mastery experiences. Successes build a robust efficacy. Failures undermine it, especially in early phases of efficacy development. If people experience only easy successes, they come to expect quick results, and are easily discouraged by failure. Resilient efficacy requires experience in overcoming obstacles, through perseverant effort. Resilience is also built by training in how to manage failure so it becomes informative rather than demoralizing.

The second way of developing self-efficacy is by social modeling. Models are sources of aspiration, competencies, and motivation. Seeing people similar to oneself succeed by perseverant effort, raises observers' beliefs in their own abilities.

Social Persuasion is the third mode of influence. Realistic boosts in efficacy can lead people to exert greater effort. This increases their chances of success. But effective efficacy builders do more than convey positive appraisals. They structure situations for others in ways that bring success, and avoid placing them, prematurely, in situations where they are likely to fail.

People also rely partly on their physical and emotional states, in judging their efficacy. They read their emotional arousal, and tension, as signs of personal vulnerability. In activities involving strength and stamina, people interpret their fatigue, aches, and pains, as indicators of low physical efficacy. The fourth way of modifying efficacy beliefs is to reduce people's stress and depression, and build their physical strength. Many of the challenges of life involve common problems that require people to work together with a collective voice to change their lives for the better. People's shared belief in their collective power to realize the futures they seek through collective effort is a key ingredient of collective agency.

Goals and Aspirations

People motivate themselves and guide their behavior by the goals, aspirations, and challenges they set for themselves (Bandura, 1986; Locke & Latham, 1990). Long-term goals set the course of personal change but they are too far removed to overrule competing current influences on behavior. Short-term goals motivate and provide direction for one's efforts in the here and now for incremental change. Goals have little impact unless they are translated into explicit plans and strategies for realizing them. Media productions, therefore, model how to translate a vision of a desired future into a set of achievable subgoals.

Outcome Expectations

Human motivation and behavior are also affected by the outcomes people expect their actions to produce (Bandura, 1986). Outcome expectations can take three major forms. One set of outcomes includes the material pleasurable and aversive effects the behavior produces. Behavior is also partly regulated by the social reactions it evokes. The social approval and disapproval the behavior produces is the second major class of outcomes. People adopt personal standards and regulate their behavior by their self-evaluative reactions. They do things that give them self-satisfaction and self-worth, and refrain from behaving in ways that breed self-dissatisfaction.

Perceived Facilitators and Impediments

Personal and social change would be easy if there were no impediments to surmount. The facilitators and obstacles people see to changing their behavior is another influential determinant. Some of the impediments are personal ones that undermine efforts at change, such as profound self-doubts that one's efforts would make a difference. Others are situational and structural impediments. Beliefs of personal efficacy affect how formidable the impediments appear.

People who have a resilient sense of efficacy figure out ways to overcome obstacles to change. Those who distrust their efficacy view impediments as insurmountable and are easily convinced of the futility of effort. They quickly abort their effort when they run into difficulties, should they even try. Efforts at socially oriented changes are designed to enhance the enabling aspects of social systems and reduce the impeding aspects.

COMPONENTS OF PSYCHOSOCIAL MODELS FOR SOCIAL CHANGE

There are three major components to this social cognitive approach to fostering society-wide changes (Bandura, 2001b). The first component is a theoretical model. It specifies the determinants of psychosocial change and the mechanisms through which they produce their effects. This knowledge provides the guiding principles. The second component is a translational and implementational model. It converts theoretical principles into an innovative operational model. It specifies the content, strategies of change, and their mode of implementation. The third component is a social diffusion model on how to promote adoption of psychosocial programs in diverse cultural milieus.

Effective psychosocial models of change usually have limited social impact because of inadequate systems for their social diffusion. As a result, we do not profit from our successes. Lack of expertise and resources in host countries further undermine perceived efficacy to produce long-running serials that can capture and hold public attention and change behavior.

Population Communications International (PCI) and the Population Media Center (PMC) remove this impediment by serving as the global diffusion mechanisms (Poindexter, 2004; Ryerson, 1999). These two nonprofit organizations raise funds from various sources to cover production costs. They provide the nations' media personnel with the enabling guidance and technical assistance to create serial dramas tailored to the particular cultural milieus. This creative process involves a close collaborative partnership with the host country's production teams. Funds to cover the production costs are sought from the UN population fund, private foundations, and donors.

PCI and PMC also promote cooperation and collaboration among nongovernmental organizations worldwide concerned with population growth, environmental and health problems, and human rights. Such alliances increase the chances of success by mobilizing and focusing people's efforts to improve the quality of life for themselves and their children. In addition, PCI and PMC work with professionals in the entertainment industry to heighten their sensitivity to ethnic stereotyping, human rights, health, population growth, and environmental degradation in their media productions. They are encouraged to include themes related to these issues in the story lines they create for their fictional dramas.

Major scientific progress and achievement of widespread social changes require pooling the knowledge and innovative expertise of diverse disciplines. In the macrosocial approach under discussion, social cognitive theory provided the theoretical model (Bandura, 1986, 1997). Miguel Sabido, a creative dramatist, devised the generic translational and implemental model (Sabido, 1981, 2002), and Poindexter (2004) and Ryerson (1994) designed the social diffusion model.

CULTURAL AND VALUE ANALYSES

As is true of any intervention, the use of mass communications to foster personal and social change raises ethical issues. Ethical evaluations will depend on who selects the types of changes to be promoted, the agents of change, the means used, and the choice and voluntariness of exposure to the influence. These are not programs foisted on nations by outsiders in pursuit of their self-interest. The dramatic serials are created only on invitation by countries seeking help with intractable problems. The host production team, drawing on a wide variety of sources, including public health systems, religious organizations, women's groups, and other constituencies identify unique cultural life conditions, values, and itemize the types of changes the dramatizations should encourage. Once a program is aired, producers monitor how viewers perceive the characters, with whom they are identifying, how they view the obstacles and the dramatized options, and the types of futures they envision.

Extensive cultural and value analyses are conducted before serial dramas are developed and implemented. In this formative phase, focus groups, representing the various constituencies in the society, identify problems of major concern to them and the obstacles they face. These interviews provide the culturally relevant information for developing realistic characters and engrossing functional plot lines.

Value disputes are often fueled by wrangling over stereotypes with emotive surplus meanings rather than deliberating about changes in real-life terms. The value issues are, therefore, cast in concrete terms of detriments and benefits of particular lifestyles. The tangible values embody respect for human dignity and equitable familial, social, health, and educational opportunities that support common human aspirations. The dramatizations are thus grounded in the internationally endorsed human values codified in United Nations covenants and resolutions. The dramatized options and consequences enable people to make informed choices to improve their lives.

ELEMENTS OF DRAMATIC SERIALS

Social Modeling

There are four basic principles guiding the construction of the dramatic serials. The first principle enlists the power of social modeling for personal and social change. Culturally admired television models exhibit the beneficial styles of behavior. Social attraction increases the impact of modeling influences. Characters representing different segments of the population are shown adopting the beneficial attitudes and behavior patterns. Seeing people similar to themselves change their lives for the better not only conveys strategies for how to do it, but raises viewers' sense of efficacy that they too can succeed. Viewers come to admire and are inspired by characters in their likenesses who struggle with difficult obstacles and eventually overcome them.

Three types of contrasting models are used to highlight the personal and social effects of different patterns of behavior. The episodes include positive models portraying beneficial lifestyles. Other characters personify negative models exhibiting detrimental views and lifestyles. Transitional models are shown transforming their lives by discarding adverse styles of behavior in favor of beneficial ones. Viewers are especially prone to draw inspiration from, and identify with, transforming models by seeing them surmount similar adverse life circumstances.

Vicarious Motivators

The second feature of the dramatic productions enlists vicarious motivators as the incentive for change. Unless people see the modeled lifestyle as improving their welfare they have little incentive to adopt it. The personal and social benefits of the favorable practices, and the costs of the detrimental ones are vividly portrayed. Depicted beneficial outcomes instill outcome expectations that serve as positive incentives for change.

Showing models discarding subservient roles and challenging inequitable dated norms requires depiction of some negative reactions to reflect the social reality. These discordant episodes serve to model strategies for managing such events successfully. Viewers come to believe they can improve the quality of their lives by similar means used perseveringly. Many efficacy-enhancing elements are incorporated in the transactional episodes. For example, in reducing gender inequities, some of the story lines depict women who struggle for more opportunities and rights for women in ways that improve their life conditions. Occasional references to accomplished women worldwide working to raise the status of women provide also a source of inspiration and support.

Efforts at social change typically challenge power relations and entrenched societal practices. Successes do not come easy. To change their lives for the better, people have to contest dated traditions and normative constraints. For example, managing sexual and reproductive life requires managing emotionally charged relationships embedded in power relations (Bandura, 1994). In societies with gendered power imbalances, women who want to limit childbearing have difficulty talking to their husbands about contraceptive methods. The challenge is to enable women to discuss family planning and to provide them with the social supports to do so. However, the major burden for contraception should not fall solely on women.

Efforts at change must address sociocultural norms and practices at the social system level. Because of the centrality of perceived efficacy in people's lives, media productions help to raise people's beliefs that they can have a hand in bringing about changes in their lives. For example, in a radio serial drama in Tanzania, many women believed they had no control over family size. It was predetermined divinely, by fate or by forces beyond their control. The drama raised viewers' perceived efficacy to manage their reproductive life through family planning (Rogers, Vaughan, Swalehe, Rao, Svenkerud, & Sood, 1999).

People must be prepared for the obstacles they will encounter by modeling prototypic problem situations and effective ways of overcoming them. There are several ways of building resilience to impediments through social modeling. People are taught how to manage setbacks by modeling how to recover from failed attempts. They are shown how to enlist guidance and social support for personal change from self-help groups and other agencies in their localities. Seeing others similar to themselves succeed through perseverant effort also boosts staying power in the face of obstacles.

Attentional and Emotional Engagement

To effect changes serial dramas have to attract and maintain regular viewership. A third principle guiding the creation of the dramatic productions concerns the attentional and emotional engagement of viewers. There are several elements that serve this purpose. The most powerful one is functional relevance. The dramas mirror the realities of people's everyday lives, the impediments with which they struggle, and model ways by which they can enhance their personal development and improve their life conditions. Personally relevant story lines with functional modeling command attention and high interest. Melodramatic embellishments of engrossing plot lines with emotive musical accompaniments give further dramatic intensity to the episodes. Ongoing engagement in the evolving lives of the models provide numerous opportunities to learn from them and to be inspired by them.

Unlike brief exposures to media presentations, that typically leave most viewers untouched, extended dramatizations that reflect viewers' life experiences, get people deeply involved in the lives of the models and attached to them. In India, 400,000 viewers sent letters supporting, advising, or criticizing the various models in the drama. In a serial in Tanzania, women spotted a negative model at a market and drove him out under a rain of tomatoes and mangos. In Brazil, 10,000 people showed up for a virtual filming of a marriage of two of the characters in a serial drama.

Environmental Supports

It is of limited value to motivate people to change if they are not provided with appropriate resources and environmental supports to realize those changes. Enlisting and creating environmental supports is an additional and especially helpful feature for promoting personal and social change. To foster large-scale changes, the dramatic productions are designed to operate through two pathways (Fig. 3.1). In the direct pathway, the serials promote changes by informing, enabling, motivating, and guiding viewers. In the socially mediated pathway, media influences are used to connect viewers to social networks and community settings. These places provide continued personalized guidance, as well as natural incentives and social supports for desired changes. The major share of behavioral and valuational changes are promoted within these social milieus.

People are socially situated in interpersonal networks. When media influences lead viewers to discuss and negotiate matters of import with others

DUAL PATH OF INFLUENCE

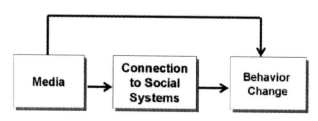

FIG. 3.1. Paths of influences through which communications affect psychosocial changes both directly and via a socially mediated pathway by linking viewers to social networks and community settings. From Bandura (2002a).

in their lives, the media set in motion transactional experiences that further shape the course of change. The socially mediated influences can have a stronger impact than the direct media influence.

Epilogues, often presented by culturally celebrated figures, provide contact information to relevant community services and support groups. For example, women who are challenging stifling traditions are provided with information about service centers and organizations that can help support their efforts. A serial drama in Mexico to promote enrollment in a national literacy program enlisted a popular actor to inform viewers about the program and to encourage them to take advantage of it. On the day after the epilogue about 25,000 people descended on the distribution center in downtown Mexico City to obtain the primers.

These socially enabling dramas are not soap operas in which arrays of characters are endlessly entangled in unseemly conflicts and moral predicaments laced with interpersonal treachery. Nor are they superficial media campaigns marketing quick fixes to intractable social problems. Rather, the sociocognitive genre dramatizes the everyday social problems with which people struggle, models realistic solutions, and provides people with incentives, support, and strategies for bettering their lives. In audience surveys, viewers report the many ways in which the characters in the dramas touch their personal lives. As an Ethiopian viewer explained the relevance and functional value of the realistic dramatizations, "I'm seeing my life in this story. My behavior really changed because of information which is helpful for my life." Functional relevance makes these serials immensely popular. In short, both genres involve storytelling but they tell entirely different types of stories serving markedly different purposes.

The sociocognitive dramatizations are not aimed at simply changing attitudes, which often bear weak relation to behavior. When self-interest conflicts with personal attitudes, people readily find reasons not to act on their attitudes that justify exemptions to them. As previously noted, the dramatizations serve more powerful functions. They inform, enable, guide, and motivate people to effect changes in their lives. The dramatizations further assist people in their efforts at personal and social change by linking them to enabling and supportive subcommunities and beneficial human services.

These serial dramas are also not "family planning" programs foisted on the women of poor nations by powerful outsiders. This communications approach addresses the problem of mounting population growth and possible solutions in broader human terms. In many societies women are treated more like property than persons, denied equitable access to education, forced into prearranged marriages, and granted little say in their reproductive lives. Therefore, one of the central themes in the dramatizations is aimed at raising the status of women so they have equitable access to educational and social opportunities, have a voice in family decisions about child bearing, and serve as active partners in their familial and social lives. This involves raising men's understanding of the legitimacy of women making decisions regarding their reproductive health and family life. Moreover, the engrossing programs serve as an excellent vehicle for modeling a variety of functional life skills woven into the familial and social transactions.

GLOBAL APPLICATIONS OF THE SOCIOCOGNITIVE MODEL

Many worldwide applications of the sociocognitive model in Africa, Asia, and Latin America are promoting personal and society-wide changes that better the lives of millions of people (Bandura, 2002; Singhal, Cody, Rogers, & Sabido, 2004). Some of these applications and formal evaluations of their effects are presented in the section that follows.

Promoting National Literacy

Literacy is vital for personal and national development. To reduce widespread illiteracy, the Mexican government launched a national self-study program. People who were skilled at reading were urged to organize small self-study groups in which they would teach others how to read with primers specifically developed for this purpose. So Sabido created a year-long serial with daily episodes to reach, enable, and motivate people with problems of illiteracy. The main story line in the dramatic series centered on the engaging and informative experiences of a self-study group. The implementation model involved creative translation of social cognitive theory into practice. A popular soap opera performer was cast in the role of the literate model, to take advantage of prestigeful modeling. To enhance the impact of modeling through perceived similarity, she recruits a cast of characters who represent the different segments of the population with problems of illiteracy. Showing people similar to themselves mastering linguistic skills helps to persuade viewers that they too possess the capabilities to master the skills that were being modeled. The serial portrayed collective mastery of competencies and the accompanying benefits.

A prior interview survey revealed several personal demotivating barriers that dissuaded people from enrolling in the national literacy program. These impeding beliefs centered on perceived self-efficacy, critical period constraints, and personal worthiness. Many believed that they lacked the capabilities to master such a complex skill. Others believed that reading skills could be acquired only when one is young. Still others felt that they were unworthy of having an educated person devote their time to help them. These self-handicapping misbeliefs were modeled by the various actors and corrected by the instructor as she persuaded them they possessed the capabilities to succeed. The televised episodes included humor, conflicts, and engrossing discussions of the subjects being read. They portrayed the characters struggling in the initial phases of learning, and then gaining progressive mastery with self-pride in their accomplishments.

To provide vicarious motivators to pursue the self-education program, the dramatic series depicted the substantial benefits of literacy both for personal development and for national efficacy and pride. Melodramatic embellishments and emotive music gave dramatic intensity to the episodes to ensure high viewer involvement.

Epilogues were used to increase memorability of the modeled messages. To facilitate media-promoted changes, the educational agency made the primers easily available. In addition, the series often used real-life settings showing the actors obtaining the primers from an actual distribution center and eventually partaking in a graduation ceremony for actual enrollees. Epilogues also informed the viewers of the national self-study program and encouraged them to take advantage of it. As previously noted, what a powerful motivator it turned out to be.

Millions of viewers watched this series faithfully. Compared to nonviewers, viewers of the dramatic series were much more informed about the national literacy program and expressed more positive attitudes about helping one another to learn. As shown in Fig. 3.2, enrollment in the literacy program was relatively low in the year before the televised series, but rose abruptly during the year of the series.

As people develop a sense of efficacy and competencies that enable them to exercise control over their lives, they serve as models, inspiration, and even tutors for others in the circles in which they travel. This concomitant socially mediated influence can vastly multiply the impact of televised modeling. In the year following the televised series, another 400,000 people enrolled in the self-study literacy program. Through the socially mediated path of influence, televised modeling can set in motion an ever-widening, reverberating process of social change.

The lead model had difficulty getting movie roles because she was considered insufficiently attractive. The serial drama brought her national fame, movie roles, and political power. She became a leading political figure in the more liberally oriented party.

Environmental Sustainability by Stemming Population Growth

Soaring population growth is wreaking havoc with the global environment, depleting natural resources, degrading the quality of life, and overwhelming efforts at social and economic development. The current world

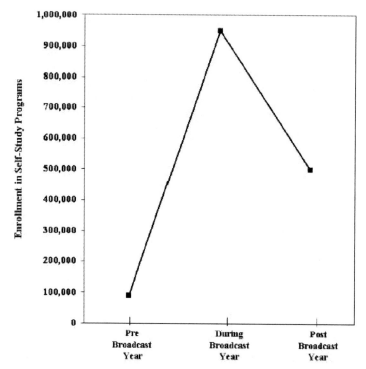

FIG. 3.2. Enrollments in the national literacy program in the year prior to, during, and following the televised serial drama. Drawn from data in Sabido (1981).

population is 6 billion and projected to increase by 50% to 9 billion within the next 50 years. Population growth has stabilized in the more developed nations, but is soaring in the less developed ones (Fig. 3.3). The massive population encumbrance underscores the need to accelerate the types of psychosocial changes that are critical to the reduction of fertility rates and to the promotion of consummatory lifestyles that ensure the sustainability of the environment.

Unless people see family planning as improving their welfare, they have little incentive to adopt it. Sabido (1981) developed a series of serial dramas in Mexico to check the cycle of poverty exacerbated by a high rate of unplanned childbearing. Through modeling with accompanying outcomes, the dramas portrayed the process as well as the personal, social, and economic benefits of family planning. The positive family life of a small family, whose wife worked in a family planning clinic, was contrasted with that of a married sister overburdened with a huge family living in impoverishment and misery.

Much of the drama focused on the married daughter from the huge family, who was beginning to experience severe marital conflicts and distress

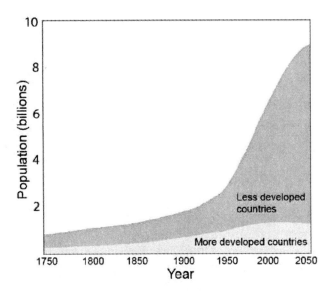

FIG. 3.3. Population growth in developed and less developed countries. From Population Reference Bureau (1998).

over a rapidly expanding family. She served as the transitional model, living in her parents' despairingly crowded and impoverished environment. In dramatic scenes she expresses emotionally her desire for a voice in her family life, to cease having more babies, and to break the cycle of poverty that will condemn her family to an inner-city slum without ability to care adequately for her children. She turns to her aunt for help, which serves as the vehicle for modeling a great deal of information about how to manage marital discord and machismo behavior, how to deal with male resistance to contraception and family planning, how to communicate openly in the family, and how to escape the many problems caused by a family overburdened with children.

As the drama unfolds, the young couple is shown gaining control over their family life and enjoying the accruing benefits with the help of a family planning center. A priest occasionally appeared in the dramas, emphasizing the need for responsible family planning by limiting the number of offspring to those the family can afford to raise adequately. At the end of some of the programs, viewers were informed in epilogues about existing family planning services to facilitate media-promoted changes.

Compared to nonviewers, heavy viewers of the dramatic serial (Sabido, 1981) were more likely to link lower childbearing to social, economic, and psychological benefits. They also developed a more positive attitude toward helping others plan their family. Records of the family planning centers revealed a 32% increase in the number of new contraceptive users over

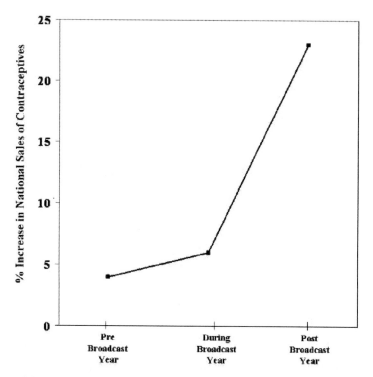

FIG. 3.4. National sales of contraceptives in the two years preceding the serial drama promoting family planning and during the year it was broadcast. Drawn from data in Sabido (1981).

the previous year before the series was televised. People reported that the television portrayal served as the impetus for consulting the health clinics. National sales of contraceptives rose from 4% and 7% in the preceding two baseline years to 23% in the year the program was aired (Fig. 3.4).

Generalization Through Functional Adaptation to Cultural Practices

Applications in India and Kenya illustrate its generalizability of the socio-cognitive model through functional tailoring to diverse cultural practices. Efforts to bring down the rate of population growth must address not only the strategies and benefits of family planning, but also the role and status of women in societies in which they are treated subserviently. In some societies, the equity problems stem from machismo dominance; in others, from marriage and pregnancy at the onset of puberty with no say in the choice of husband or the number and spacing of children; and in still others from dispossession by polygamous marriages. In some societies, women are subjugated to the point where they are repeatedly beaten and are not even allowed to turn on a family radio.

The television program in India was designed to raise the status of women, as well as to promote a smaller family norm. It addressed a variety of themes about family life in the context of broader social norms and practices (Singhal & Rogers, 1999). The subthemes devoted particular attention to family harmony amidst differences among family members, elevation of the status of women in family, social, and economic life, educational opportunities, career options for women, son preference, gender bias in child rearing, the detriment of dowry requirement, choice in spouse selection, teenage marriage and parenthood, spousal abuse, family planning to limit family size, youth delinquency, and community development. Some of the characters personified positive role models for gender equality; others were proponents of the traditional subservient role for women. Still others were transitional models. A famous Indian film actor reinforced the modeled messages in epilogues.

The melodramatic series was immensely popular, enjoying top viewership on television and a massive outpouring of letters in the hundreds of thousands from viewers offering advice and support to the characters. A random sample of viewers reported they had learned from the program that women should have equal opportunities and a say in decisions that affect their lives, programs advancing the welfare of women should be encouraged, cultural diversity should be respected, and that family size should be limited. The more aware viewers were of the messages being modeled, the greater was their support of women's freedom of choice in matters that affect them and of planning for small families (Brown & Cody, 1991; Singhal & Rogers, 1999).

Intensive interviews with villagers revealed that dramatizations sparked serious public discussions about the broadcast themes concerning child marriages, dowry requirements, education of girls, the benefits of small families, and other social issues (Papa et al., 2000). These social transactions went beyond talk to collective community action aimed at changing inequitable normative practices and improving their social future. Indeed, one village sent to the broadcast center a large poster letter signed by its inhabitants stating that they will work to eradicate the practice of dowry, child marriages, and support the education of daughters. The enrollment of girls in elementary and junior high schools rose from 10% to 38% in one year of the broadcasts.

There are many impediments to sociocultural change, but their force weakens over time as new practices gain support and collective benefits outweigh the social costs of harmful traditional practices. In another village young boys and girls created a self-help action group to promote the changes modeled in the serial drama (Law & Singhal, 1999). The system-level effects illustrate how dramatizations that address the social problems that people face in enabling ways can spawn the development of collective efficacy.

In a radio serial drama in India, with a listenership of about 25 million, a mother challenges restrictive cultural norms for her daughter Taru and promotes her education, Taru inspired ardent teenage listeners who had no access to education to become avid readers and raise their academic aspirations. Four of the teenage girls started a school for a large group of poor children in classes held regularly around the village water well. One of the mothers of the teenagers also began a school for illiterate women. The teenagers fight against gender and class discrimination and early forced marriages. Their efforts produce changes in community norms. The elders in the community acknowledge the need to alter their social practices to fit the changing times. Parents began to relax restrictive norms for their daughters. One of the teenagers explained the power of enabling modeling to inspire listeners to work for social change: "*When Taru and her mother can fight harsh circumstances, why can't we?*" Another teenager describes poetically her revered model transformed her life: "*Before Taru there was darkness. Now there is light.*"

Land ownership is highly valued in Kenya. A major story line in the serial drama revolved around the inheritance of land and the impoverishing effect of large families. The contrast modeling involves two brothers, one of whom has a wife, a son, and several daughters, whereas the other brother has multiple wives, nine sons, and even more daughters. They squabble over how to pass on the inherited family farm to the next generation. In Kenya, only sons can inherit property. The monogamous brother argues that his lone male heir is entitled to half the land, the polygamous brother insists on dividing the farm into 10 small plots. In another concurrent story line a teacher pleads with parents, who want their young daughter to quit school, be circumcised, and married off to an arranged partner, to allow her to continue her education which she desperately desires.

The serial drama, which was broadcast via radio to reach rural areas, attracted 40% of the Kenyan population each week as the most popular program on the air. Contraceptive use increased by 58%, and desired family size declined 24%. A survey of women who came to health clinics reported that the radio series helped to persuade their husbands to allow them to seek family planning. Quantitative analyses including multiple controls for possible determinants (Westoff & Rodriguez, 1995). These controls include life-cycle status, number of wives and children, and a host of socioeconomic factors such as ethnicity, religion, education, occupation, and urban–rural residence.

The impact of media exposure on adoption and consistent use of new methods of contraception is shown in Fig. 3.5. The media effect remained after applying the multiple controls. Evidence that the social impact of the dramatizations is enhanced with increased exposure to them sheds further

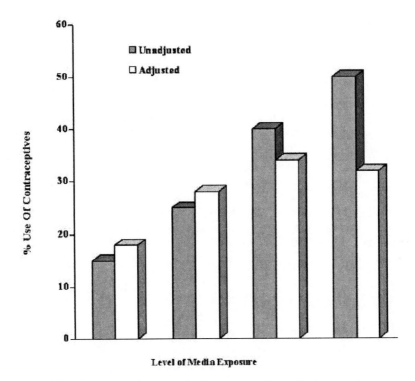

FIG. 3.5. Percentage of women adopting contraceptive methods depending on the amount of exposure to family planning communications in the media. The white bars report the level of contraceptive use after controlling for the women's demographic and socioeconomic characteristics and a host of other potential determinants. From Westoff and Rodriguez (1995).

light on functional efficacy. Internal analyses of evaluation surveys further revealed that the media influence was a major factor in raising motivation to limit birthrate and adopt contraception practices.

Countries containing regions with separate transmitters provide a natural control group. Under these conditions, the serial dramas can be aired in one region with another serving as a control. Following the formal evaluation, the serial can be aired in the control region and its effects measured. Tanzania provided a unique opportunity to conduct this type of field experiment because it contains regions with separate broadcasting transmitters. The population of Tanzania is 36 million, the fertility rate is 5.6 children per woman, and the doubling time for the population at the current rate is 25 years.

The serial drama was broadcast by radio in one major region of the country and the other region served as the control. The program targeted both family planning and sexual practices that increase vulnerability to infection with the AIDS virus. Although, at the outset, the populace was well informed about contraception and AIDS prevention and were favorably disposed toward such practices, they did not translate these attitudes into action. The problem was neither informational nor attitudinal, but motivational. The dramatic series provided the impetus for change.

Compared to the control region, the serialized dramatizations raised viewers' perceived efficacy to determine their family size, decreased the desired number of children, increased the ideal age of marriage for women, increased approval of family planning methods, stimulated spousal communication about family size, and increased use of family planning services and adoption of contraceptive methods.

Figure 3.6 shows the mean number of adopters of contraceptive methods per clinic over time in the broadcast and control regions. Both regions increased slightly at the same rate during the prebroadcast period. The adoption rate increased only slightly in the control region but at an abrupt pronounced rate in the broadcast region. These effects were replicated when the serial was later broadcast in the control region. The replicated effects

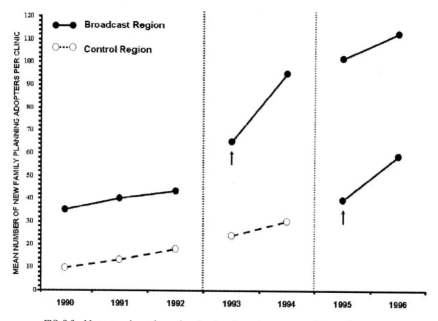

FIG. 3.6. Mean number of new family planning adopters per clinic in the Ministry of Health clinics in the broadcast region and those in the control region. The values left of the dotted line are adoption levels prior to the broadcast; the values between the dotted lines are adoption levels when the serial was aired in the broadcast region but not in the control region; the values to the right of the dotted line are the adoption levels when the serial was aired in both the broadcast region and previous control region. Drawn from data in Rogers et al. (1999).

provide further support for a genuine conditional relation. The fertility rate declined more in the 2-year period of the serial dramas than in the previous 30 years without any change in socioeconomic conditions and little change in death rate (Vaughan, 2003).

As in the Kenya findings, the more often people listened to the broadcasts, the more the married women talked to their spouses about family planning and the higher the rate of adoption of contraceptive methods (Fig. 3.7). These diverse effects remained after multiple controls for other potential determinants, including exposure to other radio programs with family planning and AIDS contents, prebroadcast levels and changes in education, increased access to family planning clinics, radio ownership, and rural–urban differences.

Seventeen segments were included to prevent the spread of the AIDS virus. A particular problem was the transmission of AIDS heterosexually by long-distance truckers at truck stop hubs with hundreds of prostitutes. About 60% of them are infected, and about one third of the truck drivers are also infected. The common belief was that AIDS is transmitted by mosquitoes. Some of the males believed that condoms caused infection and that having sexual intercourse with a virgin would cure AIDS. The program quickly debunked the false beliefs.

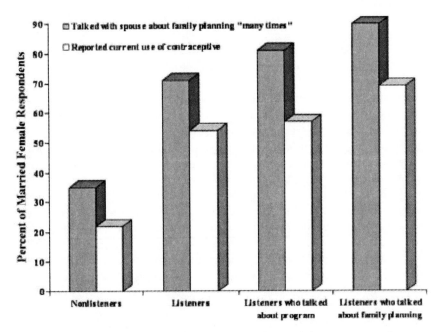

FIG. 3.7. Impact of degree of involvement in the serial drama on women's spousal discussion of family planning and use of contraceptive methods. From Rogers et al. (1999).

In the contrast modeling, the negative trucker engages in risky sex with multiple partners; the positive model adopted safer sex practices and cut back on the number of partners; and a transitional model begins with risky practices but adopts safer ones. The truckers using the safer practices try unsuccessfully to talk their friend into changing his risky ways. He refuses. His wife fears that she will get infected. The community helps her to find work to support her family. She leaves her husband who eventually gets infected and dies of AIDS.

Compared to residents in the control region, those in the broadcast region increased belief in their personal risk of HIV infection through unprotected sexual practices, talked more about HIV infection, reduced the number of sexual partners, and increased condom use (Vaughan, Rogers, Singhal, & Swalehe, 2000). The number of condoms distributed annually by the National AIDS program remained low in the control region, increased substantially in the broadcast region, and increased significantly in the control region after exposure later to the broadcast.

China is the most populous nation in the world facing a projected doubling of its current population to the two billion mark in about 70 years. This enormous population growth will have devastating effects on ecological systems. Urban areas have achieved replacement level fertility, but the inhabitants in rural areas continue to have large families. The Chinese one-child policy heightens the traditional cultural preferences for sons. The serial drama addressed the discriminatory gender bias in the society, and fostered psychosocial changes to supplant coercive institutional controls on fertility with voluntary adoption of contraceptive practices and preferences for small families.

This televised serial drama, that has won numerous prestigious awards, addressed a variety of societal issues. These include, girls' education, arranged marriages, coerced pregnancy, son preference, and women's self-determination. The dramatizations graphically portray the tragedy and injustice of social practices that force women into arranged marriages they do not want and bearing baby girls who are culturally devalued.

The central theme is aimed at altering discriminatory gender norms and practices in the society. Societies are undergoing a historic transition to the information era. It is supplanting brawn with intellect in modern work life. At times of transformative change, there is a mismatch or structural lag between dated normative practices and contemporary social reality. The serial dramas show how educated daughters and not just sons can be productive providers. The drama tries to foster a better normative match to the challenges and opportunities of this new era.

In this drama a father is desperate to receive a dowry payment, so he can buy a bride for his son, his pride and joy. He demands that his daughter agree to an arranged marriage, to an arrogant man of means. She resists because she is in love with a musician of modest means. But to spare her younger sister, who the father targets next, she eventually agrees to the arranged marriage.

As the wedding procession is going down the river, her boyfriend is running along the river bank shouting to her, and playing a tune he played when they first met. Her husband is enraged by the boyfriend's intrusion. He kicks out the guests after the wedding ceremony and rapes her. She finds herself trapped in a miserable marriage with an abusive husband. As the story unfolds, she gives birth to a female infant. He demands she get pregnant again to bear him a son. She leaves him, remarries, and pursues a successful career.

Viewers were inspired and strengthened by the determination and courage of female characters who challenge the subordinate status of women, and who strive to change detrimental cultural practices. The central figure in this serial has become a highly admired national model for raising the valuation of women and expanding opportunities for them to become active participant in the social and economic life of Chinese society.

Applications of the sociocognitive model have yielded positive results in diverse cultural milieus and across spheres of functioning. The dramatic serials are an extraordinarily effective vehicle for reaching vast numbers of people over a prolonged period. Viewers get deeply involved in the lives of the televised characters and are inspired by them to take steps that can improve their lives. Radio versions of the serial dramas can reach vast rural populations. Airing of the televised serials is typically followed by an increase in the status of women, preference for smaller families, and adoption of contraceptive methods and self-protection against sexually transmitted diseases. The strength of the social impact increases as a function of level of exposure to the broadcasts. The more that people watch a media program, the more they talk about the issues that are aired, the more supportive they are of gender equality, the higher their perceived efficacy to regulate their reproductive behavior, and the more likely they are to adopt contraceptive methods. Societies with a burgeoning population need not, nor can afford to wait until they become economically prosperous to bring birthrates down. Indeed, nations cannot achieve much national progress until they bring their population growth under control.

Extensions of the Sociocognitive Model Through Storytelling

The sociocognitive model using storytelling as the vehicle of change lends itself readily to creative spinoffs and extensions. Diverse modes of influence expand their reach and mutually reinforce their impact. For example, to curtail the transmission of HIV infection spread heterosexually in Ethiopia by long-distance truckers, PMC created a 24-episode serial drama centered on this theme. The audiocassettes were distributed to truck drivers and commercial sex workers (Ryerson & Teffera, 2004). Mobile stage dramas, that reach millions of people in all walks of life, reinforce the themes highlighted in the national radio serial. PMC has assisted in creating significant social themes that can be easily incorporated into popular, prime-time telenovelas on TV Globo which, dubbed in different languages, reach about 900 million people worldwide. The themes center on diverse issues, such as gender relations, marital conflict, domestic violence, reproductive health, contraception, risky sexual behavior, homosexuality, and adolescent sexuality (Fig. 3.8).

To reach teenagers, PCI created radio minidramas that speak to matters of concern to them. Each program in this radio series, which is aired weekly, begins with a street poll of adolescents that frames the relevant topic. It is then explored in a brief minidrama that helps listeners to make informed choices for healthier and safer lives. The minidrama is followed by listener call-ins where invited guests provide further guidance and referrals on where to go for additional information and help. The programs, which enjoy high popularity, are written, produced, and hosted by youth. The episodes address such issues as drug abuse, teenage sexuality and

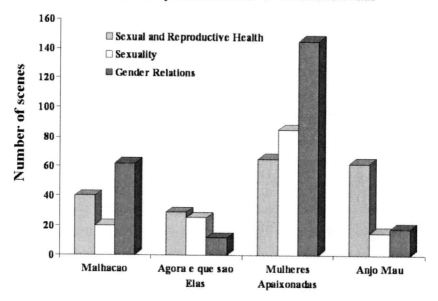

FIG. 3.8. Number of social themes incorporated in prime-time *telenovelas* broadcast by TV Globo aired in Rio de Janeiro. From Ryerson (2004).

pregnancy, disease prevention, violence, and other psychosocial issues of concern to teenagers.

Sabido (2004) has created an Internet-based model to address vexing societal problems in a timely fashion as they appear in national headlines. Brief photo dramas are used as the vehicle for this purpose. They include brief engrossing dramatizations of the problems in still photographs with hyperlinks to the social context of a current problem, its historical roots, current causes, various effects, and possible alternative solutions. For example, in response to a rash of anti-Semitism, the dramatization depicts a woman in deep conflict over her husband's involvement in anti-Semitic activities. She seeks the help of her priest. Viewers are linked to information about the Holocaust, conditions that spawn anti-Semitism, and how to deal with the problem both in the family and at the societal level. This is a highly flexible and convenient vehicle for addressing societal problems as they arise and helping people on how to deal with them.

Modification of Consummatory Lifestyles

Environmental degradation is affected not only by population size, but also by the level of consumption, and the damage to the ecosystem caused by the technologies used to supply the consumable products (Ehrlich, Ehrlich, & Daily, 1995). There are limits to the earth's carrying capacity. The global ecosystem cannot sustain burgeoning populations and high consumption of finite natural resources. The sociocognitive model lends itself readily to other types of lifestyle changes, such as environmental conservation and consummatory practices to promote environmental sustainability. For example, an Indian serial drama, that centered on environment preservation, motivated villagers to take collective action to improve sanitation, reduce potential health hazards, adopt fuel conservation practices to reduce pollution, and launch a tree-planting campaign (Papa et al., 2000). They persuaded other villages to institute similar environmental practices.

If people are to make decisions supportive of sustained development, they need to be informed of the ecological costs of their consummatory practices and enabled and motivated to turn enlightened concern into constructive courses of action. This change is best achieved through multiple modes of communication (Singhal & Rogers, 1999). Many of the lifelong consummatory habits are formed during childhood years. It is easier to prevent wasteful practices than to try to change them after they have become deeply entrenched as part of a lifestyle.

To address the environmental problems created by overconsumption, PCI produced a video, *The Cost of Cool*, for distribution to schools that focuses on the buying habits of teenagers (PCI, 2000). It tracks the ecological costs of the manufacture of everyday items such as T-shirts and sneakers.

Providing teenagers with sound information helps them make informed choices in their buying habits. As one viewer put it, *"I'll never look at a T-shirt in the same way."* Popular entertainment formats, such as music concerts, recordings, and videos, provide another vehicle for reaching mass youth populations. The themes address critical social issues, substance abuse, violence, teen sexuality, and gender equality. The impact of these complimentary approaches requires systematic evaluation. The increasing magnitude of the environmental problem calls for multifaceted efforts to alter behavioral practices that degrade the ecological supports of life.

Concluding Remarks

The research cited in this chapter provides convergent evidence from diverse cultural milieus, adaptational themes, and domains of functioning, methodologies, multiple controls for a host of other potential determinants, and multifaceted forms of assessments. The findings attest to the social utility of the sociocognitive communication model for effecting personal and social change grounded in internationally endorsed human values with sensitive adaptations to cultural diversity.

We enjoy the benefits left by those before us who collectively fought for social reforms that improved our lives. Our own collective efficacy will shape how future generations live their lives. The times call for social initiatives that enable people to play a part through their collective voice in bettering the human condition.

REFERENCES

Bandura, A. (1986). *Social foundations of thought and action: A social cognitive theory.* Englewood Cliffs, NJ: Prentice-Hall.

Bandura, A. (1994). Social cognitive theory and exercise of control over HIV infection. In R. DiClemente & J. Peterson (Eds.), *Preventing AIDS: Theories and methods of behavioral interventions* (pp. 25–59). New York: Plenum.

Bandura, A. (1997). *Self-efficacy: The exercise of control.* New York: Freeman.

Bandura, A. (2000). Exercise of human agency through collective efficacy. *Current Directions in Psychological Science, 9,* 75–78.

Bandura, A. (2001a). Social cognitive theory: An agentic perspective. *Annual Review of Psychology, 52,* 1–26.

Bandura, A. (2001b). Social cognitive theory of mass communications. In J. Bryant & D. Zillman (Eds.), *Media effects: Advances in theory and research* (2nd ed., pp. 121–153). Mahwah, NJ: Lawrence Erlbaum Associates.

Bandura, A. (2002a). Environmental sustainability by sociocognitive deceleration of population growth. In P. Schmuck & W. Schultz (Eds.), *The psychology of sustainable development* (pp. 209–238). Dordrecht, the Netherlands: Kluwer.

Bandura, A. (2002b). Growing primacy of human agency in adaptation and change in the electronic era. *European Psychologist, 7,* 2–16.

Brown, W. J., & Cody, M. J. (1991). Effects of a prosocial television soap opera in promoting women's status. *Human Communication Research, 18,* 114–142.

Ehrlich, P. R., Ehrlich, A. H., & Daily, G. C. (1995). *The stork and the plow: The equity answer to the human dilemma.* New York: Putnam.

Gerbner, G., Gross, L., Morgan, M., Signorielli, & Shanahan (2002). Growing up with television: Cultivation processes. In J. Bryant & D. Zillman (Eds.), *Media effects: Advances in theory and research* (pp. 43–68). Mahwah, NJ: Lawrence Erlbaum Associates.

Law, S., & Singhal, A. (1999). Efficacy in letter-writing to an entertainment-education radio serial. *Gazette, 61,* 355–372.

Locke, E. A., & Latham, G. P. (1990). *A theory of goal setting and task performance.* Englewood Cliffs, NJ: Prentice-Hall.

Papa, M. J., Singhal, A., Law, S., Pant, S., Sood, S., Rogers, E. M., & Shefner-Rogers, C. L. (2000). Entertainment-education and social change: An analysis of parasocial interaction, social learning, collective efficacy, and paradoxical communication. *Journal of Communication, 50,* 31–55.

PCI. (2000). *Fifteenth anniversary.* New York: Population Communications International.

Poindexter, D. O. (2004). A history of entertainment-education, 1958–2000. The origins of entertainment-education. In A. Singhal, M. J. Cody, E. M., Rogers, & M. Sabido (Eds.), *Entertainment-education and social change: History, research, and practice* (pp.). Mahwah, NJ: Lawrence Erlbaum Associates.

Population Reference Bureau. (1998). *World population: More than just numbers.* Washington, DC: Population Reference Bureau.

Rogers, E. M., Vaughan, P. W., Swalehe, R. M. A., Rao, N., Svenkerud, P., & Sood, S. (1999). Effects of an entertainment-education radio soap opera on family planning behavior in Tanzania. *Studies in Family Planning, 30,* 1193–1211.

Ryerson, W. N. (1994). Population communications international: Its role in family planning soap operas. *Population and Environment: A Journal of Interdisciplinary Studies, 15,* 255–264.

Ryerson, W. N. (1999). *Population media center.* Shelburne, Vermont.

Ryerson, W. N. (2004). *Population media center.* Shelburne, Vermont.

Ryerson, W. N., & Teffera, N. (2004). Organizing a comprehensive national plan for entertainment-education in Ethiopia. In A. Singhal, M. J. Cody, E. M. Rogers, & M. Sabido (Eds.), *Entertainment-education and social change: History, research, and practice* (pp. 177–188). Mahwah, NJ: Lawrence Erlbaum Associates.

Sabido, M. (1981). *Towards the social use of soap operas.* Mexico City, Mexico: Institute for Communication Research.

Sabido, M. (2002). *El tono* [The tone]. Mexico City: Universidad Nacional Autonoma de Mexico.

Sabido, M. (2004). The origins of entertainment-education. In A. Singhal, M. J. Cody, E. M. Rogers, & M. Sabido (Eds.), *Entertainment-education and social change: History, research, and practice* (pp. 61–74). Mahwah, NJ: Lawrence Erlbaum Associates.

Singhal, A., Cody, M. J., Rogers, E. M., & Sabido, M. (Eds.). (2004). *Entertainment-education and social change: History, research, and practice.* Mahwah, NJ: Lawrence Erlbaum Associates.

Singhal, A., & Rogers, E. M. (1999). *Entertainment-education: A communication strategy for social change.* Mahwah, NJ: Lawrence Erlbaum Associates.

Vaughn, P. W. (2003). *The onset of fertility transition in Tanzania during the 1990's: The role of two entertainment-education radio dramas.* Submitted for publication.

Vaughan, P. W., Rogers, E. M., Singhal, A., & Swalehe, R. M. A. (2000). Entertainment-education and HIV/AIDS prevention: A field experiment in Tanzania. *Journal of Health Communication, 5,* 81–100.

Westoff, C. F., & Rodriguez, G. (1995). The mass media and family planning in Kenya. *International Family Planning Perspectives, 21,* 26–31.

Using Psychological Science to Achieve Ecological Sustainability

Stuart Oskamp
Claremont Graduate University

P. Wesley Schultz
California State University, San Marcos

A great change in our stewardship of the earth and the life on it is required, if vast human misery is to be avoided and our global home on this planet is not to be irretrievably mutilated.

—Union of Concerned Scientists (1993)

This urgent statement, from the *World Scientists' Warning to Humanity*, was signed by more than 1,600 eminent scientists worldwide. It raises the prospect that the world we pass on to our descendants may not be one worth living in. This is the issue of *ecological sustainability*—using the Earth's resources in ways that will allow future generations to survive on Earth and to maintain an acceptable quality of life.

The threats to Earth's life-sustaining environment are many and diverse. In recent years they have been described by many writers (e.g., Flavin, 2001; Oskamp, 2000; Oskamp & Schultz, 2005; Schmuck & Schultz, 2002; Schneider, 1997; World Resources Institute, 2002; Worldwatch Institute, 2003, 2004; Zelezny & Schultz, 2000). In this chapter we focus on psychological contributions that can help to overcome these threats and advance the world toward sustainable patterns of human behavior—patterns that must be accomplished at all levels, individual, organizational, and national. First, for specificity, we simply list some of the main threats to ecological sustainability that have been described at length by the writers mentioned above.

THREATS TO ECOLOGICAL SUSTAINABILITY

These threats arise from three main sources: the growth of human population, which has more than tripled since 1930, reaching 6 billion in 1999
(Pimentel et al., 1994); overconsumption of natural resources, 25% of which
are used by the United States, though it has less than 5% of the Earth's population; and underconservation of the natural resources that are used
(Durning, 1992). Among the major threats are:

- Global climate change due to the greenhouse effect (IPCC, 2001);
- Destruction of much of the protective ozone layer;
- Deforestation and resulting local climate changes;
- Species extinction and loss of biodiversity;
- Exhaustion of fisheries, agricultural land, and fresh water supplies;
- Toxic pollution of air and water supplies (e.g., smog and acid rain);
- Depletion of nonrenewable energy resources, such as fossil fuels;
- Health and genetic effects of human exposure to toxic chemicals, such
  as dioxin;
- Limited access to adequate health care, nutrition, and sanitation;
- Spread of devastating diseases such as AIDS;
- Additive, interactive, or synergistic effects of ecological threats in com-
  bination;
- Possible discontinuities in environmental responses to stressors, such
  as the recent collapse of various oceanic fisheries, sudden rather than
  gradual changes in Earth's temperature, or diversion of ocean currents
  that affect climate (Taylor, 1999).

Taken together, the immensity of these problems is obvious. At the very
least, they threaten the quality of life for the current and future generations
of all living things. At the extreme, they threaten the long-term survival of
human life on this planet. Moreover, they are urgent threats, which must be
addressed immediately, particularly because some of their effects may be
irreversible once they have begun (Meadows, Meadows, & Randers, 1992;
Meadows, Randers, & Meadows, 2004; Stern, 1992).

PSYCHOLOGY'S ROLE

Psychology, in combination with the other social sciences, can be crucial in
moving the world toward sustainable patterns. Almost all of the ecological
threats just listed are caused or exacerbated by human activities, and they

can all be diminished or reversed by changes in human behavior, policies, or systems. Social scientists can offer research findings, implement and evaluate behavior-change programs, and offer policy advice aimed toward sustainability.

A broad principle that is vital in addressing ecological threats is the *precautionary principle*, which states that:

> When an activity raises threats of harm to human health or the environment, precautionary measures should be taken even if some cause and effect relationships are not fully established scientifically. In this context the proponents of an activity, rather than the public, should bear the burden of proof. (Montague, 1998, pp. 1–2)

A corollary of this approach is the *polluter pays* principle—whatever person or organization pollutes the environment must pay for the resulting damages. Some national governments have recently implemented these principles in their laws concerning environmental management (Wahlstrom, 1999).

Useful Theories

Theories are a vital ingredient, both in scientific research and in applied work that aims to solve social problems such as the earlier-mentioned threats to sustainability. Among their most important functions in science, theories:

- Guide our research procedures,
- Help us understand and interpret research findings,
- Provide a basis for predicting what will happen under certain specific conditions,
- Specify the conditions or variables that must be established or controlled to create programs or interventions that will succeed in accomplishing desired goals.

Theories are a key element in applied work and they bridge the gap between basic and applied science. Applied researchers are interested in changing specific behaviors—for example, energy conservation, recycling, use of public transportation, green buying, or donations to environmental organizations. In applied work, something needs to be done to change the behavior, and the choice of intervention strategy *must* be guided by theory. The guiding theory can be derived from personal experience with the program or behavior, from lay theories of human behavior, or ideally from psychological research that is sufficiently rigorous to be published in peer-reviewed scientific journals. Given the importance of theories, a solid background and training in the discipline of psychology can be indispensable in applied work.

Since environmental issues first emerged as pressing problems in the early 1960s, many varying theories have been applied to understand and promote proenvironmental behaviors (Vining & Ebreo, 2002). Here we briefly mention some of the theories that have successfully guided either research findings or development and implementation of programs and policies to increase proenvironmental behavior and sustainable systems. In a later section of this chapter, we provide an in-depth focus on some key findings of five major theoretical approaches.

Behavior Analysis. Behavior analysis is not a specific theory, but rather a general scientific approach to changing behavior. It involves analyzing the antecedents and consequences of a specific pattern of behavior, choosing interventions that manipulate one or more of these antecedents and/or consequences, studying the effects of these interventions, and reiteratively improving the effectiveness of the intervention until a desired change is obtained. The approach is largely based on a *rational choice* theory of human behavior, which views humans as active decision makers, weighing the costs and benefits of an action, and then acting. By increasing the perceived benefits of the action, and/or decreasing the perceived costs, the behavior analyst can facilitate change. Key findings of this approach as applied to ecological behaviors are summarized in the next section of this chapter.

Social Dilemmas. A social dilemma is a situation in which individuals, acting in their own best interest, have a negative collective consequence for their larger group. In these situations each individual benefits from pursing his or her own self-interest, but if most or all individuals cooperated it would yield a better result for the group. One example of a social dilemma is commuting by car versus carpooling or using public transportation (Van Lange, Van Vugt, Meertens, & Ruiter, 1998). Typically, driving produces a better outcome for the individual (it is faster and more convenient), but more people taking public transportation would produce a better collective outcome (less pollution, less traffic congestion, and less use of natural resources). A number of researchers have used social dilemma theory to understand environmental problems and to develop approaches to promoting the collective good (Biel, Von Borgstede, & Dahlstrand, 1999; Samuelson, 1990; Samuelson, Messick, Rutte, & Wilke, 1984). One notable series of studies in this area examined transportation decisions (Van Lange et al., 1998; Van Vugt, Van Lange, & Meertens, 1996; Van Vugt, Van Lange, Meertens, & Joireman, 1996; Joireman et al., 2001). Across a number of studies, the authors found that an individual's decision to support programs intended to reduce individual car use was related to perceived benefits to the self. However, they also found strong evidence for individual differences in the importance of benefits to oneself versus benefits to the collective. Individuals with a proself value orientation tend to emphasize the importance of self-gains (e.g., reduced commuting time), whereas people with a prosocial value orientation are more focused on collective gains (e.g., less traffic congestion for everyone).

Cognitive Dissonance. Studies of cognitive dissonance theory date back to research in the 1950s by Festinger (1954, 1957). The essence of the theory is that individuals have a desire to remain consistent in their thoughts and actions. When a person has two or more cognitions that are inconsistent, an unpleasant state of tension arises, and the individual is motivated to resolve the dissonance (e.g., by changing the behavior, adding additional cognitions, or derogating the source of one of the cognitions). An example of using dissonance theory to promote proenvironmental behavior was provided by Dickerson, Thibodeau, Aronson, and Miller (1992), who developed an intervention to arouse dissonance regarding water usage in a gym shower. As swimmers left the swimming pool, they were approached by a researcher, who inquired about their showering habits and asked them to sign a petition encouraging other people to conserve water. Participants in the dissonance condition were reminded that they didn't always conserve water (based on their reports to the survey), yet they had signed a petition stating that others should conserve—thus they were hypocrites! Results showed that swimmers in the dissonance condition took significantly shorter showers than participants in the control condition or the conditions where they received a petition alone or a reminder alone.

Persuasion. Social psychologists have had a longstanding interest in persuasion, and some of them have applied basic principles of persuasion and social influence to promote proenvironmental behavior. Although most persuasion research has focused on changing attitudes or intentions, a few studies have focused on actual behavior. This approach is well illustrated by a series of studies by Aronson and his colleagues (Aronson & Gonzales, 1990; Gonzales, Aronson, & Costanzo, 1988). In one study, the team examined compliance by householders with recommendations made by a home energy auditor. The energy auditors gave free inspections to households that requested them, concluding with recommendations on ways to save energy. (Such energy audits are still widely used by utility companies.) The persuasion techniques involved using vivid language, inducing verbal commitments, and framing the message in terms of money lost by inaction. Illustrating the use of vivid language, attics without proper insulation were described as "naked attics." Similarly, an inspector might say:

Look at the cracks under that door! It may not seem like much to you, but if you were to add all the cracks around and under each of these doors, you'd have the equivalent of a hole the size and circumference of a basketball. (Gonzales et al., 1988, p. 1054)

Baseline measures taken before the auditors were trained in these persuasion techniques showed that approximately 20% of households actually implemented the changes that were suggested. However, after the auditors were trained in these techniques, 61% of homeowners made the recommended changes.

Other Theories. In addition to these major theoretical approaches, many other theories have been applied to environmental issues (Vining & Ebreo, 2002). They include:

- Schwartz's norm activation model (Stern, Dietz, & Black, 1985–1986),
- Geller's model of actively caring (Allen & Ferrand, 1999; Geller, 1995),
- Schwartz's value system (Schultz & Zelezny, 1999),
- Deci and Ryan's self-determination theory (Pelletier, 2002),
- Ajzen's theory of planned behavior, which is discussed in a later section (Cordano & Frieze, 2000; Kaiser & Gutscher, 2003),
- theories of emotions in understanding attitudes and behaviors (Grob, 1995; Kals & Maes, 2002).

In the following sections we present examples of important research findings concerning sustainability derived from five major theoretical approaches, and we briefly discuss their theoretical underpinnings and implications.

BEHAVIOR ANALYSIS APPROACHES

In the environmental area, behavioral analytic procedures have been used to increase environmentally protective behavior patterns (e.g., carpooling, using public transportation, purchasing returnable bottles) and to decrease environmentally destructive ones (e.g., littering, electricity consumption, high private vehicle mileage) (Geller, 2002).

Research Examples

Prompts Can Reduce Littering. Prompts are visual or auditory reminders to carry out an action, such as a sticker beside a light switch saying "Please Turn Off the Lights." Many studies have shown ways to state and place prompts so that they will influence behavior. One example was a study by Houghton (1993), in which the introduction of visual and auditory prompts in a high school cafeteria significantly decreased littering (i.e., misplaced solid waste), and a combination of the two types of prompts decreased littering by a larger proportion.

Variable Fees Improved Efficiency of Trash Collection. In the early 1980s, Seattle's trash collection service charged each household the same amount, and the average number of cans of garbage collected from households was 3.5 per week. But then the city began a free curbside pickup program for recyclable materials, and it began charging a variable fee for trash collection, depending on the number of cans of garbage that each household put out. As a result, by 1992, the city collected huge amounts of recyclables and decreased its costs for trash disposal, the amount of trash collected was sharply decreased, lengthening the useful lifespan of the garbage landfills, and the average number of cans of garbage collected each week dropped drastically to only 1 per household (Cuthbert, 1994; Shireman, 1993).

Television Feedback to Large Regional Groups. During the international oil crisis in the summer of 1979, daily feedback about regional gas consumption was provided by a major TV station in the Midland–Odessa area of Texas (population 300,000). Every weekday evening in the 6 o'clock news program, the station ran a 30-second announcement that included a graph showing each day's total gasoline consumption in the area, gave praise for reduced consumption and a conservation tip from the announcer, and encouraged competition in conservation between the two main cities in the area. The gas consumption data were obtained from a random sample of gas stations in the area, whose managers computed total consumption in the previous 24-hour period ending at 3 p.m. from automatic pump meters. Research assistants obtained these reports by phone, computed total regional consumption, and relayed the figures to the TV station in time for the 6 p.m. news.

The study design used an ABABA repeated-treatment-and-withdrawal procedure (Rothstein, 1980). By agreement with the TV station, there was a 2-week period of baseline data collection, then 3 weeks of the daily consumption feedback, then 2 weeks when the feedback was withdrawn, then a further 3 weeks of daily feedback, then discontinuation of the feedback, and finally 1 week of follow-up data collection 3 months later. The baseline daily consumption of gas in the whole region was about 237,000 gallons. During the first feedback period consumption dropped by 30%, to 70% of the baseline; during the 2-week withdrawal period it increased slightly to 71%; in the next feedback period it dropped further to 67%; and at the 3-month follow-up it increased to 85% of baseline. The overall daily savings during the feed-back periods averaged 31.5% of baseline, or 75,000 gallons of gas per day—a figure that was much greater than the reduction in other areas of the country during this oil-crisis period.

Conceptual Conclusions

Research findings such as these have a clear value in helping society to change environmentally destructive patterns. However, a recent review lamented that behavior analysis methods have not been used enough in applications relevant to environmental policies and problems (Geller, 2002). The review suggested several reasons for this relative neglect. First is the fact that most behavior analysis studies are published in professional journals that are read mostly by other psychologists, and their authors rarely attempt to impress their findings on decision makers who are responsible for determining policies concerning large-scale environmentally relevant procedures. (An exception is the social marketing work described in the next section.)

A second reason why promising research findings have too seldom been used in practical environmental programs is that behavior analysts have most often aimed their studies at curtailment behaviors (repetitive behaviors such as turning off lights, or reducing vehicle mileage) rather than one-time efficiency behaviors (such as purchasing a more fuel-efficient auto or insulating one's house). However, the one-time efficiency procedures usually save much more energy or other environmental resources than do the repetitive curtailment behaviors (Gardner & Stern, 2002). Also, researchers have studied the actions of individuals and households much more often than the actions of corporations, organizations, or governments; but the large-scale actions of corporations, organizations, and governments have much greater detrimental effects on the environment than do the actions of individuals. Furthermore, the long-term maintenance and diffusion of behavior-change procedures have rarely been studied, and careful longitudinal evaluation studies of the long-term effects of environment-protective programs are badly needed (Geller, 2002).

In surveying the results of many behavior-change programs, Geller (2002) summarized several principles that affect their success. He emphasized that behavior is most likely to be influenced by consequences that occur soon and with relative certainty. Most environmentally *destructive* behavior has consequences of this sort, such as convenience, comfort, or apparent efficiency. Unfortunately, environmentally protective actions often have consequences that are hard to notice because they are far removed in time or dependent on the combined actions of huge numbers of people, so that any one individual's contribution is invisible. One result of weak expected consequences is that people often ignore the desirability of proenvironmental behaviors until an emergency occurs, in which the punishing consequences of continued waste are apparent, such as droughts or gas shortages.

In analyzing the effects of various interventions, Geller (2002) emphasized that behavior-change programs should utilize positive, rather than negative, consequences of people's actions. Such positive consequences favorably affect people's attitudes as well as their behavior, and they are more likely to lead to a voluntarily accepted social norm. However, governmental attempts to protect the environment usually take the form of laws or regulations that emphasize penalties or disincentives and require continuing enforcement efforts. (One exception is the "bottle bills" passed by 11 states and several Canadian provinces, which give monetary rewards for returning beverage containers instead of throwing them away. Even if the first user throws the bottle away, other individuals often find the reward sufficiently motivating for them to pick up and return discarded containers.) In general, strategies using positive rewards have to continue the reward indefinitely, for otherwise the desired behavior usually quickly returns to its former level when the reward is discontinued.

A limitation of behavior-change programs that are aimed at individual-level behavior, if they do not utilize laws or regulations, is that they require a large number of intervention agents in order to achieve major increases in environmentally protective behavior (Geller, 2002). One way in which this has sometimes been successfully accomplished has been to enlist numerous neighborhood "block leaders" or other volunteers to contact their neighbors and friends and advocate the desired behavior patterns. This approach has often been combined with a commitment procedure, by having the intervention agents request other participants to sign a pledge statement or post a small sticker indicating their support of the behavioral goal.

Extending this commitment strategy, Geller (2002) has emphasized that individuals can utilize a behavior-analytic approach to help *themselves* internalize a behavioral norm through a process of *self*-persuasion and *self*-management. Eventually this self-directed pattern of behavior will be transformed to an automatic habit. This process can be considerably aided by support from others, particularly peer-group members. However, too much external pressure can prevent the development of internal motivation and self-direction (Lepper & Greene, 1978). In contrast, Geller (2002) stressed that personal commitment and self-persuasion can lead to a feeling of *responsibility* in which individuals go beyond "the call of duty" in protecting environmental resources (cf. Aronson, 1999). Environmental protection often requires inconvenient or effortful actions, and in such situations external pressure through persuasion techniques has often been found to be relatively unsuccessful.

SOCIAL MARKETING

A coherent system for accomplishing socially desirable goals such as promoting sustainable behavior has been designed by McKenzie-Mohr (2000). This system begins with psychological research knowledge and expertise, which is then applied to planning and delivering a program to achieve a specific desirable environmental goal. McKenzie-Mohr terms this process *community-based social marketing* because the programs are usually organized on a city or county scale, rather than a national one, and they take account of local conditions, attitudes, and history. Also, these programs usually avoid or de-emphasize the common information-intensive approach of using mass-media advertising campaigns to enhance public knowledge of an issue and change attitudes toward it. They avoid that approach because much psychological research has shown that such information campaigns typically have weak or no effects on the desired behaviors (Aronson & Gonzales, 1990; Costanzo, Archer, Aronson, & Pettigrew, 1986; Schultz, 2002).

The conceptual framework of this social marketing system comprises four essential steps, each of which involves psychological expertise. It also emphasizes that programs should be tailored to and aimed at specific segments of the public, and that they must be designed so as to overcome whatever barriers prevent that segment from engaging in the desired behaviors. The four steps in the system are as follows (McKenzie-Mohr, 2000):

I. Uncovering Barriers and Selecting Target Behaviors. Any broad goal, such as decreasing fossil fuel use, can be achieved through various activities (e.g., encouraging carpooling, or increasing household insulation). Because it is usually infeasible to emphasize all of these activities at once, an informed decision must be made about which activity to target in the planned program. That decision should be based on the answers to three questions: (a) the potential impact of the behavior, (b) the barriers that impede the behavior, and (c) whether there are sufficient resources to overcome these barriers. For each proposed target behavior, research is usually necessary to identify the barriers to it that affect a substantial segment of the public. This may be done through focus groups, observational studies, or survey research. Barriers may be either internal (e.g., lack of motivation) or external (e.g., no carpool program in one's region). Understanding the barriers and resources will make it possible for social scientists to design behavior-change strategies that are likely to be effective. For instance, it is usually harder to change and maintain a repetitive behavior (e.g., daily setting of a thermostat) than it is to accomplish a one-time change, such as installing a programmable thermostat that doesn't require daily setting changes (Kempton, Darley, & Stern, 1992).

2. Designing Strategies. Strategies should be designed to remove as many of the identified barriers to the target behavior as possible. Psychological research findings are often valuable in this process. For instance, if the barrier is low motivation, a strategy utilizing a commitment procedure may be effective. If the barrier is doubt about the desirable behavior, a strategy emphasizing social norms may be used. Or, if the barrier is lack of knowledge, a strategy of presenting clear-cut information may be a good choice.

3. Piloting the Program. Though past research findings may point to selection of a particular strategy, it is essential to do a pilot test of the proposed program to see if it actually works with the particular population segment at hand. In this process, use of appropriate psychological research methods and statistical tests can lead to effective procedures and definitive pilot results. Moreover, if the pilot shows insufficient behavior changes, the proposed program must be modified and further pilot tests must be conducted until the desired behavioral effects are achieved. Only then should the program be presented to the whole target community.

4. Evaluation of Program Results. After the program has run for a reasonable period, it is essential to conduct evaluation research to see what its actual effects have been. Again, this process requires psychological expertise to obtain relevant and definitive findings. Furthermore, it should focus on actual behavior or its consequences (e.g., observed carpooling, or insulation purchases) rather than self-reports of these behaviors, which are often biased or unreliable.

Research Example

Some excellent examples of community-based social marketing (CBSM) come from programs to increase water-use efficiency in Canadian cities (Bach, 2004; McKenzie-Mohr, 2000). Local officials in the province of Ontario wanted to decrease summer lawn watering in order to avoid the necessity of building a new water-processing plant. Survey research and observation were used to identify barriers to reduced lawn watering. The first barrier found by researchers was that residents were not aware of when they had watered their lawn enough; this barrier was overcome by giving them a water gauge that provided that answer. A second barrier, weak motivation, was attacked by asking householders to make a commitment to use less water. The commitment involved signing a pledge statement that they agreed to water their lawns only on odd (or even) days, only to a one-inch depth, and only when there had been no rain in the previous week; 72% of those approached signed this commitment. Furthermore, an additional feature of personal communication was employed by having the gauge, the commitment procedure, and a personal discussion of efficient water use all delivered to residents by a student employee on a bicycle. The cyclist also delivered a "prompt"—a cap with a printed reminder of when and how much to water—which was to be placed over the outside water faucet.

All of these procedures were used with a randomly selected experimental group of residents, while a comparable control group received information only, in the form of a packet of materials discussing efficient water use. Comparing data collected before the program with later data collected in the summer months, the results showed that households in the experimental group decreased lawn watering by 54% while the control group *increased* by 15%. Moreover, watering lawns for more than one hour decreased by 66% in the experimental group, whereas it *increased* by 96% in the control group. These impressive results were calculated to have achieved a reduction in peak water usage that saved nearly $1 million in water plant development costs, whereas the total research and intervention cost was only $80,000.

Continuing this work, a large-scale intervention to decrease the demand for residential water (mostly lawn watering) was conducted in three regions of Ontario, Canada (Bach, 2004). In this study, bulk water meters were installed in neighborhoods to measure overall water usage. The meters were installed without informing the residents, since the mere awareness of the meters might have been sufficient to induce behavior change. The research was done in three demographically similar regions of the province, measuring approximately 500 households in each region. In the control region, program staff members brought each household a rain gauge, a flyer promoting decreased water usage, and an outdoor hose tag reminding residents of the program (program cost: $22 per household). In the second community, CBSM techniques were used, in which households received frequent personal contact from the research team (university students) along with the rain gauge and educational materials (program cost: $44 per household). Finally, in the third region, less-intense CBSM techniques were used, with mailed letters about the program and less-frequent personal contact from students, who gave each household a free rain gauge and educational materials (program cost: $18 per household).

Baseline data showed that residents in the control region were initially using less water. However, the key comparison of water usage prior to the summer with that during the summer-months intervention period showed that the two CBSM regions had substantially decreased their levels of water consumption. As shown in Fig. 4.1, the information-only approach yielded an average decrease of only 3 liters per household, whereas the two CBSM regions reduced consumption by 215 and 220 liters per household respectively—32% and 45% reductions in water use!

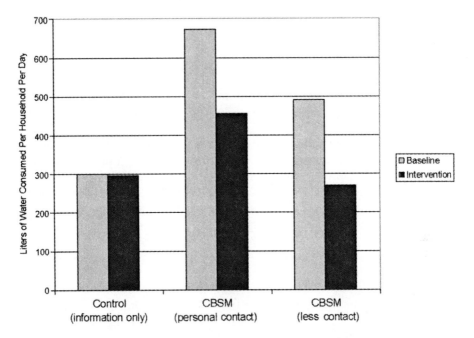

FIG. 4.1. Results from a community-based social marketing (CBSM) intervention to reduce residential water consumption.

Other examples of applied research projects using this approach can be found at www.cbsm.com

EMPHASIZING SOCIAL NORMS

There is strong evidence from a number of areas of psychological research that a person's decision to engage in a behavior is strongly influenced by perceptions of what other people do (i.e., social norms). The research shows that social norms can both facilitate behavior and cause people to engage in behaviors that they otherwise would not (Aarts & Dijksterhuis, 2003; Allison & Kerr, 1994; Kerr, 1995). Social norms are standards that are understood by members of a group, and that guide or constrain behavior without the force of law (Cialdini & Trost, 1998). *Descriptive* social norms are beliefs about what other people do, whereas *injunctive* social norms are beliefs about what other people think *ought* to be done. Cialdini and his colleagues (Cialdini, Reno, & Kallgren, 1990; Cialdini, Kallgren, & Reno, 1991) developed a focus theory of normative conduct, which proposes that while normative beliefs are generally predictive of behavior, they can be particularly powerful when they are focal in attention. A number of applied studies have used descriptive and injunctive norms to promote proenvironmental behavior.

Reducing Littering. Despite the strong social prohibition against littering, it is a persistent social and environmental problem. Cialdini and his colleagues conducted a number of studies examining the role of social norms and norm focus on littering behavior. In these studies, participants were visitors to a local hospital or library who, upon returning to their car, found a handbill on the windshield. Their decision to litter by dropping the handbill (or not) was observed from a hidden vantage point. A number of findings from these studies warrant mention. First, participants were more likely to litter into a littered environment (because the littered environment conveyed a descriptive social norm). Second, participants were more likely to litter after witnessing a confederate litter into a littered environment. However, participants were *least* likely to litter after observing a confederate litter into a clean environment—whereas 54% of the participants littered into the dirty environment after seeing a confederate litter, only 6% did so when the confederate littered into a clean environment. Cialdini and his colleagues argued that this is because seeing the confederate littering made focal the social norm of the situation, which in the case of the clean environment was not to litter.

Unfortunately, this finding suggests that many widely used antilittering campaigns may be ineffective. Most antilittering media messages depict an individual (an owl, "Iron Eyes Cody," Tony Hawk) in a highly littered environment, lamenting the conditions. Although such an image clearly conveys an injunctive norm against littering, it also presents a descriptive norm that is counterproductive—"other people litter." This image is often followed by an image of someone throwing litter into the environment—exactly the condition that the foregoing experiments found produced *the most* littering! In coming years, we hope that these research findings will be better utilized in large-scale antilittering campaigns.

Promoting Recycling. In the past 10 years, curbside recycling has become commonplace. Nearly all major cities in the United States offer residents curbside collection of recyclable materials, but many of these programs have experienced a ceiling to their effectiveness. Schultz (1999) reported a field experiment in which descriptive and injunctive norms about local recycling were conveyed to householders by providing them with normative feedback delivered to their homes weekly for a 4-week period. Results showed that participants who received the normative feedback (i.e., information about what others in their local area of the community were doing) recycled significantly more material than participants in the control condition or a condition which merely provided a weekly set of facts about recycling procedures and recyclable materials. Participants in the descriptive and injunctive norm conditions recycled 19% and 23% more material respectively following the intervention, compared with a 4% increase for the control condition. These results demonstrate that social norms can be invoked in printed messages—not just activated by witnessing the behavior of others.

Other studies have integrated normative messages into televised public service announcements (PSAs) to promote recycling (Cialdini, 2003; Cialdini et al., 2004). In one large-scale intervention, public service announcements were aired in four Arizona communities. Each PSA portrayed a scene in which the majority of depicted individuals engaged in recycling, spoke approvingly of it, and spoke disparagingly of a single individual in the scene who failed to recycle. Results showed a dramatic increase of 25% in the recycling tonnage collected, compared with matched control communities not exposed to the messages (Cialdini & ASU Recycling Group, 1999).

Reducing Energy Consumption. The studies summarized so far show the power of social norms to change behavior. But would normative interventions work for private behaviors, like energy conservation, which generally are not done in public places? A series of studies by Cialdini and Schultz (2003) demonstrated that normative messages can be applied to reduce energy consumption. The studies were conducted with hotel guests and measured their reuse of towels (which reduced the energy required to launder them). Across several studies, the results showed that integrating a normative element into placards placed in the hotel rooms produced an increase in towel reuse by hotel guests, compared to a control message that just provided information about how to reuse their towels. To illustrate, one of the experimental messages stated that:

> Many of our hotel guests have expressed to us the importance of conserving energy. When given the opportunity, nearly 75% of guests at this hotel choose to reuse their towels each day. Because so many guests value conservation and want to conserve, this hotel has initiated a conservation program. If you would like your towels replaced, please leave your used towels on the bathroom floor. Towels left hanging on the towel rack tell us that you want to reuse them.

The control message was identical in the last two procedural sentences, but omitted the first three normative sentences. Interestingly, the same normative effects were even found for upscale timeshare resorts, where guests might have been expected to feel that they had paid for the luxury of using extra towels. In the timeshare facilities, an average of 1.94 towels were replaced by the cleaning staff in rooms with the control message, whereas an

average of 1.52 towels were replaced in rooms with the normative message—a 20% decrease!

USING THE THEORY OF PLANNED BEHAVIOR

One of the most widely applied social psychological theories is the Theory
of Planned Behavior (TPB—Ajzen, 2001; Ajzen & Madden, 1986). It posits that
a person's intention to act is the best determinant of his or her actual behavior, and it presents a formula indicating how intentions are determined
by a person's attitudes, normative beliefs, and perceived behavioral control
concerning a target behavior. The theory has been used extensively in basic research, and applied to a number of social issues—most notably health
behaviors like condom use, alcohol consumption, and seatbelt use, but also
environmental behaviors like recycling and water conservation. A meta-
analysis of 185 published studies using the TPB found it worked very well,
with a multiple correlation of .63 for predicting behavioral intentions (Armitage & Conner, 2001). We now summarize a few studies that have applied
the theory to issues of environmental protection.

Most TPB studies have predicted behavior or behavioral intentions, but
only a few have conducted interventions to change behavior. One area
where interventions have been conducted is in promoting the use of public
transportation. Several studies have shown that a person's decision to use
public transportation can be explained quite well using TPB (Bamberg,
1996; Bamberg, Ajzen, & Schmidt, 2003; Bamberg & Schmidt, 2003; Heath &
Gifford, 2002). For example, Heath and Gifford reported that 70% of the variance in intentions to use public transportation was explained by attitudes
(*beta* = .34), subjective norms (*beta* = .66), and perceived behavioral control
(*beta* = .43).

Going beyond prediction, Bamberg and Schmidt (2001) conducted an intervention designed to reduce private car use. The intervention was a "semester ticket" which allowed all students at a university to use the public
transportation system without a charge—they just needed to show their student ID card. In a panel design a large sample of students was measured
twice, once before the start of the intervention, and a second time 10
months after the introduction of the semester ticket. The final sample was
1,036 students, who answered questionnaire items measuring attitudes,
subjective norms, perceived behavioral control, intention to use the public
transportation system, and self-reported bus use. Results showed that the
intervention was a success: Before the intervention 15% of the sample reported using public transportation, compared to 31% afterward. Similarly,
private car use dropped from 44% before the intervention to 30% afterward.
Additional analyses showed that following the intervention, students had a

more favorable attitude toward public transportation, and both subjective norms and perceived behavioral control increased. At that point the bus was seen as more comfortable, faster, cheaper, and more ecological; and students knew more about the procedure for riding the bus.

Heath and Gifford (2002) conducted a similar pre–post study, in which university students were given free access to the bus system with their student ID card. Data from 387 students showed that the intervention was effective, with an increase in bus usage from 32% prior to intervention to 43% following. There was also a decrease in car use, from 33% to 26%, and an increase in intention to use the bus. After the intervention, the bus was seen as more comfortable, convenient, and cheap; and students knew more about the bus system.

PUBLIC POLICY APPLICATIONS

An especially important type of contribution toward ecological sustainability is research that results in policy advice or has been applied to topics related to public policy. In this section we summarize a number of such contributions, stemming from a variety of topic areas, all of which have been applied effectively in real-world field settings.

Modeling Changed Farming Practices. During the "dustbowl" period of extreme drought in the 1930s, huge quantities of topsoil were blowing away from American farms. The U.S. government tried to improve the situation by distributing brochures to farmers suggesting helpful actions, such as contour plowing and planting rows of trees to serve as windscreens. However, like many information campaigns, this one had very little effect in changing farm practices. When that became clear, the government changed its approach and appointed county agricultural agents in farming areas. These well-informed agents worked intensively with a few farmers, advising and assisting them to adopt the desirable practices. These farmers then served as models for their neighbors who, after seeing and discussing the results of the new practices, often eagerly adopted them. Through this process of social dissemination, the improved practices spread quickly and widely (Nisbett, Borgida, Crandall, & Reed, 1976).

Energy Conservation Programs Can Save Money and Energy. In 1983, the Bonneville Power Administration began a demonstration project to see if strenuous energy conservation measures could reduce electricity demand enough to avoid the huge costs and long time required to build a major new power plant (Hirst, 1987). It chose the town of Hood River, Oregon (population 15,000), as the site for the conservation program and studied two similar towns for comparison purposes. The program began with a publicity blitz offering all the electrically heated households in Hood River a free energy-efficiency audit and later free installation of high levels of ceiling insulation and floor insulation, triple-glazed windows, and other strong energy-saving measures. In response to the many channels of publicity, 85% of the eligible homes volunteered and actually had major energy improvements installed within a period of 27 months. This was an extremely high rate of participation, and the time span was far less than the 10 years it generally takes to build a major power plant.

The cost of the program averaged more than $4,000 per house, but it was worthwhile to the power company because achieving the power savings cost less than the same amount of generating capacity would have cost. The amount of electricity saved averaged 15% in the participating homes. In addition, there were other benefits: Because many homes had previously been using wood as a supplementary fuel, there were further energy savings due to less wood being burned, and that improved the local air quality. Finally, the average home increased its winter temperature slightly, providing greater comfort than before (Hirst, 1987).

Factual Data Promote Good Public Policies. Governments and industries often attempt to conceal information or mislead the public about their environmental depredations. In such situations factual data are vital to improving environmental policies and conditions. An excellent example in the United States is a law passed in 1986 that required collection and publication of data about toxic chemical emissions from industrial plants. The result, called the Toxic Release Inventory, provided citizens with their first factual information about toxic pollution from local industries. The publicity that was generated by these data depressed offending companies' stock prices and stimulated them to reduce their toxic emissions. Similar laws have since been passed in many other nations (Young, 1994).

Organized Group Pressures Can Influence Large Corporations. Proenvironmental boycotts and other pressure campaigns have moved some major companies toward more sustainable practices (Friedman, 1995). One good example is a 1988 consumer boycott of Burger King restaurants because they imported cheap beef from tropical countries, where rainforests had been clear-cut and converted to cattle ranches, causing huge ecological damage. Burger King's sales decreased by 12% during the boycott, and soon the company canceled its contracts for Central American beef and announced that it would no longer buy beef from rainforest countries (http://rainforestweb.org).

Laws and Regulations Are Potent Forces in Environmental Improvement. An excellent example of this principle is the corporate average fuel efficiency (CAFE) standards for automobiles passed by Congress in the 1970s. The requirement that each auto manufacturer had to achieve an average efficiency of 27.5 miles per gallon (mpg) for its whole fleet of cars saved enormous amounts of oil and lessened U.S. dependence on petroleum imports from the Mideast. This requirement also changed the production practices of the huge auto corporations and gave consumers a much broader range of choices when purchasing cars.

It would be highly beneficial to the environment and to U.S. independence from foreign oil to extend these fuel efficiency standards and take advantage of current improved technology. In the 2000s, much higher gas mileage is now available in many cars, and an increase of less than 3 mpg in all U.S. cars' fuel efficiency would eliminate our need to import *any* Persian Gulf oil (Chandler, Geller, & Ledbetter, 1988; Kennedy, 2001). Sadly, however, in 2002, Congress yielded to pressure from the oil and automobile companies and refused to pass a bill requiring higher automobile fuel efficiency standards in the future (Masterson, 2002).

"Bottle Bills" Have Saved Natural Resources and Energy. Eleven states and several Canadian provinces have passed laws requiring a refundable deposit on beverage cans and bottles. The refund provides a monetary reward for returning the containers instead of throwing them away. These bills have been outstandingly successful in increasing the percentages of returned containers, to levels as high as 90% in some states. Consequently they have dramatically decreased the amount of roadside litter, markedly increased the reuse of materials such as aluminum and plastics, thereby saving huge amounts of energy that would be required to produce new materials, and also provided many new jobs in the recycling industry (Shireman, 1993). Examples of studies that have documented these effects are provided by Institute of Applied Research (1980) and Levitt and Leventhal (1986).

Ecological Tax Reform Has Great Potential for Environmental Improvement. Ecological tax reform may be defined as increasing taxes on processes that harm the environment, such as high consumption of fossil fuels, minerals, water, and other natural resources, as well as on toxic emissions and waste of resources, *combined with reducing other taxes on desirable products and processes*, such as income taxes and value-added taxes. Advocates of this approach often specify that the net result should be *revenue-neutral* (i.e., a tax shift, rather than an increase in the overall tax burden—von Weizsacker & Jesinghaus, 1992).

Many countries have begun to use such ecological taxes in a small way. One of the earliest was the Netherlands, which in 1970 imposed a tax on water pollution. That tax was credited as the main factor in a 72% to 99% drop over a 20-year period in industrial discharges of various toxic heavy metals into waterways. Similarly, Germany in 1991 established a tax on toxic waste production, which then fell by 15% in 3 years. As examples of ecological tax *shifts*, Sweden in 1991 cut taxes on personal income and raised them on carbon and sulfur emissions, while Spain in 1995 lowered taxes on wages and raised them on gasoline sales. In these initial cases, the environmental results of such taxes seem very promising (Roodman, 1999).

A carefully thought-out proposal for ecological tax reform has been presented by von Weizsacker and Jesinghaus (1992). They pointed out that, in our current world, the greatest "steering effect" or environmental benefit would be obtained from raising taxes on fossil fuels, which would reduce their use as well as their predominant contribution to global climate change through the greenhouse effect, and would also reduce national expenditures for them and national dependence on potentially interruptible Mideast oil supplies. At the same time, these authors advocated reducing the many huge national subsidies that are environmentally harmful, such as subsidies or tax breaks for the consumption of electricity, coal, and water, for the production of aluminum and farm products, and for automobile users. The subsidies for automobile use, in particular, tend to stifle public transportation systems, which are far more energy-efficient than motor vehicles.

von Weizsacker and Jesinghaus have made detailed computations of the likely effects of such ecological tax reforms. As a result, they advocated a steady increase (and thus, importantly, one that is dependable for businesses' planning purposes) in fossil fuel taxes of 5% a year, continued for 30 to 40 years. They pointed out that many nations already have fuel prices 2 to 3 times those in the United States, and their research comparisons of nations that already have marked differences in fuel prices indicate that the long-term "price elasticity" (i.e., changes in consumption rates based upon price levels) is quite large. For instance, with higher fuel prices, many people will buy smaller or more fuel-efficient cars, drive fewer miles, or switch to other forms of transportation; and new fuel sources will become practical, such as electric- or hydrogen-powered cars, thus sharply reducing the consumption of gasoline. The authors' research showed that, across major industrial nations, the correlation between fuel prices and *efficient* use of fuel is about +.85. Two other factors, population density and national wealth (i.e., per capita income), also influence fossil fuel usage; and the authors showed that combining them with fuel prices in a single equation yielded a very good prediction of fuel usage.

The projections of von Weizsacker and Jesinghaus (1992) indicate that a steady 5% annual increase in the price of gasoline, maintained by most industrialized nations, would decrease their gas consumption by at least 50% by the end of a 30-year period, while an annual 7% price increase would decrease consumption by about 70%. The authors considered a wide range of possible objections to such ecological tax shifts, and concluded that none of them would impair their plan severely if most industrial nations agreed to implement it. Indeed, they suggested that industrial and commercial companies might appreciate its long-term price predictability and its promise of profits due to increased efficiency. As Roodman (1999) summarized, Japan and the European Union nations have already taken many steps toward such types of ecological taxes.

Alternative Energy Sources Can Be Successfully Encouraged. Some actual results of national stimulation of alternative energy sources have been summarized by Sawin (2004). She pointed out that in the past 10 years Germany has moved from having virtually no renewable energy to being the world leader in wind power (having twice the installed capacity of the United States), and has also become one of the leading nations in solar power generated by photovoltaic (PV) cells (see Fig. 4.2). Similarly, Japan started the 1990s as a minor player in solar power, but by 2003 it was the world leader, with more than three times the PV capacity of the United States despite its much smaller land area and exposure to sunlight.

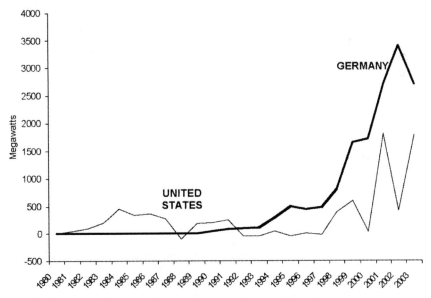

FIG. 4.2. Annual wind power capacity additions in Germany and the United States, 1980–2003. *Source:* Worldwatch Institute, www.worldwatch.org "Mainstreaming Renewable Energy in the 21st Century," 2004.

In both nations, new laws were crucial in creating the business climate for these growth spurts. In 1990, Germany passed a law that required electric utilities to purchase all electricity generated from renewable sources in their geographic areas, at a price at least 90% of the retail price. This dramatically encouraged renewable energy by making its financial prospects dependable, and later government programs facilitated siting and financing of renewable energy facilities. In Japan, policies to promote PV installations on 70,000 roofs set regional targets, required utilities to purchase PV power at the retail rate, gave low-interest loans and rebates to residential PV facilities, and promoted solar energy through publicity and government subsidies. By 2002, the program's installations had more than doubled its goal of 70,000 residential PV systems. In Japan, the costs for PV installations have dropped so much that PV on-grid power is now cheaper than retail electricity, while Germany aims to produce 25% of its electricity from wind power by 2025, and it has pledged to reduce its CO_2 emissions at least 21% by 2010 (Sawin, 2004).

CONCLUSION

As the foregoing examples show, important steps toward sustainability can be strongly aided by the use of psychological theories and research findings. Among the approaches that have been found fruitful are applied behavior analysis, social marketing programs, techniques of feedback and persuasion, emphasis on social norms and the Theory of Planned Behavior in designing interventions, and application of a wide variety of procedures to influence public policy in proenvironmental directions. Much more intensive and far-reaching applications of these approaches will be needed in the near future if the Earth is to avoid the many threats to ecological sustainability listed at the beginning of this chapter.

REFERENCES

Aarts, H., & Dijksterhuis, A. (2003). The silence of the library: Environment, situational norm and social behavior. *Journal of Personality and Social Psychology, 84*, 18–28.

Ajzen, I. (2001). Nature and operation of attitudes. *Annual Review of Psychology, 52*, 27–58.

Ajzen, I., & Madden, T. J. (1986). Prediction of goal-directed behavior: Attitudes, intentions, and perceived behavioral control. *Journal of Experimental Social Psychology, 22*, 453–474.

Allen, J., & Ferrand, J. (1999). Environmental locus of control, sympathy, and proenvironmental behavior: A test of Geller's actively caring hypothesis. *Environment and Behavior, 31*, 338–353.

Allison, S. T., & Kerr, N. L. (1994). Group correspondence biases and the provision of public goals. *Journal of Personality and Social Psychology, 66*, 688–698.

Armitage, C. J., & Conner, M. (2001). Efficacy of the theory of planned behavior: A meta-analytic review. *British Journal of Social Psychology, 40*, 471–499.

Aronson, E. (1999). The power of self-persuasion. *American Psychologist, 54*, 875–884.

Aronson, E., & Gonzales, M. H. (1990). Alternative social influence processes applied to energy conservation. In J. Edwards, R. S. Tindale, L. Heath, & E. J. Posavac (Eds.), *Social influence processes and prevention* (pp. 301–325). New York: Plenum.

Bach, C. (2004). *Outdoor residential water reduction programs: Do they really work?* Ontario, Canada: Regional Municipality of Halton.

Bamberg, S. (1996). An empirical test of the Theory of Planned Behavior in two choice situations with two behavioral alternatives: Bike vs. car and container vs. garbage can. *Zeitschrift für Socialpsychologie, 27*, 32–46.

Bamberg, S., Ajzen, I., & Schmidt, P. (2003). Choice of travel mode in the Theory of Planned Behavior: The roles of past behavior, habit, and reasoned action. *Basic and Applied Social Psychology, 25*(3), 175–187.

Bamberg, S., & Schmidt, P. (2001). Theory-driven subgroup-specific evaluation of an intervention to reduce private car use. *Journal of Applied Social Psychology, 31*, 1300–1329.

Bamberg, S., & Schmidt, P. (2003). Incentives, morality, or habit? Predicting students' car use for university routes with models of Ajzen, Schwartz, and Triandis. *Environment and Behavior, 35*, 264–285.

Biel, A., Von Borgstede, C., & Dahlstrand, U. (1999). Norm perception and cooperation in large scale social dilemmas. In M. Foddy, M. Smithson, S. Schneider, & M. Hogg (Eds.), *Resolving social dilemmas* (pp. 245–252). Philadelphia: Taylor & Francis.

Chandler, W. U., Geller, E. S., & Ledbetter, M. R. (1988). *Energy efficiency: A new agenda.* Washington, DC: American Council for an Energy-Efficient Economy.

Cialdini, R. B. (2003). Crafting normative messages to protect the environment. *Psychological Science, 12*, 105–109.

Cialdini, R. B., & ASU Recycling Group. (1999). *Influencing behavior through public service announcements* (Report to the Arizona Department of Environmental Quality). Tempe: Arizona State University, Department of Psychology.

Cialdini, R. B., Barrett, D., Bator, R., Demaine, L., Sagarin, B., & Rhoads, K. (2004). *Activating and aligning social norms for persuasive impact.* Unpublished manuscript, University of Arizona.

Cialdini, R. B., Kallgren, C. A., & Reno, R. R. (1991). A focus theory of normative conduct: A theoretical refinement and reevaluation of the role of norms in human behavior. In L. Berkowitz (Ed.), *Advances in experimental social psychology* (Vol. 24, pp. 201–234). San Diego, CA: Academic Press.

Cialdini, R. B., Reno, R. R., & Kallgren, C. A. (1990). A focus theory of normative conduct: Recycling the concept of norms to reduce littering in public places. *Journal of Personality and Social Psychology, 58*, 1015–1026.

Cialdini, R. B., & Schultz, P. W. (2003). *Understanding and motivating energy conservation via social norms.* Technical report submitted to the William and Flora Hewlett Foundation.

Cialdini, R. B., & Trost, M. R. (1998). Social influence: Social norms, conformity, and compliance. In D. T. Gilbert, S. T. Fiske, & G. Lindzey (Eds.), *Handbook of social psychology* (4th ed., Vol. 2, pp. 151–193). New York: McGraw-Hill.

Cordano, M., & Frieze, I. (2000). Pollution reduction preferences of U.S. environmental managers: Applying Ajzen's Theory of Planned Behavior. *Academy of Management Journal, 43*, 627–641.

Costanzo, M., Archer, D., Aronson, E., & Pettigrew, T. (1986). Energy conservation behavior: The difficult path from information to action. *American Psychologist, 41*, 521–528.

Cuthbert, R. (1994, May). Variable disposal fee impact. *BioCycle*, pp. 63–65.

Dickerson, C., Thibodeau, R., Aronson, E., & Miller, D. (1992). Using cognitive dissonance to encourage water conservation. *Journal of Applied Social Psychology, 22*, 851–854.

Durning, A. T. (1992). *How much is enough? The consumer society and the future of the earth.* New York: Norton.

Festinger, L. (1954). A theory of social comparison processes. *Human Relations, 7*, 117–140.

Festinger, L. (1957). *A theory of cognitive dissonance.* Stanford, CA: Stanford University Press.

Flavin, C. (2001). Rich planet, poor planet. In L. R. Brown et al., *State of the world 2001* (pp. 3–20). New York: Norton.

Friedman, M. (1995). On promoting a sustainable future through consumer activism. *Journal of Social Issues, 51*(4), 197–215.

Gardner, G. T., & Stern, P. C. (2002). *Environmental problems and human behavior* (2nd ed.). Boston: Pearson.

Geller, E. S. (1995). Integrating behaviorism and humanism for environmental protection. *Journal of Social Issues, 51*(4), 179–195.

Geller, E. S. (2002). The challenge of increasing proenvironment behavior. In R. B. Bechtel & A. Churchman (Eds.), *Handbook of environmental psychology* (pp. 525–540). New York: Wiley.

Gonzales, M., Aronson, E., & Costanzo, M. (1988). Using social cognition and persuasion to promote energy conservation: A quasi experiment. *Journal of Applied Social Psychology, 18*, 1049–1066.

Grob, A. (1995). A structural model of environmental attitudes and behaviors. *Journal of Environmental Psychology, 15*, 209–220.

Heath, Y., & Gifford, R. (2002). Extending the Theory of Planned Behavior: Predicting the use of public transportation. *Journal of Applied Social Psychology, 32*, 2154–2185.

Hirst, E. (1987). *Cooperation and community conservation: The Hood River Conservation Project* (ORNL/CON-235; DOE/BP-11287-16). Oak Ridge, TN: Oak Ridge National Laboratory.

Houghton, S. (1993). Using verbal and visual prompts to control littering in high schools. *Educational Studies (UK), 19*, 247–254.

Institute of Applied Research. (1980). *Michigan litter: After*. Sacramento, CA: Author.

Intergovernmental Panel on Climate Change. (2001). *Climate change 2001: Impacts, adaptation, and vulnerability*. Geneva, Switzerland: Author.

Joireman, J., Van Lange, P., Van Vugt, M., Wood, A., Leest, T., & Lambert, C. (2001). Structural solutions to social dilemmas: A field study on commuters' willingness to fund improvements in public transit. *Journal of Applied Social Psychology, 31*, 504–526.

Kaiser, F., & Gutscher, H. (2003). The proposition of a general version of the Theory of Planned Behavior: Predicting ecological behavior. *Journal of Applied Psychology, 33*, 586–603.

Kals, E., & Maes, J. (2002). Sustainable development and emotions. In P. Schmuck & P. W. Schultz (Eds.), *Psychology of sustainable development* (pp. 97–122). Norwell, MA: Kluwer.

Keep America Beautiful, Inc. (1968). *Who litters and why*. New York: Public Opinion Surveys.

Kempton, W., Darley, J. M., & Stern, P. C. (1992). Psychological research for the new energy problems: Strategies and opportunities. *American Psychologist, 47*, 1213–1223.

Kennedy, R. F., Jr. (2001, November 24). Better gas mileage, greater security. *New York Times*, p. 27.

Kerr, N. L. (1995). Norms in social dilemmas. In D. Schroeder (Ed.), *Social dilemmas: Perspectives on individuals and groups* (pp. 31–48). Westport, CT: Praeger.

Lepper, M. R., & Greene, D. (1978). *The hidden costs of reward: New perspectives on the psychology of human motivation*. Hillsdale, NJ: Lawrence Erlbaum Associates.

Levitt, L., & Leventhal, G. (1986). Litter reduction: How effective is the New York State bottle bill? *Environment and Behavior, 18*, 467–479.

Masterson, K. (2002, March 14). Fuel efficiency rules cut out of energy bill: Lawmakers yield to auto industry. *Houston Chronicle*, p. 1.

McKenzie-Mohr, D. (2000). Promoting sustainable behavior: An introduction to community-based social marketing. *Journal of Social Issues, 56*, 543–554.

Meadows, D. H., Meadows, D. L., & Randers, J. (1992). *Beyond the limits: Confronting global collapse; envisioning a sustainable future*. Post Mills, VT: Chelsea Green.

Meadows, D. H., Randers, J., & Meadows, D. L. (2004). *Limits to growth: The 30-year global update*. White River, VT: Chelsea Green.

Montague, P. (1998, February 19). The precautionary principle. *Rachel's Environment and Health Weekly*, No. 586, pp. 1–6.

Nisbett, R. E., Borgida, E., Crandall, R., & Reed, H. (1976). Popular induction: Information is not necessarily informative. In J. S. Carroll & J. W. Payne (Eds.), *Cognition and social behavior* (pp. 113–133). Hillsdale, NJ: Lawrence Erlbaum Associates.

Oskamp, S. (2000). A sustainable future for humanity? How can psychology help? *American Psychologist, 55,* 496–508.

Oskamp, S., & Schultz, P. W. (2005). *Attitudes and opinions* (3rd ed.). Mahwah, NJ: Lawrence Erlbaum Associates.

Pelletier, L. (2002). A motivational analysis of self-determination for pro-environmental behaviors. In E. Deci & R. Ryan (Eds.), *Handbook of self-determination research* (pp. 205–232). Rochester, NY: University of Rochester Press.

Pimentel, D., Harman, R., Pacenza, M., Pacarsky, J., & Pimentel, M. (1994). Natural resources and an optimum human population. *Population and Environment, 15,* 347–369.

Roodman, D. M. (1999). Building a sustainable society. In L. R. Brown et al., *State of the world 1999* (pp. 169–188). New York: Norton.

Rothstein, R. N. (1980). Television feedback used to modify gasoline consumption. *Behavior Therapy, 11,* 683–688.

Samuelson, C. D. (1990). Energy conservation: A social dilemma approach. *Social Behaviour, 5,* 207–230.

Samuelson, C. D., Messick, D. M., Rutte, C. G., & Wilke, H. (1984). Individual and structural solutions to resource dilemmas in two cultures. *Journal of Personality and Social Psychology, 47,* 94–104.

Sawin, J. L. (2004, May). *Mainstreaming renewable energy in the 21st century* (Worldwatch Paper 169). Washington, DC: Worldwatch Institute.

Schmuck, P., & Schultz, P. W. (Eds.). (2002). *Psychology of sustainable development.* Boston: Kluwer.

Schneider, S. H. (1997). *Laboratory earth: The planetary gamble we can't afford to lose.* New York: Basic Books.

Schultz, P. W. (1999). Changing behavior with normative feedback interventions: A field experiment on curbside recycling. *Basic and Applied Social Psychology, 21,* 25–36.

Schultz, P. W. (2002). Knowledge, education, and household recycling: Examining the knowledge-deficit model of behavior change. In T. Dietz & P. Stern (Eds.), *Education, information, and voluntary measures in environmental protection* (pp. 67–82). Washington, DC: National Academy of Sciences.

Schultz, P. W., & Zelezny, L. C. (1999). Values as predictors of environmental attitudes: Evidence for consistency across 14 countries. *Journal of Environmental Psychology, 19,* 255–265.

Shireman, W. K. (1993). Solid waste: To recycle or to bury California? In T. Palmer (Ed.), *California's threatened environment: Restoring the dream* (pp. 170–181). Washington, DC: Island.

Stern, P. C. (1992). Psychological dimensions of global environmental change. *Annual Review of Psychology, 43,* 369–402.

Stern, P. C., Dietz, T., & Black, J. S. (1985–1986). Support for environmental protection: The role of moral norms. *Population and Environment: Behavioral and Social Issues, 8*(3–4), 204–222.

Taylor, K. (1999). Rapid climate change. *American Scientist, 87,* 320–327.

Union of Concerned Scientists. (1993, April). *World scientists' warning to humanity* [Statement]. Cambridge, MA: Author.

Van Lange, P., Van Vugt, M., Meertens, R., & Ruiter, R. (1998). A social dilemma analysis of commuting preferences: The role of social value orientation and trust. *Journal of Applied Social Psychology, 28,* 796–820.

Van Vugt, M., Van Lange, P. A. M., & Meertens, R. M. (1996). Commuting by car or public transportation? A social dilemma analysis of travel mode judgments. *European Journal of Social Psychology, 26,* 373–395.

Van Vugt, M., Van Lange, P. A. M., Meertens, R. M., & Joireman, J. A. (1996). How a structural solution to a social dilemma failed: A field experiment on the first carpool lane in Europe. *Social Psychology Quarterly, 59*, 364–374.

Vining, J., & Ebreo, A. (2002). Emerging theoretical and methodological perspectives on conservation behavior. In R. B. Bechtel & A. Churchman (Eds.), *Handbook of environmental psychology* (pp. 541–558). New York: Wiley.

von Weizsacker, E. U., & Jesinghaus, J. (1992). *Ecological tax reform: A policy proposal for sustainable development.* London, UK: Zed.

Wahlstrom, B. (1999). The precautionary approach to chemicals management: A Swedish perspective. In C. Raffensperger & J. A. Ticknor (Eds.), *Protecting public health and the environment: Implementing the precautionary principle* (pp. 51–69). Washington, DC: Island Press.

World Resources Institute. (2002). *World resources 2000–2001.* Available on-line at: http://www.wri.org/wri/wr2000/index.html

Worldwatch Institute. (2003). *State of the world 2003: A Worldwatch Institute report on progress toward a sustainable society.* New York: Norton.

Worldwatch Institute. (2004). *State of the world 2004: The consumer society.* New York: Norton.

Young, J. E. (1994). Using computers for the environment. In L. R. Brown et al., *State of the world 1994* (pp. 99–116). New York: Norton.

Zelezny, L. C., & Schultz, P. W. (Eds.). (2000). Promoting environmentalism. *Journal of Social Issues, 56*, 365–578.

5

Applying Psychological Research on Interpersonal Expectations and Covert Communication in Classrooms, Clinics, Corporations, and Courtrooms

Robert Rosenthal
University of California, Riverside

In the mid 1950s I nearly ruined the results of my doctoral dissertation at UCLA. The sordid details are available elsewhere (Rosenthal, 1985) but briefly, it appeared that I might have treated my research participants in such a way as to lead them to respond in accordance with my experimental hypothesis or expectancy. All of this was quite unwitting, of course, but it did raise a sobering question about the possibility of interpersonal expectancy effects in the psychological laboratory. If it were my unintentional interpersonal expectancy effect that had led to the puzzling and disconcerting results of my dissertation, then presumably we could produce the phenomenon in our own laboratory and with several experimenters rather that just one. Producing the phenomenon in this way would yield not only the scientific benefit of demonstrating an interesting and important concept; it would also yield the very considerable personal benefit of showing that I was not alone in having unintentionally affected the results of my research by virtue of my bias or expectancy.

SOME EARLY RESULTS

Human Subjects

In the first of our studies employing human subjects, 10 students of psychology, both undergraduate and graduate, served as the experimenters

(Rosenthal & Fode, 1963b). All were enrolled in an advanced course in experimental psychology and were already involved in conducting research. Each student-experimenter was assigned as his or her research participants about 20 students of introductory psychology. The procedure was for the experimenters to show a series of 10 photographs of people's faces to each of their participants individually. Participants were to rate the degree of success or failure shown in the face of each person pictured in the photos. Each face could be rated as any value from −10 to +10, with −10 meaning *extreme failure* and +10 meaning *extreme success*. The 10 photos had been selected so that, on the average, they would be seen as neither successful nor unsuccessful, but quite neutral, with an average rating of zero.

All 10 experimenters were given identical instructions on how to administer the task to their participants and were given identical instructions to read to them. They were cautioned not to deviate from these instructions. The purpose of their participation, it was explained to all experimenters, was to see how well they could duplicate experimental results which were already well established. Half the experimenters were told that the "well-established" finding was such that their participants should rate the photos as of successful people (ratings of +5) and half the experimenters were told that their participants should rate the photos as being of unsuccessful people (ratings of −5). Results showed that experimenters expecting higher photo ratings obtained higher photo ratings than did experimenters expecting lower photo ratings. Subsequent studies tended to obtain generally similar results (Rosenthal, 1969; Rosenthal & Rubin, 1978).

Animal Subjects

Pfungst's work with Clever Hans, and Pavlov's work on the inheritance of acquired characteristics had both suggested the possibility of experimenter expectancy effects with animal subjects (Gruenberg, 1929; Pfungst, 1911/1965). In addition, Bertrand Russell (1927) had noted this possibility, adding that animal subjects take on the national character of the experimenter. As he put it: "Animals studied by Americans rush about frantically, with an incredible display of hustle and pep, and at last achieve the desired result by chance. Animals observed by Germans sit still and think, and at last evolve the solution out of their inner consciousness" (pp. 29–30).

But it was not only the work of Pavlov, Pfungst, and Russell that made us test the generality of experimenter expectancy effects by working with animal subjects. It was also the reaction of my friends and colleagues who themselves worked with animal subjects. That reaction was: "Well of course you'd find expectancy effects and other artifacts when you work with humans; that's why we work with rats."

A good beginning might have been to replicate with a larger sample size Pfungst's research with Clever Hans; but with horses hard to come by, rats were made to do (Rosenthal & Fode, 1963a).

A class in experimental psychology had been performing experiments with human participants for most of a semester. Now they were asked to perform one more experiment, the last in the course, and the first employing animal subjects. The experimenters were told of studies that had shown that maze-brightness and maze-dullness could be developed in strains of rats by successive inbreeding of the well and the poorly performing maze-runners. Sixty laboratory rats were equally divided among the 12 experimenters. Half the experimenters were told that their rats were maze-bright while the other half were told their rats were maze-dull. The animal's task was to learn to run to the darker of two arms of an elevated T maze. The two arms of the maze, one white and one gray, were interchangeable; and the "correct" or rewarded arm was equally often on the right as on the left. Whenever animals ran to the correct side they obtained a food reward. Each rat was given 10 trials each day for 5 days to learn that the darker side of the maze was the one that led to the food.

Beginning with the first day and continuing on through the experiment, animals believed to be better performers became better performers. Animals believed to be bright showed a daily improvement in their performance, while those believed to be dull improved only to the third day and then showed a worsening of performance. Sometimes an animal refused to budge from the starting position. This happened 11% of the time among the allegedly bright rats; but among the allegedly dull rats it happened 29% of the time. When animals did respond and correctly so, those believed to be brighter ran faster to the rewarded side of the maze than did even the correctly responding rats believed to be dull.

When the experiment was over, all experimenters made ratings of their rats and of their own attitudes and behavior vis-à-vis their animals. Those experimenters who had been led to expect better performance viewed their animals as brighter, more pleasant, and more likable. These same experimenters felt more relaxed in their contacts with the animals and described their behavior toward them as more pleasant, friendly, enthusiastic, and less talkative. They also stated that they handled their rats more and also more gently than did the experimenters expecting poor performance. Our next experiment with animal subjects also employed rats, this time using not mazes but Skinner boxes (Rosenthal & Lawson, 1964), but the results were essentially the same (with effect size rs of .47 and .54 for the first and second studies, respectively).

TEACHER EXPECTATION EFFECTS

If rats became brighter when expected to then it would not be farfetched to think that children might become brighter when expected to by their teachers. Indeed, Kenneth Clark (1963) had for years been saying that teachers' expectations could be very important determinants of intellectual performance. Clark's ideas and our research should have sent us right into the schools to study teacher expectations; but that's not what happened. What did happen was that a brilliant educational scholar and administrator, Lenore Jacobson, suggested a collaborative study in which we would experimentally raise the level of teachers' expectations for some of the children in their classrooms and measure the effect of these raised expectations on children's subsequent intellectual performance.

The Pygmalion Experiment

All of the children in the study were administered a nonverbal test of intelligence, which was disguised as a test that would predict intellectual "blooming." The test was labeled as "The Harvard Test of Inflected Acquisition." There were 18 classrooms in the school, three at each of the six grade levels. Within each grade level the three classrooms were composed of children with above average ability, average ability, and below average ability, respectively. Within each of the 18 classrooms approximately 20% of the children were chosen at random to form the experimental group. Each teacher was given the names of the children from his or her class who were in the experimental condition. The teacher was told that these children had scored on the "Test of Inflected Acquisition" such that they would show surprising gains in intellectual competence during the next 8 months of school. The only difference between the experimental group children and the control group children, then, was in the mind of the teacher.

At the end of the school year, 8 months later, all the children were re-tested with the same test of intelligence. Considering the school as a whole, the children from whom the teachers had been led to expect greater intellectual gain showed a greater intellectual gain than did the children of the control group (Rosenthal & Jacobson, 1966, 1968, 1992).

Reactions to Pygmalion

Reactions to Pygmalion were extreme. Many were very favorable, many were very unfavorable. Elsewhere we have noted the best known of these negative criticisms and given reasons why they were not compelling (Rosenthal, 1985, 1987b, 1995, 2002; Rosenthal & Rubin, 1971, 1978). However, the strongest defense of Pygmalion effects comes not from statistical arguments but from the hundreds of studies showing the replicability of these effects of interpersonal expectations.

THE META-ANALYTIC EVIDENCE

Meta-analysis is the rapidly developing area of data analysis in which the entire body of research literature on a given question is summarized quantitatively (Cooper & Hedges, 1994; Glass, McGaw, & Smith, 1981; Rosenthal, 1984, 1987a, 1991a). Table 5.1 summarizes eight meta-analyses of the literature on interpersonal expectancy effects, with each meta-analysis conducted on a different domain of the research. For each domain the table shows the mean effect size (r) and gives an example of the type of study included in each domain. The effect size r can be interpreted as the point biserial correlation, r_{pb}, between experimental versus control group status (e.g., coded 1 or 0) and the outcome score (say, gain in performance). In an updated meta-analysis of 479 studies conducted nearly 20 years later, the average effect size r was .30 (Rosenthal, 1998).

THE 10 ARROW MODEL

For many years the central question in the study of interpersonal expectancy effects was whether there was any such thing. The meta-analytic evidence has answered that question sufficiently (e.g., $p < 1/10^{175}$, mean $r = .30$, based on the current full N of 479 studies) so that simple additional replications will add little new knowledge. The central questions in the study of interpersonal

TABLE 5.1
Magnitude of Interpersonal Expectancy Effects in Eight Research Domains

Domain	Mean Effect Size r	Example of Type of Study
Laboratory interviews	.07	Effects of sensory restriction
Reaction time	.08	Latency of word association
Learning and ability	.26	IQ test scores; verbal conditioning
Person perception	.27	Perception of others' success
Inkblot tests	.39	Ratio of animal to human Rorschach responses
Everyday situations	.40	Symbol learning; athletic performance
Psychophysical judgments	.46	Ability to discriminate tones
Animal learning	.65	Learning in mazes and Skinner boxes
Weighted mean[a]	.33	
Unweighted mean	.35	
Weighted median[a]	.39	
Unweighted median	.33	

[a]Weighting is by number of studies in each domain.

expectancy effects have changed so that now the more interesting questions include the specification of the variables that (a) *moderate* expectancy effects and (b) *mediate* expectancy effects. Moderator variables are pre-existing variables such as sex, age, and personality that are associated with the magnitude of interpersonal expectancy effects; mediating variables refer to the behaviors by which expectations are communicated. The basic elements of the 10 arrow model designed to clarify the study of interpersonal expectancy effects are (a) distal independent variables (e.g., stable attributes of the expecter and expectee), (b) proximal independent variables (the expectancy), (c) mediating variables, (d) proximal dependent variables (e.g., outcome measures such as achievement on tests, etc.), and (e) distal dependent variables (longer term outcome variables). A useful feature of this model is that the 10 arrows of the model represent the types of relationships that can be examined in research on expectancy effects (see Fig. 5.1).

These arrows are described in detail elsewhere (Rosenthal, 1981, 1985, 1991b) so we discuss here only the two links relevant to the topic of mediation: the B–C and C–D arrows. B–C relationships describe the effect the expectancy has on the expecter's behavior, the relationships most often investigated in research on mediation. Equally important to understanding mediation, however, are the C–D relationships between the expecter's behavior and outcome variables. Research bearing on the B–C link tells us which behaviors are induced by a given expectancy, but research bearing on the C–D link assures us that these behaviors affect the expectee so as to create a self-fulfilling prophecy. As is evident, the two types of relationships address different questions, making the B–C/C–D distinction critical. In a detailed series of meta-analyses on the mediation of interpersonal expec-

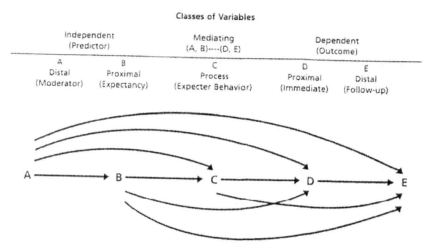

FIG. 5.1. The 10 Arrow Model for the study of interpersonal expectancy effects.

tancy effects, Harris and Rosenthal (1985, 1986) acknowledged the B–C/C–D distinction by discussing results for the B–C and C–D links separately.

THE FOUR FACTOR "THEORY"

On the basis of the first 30 or so published studies relevant to mediation, a four-factor "theory" of the mediation of teacher expectancy effects was proposed (Rosenthal, 1973, 1974). The theory describes four major groupings of teacher behaviors hypothesized to be involved in mediation. The first factor, *climate*, refers to the warmer socioemotional climate that teachers tend to create for high-expectancy students, a warmth that can be communicated both verbally and nonverbally. The *input* factor refers to the tendency for teachers to teach more material to their "special" students. The *output* factor refers to the tendency for teachers to give their special students greater opportunities for responding. Finally, the *feedback* factor refers to the tendency for teachers to give more differentiated feedback to their "special," high-expectancy students. By differentiated, we mean that the feedback will be contingent on the correctness or incorrectness of the student's response and that the content of the feedback will tend to be directly related to what the student has said.

The meta-analyses conducted by Harris and Rosenthal were designed to summarize the many studies examining either the B–C or C–D links (or both) and to come up with a quantitative estimate of the importance of each of the four factors in the mediation of interpersonal expectancy effects. Table 5.2 summarizes the qualitative evidence for each of the four fac-

TABLE 5.2
Summary of Four Factors in the Mediation of Teacher Expectancy Effects

Factor	Brief Summary of the Evidence
Central Factors:	
Climate (Affect)	Teachers appear to create a warmer socio-emotional climate for their "special" students. This warmth appears to be at least partially communicated by nonverbal cues.
Input (Effort)	Teachers appear to teach more material and more difficult material to their "special" students.
Additional Factors:	
Output	Teachers appear to give their "special" students greater opportunities for responding. These opportunities are offered both verbally and nonverbally (e.g., giving a student more time in which to answer a teacher's question).
Feedback	Teachers appear to give their "special" students more differentiated feedback, both verbal and nonverbal, as to how these students have been performing.

TABLE 5.3
Meta-Analytically Derived Average Correlations Indexing
the Effect Sizes of the Four Factor Theory

Factor	B–C Link[a]	C–D Link[b]	Mean[c]
1. Climate (affect)	.23	.36	.29
2. Input (effort)	.26	.28	.27
3. Output	.18	.16	.17
4. Feedback	.13	.08	.10

Note. All correlations are significantly greater than zero at $p < .002$. The correlation between the magnitudes of the average B–C and C–D links is .88. From Harris and Rosenthal (1986).
[a]Correlation between expectation and expecter's behavior.
[b]Correlation between behavior of expecter and response of expectee.
[c]Geometric mean correlation.

tors based on the meta-analyses, and Table 5.3 gives the average magnitude of the role of each factor separately for the B–C and C–D links. While all four factors received ample support in terms of significance testing, the magnitudes of the effects for the *climate* and *input* factors were especially impressive. Teachers appear to teach more and to teach it more warmly to students for whom they have more favorable expectations.

From these results we cannot infer that if we select warmer and more material-presenting teachers our nation's children will learn more. We also cannot infer from these results that training teachers to be warmer and more material-presenting will lead to improved learning on the part of our nation's children. Our results do suggest, however, that conducting the research required to determine the benefits of selection and training for *climate* (or affect) and *input* (or effort) may well yield substantial benefits both for science and for society.

BEYOND CLASSROOMS AND LABORATORIES

The covert communication mediating one person's expectation for the behavior of another occurs well beyond the confines of our classrooms or our laboratories. A recent meta-analysis of 13 Pygmalion studies conducted in work organizations found a mean overall effect size r of .38 (Kierein & Gold, 2000). A mean effect size r of that magnitude is associated with improving a success rate from 31% to 69% (Rosenthal & Rubin, 1982). Kierein and Gold found larger effects of interpersonal expectations when workers' initial levels of performance were low. They also found larger effects when the experiments were conducted in military rather than in business settings. For a fuller discussion of Pygmalion in management contexts see Eden (1990).

Several studies have investigated the effects of judges' beliefs about the guilt of the defendant on the way in which judges deliver their instructions to jurors (i.e., the B–C links described earlier), and the way in which these instructions influence jurors in how they decide on the defendant's guilt (i.e., the C–D link described earlier); see Blanck, Rosenthal, Hart, and Bernieri (1990) and Halverson, Hallahan, Hart, and Rosenthal (1997). In a meta-analysis of the four studies reported to date, the median effect size r was .14, combined $p = .0006$. In terms of the Binomial Effect Size Display (BESD) introduced as a means of displaying the practical effect of any given r (Rosenthal & Rubin, 1982), the obtained median effect size r is associated with a change in the rate of findings of guilty from 43% to 57% as a function of being instructed by a judge who believes a defendant to be guilty rather than not guilty. It should be added as a methodological note that the defendant the judge believed to be guilty versus not guilty was not the same defendant whose case the jurors were trying to decide. Jurors saw a videotaped trial with defendant A but were given their instructions via videotape by a judge who was actually instructing a different jury with a different defendant, B.

There have been few randomized experiments in which health care workers' expectations have been raised for the health outcomes of their patients. One such study was conducted in a nursing home context; it was found that raising caretakers' expectations led to a reduction in the depression levels of the residents (Learman, Avorn, Everitt, & Rosenthal, 1990).

Not all of our research on covert communication has been in the context of the mediation of interpersonal expectancy effects. For example, some of our most recent work on what we call "thin slices of nonverbal behavior" has dealt with the tone of voice that primary care physicians and surgeons employ when talking with their patients. We compared the clinicians who had never been sued with those who had been sued at least twice. We found that surgeons who were more bossy in tone of voice, and primary care physicians who seemed to care less about their patients, judging from their tone of voice, were those more likely to be sued (Ambady, LaPlante, Nguyen, Rosenthal, Chaumeton, & Levinson, 2002). A good deal earlier we had found that physicians' tone of voice in talking about patients postdicted quite accurately their success rate in getting alcoholic patients to enter treatment (Milmoe, Rosenthal, Blane, Chafetz, & Wolf, 1967).

Of special interest to those of us who teach and are evaluated at the end of the term by our students is the research showing just how easy it is to predict how our students will evaluate our overall effectiveness at the end of the term. All it takes is showing 30 seconds of a videotape of our teaching behavior, with the sound turned off, to undergraduate raters of our nonverbal behavior. Our nonverbal warmth, enthusiasm, likeability, etc. as rated by these undergraduate raters predicts our subsequent overall effectiveness ratings made by our students with $r = .76$; a replication study in a high school rather than a college setting yielded $r = .68$ (Ambady & Rosenthal, 1993). In further studies, when the 30 seconds of silent videotape was reduced to 6 seconds, predictive accuracy decreased but remained remarkably high: $r = .71$ for college teachers, $r = .31$ for high school teachers.

These studies turned out not to be aberrant. In a meta-analysis of 38 independent studies employing thin slices of behavior (5 minutes or less), we found considerable accuracy of predictions of various objective outcomes in the areas of social and clinical psychology, with an overall mean effect size r of about .40 (Ambady & Rosenthal, 1992). Perhaps most surprising was the result that accuracy did not increase as exposure length was increased from 30 seconds to 5 minutes; nor did it increase for a series of studies based on quite thick slices of behavior covering spans of hours and even days (Ambady & Rosenthal, 1992).

CONCLUSION

We have had an overview of some processes of covert communication in classrooms, clinics, and courtrooms, and in the cubicles of corporations and of laboratories. Our primary emphasis has been on processes in which the expectation of one person (a teacher, a health care provider, a judge, an executive, or an experimenter), for the behavior of another person (a pupil, a patient, a juror, an employee, or a research participant), has come to serve as a self-fulfilling prophecy. The behavior expected actually came to pass *because* the expecter expected it.

We can draw that causal conclusion because of the hundreds of randomized experiments that have been conducted, reported, and summarized quantitatively. However, there is still much that we do not know. We do not know precisely what changes in the expecter's verbal and nonverbal behavior are brought about by changed expectations nor do we know precisely what elements of these changes are causal in bringing about the behavior changes we see in expectees.

We keep learning more about various processes of covert communication but, as we do, we keep learning more about what it is we do *not* yet know. But that should not be discouraging; it just shows we are making good progress!

Author's Note

This chapter is based in part on two recent papers: Rosenthal (2003), and an award address delivered at the 110th annual meeting of the American Psychological Association held August 22–25, 2002 in Chicago. The award was for Distinguished Scientific Applications of Psychology.

REFERENCES

Ambady, N., LaPlante, D., Nguyen, T., Rosenthal, R., Chaumeton, N., & Levinson, W. (2002). Surgeons' tone of voice: A clue to malpractice history. *Surgery, 132*(1), 5–9.

Ambady, N., & Rosenthal, R. (1992). Thin slices of expressive behavior as predictors of interpersonal consequences: A meta-analysis. *Psychological Bulletin, 111,* 256–274.

Ambady, N., & Rosenthal, R. (1993). Half a minute: Predicting teacher evaluations from thin slices of nonverbal behavior and physical attractiveness. *Journal of Personality and Social Psychology, 64,* 431–441.

Blanck, P. D., Rosenthal, R., Hart, A. J., & Bernieri, F. (1990). The measure of the judge: An empirically-based framework for exploring trial judges' behavior. *Iowa Law Review, 75,* 653–684.

Clark, K. B. (1963). Educational stimulation of racially disadvantaged children. In A. H. Passow (Ed.), *Education in depressed areas* (pp. 142–162). New York: Bureau of Publications, Teachers College, Columbia University.

Cooper, H., & Hedges, L. V. (Eds.). (1994). *Handbook of research synthesis.* New York: Russell Sage Foundation.

Eden, D. (1990). *Pygmalion in management: Productivity as a self-fulfilling prophecy.* Lexington, MA: D. C. Heath.

Glass, G. V, McGaw, B., & Smith, M. L. (1981). *Meta-analysis in social research.* Beverly Hills, CA: Sage.

Gruenberg, B. C. (1929). *The story of evolution.* Princeton, NJ: Van Nostrand.

Halverson, A. M., Hallahan, M., Hart, A. J., & Rosenthal, R. (1997). Reducing the biasing effects of judges' nonverbal behavior with simplified jury instruction. *Journal of Applied Psychology, 82,* 590–598.

Harris, M. J., & Rosenthal, R. (1985). The mediation of interpersonal expectancy effects: 31 meta-analyses. *Psychological Bulletin, 97,* 363–386.

Harris, M. J., & Rosenthal, R. (1986). Four factors in the mediation of teacher expectancy effects. In R. S. Feldman (Ed.), *The social psychology of education* (pp. 91–114). New York: Cambridge University Press.

Kierein, N. M., & Gold, M. A. (2000). Pygmalion in work organizations: A meta-analysis. *Journal of Organizational Behavior, 21,* 913–928.

Learman, L. A., Avorn, J., Everitt, D. E., & Rosenthal, R. (1990). Pygmalion in the nursing home: The effects of caregiver expectations on patient outcomes. *Journal of the American Geriatrics Society, 38,* 797–803.

Milmoe, S., Rosenthal, R., Blane, H. T., Chafetz, M. E., & Wolf, I. (1967). The doctor's voice: Postdictor of successful referral of alcoholic patients. *Journal of Abnormal Psychology, 72,* 78–84.

Pfungst, O. (1965). *Clever Hans* (C. L. Rahn, Trans.). New York: Holt, 1911; Holt, Rinehart & Winston.

Rosenthal, R. (1969). Interpersonal expectations. In R. Rosenthal & R. L. Rosnow (Eds.), *Artifact in behavioral research* (pp. 181–277). New York: Academic Press.

Rosenthal, R. (1973). The mediation of Pygmalion effects: A four factor "theory." *Papua New Guinea Journal of Education, 9,* 1–12.

Rosenthal, R. (1974). *On the social psychology of the self-fulfilling prophecy: Further evidence for Pygmalion effects and their mediating mechanisms* (pp. 1–28) Module 53. New York: MSS Modular Publications.

Rosenthal, R. (1981). Pavlov's mice, Pfungst's horse, and Pygmalion's PONS: Some models for the study of interpersonal expectancy effects. In T. A. Sebeok & R. Rosenthal (Eds.), *The Clever Hans Phenomenon* (pp. 182–198). Annals of the New York Academy of Sciences, No. 364.

Rosenthal, R. (1984). *Meta-analytic procedures for social research.* Newbury Park, CA: Sage.

Rosenthal, R. (1985). From unconscious experimenter bias to teacher expectancy effects. In J. G. Dusek, V. C. Hall, & W. J. Meyer (Eds.), *Teacher expectancies* (pp. 37–65). Hillsdale, NJ: Lawrence Erlbaum Associates.

Rosenthal, R. (1987a). *Judgment studies: Design, analysis, and meta-analysis.* New York: Cambridge University Press.

Rosenthal, R. (1987b). Pygmalion effects: Existence, magnitude, and social importance. *Educational Researcher, 16,* 37–41.

Rosenthal, R. (1991a). *Meta-analytic procedures for social research* (rev. ed.). Newbury Park, CA: Sage.

Rosenthal, R. (1991b). Teacher expectancy effects: A brief update 25 years after the Pygmalion experiment. *Journal of Research in Education, 1,* 3–12.

Rosenthal, R. (1995). Critiquing Pygmalion: A 25-year perspective. *Current Directions in Psychological Science, 4,* 171–172.

Rosenthal, R. (1998). Interpersonal expectancy effects: A forty year perspective. *Psychology Teacher Network, 8,* 2–4, 9.

Rosenthal, R. (2002). The Pygmalion Effect and its mediating mechanisms. In J. Aronson (Ed.), *Improving academic achievement* (pp. 25–36). San Diego, CA: Academic Press.

Rosenthal, R. (2003). Covert communication in laboratories, classrooms, and the truly real world. *Current Directions in Psychological Science, 12,* 151–154.

Rosenthal, R., & Fode, K. L. (1963a). The effect of experimenter bias on the performance of the albino rat. *Behavioral Science, 8,* 183–189.

Rosenthal, R., & Fode, K. L. (1963b). Three experiments in experimenter bias. *Psychological Reports, 12,* 491–511.

Rosenthal, R., & Jacobson, L. (1966). Teachers' expectancies: Determinants of pupils' IQ gains. *Psychological Reports, 19,* 115–118.

Rosenthal, R., & Jacobson, L. (1968). *Pygmalion in the classroom.* New York: Holt, Rinehart and Winston.

Rosenthal, R., & Jacobson, L. (1992). *Pygmalion in the classroom* (expanded ed.). New York: Irvington.

Rosenthal, R., & Lawson, R. (1964). A longitudinal study of the effects of experimenter bias on the operant learning of laboratory rats. *Journal of Psychiatric Research, 2,* 61–72.

Rosenthal, R., & Rubin, D. B. (1971). Pygmalion reaffirmed. In J. D. Elashoff & R. E. Snow (Eds.), *Pygmalion reconsidered* (pp. 139–155). Worthington, OH: C. A. Jones.

Rosenthal, R., & Rubin, D. B. (1978). Interpersonal expectancy effects: The first 345 studies. *The Behavioral and Brain Sciences, 3,* 377–386.

Rosenthal, R., & Rubin, D. B. (1982). A simple, general purpose display of magnitude of experimental effect. *Journal of Educational Psychology, 74,* 66–169.

Russell, B. (1927). *Philosophy.* New York: Norton.

6

Research to Address Racial and Ethnic Disparities in Mental Health: Some Lessons Learned

Stanley Sue

University of California, Davis

The noted journalist Theodore H. White (1979) concluded that three issues have always plagued American society: Bread and butter, war and peace, and Black and White. This last issue concerns race and ethnic relations. Why have ethnic and racial conflicts persisted for centuries, when during this time period we have made unprecedented technological advances and solved many perplexing problems? We have evolved a Constitution and democratic society that attempt to hold the high ideals of freedom and justice for all. We have sent human beings to the moon, connected the world through an Internet system, and mapped the human genome. Yet, our society as well as those throughout the world continues to grapple with ethnic and racial prejudice and discrimination, slurs, violence, ethnic cleansing, and disparities in privilege and the quality of life.

ETHNICITY AND MENTAL HEALTH

In many ways, the problems concerning race and ethnic relations in society are reflected in the mental health arena. Racial and ethnic disparities and inequities in mental health services have been identified in reports by the U.S. Surgeon General (2001) and by the President's New Freedom Commission (2003). The reports noted that racial and ethnic minority groups (e.g., African Americans, American Indians and Alaska Natives, Asian Americans and Pacific Islanders, and Hispanic Americans) experienced a greater disability burden from unmet mental health needs and that these groups received poor quality of care. Therefore, a major challenge facing the mental health field is how to use research to increase knowledge of the nature of disparities and to reduce these disparities.

In this chapter, I discuss our past and present research program to address mental health needs of ethnic minority group individuals. Particular attention is placed on the process involved in the application of research to help solve major social and health problems. The lessons learned in this process are especially instructive because they reveal challenges encountered in applied research in general and ethnic minority research in particular. From the outset, it should be noted that mental health disparities have not been "solved" through our research work or through the work of others. Rather, this chapter points to the problems and issues involved in the process of conducting applied research on ethnic minority populations.

The Nature of Disparities

For decades, researchers and practitioners have observed that racial and ethnic minority groups were receiving inadequate and low quality mental health care. For example, the President's Commission on Mental Health (1978) found that mental health services were often inappropriate for the cultural and linguistics traditions of these groups. However, most of the conclusions regarding the quality of care were derived from anecdotes, observations, or preliminary empirical research that was largely based on small samples of clients, measures with unknown cross-cultural validity, limited to one ethnic minority group, and so forth. Given these problems and our desire to address treatment disparities, we wanted to first understand the nature of the disparities and then discover means of reducing these disparities.

We found a unique opportunity to study ethnicity and treatment variables in the Seattle area. In our Seattle project, the state of Washington supplied us with data on nearly 14,000 clients seen in 17 community mental health facilities. Records were kept on African American, American Indian, Asian American, Hispanic American, and non-Hispanic White clients. Herman McKinney and I examined utilization patterns, client characteristics, services received, length of treatment, and outcomes of clients. We could find no other studies that were based on such extensive data. After making ethnic comparisons, we concluded that ethnic minority clients were not faring well in the mental health system (Sue, 1977). They tended to prematurely terminate from treatment and to average fewer number of treatment sessions than did Whites. From 42% to 55% of clients from each of the ethnic minority groups failed to return for services after one session compared to a 30% drop-out rate for Whites. The ethnic–White differences in premature termination rates persisted, even after controlling for variables such as clients' socioeconomic class, age, gender, marital status, referral source, initial diagnosis, type of treatment received, type of therapist seen, and so on. Because the treatment outcome measures used by the mental health facilities proved to be problematic and quantifying the degree of improvement was not possible, we examined using length of treatment as a proxy variable for treatment outcome. In several major reviews, length of treatment has been found to be positively related to outcome (Baekelund & Lundwall, 1975; Luborsky, Chandler, Auerbach, Cohen, & Bachrach, 1971; Orlinsky, Ronnestad, & Willutzki, 2004). The findings indicated that ethnicity was a strong predictor of premature termination and fewer sessions. We concluded that ethnic minority groups were receiving inadequate services.

The research received a great deal of attention and praise. O'Sullivan, Peterson, Cox, and Kirkeby (1989) noted that Sue's work was "cited as the key investigation of CMHS services for minority groups ..." (p. 19). Snowden (1987) regarded the investigations as "perhaps the most comprehensive and detailed of evaluations ..." (p. 577). The praise we received was not attributable to the methodological rigor or the deep insights gained from the project. The investigations yielded descriptive information and were not grounded in methodological sophistication and rigor. Rather, two other factors drew attention to the project. First, the research was pioneering. Prior to this work, ethnic services research was based on small samples, compared Whites with non-Whites as a general category, or failed to control for other variables (e.g., social class, diagnosis, etc.) that might be confounded with ethnicity. Our studies included large samples of clients who were broken down by ethnicity and who had sufficient information permitting control of various demographic variables. Second, the work proved to be highly controversial, which added to its visibility. The controversy concerned our conclusion that services were not meeting the needs of ethnic minority groups. Unknown to us, the National Institute of Mental Health (NIMH), which funded our project, was extremely concerned about the observed inequities in service delivery that were uncovered by our analysis. It contacted the Washington State Department of Social and Health Services and raised issues over the State's lack of compliance with civil rights goals involving the delivery of quality services to different populations. Because NIMH was involved and concerned, the State apparently grew fearful that future NIMH funding opportunities for research might be jeopardized and that the general public as well as legislators might have adverse reactions to the State's mental health system. In any event, the State Department of Social and Health Services then challenged the validity of our findings. It stated that 1 of the 17 mental health facilities may have provided inaccurate data. Thus the State questioned the validity of the data it had given us.

Those of us involved in the research seemed to be the last to become informed of the controversy. I was unaware of these events until I was asked by the Washington State Psychological Association to testify at a hearing of the Senate Subcommittee on Mental Health. The Subcommittee wanted to investigate the adequacy of services for different client populations and the validity of our findings. Prior to the hearings, we quickly reanalyzed the data. By excluding the data from the one facility in question, we addressed the challenge that the State made. The reanalysis did not change our original conclusions. Yet, the situation was awkward for everyone involved in the study, as noted in Sue (1992).

On the one hand, the data revealed some problems in the provision of mental health services and enabled us to make policy and program recommendations. On the other hand, the State could be singled out for criticism, when, from all available evidence, other states and systems were encountering similar problems in responding to ethnic minority populations. Furthermore, I was concerned that, based on our experience, various states and mental health programs might be reluctant to conduct evaluation research or to turn over data to researchers fearing the implications of the findings. The purpose of our research was to examine problems in the mental health system and to make recommendations. We and the State, which fully cooperated with the research project, did not anticipate that the findings would be used for compliance purposes, that is, whether the State was complying with federal guidelines and goals for providing services to ethnic minority populations.

Happily, the situation ended with some positive notes. After my testimony, officials from the State Department of Social and Health Services met with me and indicated they were concerned over the plight of ethnic minority populations and that I could have access to any of their data in the future. More importantly, the State initiated several programs intended to offer culturally responsive services for ethnic minority group populations. O'Sullivan et al. (1989) conducted a 10-year followup investigation of our Seattle project. They found that the high drop-out rates for ethnic minority clients had now been reduced and were not much different from Whites. They attributed the improvement to the hiring of more ethnic minority service providers, to the creation of ethnic specific services, and to other innovative programs. I was quite pleased that the State had initiated culturally responsive services and sponsored additional research work on the matter (see pp. 193–194).

Reflections

Several lessons are apparent from our experience with the research. First, at that time, there was a low baseline of knowledge on ethnic minority groups. Relatively little research had been conducted. Although more research is presently available, the field of ethnic mental health still suffers from a paucity of knowledge (U.S. Surgeon General, 2001). Second, ethnic research is controversial. The uncovering of inequities in services is likely to be uncomfortable for those in the mental health system. Again, the issues reflect larger societal concerns over prejudice and discrimination, social justice, and rights and privileges for ethnic minorities. Ethnic researchers must be prepared for possible debate and controversy over their work. Third, researchers must be aware of the implications of research. We had no idea that our research would be used for civil rights compliance purposes, and the analyses had effects on the state of Washington. Applied research on ethnic minority groups may be used for many different purposes than intended by the investigators. I return to this point later in the chapter.

Policies and Practices

If, as suggested by our research and those of other investigators, there is convergent evidence of disparities or inequities in the delivery of mental health services, how can these disparities be reduced? This is an important topic for applied research. One well-recognized paradigm for applying research to solve problems was proposed by George Fairweather (Fairweather & Fergus, 1993). According to Fairweather's Experimental Social Innovations approach, there are sequential steps that are important in finding solutions to social problems through research:

1. Problem definition—identifying a human problem of concern and potential interventive approaches for dealing with it through information gathering and synthesis;
2. Design—using the acquired information base and disciplined creativity to shape potential interventive solutions;
3. Comparison—use of experimental comparisons of proposed interventions with existing or traditional interventions;
4. Evaluation—extensive and controlled field testing of the interventions;
5. Implementation and dissemination—determining potential users of the intervention and preparing and packaging the intervention for use.

The approach systematically uncovers interventions that can be tested for their value in addressing social problems.

Why not use such a systematic approach to find out how to address the service inequities and disparities for ethnic minority populations? The appropriateness of the approach hinges on the availability of information and the feasibility of conducting research tests of interventions. The knowledge base on mental health interventions for ethnic minority populations has been sparse (Chambless et al., 1996; President's New Freedom Commission,

2003; U.S. Surgeon General, 2001). Thus, the knowledge on which to base interventions is limited. Even more important is the fact that ethnic mental health research is extremely difficult to conduct. Numerous problems are encountered by ethnic researchers. For example, finding representative samples or even adequate sample sizes may be difficult. Consider the situation of a researcher who wants to study the effects of psychotropic medication on Southeast Asian refugees with schizophrenia. Where does one find such individuals, will sample sizes be large enough to make experimental comparisons, and are the located samples representative of the general population of Southeast Asian refugees? Furthermore, if questionnaires or interviews are used, should English or a Southeast Asian language be used? How can the validity of language translations be assured? Are the measures themselves cross-culturally valid? What kinds of cultural response sets may exist among Southeast Asians? The point is that ethnic mental health research is frequently difficult and costly to conduct. Designing rigorous experimental studies is especially problematic and costly because of the sophistication and control of variables that are required. Thus, using the Fairweather paradigm is often not feasible or practically possible unless substantial resources are made available.

Given these considerations, we felt that it was still possible to understand the possible effects of intervention by examining effectiveness research. That is, we could test the possible effects of interventions by noting the relationships between certain treatment variables and outcomes in the mental health setting. Although effectiveness research is less credible in establishing causality (e.g., the effects of intervention on outcomes) than efficacy research, it would nevertheless provide valuable information about plausible hypotheses to subject to further testing or about possible strategies to use in improving treatment outcomes for ethnic minority groups. We first wanted to identify factors that may be associated with positive treatment outcomes for these groups before subjecting these factors to empirical testing.

From a review of the ethnic mental health services literature, one of the most common themes was that services were culturally insensitive, inappropriate, or incompatible (e.g., see U.S. Surgeon General, 2001 for a review). The conceptual rationale for the theme was that services lacked match or fit with the culture, language, or background of ethnic minority clients such as African Americans, American Indians, Asian Americans, and Latinos. Cultural mismatches could affect the validity of assessment as well as the development of therapist–client rapport, therapeutic alliance, and treatment effectiveness.

In view of these problems, a series of recommendations were made to facilitate the provision of more culturally responsive treatments. The recommendations, based on match or fit, included the necessity to know the culture of clients, to be sensitive and flexible in dealing with clients, and to achieve credibility (Bernal & Scharron-del-Rio, 2001; D'Andrea & Daniels, 1991; Ponterotto & Alexander, 1996; Sue & Sue, 1999). In particular, three kinds of match seemed important: *Service match*—ethnic specific services (ESS). In ESS the mental health services are particularly targeted for a particular ethnic population. For example, in a community composed largely of Mexican Americans, a mental health clinic may target that population by having bilingual and bicultural personnel, treatment approaches to take the client's cultural background into consideration, notices written in Spanish, etc. The services match the ethnicity or culture of clients. One particular ESS is located at San Francisco General Hospital. The hospital has several psychiatric wards that are focused on particular ethnic clients (e.g., an African American ward, an Asian American ward, etc.). Ethnic clients can be treated on these wards if it is felt that the ESS wards are more beneficial than general wards not focused on a particular ethnic group. If a client can only speak Chinese, that client may be assigned to the Asian American ward where there are Chinese speaking therapists and Chinese cultural amenities (Chinese meals, Chinese television programs, etc.).

Another recommended strategy that was found in the mental health literature was *ethnic match* between therapist and client. This strategy was based on the assumption that an ethnic client may prefer to work with, and benefit from, a therapist of the same ethnicity and culture. Indeed, mental health training programs started to recruit and train more ethnic minority providers in an attempt not only to increase diversity of the workforce but also to increase the likelihood that ethnic clients could work with therapists who shared the same ethnicity or culture. Presumably, ethnic clients would feel more comfortable and better understood, and therapists would conduct better assessments and provide more culturally consistent interventions if clients and therapists matched ethnically and culturally.

Finally, the literature also identified the importance of *cognitive match*—that is, the shared thinking or understanding of therapists and clients. This form of match occurs when the therapist knows or shares the explanatory and cultural beliefs of the client. By understanding these cultural beliefs, the therapist is able to make interventions or recommendations that are more culturally consistent and credible to the client. Cognitive match is the rationale for training therapists to understand the cultural background, attitudes, and lifestyles of ethnic clients.

Our Research Program

In our program of research, we wanted to test whether ethnic specific services, ethnic match, and cognitive match might reduce the mental health treatment disparities found among ethnic minority clients. Because of the problems in conducting rigorous experimental tests of these interventions, we decided to investigate the relationship between these match variables and treatment outcomes in mental health settings. Three questions were addressed: First, when therapists and clients are ethnically matched, are treatment outcomes better than when therapists and clients differ in ethnicity? Is there evidence that ethnic clients benefit from seeing an ethnically similar therapist? Under what conditions is ethnic match beneficial? Match presumably may not be effective for all clients, so it is important to determine the conditions under which match is important. Second, when ethnic clients utilize an ethnic-specific service, are outcomes better than if they utilize a non-ethnic specific (mainstream service)? Many ethnic specific services have been established throughout the country. Are these services effective, and what is it about such services that is effective? Third, when therapists and clients think the same (i.e., exhibit cognitive match) regardless of ethnicity, are treatment outcomes more favorable? Table 6.1 shows the three areas of investigation. Interestingly, prior to our research, we found little in the way of empirical tests of these recommendations or assumptions.

To examine the first question regarding ethnic match, we analyzed data on thousands of African American, Asian American, Mexican American, and White clients seen in the Los Angeles County Mental Health System (Sue, Fujino, Hu, Takeuchi, & Zane, 1991). We were able to determine whether clients worked with therapists who were of the same ethnicity. Ethnic match was then used as a predictor of dropping out of treatment, number of treatment sessions, and treatment outcomes. The treatment outcome measure was the Global Assessment Scale (GAS) on which therapists rate their clients in terms of level of functioning on a 100-point scale. A number of other client variables were controlled such as social class, initial level of functioning, diagnosis, gender, age, and so forth. Results revealed that Asian Americans generally fared better in terms of more sessions, less dropping out, and

TABLE 6.1
Past Recommendations

Ethnic Specific Services	Ethnic Match	Cognitive Match
Services and programs are specially designed to serve ethnic populations. The services are culturally consistent with the local ethnic population.	Therapists and clients are similar in ethnicity, language, or background. The match involves demographic or background variables.	Therapists and clients are similar in world views and perspectives; or therapists understand those of the clients. They may match in terms of problem conceptualizations, means for resolving problems, or goals for treatment.

better treatment outcomes, when they saw a therapist who was matched ethnically. Match was also a predictor of outcomes for Mexican Americans, although the effects were less dramatic. Interestingly, we were able to examine ethnic match and language match for Asian Americans and Mexican Americans. Both were important predictors, especially for clients who were less acculturated. This finding is important because it points to individual differences. Match may be especially important if clients are less acculturated and may be of less importance for clients who are acculturated and "Americanized." Ethnic matches were significantly related to more sessions for African Americans and Whites. Ethnic match also predicted lower rates of premature termination among Whites, although match was unrelated to premature termination among African Americans. When the results for match and number of sessions or premature termination reached statistically significant, most of the effect sizes were large, indicating clinical significance of the findings. As noted earlier, both number of sessions and dropping out have been used as indicators because they are directly related to treatment outcomes (Orlinsky et al., 2004; Sue et al., 1991). Finally, ethnic match failed to predict treatment outcomes on the GAS for African Americans and Whites. We do not know why matching is related to the GAS for some groups but not others. Perhaps, in this study, the GAS lacked sufficient sensitivity to measure treatment outcomes in a valid manner. On the other hand, the benefits of ethnic match may depend heavily on the acculturation level, ethnic–cultural identity, or ethnicity of clients. That is, individual differences exist as to the value of ethnic match in treatment.

The second question involved the benefits of ethnic specific services. Using the Los Angeles County data set with thousands of ethnic minority clients, we compared the outcomes of ethnic clients who utilized ethnic specific services (e.g., an African American client using a mental health program especially designed for the local African American community) with those of ethnic clients using mainstream, nonethnic specific programs (Takeuchi, Sue, & Yeh, 1995; Yeh, Takeuchi, & Sue, 1994). The criterion variables again were dropout rates, length of treatment, and GAS scores. Because ethnic match was associated with these variables, we controlled for ethnic match as well as for diagnosis, gender, age, and social class. In general, the results indicated that ethnic clients who attend ethnic-specific programs had lower dropout rates and stayed in the programs longer than those using mainstream services. The findings were not clear-cut when the GAS measure was examined. Thus, the results largely show that ethnic match and ethnic specific services are associated with favorable treatment outcomes. Because the research design was not experimental, we cannot assert with confidence that match affects outcomes. However, the findings do support such a conclusion. Experimental studies of match are, of course, needed to help establish causality.

The final question we addressed was whether clients whose therapists think in a similar manner (cognitive match) have better outcomes than those whose therapists think differently. One obstacle to the provision of adequate services for ethnic minority clients is that therapists and clients may not share common assumptions, attitudes, and beliefs about therapy and about the problems that are presented in treatment. In one of our studies, we investigated client–therapist similarity (Zane et al., 2005). By measuring therapist and client perceptions of the presenting problem, coping orientation, and treatment goals, we could determine the extent of similarity between therapists and clients. Similarity was then used as a predictor of treatment outcomes and processes. This study was prospective in nature, used separate and independent sources for the cognitive predictors, employed multiple-outcome measures, and focused on specific attitudes and perceptions that are quite salient and relevant to treatment. Cognitive similarities between clients and their therapists on several of the attitudinal and perceptual measures were predictive of treatment outcomes. In various comparisons, therapist–client matches on goals for treatment and on coping styles were related to better adjustment and more positive impressions of the sessions. In no case did a cognitive mismatch predict better process or treatment outcome. This study demonstrates that therapist conceptions and their congruence with those of clients are related to therapeutic outcomes. Whereas our previous studies demonstrated that ethnic match and service match are important, we now have additional knowledge about the conditions that are related to favorable outcomes within ethnic match, that is, cognitive match. Our most recent research project tries to identify those characteristics of therapists that are related to positive treatment outcomes across different ethnic populations in the State of California.

LESSONS LEARNED

In conducting the research, several lessons were learned that are germane to our discussion of applied research. Some of these lessons have already been discussed. The research frequently involves controversy, has unanticipated side effects, and is difficult to conduct. I would like to further elaborate on these lessons and then conclude by indicating that the research has also been meaningful, exciting, and valuable.

Controversial Nature and Side Effects

Earlier, it was noted that a controversy arose from the research findings that ethnic minority clients were not faring well in the mental health system. Two other important controversies arose from our work. First, some interpreted our research as supporting segregation. Our conclusion that ethnic specific services were beneficial draws concerns that we were advocating a dualism of services—one for mainstream Americans and one for ethnic minorities. Kramer (1984) argued that ethnic specific programs perpetuated segregation. He felt that the mental health system should encourage clinics and hospitals to provide culturally appropriate services for all groups. His objection was that: "In our efforts to provide distinctive help along residential lines to distinctive racial–ethnic groups, we may be contributing and adding to the very segregation that has been a curse to our emotional existence" (p. 261). Second, the issue of segregation was also raised from our finding that ethnic match is associated with favorable treatment outcomes. During a discussion of the research, one investigator from South Africa mentioned that in his country, the finding was being used to justify segregation. That is, from our findings that ethnic match may be beneficial, some in South Africa were arguing that "Whites should take care of Whites and Blacks should only work with Blacks."

Both conclusions from our match research were incorrect. We wanted to test whether service and ethnic match were beneficial. We were not arguing for segregation or for the necessity of having match. In fact, our position was that individual differences were important, and research should examine the conditions under which match is important—not that all ethnic clients needed ethnic specific services or ethnically matched therapists.

Second, a controversy arose over the importance of responding to the cultural differences that ethnic minority clients may have. Satel (2000; Satel & Forster, 1999) has attacked the cultural competency attempts to improve the quality of services provided to ethnic minority clients.

> Cultural competence ranges from the gratuitous (advising clinicians to "respect" a patient's cultural heritage) to the misguided (believing that human identity and behavior are primarily culture-dependent) to the near-paranoid (presuming that therapists and patients of different racial groups will experience so much miscommunication and mistrust that the therapist must learn a different set of rules for treating patients of a different race or better yet, that the clinician and the patient should be from the same racial or ethnic group). The most radical vision of cultural competence claims that membership in an oppressed group is a patient's most clinically important attribute and that white therapists are racist whether they know it or not. (Satel & Forster, 1999, p. 1)

In a subsequent argument, Satel (2000) challenged cultural competency by pointing to the lack of experimental tests. She stated that: "Multicultural counseling has not been put to any kind of test.... I could find no controlled studies of patients wherein half are randomly assigned to multicultural counseling and half to conventional counseling" (p. 187).

There are a few experimental studies of cultural competency (Zane et al., 2004). These along with field and clinical research provide substantial evidence for the value of interventions intended to improve cultural competency (Hall, 2001, 2003). However, it is likely that the debate over cultural competency will continue at least in the near future. Conflict seems to accompany ethnic and racial issues.

Another example of controversy over research conclusions occurred over the National Healthcare Disparities Report (NHDR) released by Health and Human Services (HHS) in 2003. Initially, the scientists who drafted the report noted in the executive summary the magnitude of disparities in health care. The conclusions were similar to those found in the Institute of Medicine's *"Unequal Treatment: Confronting Racial and Ethnic Disparities in Health Care"* (Smedley, Stith, & Nelson, 2003). However, before the NHDR report was released, there were attempts by some staff at the Department of Health and Human Services (HHS) to modify the conclusions of the report to downplay the extent of disparities. For example, in one draft of the report, the conclusion was that significant inequalities were found in health care in the United States and health care disparities constituted national problems. However, after the modifications by HHS staff, none of these conclusions appeared. Furthermore, nearly all mentions of the word "disparity," cited about 30 times in the "key findings" section, were deleted.

A number of political figures protested the modifications made by HHS staff and argued that the Bush administration was trying to "whitewash" and hide disparities uncovered by scientists:

"Just like a tumor cannot be healed by covering it with a bandage, healthcare disparities cannot be eliminated with misrepresented facts," said Rep. Elijah E. Cummings, Chair of the Congressional Black Caucus. "I urge the Bush Administration to stand by its commitment to eliminating racially-defined healthcare disparities by 2010. Disparities do not disappear by concealing information."

"It's inconceivable that HHS could, in good conscience, remove the word that describes not only the shortcomings, but the pain caused by the holes in our current healthcare system," said Rep. Ciro D. Rodriguez, Chair of the Congressional Hispanic Caucus. "It's vital to receive accurate information in order to correct our current system and to guarantee a better one for our children. Removing the word does not remove the issue."

"Instead of leading the fight against healthcare disparities, HHS is downplaying the serious inequities faced by racial and ethnic minorities," said Rep. Michael M. Honda, Chair of the Congressional Asian Pacific American Caucus. "By tampering with the conclusions of its own scientists, HHS is placing politics before social justice."

After numerous protests regarding the changes to the Report were sent to HHS Secretary Tommy Thompson, he said that his department had erred in rewriting a report on racial and socioeconomic health disparities and that he planned to release the report as originally written.

Why Bother?

Given the conflicts and the methodological and conceptual problems that often accompany ethnic research, why bother doing such research? For several reasons, I have found the research to be personally and professionally meaningful. First, the research is intended to promote human welfare in finding ways of addressing ethnic and racial disparities. Many psychologists enter the field with desires to help people, particularly those in the clinical or educational psychology area. Through research, one can gain understanding of the nature of problems, discover ways of increasing equity and human functioning, and make original contributions both as a psychologist and as a citizen. Second, the research can have an impact on policies and programs. As a result of research, I have been asked to serve on policy boards and committees (e.g., on the Planning Board for the U.S. Surgeon General's Mental Health Report), and I have seen social service agencies and mental health clinics use the research findings to argue for increased resources. Although it is true, as discussed previously, that there are often unintended side effects to one's research, I have always felt that the research has influence and impact. Third, even though the research is identified as being "applied," the relationship between applied and theoretical research is intimate. Through the research, implications for theory and practice can be drawn. Furthermore, although ethnic research is intended to provide knowledge about ethnic groups, it frequently carries implications for all human beings. For example, the universality of theories and practices can never be established simply by examining one population.

In summary, research on ethnicity and mental health has been gratifying despite the controversies that are encountered and the methodological and conceptual problems that accompany such research. More knowledge is accumulating that can address the disparities and inequities found in services to ethnic minority groups.

REFERENCES

Baekelund, F., & Lundwall, L. (1975). Dropping out of treatment: A critical review. *Psychological Bulletin, 82,* 738–783.

Bernal, G., & Scharron-del-Rio, M. R. (2001). Are empirically supported treatments valid for ethnic minorities? Toward an alternative approach for treatment research. *Cultural Diversity and Ethnic Minority Psychology, 7,* 328–342.

Chambless, D. L., Sanderson, W. C., Shoham, V., Bennett-Johnson, S., Pope, K. S., & Crits-Christoph, P. (1996). An update on empirically validated therapies. *Clinical Psychologist, 49,* 5–18.

D'Andrea, M., & Daniels, J. (1991). Exploring the different levels of multicultural counseling training in counselor education. *Journal of Counseling and Development, 70,* 78–85.

Fairweather, G. W., & Fergus, E. O. (1993). *Empowering the mentally ill.* Austin, TX: Fairweather Publishing.

Hall, G. N. (2001). Psychotherapy research with ethnic minorities: Empirical, ethical, and conceptual issues. *Journal of Consulting and Clinical Psychology, 69,* 502–510.

Hall, G. N. (2003). Cultural competence in clinical psychology research. *Clinical Psychologist, 56,* 11–16.

Kramer, B. M. (1984). Community mental health in a dual society. In S. Sue & T. Moore (Eds.), *The pluralistic society: A community mental health perspective* (pp. 254–262). New York: Human Sciences Press.

Luborsky, L., Chandler, M., Auerbach, A. H., Cohen, J., & Bachrach, H. M. (1971). Factors influencing the outcome of psychotherapy: A review of quantitative research. *Psychological Bulletin, 75,* 145–185.

Orlinsky, D. E., Ronnestad, M. H., & Willutzki, U. (2004). Fifty years of psychotherapy process-outcome research: Continuity and change. In M. J. Lambert (Ed.), *Bergin and Garfield's handbook of psychotherapy and behavior change* (5th ed., pp. 307–389). New York: Wiley.

O'Sullivan, M. J., Peterson, P. D., Cox, G. B., & Kirkeby, J. (1989). Ethnic populations: Community mental health services ten years later. *American Journal of Community Psychology, 17,* 17–30.

Ponterotto, J. G., & Alexander, C. M. (1996). Assessing the multicultural competence of counselors and clinicians. In L. A. Suzuki, P. J. Meller, & J. G. Ponterotto (Eds.), *Handbook of multicultural assessment: Clinical, psychological, and educational applications* (pp. 651–672). San Francisco: Jossey-Bass.

President's Commission on Mental Health. (1978). *Report to the President.* Washington, DC: U.S. Government Printing Office.

President's New Freedom Commission on Mental Health. (2003). *Achieving the promise: Transforming mental health care in America.* Report of the President's New Freedom Commission on Mental Health. Rockville, Maryland.

Satel, S. (2000). *PC, M.D.: How political correctness is corrupting medicine.* New York: Basic Books.

Satel, S., & Forster, G. (1999). *Multicultural mental health: Does your skin color matter more than your mind?* Retrieved December 18, 2001, from http://www.ceousa.org/html/health.html

Smedley, B. D., Stith, A. Y., & Nelson, A. R. (2003). *Unequal treatment: Confronting racial and ethnic disparities in health care.* Washington, DC: National Academies Press.

Snowden, L. (1987). The peculiar successes of community psychology: Service delivery to minorities and the poor. *American Journal of Community Psychology, 15,* 575–586.

Sue, D. W., & Sue, D. (1999). *Counseling the culturally different: Theory and practice.* New York: Wiley.

Sue, S. (1977). Community mental health services to minority groups: Some optimism, some pessimism. *American Psychologist, 32,* 616–624.

Sue, S. (1992). Ethnicity and mental health: Research and policy issues. *Journal of Social Issues, 48,* 187–205.

Sue, S., Fujino, D., Hu, L., Takeuchi, D., & Zane, N. (1991). Community mental health services for ethnic minority groups: A test of the cultural responsiveness hypothesis. *Journal of Clinical and Consulting Psychology, 59,* 533–540.

Takeuchi, D. T., Sue, S., & Yeh, M. (1995). Return rates and outcomes from ethnicity-specific mental health programs in Los Angeles. *American Journal of Public Health, 85,* 638–643.

U.S. Surgeon General. (2001). *Mental health: Culture, race, and ethnicity—A supplement to Mental Health: A Report of the Surgeon General.* Rockville, MD: U.S. Department of Health and Human Services.

White, T. H. (1979). A conversation with Theodore H. White. *Book Digest Magazine, 6,* 19–27.

Yeh, M., Takeuchi, D. T., & Sue, S. (1994). Asian American children in the mental health system: A comparison of parallel and mainstream outpatient service centers. *Journal of Clinical Child Psychology, 23,* 5–12.

Zane, N., Hall, G. N., Sue, S., Young, K., & Nunez, J. (2004). Research on psychotherapy with culturally diverse populations. In M. J. Lambert (Ed.), *Bergin and Garfield's handbook of psychotherapy and behavior change* (5th ed., pp. 767–804). New York: Wiley.

Zane, N., Sue, S., Huang, L., Huang, J., Lowe, S., Srinivasan, S., Chun, K., Kurasaki, K., & Lee, E. (2005). *Beyond ethnic match: Effects of client-therapist similarities in problem perception, coping orientation, and therapy goals on treatment outcomes.*

7

Applying Developmental Psychology to Bridge Cultures in the Classroom

Patricia M. Greenfield
University of California, Los Angeles
Center for Advanced Study in the Behavioral Sciences,
Stanford, California

Applied developmental psychology provides an opportunity to use what is known from developmental research and apply this knowledge to solving social problems. This chapter provides the reader with a tangible example of how developmental psychology can be used in this way. The example utilizes basic developmental research demonstrating cross-cultural value conflict between Latino immigrant families and U.S. schools. This research serves as the foundation for a cross-cultural teacher training program entitled Bridging Cultures. Bridging Cultures was designed to ameliorate this cross-cultural value conflict, thereby improving the lives of Latino immigrant children, their parents, and their teachers.

WHAT IS BRIDGING CULTURES?

Bridging Cultures is a research-based cross-cultural training program for educators based on the notion that implicit value differences between school and home cause the most basic problems for immigrant or Native American children and their families, and, specifically, for most of the Latino immigrant population that comes to California. In particular, our project focuses on the difference between a collectivistic value orientation and an individualistic value orientation in order to conceptualize and organize these implicit value differences. Here, we use constructs that have a venerable history in cross-cultural psychology in a new way. The fundamental

TABLE 7.1
Contrasts Between Collectivism and Individualism

Collectivism	Individualism
Helping/being helped	Independent task completion
Social responsibility	Choice, personal responsibility
Sharing	Personal property
Narrative knowledge with a social purpose	Factual knowledge for its own sake

value orientations of individualism and collectivism lead to differences in many domains, a number of which are pertinent to the educational setting. Table 7.1 shows a few that we have found relevant in the elementary school context.

But the news in our research is not to put everyone in a box labeled individualism or collectivism (and there are of course individual differences in every group). Instead, the news is to demonstrate how these two orientations meet and clash in educational settings when immigrant families send their children to school. The news is in figuring out that these orientations apply to a dynamic real-world problem and how they animate real-world, lived experience.

The other news in Bridging Cultures is to demonstrate how an awareness of these two value orientations can result in a constant stream of innovative practices created by teachers and other school personnel, practices that create a bridge between the two cultures, between the culture of individualism, the dominant culture in the United States, and the culture of collectivism, brought from Mexico and Central America, as well as from other immigrant-sending countries.

CROSS-CULTURAL DISTRIBUTION
OF INDIVIDUALISM AND COLLECTIVISM

Between 1967 and 1973, IBM gave a questionnaire assessing individualism and collectivism to thousands of its middle-class workers around the world (Hofstede, 2001). Table 7.2 presents selected results. Note first how the United States scored as the most individualistic country in the world. Note second how all of the countries currently sending large numbers of immigrants to the United States in general and to California in particular were high on collectivism. For example, the Latin American countries of Mexico, El Salvador, and Guatemala were high on collectivism. But so were Asian countries such as the Philippines and Korea. This situation sets the stage for cross-cultural value conflict, not just in the schools, but in society at large.

TABLE 7.2
Country Rankings on Individualism and Collectivism

USA	1	Most individualistic
Australia	2	
Great Britain	3	
Canada, Netherlands	4.5	
Italy	7	
France, Sweden	10.5	
Germany	15	
Israel	19	
Spain	20	
· ·		Median
Philippines	31	
Mexico	32	
Hong Kong	37	
Singapore, Thailand, West African countries	34	
El Salvador	42	
South Korea	43	
Taiwan	44	
Pakistan, Indonesia	47.5	
Guatemala	53	Most collectivistic

Note. This table presents selected results based on factor analysis of questionnaire items given to IBM workers concerning work goals (Hofstede, 2001). Hofstede's full sample contains 53 countries.

Although the Hofstede analysis focused primarily on nationality, Hofstede and others have noted other factors that seem to influence basic value orientations. The first is socioeconomics: The rich tend to be more individualistic, the poor tend to be more collectivistic (Hofstede, 2001; Lustig & Koester, 1999). The second is demographics: Urban people tend to be more individualistic, rural people tend to be more collectivistic (Hofstede, 2001). The third factor is education: Formal education tends to make people more individualistic and less collectivistic (Tapia-Uribe, LeVine, & LeVine, 1994).

But the collectivistic side of this equation constitutes a demographic portrait of the overwhelming majority of people who come to California from Mexico, and even Central America. They are poor, rural, and have had little opportunity for formal education: Their collectivism is multiply determined. And so is the individualism of the United States. We not only inherited from northern Europe an ideology of rugged individualism, but we are predominantly rich, urban, and well educated. These contrasting demographic portraits explain why the value conflict is especially severe for Latino immigrants from Mexico and Central America.

Note too that the Latino immigrant population in our studies and in our Bridging Cultures classrooms is much more homogenous, compared with many Latino populations elsewhere in the United States. Our population, mainly from Mexico, is also poorer and has had less opportunity for formal education in their home countries. For example, in the scenario study presented shortly, the average educational level of the parents was fifth grade.

RESEARCH FOUNDATION OF THE BRIDGING CULTURES PROJECT

Methodologically, the Bridging Cultures Project utilizes mixed methods, integrating qualitative and quantitative techniques. We began with qualitative ethnographic classroom research (Greenfield, Raeff, & Quiroz, 1996), which was ongoing throughout the project. We then proceeded to a quantitative study of social dilemmas (Raeff, Greenfield, & Quiroz, 2000) and a discourse study of parent–teacher conferences (Greenfield, Quiroz, & Raeff, 2000). The results of these basic studies were then used in training our seven core teachers during the Bridging Cultures workshops (Trumbull, Rothstein-Fisch, Greenfield, & Quiroz, 2001).

The workshops and their effects also became a focus of study. We carried out before–after questionnaire assessments and also videotaped the workshops for later discourse analysis of change processes (Trumbull, Diaz-Meza, Hasan, & Rothstein-Fisch, 2001). By the end of the workshops, our teachers had become full participants in our research, and their changed practices became research data documenting effects of the training. Following the workshop series and over a period of about 5 years, they helped us document their new practices in longitudinal ethnographies that included teacher reports in our periodic group meetings and researcher observations in the teachers' classrooms, followed by an interview with each Bridging Culture teacher who had been observed.

Finally, Isaac (1999) and Correa-Chávez (1999) carried out quasi-experimental discourse studies comparing teacher–student and student–student interaction in a Bridging Cultures and a non–Bridging Cultures classroom (Correa-Chávez, 1999; Isaac, 1999). All of these data sources have contributed directly or indirectly to the present overview.

THE WORKSHOPS AND THE TEACHERS

With funding from WestEd, a federally funded regional educational R&D center with headquarters in Northern California, we held a series of three workshops over a 4-month period. Our trainees were seven elementary school teachers from all over Southern California, all teaching in bilingual Spanish–English classrooms (see acknowledgments for the list of participants). Participation was by invitation, and we selected teachers based on reputation and interest in cultural issues in teaching. Our seven participants stretched from two schools centrally located near downtown Los Angeles north to a farm worker school in Ventura County, south to Whittier, and west, just two blocks from the Pacific Ocean, to a school serving a poor immigrant community, many of indigenous origin in the Mexican state of Oaxaca. An eighth teacher, from a university elementary school, did not continue after the first workshop; this is relevant to the point that successful training probably depends on a certain amount of selectivity and self-selection in choosing trainees. Grade levels varied from kindergarten through fifth grade. We paid our teachers for their participation and always served breakfast and lunch at the workshops, which were held at UCLA. The food was important because it made the teachers feel respected, in that their needs were being taken care of, something that they felt they did not experience in their public school systems.

In Workshop 1, teachers were asked to complete several home–school scenarios as a pretest (based on Raeff, Greenfield, & Quiroz, 2000, 2003). Bridging Cultures researcher, Blanca Quiroz, and I presented the teachers with our research findings on cross-cultural value conflict between individualism and collectivism in schools serving Latino immigrant families (Raeff, Greenfield, & Quiroz, 2000; Greenfield, Quiroz, & Raeff, 2000); these findings are a key component of the present chapter. At the end of Workshop 1, we gave the teachers a homework assignment. We asked them to look for and observe in their school settings in the coming weeks examples of individualism and collectivism in conflict. Discussion of their reports constituted the main activity of Workshop 2. At the end of Workshop 2, we gave another assignment, this a very creative one: We asked the teachers to utilize the Bridging Cultures paradigm to make a change in their own educational practice, with the goal of better bridging between the home culture of collectivism and the school culture of individualism. Reports and discussion of their new practices and attitudes was the major activity of Workshop 3.

During Workshop 3, the teachers also requested that we continue to meet as an ongoing support group and they completed a posttest of additional scenarios from previous research (Raeff, Greenfield, & Quiroz, 2000) The results indicated that the teachers' individualistic perspective in problem solving was initially very strong (86%), whether they were Latino or Euro-American in background, whereas collectivistic responses were rare (7%) (Rothstein-Fisch, Trumbull, Quiroz, & Greenfield, 1997).

FROM RESEARCH TO PRACTICE: THE PROCESS OF TEACHER CHANGE

In the posttest, individualistic responses decreased to 21%, whereas collectivistic problem solving increased to 57% after the third workshop (Rothstein-Fisch, Trumbull, Quiroz, & Greenfield, 1997). In other words, the teachers went from an overwhelmingly individualistic perspective to a perspective that was more balanced between individualism and collectivism. The Latino teachers were able to once again express their home–culture perspective, whereas the Euro-American teachers were able to realize that they had a culture too. One Latina teacher later told us that she had been taught in school that her home culture would be a detriment to her education, and so she felt that she should also eradicate it from her young pupils. The Bridging Cultures experience had, for the first time, made her realize that home culture could be of value in the education of children from Latino immigrant homes.

We did continue to meet after the workshops ended, and the teachers continued to develop new practices inspired and informed by the Bridging Cultures paradigm. Examples of these practices constitute a significant aspect of the Bridging Cultures effect and the second key component of the present chapter.

The seven teachers also began to become principal disseminators of Bridging Cultures to other teachers, to teacher trainers, and to educational researchers; whether in their schools, in their school systems, or at regional and national meetings. In taking on these new tasks, the teachers began and completed a transformation from trainees to collaborators. At the same time, the teachers' new roles, practices, and attitudes became key data concerning the real-world effect of our training.

In sum, the research before the Bridging Cultures training documents cross-cultural value conflict between Latino immigrant families and the schools. The research during and after the Bridging Cultures training documents the effects of learning about research on cross-cultural value conflict on teacher behavior. Therefore, instead of presenting results in the standard way, I present a few key findings concerning cross-cultural value conflict in school and show how the Bridging Cultures teachers responded to these findings with altered attitudes and practices in their school settings. The organizing construct and link between research and practice will be the particular value conflict(s) in play.

Value Conflict #1: Helping Versus Independent Task Completion; Social Responsibility Versus Choice

The Research. I begin with a quasi-experimental study. This cross-cultural comparative study took place in two elementary schools; one served a mainly Euro-American population, while the other served a Latino immigrant community (Raeff, Greenfield, & Quiroz, 2000). We gave parents, teachers, and fifth-grade students a set of eight scenarios. Each scenario presented a dilemma that could be resolved either by collectivistic or individualistic means. To illustrate this research, I present a scenario that involves two major issues, helping vs. independent task completion, and social responsibility vs. choice, as seen in Table 7.1. We embedded these issues in our "jobs scenario," which went as follows:

> It is the end of the school day, and the class is cleaning up. Denise isn't feeling well and she asks Jasmine to help her with her job for the day, which is cleaning the blackboard. Jasmine isn't sure that she will have time to do both jobs.
> What do you think the teacher should do?

Note that both Denise and Jasmine have jobs to do. The issue is whether Jasmine should help Denise even if it means not being able to complete her own job. One frequent response which we called "find third" was the idea that a third party would be found who would volunteer to help, so that Jasmine could finish her own job. The other major response category we called "help"; the idea was that Jasmine should help no matter what her own situation.

Parallel to the way we presented our results to the teachers in the first Bridging Cultures workshop, I first summarize responses in the Euro-American school when we gave this scenario to Euro-American children, to their parents, and to teachers in their school. Figure 7.1 presents the three most frequent categories of response. Note that the dominant response in all three groups is "find third." In essence, "find third" expressed the idea that a volunteer should be found so that Jasmine could complete her own job. The notion of finding a volunteer indicates a priority placed on choice. The notion of enabling Jasmine to complete her own job indicates a priority

School 1: Euro-American Families

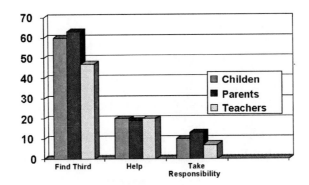

FIG. 7.1. Percentages of the three major categories of response by parents, children, and teachers to the "Jobs Scenario" in a predominantly Euro-American school. (Percentages do not add up to 100 because infrequent categories have not been included.)

placed on task completion. These are both part of the individualistic value complex (Fig. 7.1).

There are also minority responses as well. "Take responsibility" was a second response type we coded as individualistic (Fig. 7.1). This response type meant that Denise should take the personal responsibility of completing her own job even though she was sick. "Help" was another minority response. This code meant that Jasmine should help no matter what her own situation; it was classified as collectivistic (Fig. 7.1).

The most important point from the Bridging Cultures perspective is that there is cross-cultural harmony. The data show that in this school parents support the value system of the teachers, and vice versa. The dominant response of both groups is the same—the individualistic response "find third"—and individualistic responding is even greater if one adds in the category of "take responsibility." Note too that the children follow in the same footsteps as their two primary socializing agents. But also note the within-group variability. About one fifth of parents, teachers, and children choose the collectivistic pathway of the "help" response.

Figure 7.2 depicts the results in the Latino immigrant school. Here the situation is very different; parents and teachers do not agree most of the time. These results indicate that the child is pulled in two directions—between parents who say Jasmine should help no matter what and the teachers who say the teacher should respect Jasmine's right to complete her own job and helping is a matter of personal choice, not social responsibility. The graph indicates that school tends to win this battle between the two developmental

School 2: Latino Families

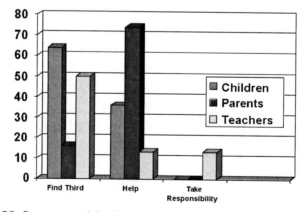

FIG. 7.2. Percentages of the three major categories of response by parents, children, and teachers to the "Jobs Scenario" in a Latino immigrant school. (Percentages do not add up to 100 because infrequent categories have not been included.)

pathways; that is, the Latino children select "find third" even more often than their parents. They have been taught and internalized the rules of the school, to the point of abandoning, in this instance, their parents' socialization goals.

Let us turn for a moment to the teachers. One final point concerning the results has important implications for cross-cultural teacher training. The teachers were multiethnic, including Latino teachers in both schools—yet the Latino or other ethnic minority teachers were no less individualistic in their responses. This finding was replicated in our Bridging Cultures teachers, as we saw earlier. School, especially teacher training, appears to enculturate teachers to the dominant culture, at least on the level assessed by our scenarios.

In sum, our findings indicated a conflict between prioritizing help as a social responsibility and prioritizing individual task completion, help being optional. We found that Latino immigrant parents generally favored helpfulness, whereas their children's teachers favored independent task completion.

The Bridging Cultures Teachers Respond to the Research Findings.
When we presented the results in Figs. 7.1 and 7.2 in the workshop, the Bridging Cultures trainees had already responded to this scenario on the pretest and discussed their responses in the workshop. Because every single trainee had responded in a uniformly individualistic manner, the Latino immigrant results (Fig. 7.2) provoked shocked surprise and an "ahaa" experience. At that moment, we, the researchers and trainers, knew the Bridging Cultures workshops were going to have an impact.

Indeed, in response to the results from the jobs scenario, teachers expressed some new insights into their own practices in the course of the workshop. For the first time they realized that they were in fact restricting helpfulness in their Latino immigrant classrooms. One example of such restriction that came up in the group discussion was the standard public school system of classroom monitors. Monitors are children who are assigned specific classroom jobs (e.g., cleaning the chalkboard or collecting homework). As was standard school practice, our Bridging Cultures trainees were in the habit of assigning only one child to each job. But in these Latino immigrant classrooms, the teachers reported that everyone wanted to help. Until the Bridging Cultures workshops, the teachers had all considered this a classroom management problem. However, once the scenario results made them aware of its source—in the Latino families' strong commitment to helpfulness as a value—our teachers developed new practices. One Bridging Cultures teacher, Giancarlo Mercado, went from single monitors to pairs of monitors, allowing greater participation in helping and permitting the monitors to help each other. Other teachers abandoned assigning tasks to individuals and allowed all who so desired to help.

This variability reflects another important point about the Bridging Cultures training methodology. We did not present any cookbook practices or "how to" material. We gave the teachers nothing but a research-based theoretical paradigm for understanding and changing the cultural dynamics of their classrooms. The teachers utilized this paradigm creatively; out of it came new attitudes toward parents (Trumbull, Rothstein-Fisch, & Greenfield, 2000) and children and a plethora of new practices (e.g., Quiroz, Greenfield, & Altchech, 1999; Rothstein-Fisch, Greenfield, & Quiroz, 1999). We, the researcher-trainers, were amazed; we had had no preset ideas of what would come out of the paradigm. The new practices varied from teacher to teacher, from situation to situation, and from grade level to grade level; however, all were based on the paradigmatic conflict between individualistic and collectivistic values. The paradigm of cross-cultural value conflict presented was generative in the same way that grammatical rules generate an infinite variety of sentences. For this reason, the teachers' generation of new practices has never stopped to this day.

The teachers not only created new practices as a result of the training. They also, with the research team's encouragement, engaged in efforts—local, regional, and national—to disseminate Bridging Cultures to other school personnel (about 50 in the first 5 years of the project; Trumbull et al., 2000). In so doing, they made ethnographic discoveries of manifestations of cross-cultural value conflict in other teachers and other schools. One example of such discoveries relates to the value conflict under discussion: helpfulness vs. individual task completion.

Often in U.S. schools, helpfulness is considered cheating; however, this may not always be true in more collectivistic countries of origin (Rothstein-Fisch, Trumbull, Isaac, Daley, & Perez, 2003). One of the Bridging Cultures teachers, Giancarlo Mercado, in the course of his own Bridging Cultures workshop for local colleagues, elicited the following autobiographical narrative from a fellow teacher of immigrant origins in South America:

My first experience in the public school was not a very positive one. I migrated to this country in 1981 and entered the eighth grade. I arrived with very good academic skills and a sense of a collectivist approach. I was very used to working with partners in solving problems. Even the homework required the sharing of ideas but most importantly sharing our materials. Our economic situation did not allow us to have pencils and crayons readily available.

I met this friend in a math class who had been here for more than a year. Naturally he had a good grasp of the language. I was exceptionally good at math computations. However, because of the language, I had a hard time solving word problems. I would immediately turn to my friend for help in understanding the problem. Once I understood the word problem, I was very good at coming up with a solution. I always assumed it was all right with my teacher until one day when he accused us of copying each other during a test. Both of us were sent to the office and were scolded by the principal. No matter how many times I tried to explain my situation, my teacher didn't want to hear it. Somehow this math class was never the same. I felt humiliated and embarrassed over this whole incident.

Clearly, this kind of incident is an extremely negative experience, with potentially damaging consequences for self and education.

What can be done to prevent this kind of experience? Once they had understood that helping another with academic work was considered a positive quality and practice in a collectivistic framework, the seven Bridging Cultures teachers encouraged, rather than discouraged, this kind of helping. For example, in a fourth grade taught by Bridging Cultures teacher, Marie Altchech, a Bridging Cultures researcher observed a student who knew more English helping a student who knew less with her writing. In a kindergarten taught by Bridging Cultures teacher, Kathy Eyler, a Bridging Cultures researcher observed one boy helping another with a math puzzle.

The teachers were very conscious about this change of attitudes toward helping behavior. One teacher said:

> *When I first started teaching at the school, I, they . . . were "no cheating nobody helps, you're doing their own work, so I know what you're capable of doing." Nobody was capable of doing anything. So it seemed to me, that's because I didn't even let them use that which makes them the best learner, each other. So I got rid of the whole idea of cheating, except when I use the test . . . but aside from that, when we're learning how to take the test, help each other please, help each other out. I don't care if you copied the answer, that's fine with me.*

In their UCLA honors theses, Correa-Chávez (1999) and Isaac (1999) compared this teacher with another teacher who taught the same level (second grade) to the same population, but had not received the Bridging Cultures training. In line with the dominant culture and our findings in the scenario study, the non–Bridging Cultures teacher expressed an ideology of individual learning and achievement. The following is an observation made by Isaac (1999).

> The children are whispering answers among themselves after one student is called on to respond to the teacher. The teacher then announces to the classroom, "I have heard people whispering and I really don't like it because why? They need to learn by themselves and you really aren't helping them learn."

This attitude on the part of the teacher led children to conflicted emotions about helping itself. Isaac (1999) observed that, in this non–Bridging Cultures class, the children were very conscious of the teacher's do-it-by-yourself values when she was around and showed signs of internal conflict between helping other students and requiring them to show independence. However, they helped each other freely when she was not around.

Value Conflict Situation #2: Sharing Versus Personal Property

Another key cross-cultural value conflict involved a collectivistic emphasis on sharing, in contrast with an individualistic emphasis on personal property.

The Research. One of the dilemmas in the scenario study related to the issue of sharing. The scenario, presented to the same samples of elementary school teachers, children, and the children's parents, went as follows:

> Adam and Johnny each get $20 from their mother, and Johnny buys a t-shirt. A week later, Adam wants to borrow Johnny's t-shirt, and Johnny says "No, this is my t-shirt, and I bought it with my own money." And Adam says, "But you're not using it now."
>
> What do you think the mother should do?

The key results are presented in Table 7.3. In the Latino immigrant school, the dominant response for the parents was to insist that the children share. In contrast, the dominant response for the teachers was that this was personal property and sharing should be only by personal choice, not out of social obligation. In this scenario, unlike the first one, the children's distribution of responses fell in between that of their parents and that of their teachers. If we compare this pattern of responding to that in response to the helping scenario, we note that children are more like their parents in the "t-shirt" scenario, more like their teachers in the "helping" scenario. This could illustrate domain-specific rates of acculturation in which children's acculturation to the host culture is more rapid in the domain of school than in the domain of home (Angela Nguyen, personal communication, May, 2005).

TABLE 7.3
Distribution of Responses by Parents, Children, and Teachers
to the "T-shirt Scenario" in a Latino Immigrant School

	Share	*Choice/Property*
Parents	58%	42%
Children	32%	50%
Teachers	6%	69%

Note. Row totals can be less than 100% because only the two most popular categories are shown in the table.

Sharing Versus Personal Property at School. This conflict between home values and school values was visible in the school itself. A.B. became an apprentice bilingual kindergarten teacher. She had immigrated as an adult from Mexico. As we all do, she began, quite naturally and without training, to construct teaching practices that came out of her own cultural background. Unconsciously and automatically, she began to develop practices that built on the strengths of the collectivistic orientation that many Latino children bring from home to school. What happened next shows the need for systemic change that goes beyond individual teachers in individual classrooms. The positive responses of the children were very encouraging. However, the negative responses of supervisors and administrators were equally discouraging.

The example that follows takes the collectivistic value of *sharing* as an expected behavior and instantiates it in a basic classroom practice. In contrast, the teacher's mentor treats *personal property* as the expected behavior.

Crayons in the kindergarten classroom

A teacher–mentor came to visit A.B.'s bilingual kindergarten classroom. The mentor observed that A.B. had arranged the crayons in cups by colors, all the red crayons in one cup, all the blue in another, etc. and that the class was sharing each cup of crayons as needed. The mentor suggested putting each child's name on an individual cup that would contain multicolored crayons and would be used only by that particular child. The reason for doing this, the mentor said, was that it was very important for children to have their own property because it made them feel good. She also said that this practice would help children take care of their own property and that it was only fair that children who took care of their things would not have to use the "crappy" (her word) material of children who did not know how to take care of their things.

However, the response of the mainly Latino children in the classroom may have surprised the mentor–teacher. In a respectful fashion, A.B. followed her mentor's suggestion.

However, the children did not seem happier or more enthusiastic with the materials than they had been before. Furthermore, they did not care if their materials were misplaced, so their "personal" materials ended up having to be rearranged by the teacher every day. It was not that the children were incapable of arranging their materials in a systematic fashion, because they had done so before. However, the category "personal material" simply was not important to them.

Crayons as personal property did not fit with the orientation to sharing they had brought from their home culture. Our conclusion was that this was an example of building-from-weakness unconsciously embodied in teacher-training methods.

The crayons incident shows how established educational practices often go against the grain of Latino immigrant students. The children kept their crayons better and were more interested in them when they were treated as communal property; it made teaching harder to transform the crayons into individual property. The Bridging Cultures training helps teachers to utilize children's collectivistic practices and values as strengths, rather than trying to eradicate ingrained values, treating them as weaknesses (Quiroz & Greenfield, 1995).

Value Conflict Situation #3: Narrative Knowledge With a Social Purpose Versus Factual Knowledge Valued for Its Own Sake

The following observation illustrates a cultural difference in the kind of knowledge that is valued in the two cultures. It is a difference between prioritizing narrative knowledge with a social purpose vs. prioritizing factual knowledge valued for its own sake (Table 7.1). This difference has many ramifications in academic settings. During one of our observations of a Los Angeles prekindergarten class made up of mostly Latino children,

the teacher was showing a real chicken egg that would soon hatch. While teaching the physical properties of the egg, she asked children to describe eggs by thinking about the times they had cooked and eaten them. One child tried three times to talk about how she cooked eggs with her grandmother, but the teacher disregarded these comments in favor of a child who explained that the insides of eggs are white and yellow.

The disregarded child was expressing knowledge in narrative form; the teacher wanted knowledge of the factual type. The disregarded child saw the eggs as a means to talk about a relationship with her grandmother; the teacher saw the bare facts about eggs as important in themselves.

This incident has a number of educational implications. Let me mention just one. Because the teacher did not even see the invisible culture that generated the description of cooking eggs with grandmother, the teacher devalued the child's contribution and, implicitly, the value orientation it reflected. Indeed, we have observed that teachers frequently make disparaging comments to each other about this socially oriented narrative style: "They're off the subject." "They can't think straight." "I can't stand it." They are critical of Latino immigrant students' cognitive and communicative style, without understanding the social values these children are expressing.

After the Bridging Cultures training, the seven Bridging Cultures teachers did indeed understand. The "eggs" incident had been presented and analyzed in one of the workshops. As a result, the teachers not only listened to and validated children's family-oriented narratives in the classroom; but, equally important, they also used these narratives as a bridge to factual knowledge for its own sake, as for example in science lessons (Rothstein-Fisch, 2003).

WHY AND HOW DID BRIDGING CULTURES WORK?

Our best answer to these questions is to enumerate the distinctive features of the Bridging Cultures approach to teacher training in general and to cross-cultural teacher training in particular.

1. *Bridging Cultures is based on research.* We presented real-world data to the teachers, and the data came from schools with populations just like those of the Bridging Cultures teachers.

2. *Bridging Cultures is an economical framework.* It is economical because it is based on only two concepts, individualism and collectivism. It is simple and easy to learn, but not simple-minded, as I hope this chapter makes clear.

3. *Bridging Cultures makes teaching easier.* Because it goes with the flow of children's home culture, it makes teaching easier. Instead of beating out home culture, teachers are building on students' home-based strengths to facilitate learning.

4. *Bridging Cultures is a generative theoretical paradigm.* Teachers have invented new practices in all aspects of their classrooms, from working with families to assessment (Trumbull, Rothstein-Fisch, Greenfield, & Quiroz, 2001; Rothstein-Fisch, Trumbull, Isaac, Daley, & Perez, 2003).

5. *Teachers continue using the paradigm after the training ends.* This is highly unusual!

6. *It is applicable on a systemic level.* For example, beyond the work in elementary education which I have detailed in this chapter, we have found that the same implicit value differences between individualism and collectivism lead to misunderstanding and subtle conflict in multiethnic peer relations at the high school level in multiethnic sports teams (Greenfield, Davis, Suzuki, & Boutakidis, 2002). We have successfully extended the Bridging Cultures framework to parent training (Esau, Greenfield, Daley, & Tynes, 2004), as well as to early education (Zepeda, Gonzalez-Mena, Rothstein-Fisch, & Trumbull, in press) and to the Korean immigrant community.

Psychological Ramifications of Conflicting Value Socialization

A major goal of Bridging Cultures is to reduce cultural conflict between home and school. Such conflict becomes internalized in the psyche of a single person. The psychological reality of this conflict is best seen in this quote from one of our Bridging Cultures teachers, herself a Latina immigrant:

> I remember going through it [the conflict] as a child—as an immigrant child—and trying to become, to understand this system. And in my family it ended up where the school was right and the teachers were right, and their value became more important ... and because of that many of my brothers just stopped communicating completely with my father, because he represented the bad, the wrong way, and that was hard.

CONCLUSIONS

I here draw four conclusions from our work with Bridging Cultures. First, it is possible to build from strengths that children bring from a collectivistic value system, rather than treating these characteristics as educational weaknesses. Second, rather than creating divided loyalties between home and school, it is possible to create harmony between these two important social forces. Third, it is also possible to give back research findings to the community and let practitioners make them their own. The fourth conclusion is more general: The sequence from basic to applied research in the Bridging Cultures Project exemplifies how basic developmental research can be applied to solving an important real-world social problem.

ACKNOWLEDGMENTS

Grateful thanks for their collaboration over the years to all of my Bridging Cultures colleagues: researchers Elise Trumbull, WestEd; Carrie Rothstein-Fisch, California State University, Northridge; and Blanca Quiroz, Harvard University; teachers Marie Altchech, Stoner Ave. School; Catherine Daley, Magnolia Ave. School; Giancarlo Mercado, Westminster School; Amada Pérez, Mar Vista School; Kathy Eyler, Hoover Street School; Elvia Hernandez, Ada B. Nelson School; and Pearl Saitzyk, Westminster School. Special thanks to Carrie Rothstein-Fisch and Elise Trumbull for the help they provided in preparing this chapter. My thanks to WestEd for their financial support and other important contributions to Bridging Cultures. I would also like to thank the Center for the Study of Evolution and the Origin of Life for use of their library for our Bridging Cultures workshops. This chapter is based on a presentation originally prepared for the Bridging Cultures Institute, WestEd, San Francisco. It was written during a fellowship year at the Center for Advanced Study in the Behavioral Sciences, Stanford, CA. The author is a member of the FPR-UCLA Center for Culture, Brain, and Development. Last but not least, thanks to Ioakim Boutakidis and the 2005 University of California Mellon Workshop on Acculturation and Ethnic Identity for some new insights into the complex issue of acculturation.

REFERENCES

Correa-Chávez, M. (1999). *Bridging Cultures between home and school: Assessment of an intervention program*. Honors thesis, Department of Psychology, UCLA.

Esau, P. C., Greenfield, P., Daley, C., & Tynes, B. (2004, May). *Bridging Cultures parent workshops: Developing cross-cultural harmony in minority school communities*. Paper presented at University of California Linguistic Minority Research Institute Conference, Santa Barbara, CA.

Greenfield, P. M., Davis, H., Suzuki, L., & Boutakidis, I. (2002). Understanding intercultural relations on multiethnic high school sports teams. In M. Gatz, M. A. Messner, & S. Ball-Rokeach (Eds.), *Paradoxes of youth and sport* (pp. 141–157). Albany: SUNY Press.

Greenfield, P. M., Quiroz, B., & Raeff, C. (2000). Cross-cultural harmony and conflict in the social construction of the child. In S. Harkness, C. Raeff, & C. M. Super (Eds.), *Variability in the social construction of the child, New Directions in Child and Adolescent Development, 87,* 93–108. San Francisco: Jossey-Bass.

Greenfield, P. M., Raeff, C., & Quiroz, B. (1996). Cultural values in learning and education. In B. Williams (Ed.), *Closing the achievement gap: A vision for changing beliefs and practices* (pp. 37–55). Alexandria, VA: Association for Supervision and Curriculum Development.

Hofstede, G. (2001). *Culture's consequences: Comparing values, behaviors, institutions, and organizations across nations* (2nd ed.). Thousand Oaks, CA: Sage.

Isaac, A. (1999). *How teachers' cultural ideologies influence children's relationships inside the classroom: The effects of a cultural awareness teacher-training program in two classrooms*. Honors thesis, Department of Psychology, UCLA.

Lustig, M. W., & Koester, J. (1999). *Intercultural competence*. New York: Longman.

Quiroz, B., & Greenfield, P. M. (1995). *Cross-cultural value conflict: Removing a barrier to Latino school achievement*. Unpublished paper, Department of Psychology, UCLA.

Quiroz, B., Greenfield, P. M., & Altchech, M. (1999). Bridging cultures with a parent–teacher conference. *Educational Leadership, 56*(7), 68–70.

Raeff, C., Greenfield, P. M., & Quiroz, B. (2000). Conceptualizing interpersonal relationships in the cultural contexts of individualism and collectivism. In S. Harkness, C. Raeff, & C. M. Super (Eds.), *Variability in the social construction of the child, New Directions in Child and Adolescent Development, 87,* 59–74. San Francisco: Jossey-Bass.

Raeff, C., Greenfield, P. M., & Quiroz, B. (2003). *Conceptualizing personal achievement in the cultural contexts of individualism and collectivism*. Unpublished paper, Department of Psychology, UCLA.

Rothstein-Fisch, C. (2003). *Bridging Cultures teacher education module*. Mahwah, NJ: Lawrence Erlbaum Associates.

Rothstein-Fisch, C., Greenfield, P. M., & Trumbull, E. (1999). Bridging cultures with classroom strategies. *Educational Leadership, 56*(7), 64–67.

Rothstein-Fisch, C., Trumbull, E., Isaac, A., Daley, C., & Perez, A. (2003). When "helping someone else" is the right answer: Bridging cultures in assessment. *Journal of Latinos and Education,* 2(3), 123–140.

Rothstein-Fisch, C., Trumbull, E., Quiroz, B., & Greenfield, P. M. (1997, June). *Bridging cultures in the classroom.* Poster presentation at the Jean Piaget Society, Santa Monica, CA.

Tapia-Uribe, F. M., LeVine, R. A., & LeVine, S. E. (1994). Maternal behavior in a Mexican community: The changing environments of children. In P. M. Greenfield & R. R. Cocking (Eds.), *Cross-cultural roots of minority child development* (pp. 41–54). Hillsdale, NJ: Lawrence Erlbaum Associates.

Trumbull, E., Diaz-Meza, R., Hasan, A., & Rothstein-Fisch, C. (2000). *The Bridging culture project: Five year report 1996–2000.* San Francisco: WestEd.

Trumbull, E., Rothstein-Fisch, C., & Greenfield, P. M. (2000). Bridging cultures in our schools: New approaches that work. *Knowledge Brief.* San Francisco: WestEd.

Trumbull, E., Rothstein-Fisch, C., Greenfield, P. M., & Quiroz, B. (2001). *Bridging cultures between home and school: A guide for teachers.* Mahwah, NJ: Lawrence Erlbaum Associates.

Zepeda, M., Gonzalez-Mena, J., Rothstein-Fisch, C., & Trumbull, E. (in press). *Bridging cultures in early care and education.* Mahwah, NJ: Lawrence Erlbaum Associates.

8

Applying the Science of Psychology to a Public That Distrusts Science

Sherylle J. Tan
Diane F. Halpern
Berger Institute for Work, Family, and Children
Claremont McKenna College

In some ways, writing a chapter about "Applied Psychology" is like writing only half a sentence or interrupting a speaker before the main point is made. *Applied psychology* needs a predicate, or at least an answer to the question—what aspect of psychology is being applied to what real-world problem? Applied psychology is not a content area or academic discipline like developmental psychology or social psychology. There are no chapters in introductory psychology textbooks devoted to applied psychology nor are there any great theorists or "pioneers" identified (exclusively) as applied psychologists, although there are many applied psychologists doing outstanding work. The term is more accurately used as a label for a decision about the type of problem that a researcher is willing to solve. Applied psychologists are interested in finding answers for only a subset of those questions that rightfully fall under the broad psychology rubric.

Applied psychologists are pragmatists who use the research and statistical methods of psychology and other social sciences to answer those contemporary questions where answers will have immediate practical use. They have the power to bring evidence and "hard data" to emotional debates, so that we can have reasoned discussions about hot topics. They do research that "makes a difference," and as trite as that may sound, it is the ultimate purpose of applied psychology. In somewhat loftier language, applied psychologists conduct research that will help to "alleviate human suffering and promote human health and happiness" (Hayes & Berens, 2003, p. 3), although we note that this overly sanguine view seems to ignore the fact that much of the applied research is done for profit in business and laboratory settings and funded by various industries. The extent of one's devotion to general public good or societal standards is not part of the definition.

The range of practical problems psychologists are asked to solve may be broader than any other discipline because it is difficult to think of a human or any other endeavor that does not, at least in part, rely on basic psychological processes like motivation, learning, relationship building, prejudice, thinking, trusting, and so on. Applied psychologists work in industry designing more efficient workplaces, in private settings helping people become less depressed or anxious, in schools to enhance learning, in the air force to make pilot training more efficient, with athletes to help them perform better, with couples to get them to improve their relationships, in hospitals to help patients learn better health behaviors, and many more settings. The "what" applied psychology is being applied to is an almost endless list.

A CHALLENGE: PUBLIC'S ACCEPTANCE OF RESEARCH

A few years ago, Diane Halpern was asked to present testimony to the United States House of Representatives Committee on Science. The topic of her testimony was "applying the science of learning." Because her presentation time was short, she prepared a few main points that would make the strongest case for science. She prepared charts with data to help her make her case. She was well prepared with research and data to back up her points for advocating the science of learning. On the way into the hearing room, a helpful legislative aide coached her about how to provide effective testimony to the Committee on Science. More than once Diane was warned not to present "too many numbers" because they tend to get bored and confused by data. A good story works best; an anecdote about someone who showed great gains in learning and then went on to become a solid citizen because a teacher used the methods that she was advocating. Don't present "too much data?" This was, after all, the U.S. House of Representatives Committee on Science. Yes indeed, what the committee wanted to hear were anecdotes, not empirically based evidence. Practices based in empirical research were not going to win anyone over.

Applied psychologists have provided answers for many important questions with broader implications for public policy *based* on research and data. However, not all the efforts of applied psychologists make tangible contributions to policies nor do they capture the attention of policymakers, politicians, and the public (Woodhead, 1988). The million dollar question is: Why? As applied researchers and scientists we have been taught to take the research and data to make informed decisions to help inform policy and practice. However from Diane's experience, we learn that "hard data" does not always sway the public.

The public has an abysmal understanding of and appreciation for the research findings from hundreds of thousands of people studied by scientists. In general, the public distrusts science, and they distrust scientists. They prefer their own personal experiences, and they especially prefer anecdotes. Newspaper reporters either share the general misunderstanding of science or they take advantage of it by using one or two vivid "person-on-the-street interviews" to make a point, instead of reporting data from large-scale studies. Given the relative popularity of different ways of obtaining information, it seems that many people prefer to have their palms read rather than read a journal article. Many do not understand the purpose of research and the potential implications that research has to offer (Field & Powell, 2001).

Why is it that the public would prefer personal experiences to knowledge based on empirical research? One argument may have to do with critical thinking skills. Many people in society consistently engage in flawed thinking (Halpern, 1998). Some common flaws that occur in thinking: (a) using an anecdote or a personal story to support or refute a general point; (b) using correlational data as causal, regardless of whether the data are factual; (c) using emotional language instead of providing reasons and evidence; and (d) viewing the alternatives in terms of black or white or good or bad, without considering "shades of gray" or possible covariates that might determine certain conditions.

These flaws contribute to people's understanding of research. If data or research contradicts one's personal belief system, the uncomfortable state of cognitive (and affective) dissonance would result. It is easier to disregard and disrespect the data than it is to change their personal belief system. Everyone has some experiences or opinions on the various topics that are researched by applied psychologists, such as child care, work and family balance, etc. People are more likely to believe their experiences than the experiences of hundreds of people from large scale studies who they do not know.

Confusing Data and Preference for Anecdotes

Data, statistics, and *numbers* are often boring and confusing terms for most people who believe that numbers are easily manipulated. Scientists know that numerical information is often misinterpreted. When there are too many numbers, people often report they become confused, bored, and even scared. Often, they do not understand the numbers that are being thrown at them. Most people, even the United States House of Representatives Committee on Science, prefer "just a little data."

From Diane's experience, we learn that data and numbers do not sway people, stories and anecdotes do. Public policies are often made by anecdote. The truth is that we like stories—they make abstract concepts come alive and provide meaning and humanity to boring and confusing data. It is amazing how a single vivid example can often outweigh a huge body of data collected from a random sample of a population. Anecdotes are self-selected, based on a sample size of 1, subject to all the biases of memory, and are often told because they represent the expected outcome. These stories can be powerful and possibly emotional.

There are few people (mostly, researchers and scientists) who understand why the personal experience of one person is less valid than the impersonal data collected from hundreds or thousand of people. Most statistical concepts and fundamental components of quality research run counter to the public's intuitive notions of what matters. These concepts need to be deliberately taught as transferable thinking skills to the general public. Thus, our job as applied psychologists becomes more difficult because statistical principles are the tools we use to provide answers to questions real people care about. Real people need to understand and value those answers.

Sample size in research is a very important factor both statistically and methodologically. If the sample size is too small, generalizations from the findings to the population are invalid, but without instruction, few people spontaneously understand why. There is much advance planning that goes into deciding upon the nature of the sample and the size of the sample. Sample size often depends on confidence level and power and other statistical considerations that most people have difficulty understanding and generally do not need to understand. The public is not clear on what constitutes as "too small" a sample size, and even those in research argue among themselves about the value of studying a single individual. Even more confusing is the concept of "statistical significance." People find it difficult to understand that because no "statistical" differences are found between two differing groups does not necessarily mean there are no differences. Dissemination of research findings has to be such that it is communicated in clear and simple terms.

It is important to understand how the sample was collected and what population the sample represents. For example, findings from a study that samples 10th-grade students from southern California with a large Hispanic/Latino population may not necessarily generalize to 10th-grade students from upstate New York. There are certain factors, such as environmental, socioeconomic, and cultural differences that may impact the nature of the results. These are considerations that we as researchers understand, but not something the general public will necessarily think about.

Causation Versus Correlation

Causation and correlation is a confusing concept and a common flaw that occurs in thinking. The public has little understanding that a correlation between two variables does not mean that one causes the other, *when the causal nature is perfectly obvious to the individual.* Causation is very difficult to find, however, causation is exactly what policymakers and the public want to know. They want to know the causes of human problems. They want clear and direct answers. Researchers need to state clearly that causation usually cannot be determined. In the human condition, there are many factors that influence various outcomes. Many of these factors cannot simply be accounted for in research; even truly experimental research can have difficulties controlling for multiple factors.

An example of this flaw in thinking is the popular assumption that the children of working mothers are more likely to become involved in criminal activity. It is commonly believed by many that since mothers have started working and placing their children in child care, there has been an increase in crime. People interpret that link to mean that maternal employment *causes* children to become criminals and engage in criminal behaviors. This is a fairly pervasive belief by many (Greenberger, Goldberg, Crawford, & Granger, 1988). Because this is a belief and people expect to find a confirmation with research, applied psychologists and social scientist research this issue. There is no research that blankly states that maternal employment causes criminal behaviors in children. However, there is some research that has found correlational relationships with maternal employment and delinquency when mothers work in coercive and alienating environments (e.g., Vander Ven & Cullen, 2004). It is not so much employment that is criminogenic but rather the type of employment that mothers engage in (i.e., menial, coercive, unsatisfying, and low-paying maternal employment), which may correlate with type of mothering in ways we have not yet identified. However, recent research has also found that maternal employment has no measurable influence on adolescent criminal involvement or risky behaviors (i.e., Aughinbaugh & Gittleman, 2003; Vander Ven & Cullen, 2004).

Maternal employment does *not* cause the delinquency of children, any more than it causes behavioral problems in children (Vander Ven, Cullen, Carrozza, & Wright, 2001). These findings hold true whether maternal employment is in children's preschool years or in adolescence. This problem of maternal employment is a socially constructed problem, rather than a problem that is supported by data and research. Yet, it is a pervasive belief that exists based on linkages and correlations rather than causation.

Controversies and Debates in Science

As science becomes more sophisticated, new research and data are produced that might clash with older data, creating doubt and confusion and undermining the public's already low degree of trust in research and data. Different research methods, approaches, samples, confounding variables, and so on may produce different findings than were previously found, and many times the public do not understand why this is so. However, many researchers, applied psychologists included, deliver the data and the findings presuming that all is understood about the research process and when the data show something that is conflicting with past data, confusion sets in. The public becomes confused and doesn't quite know what to trust.

The public is often confused and wary of research that is inconsistent and contradictory, and doubly so when the bulk of findings runs counter to commonly held beliefs. For the last several decades, applied psychologists and social scientists have tackled the issue of maternal employment and child care. This has been a hot controversy in work–family research. The most dramatic change in families in the last 30 years is the increased rate of maternal employment. From 1970 to 2000, the overall maternal employment rate rose from 38% to 67% (Smolensky & Gootman, 2003). This increase in maternal employment has led to strong controversy and debate among many regarding the effects that maternal employment and child care would have on children's development; the popular concern was that children's separation from the mother due to maternal employment and placement into day care at an early age would disrupt the bonding process with the mother, thus, being harmful to the child and compromising children's attachment to their mother and the development of children. This concern led to large fear in the detrimental effects of separating mothers from their children (Friedman, Randolph, & Kochanoff, 2001) and stemmed questions regarding the detrimental impacts of maternal employment and child care on children's developmental outcomes.

Working mothers are the realities of modern society. Mothers do work and child care is a necessity. Many families, especially low-income families, do not have a choice. We do have some unambiguous answers: Maternal employment is not bad for our children as was once thought. In fact, extensive research by applied psychologist has found positive impacts of maternal employment. Having a working mother has been found to lead to increased academic achievement and enhanced cognitive outcomes (Makri-Botsari & Makri, 2003; Vandell & Ramanan, 1992) and fewer behavior problems (Youngblut et al., 2001) in children. Furthermore, early maternal employment has been found to be more beneficial for single mothers and lower income families by increasing family income (Harvey, 1999; Vandell &

Ramanan, 1992) and improving the mother's mental health (Makri-Botsari & Makri, 2003).

However, there have been controversial findings with regard to the data on child care. Some early applied research on child care has found that participation in child care was not detrimental to children's development and has not documented the negative consequences of child care (Silverstein, 1991). And later findings from a large-scale study have maintained that child care is unrelated to the attachment of children to their mothers (NICHD, 1997). However, there have been inconsistent findings regarding the relation of child care to children's development and behavior problems. Other studies report negative cognitive and social outcomes from the relation with early maternal employment in the child's first year of life (e.g., Belsky, 1988; Belsky & Eggbeen, 1991; Brooks-Gunn, Han, & Waldfogel, 2002). And there are those that maintain that child care can be a risk factor in children's development and in the child's attachment to their mother (Belsky, 1988). However, many applied psychologists continue to maintain that those findings are inconclusive, that they pertain to a small number of children (i.e., most are doing fine) and that further research is warranted. The debate on child care continues.

This debate among psychologists has not assisted in the public's understanding of the effects of child care or maternal employment nor has it assisted families to be less concerned for their children in child care. As the psychological community understands, there are many factors and intervening variables that are seen to be related to the developmental outcomes of children (Silverstein, 1991). Because families and the public are not always given this information, families have increased concerns and oftentimes guilt for the necessity of placing their children in nonmaternal care despite the positive impact of maternal employment found by various research studies.

The reason for many controversies among research findings are not explained well in lay terms. The controversies stir up distrust among the public, as well as confusion. The general public is already wary of research, and when so-called experts cannot agree on what the research means or maintain that other findings are inconclusive, the public loses trust in the research itself.

Controversy leads to debates among researchers and experts. These debates add to the confusion among the public. People cannot figure out who is correct among all the psychobabble and disregard all findings in favor of personal experiences and anecdotes from friends. If the researchers cannot agree on what is correct, why trust either side? How can they depend on the research or the data? The general public does not understand the reasons why there are disagreements; they cannot understand how two credible psychologists can come up with conflicting findings. Researchers know that samples, confounding variables, and different methods and measures can lead to different conclusions, but the public is unaware of this. The public is confused and they have lost trust in the data, in research. The public needs to be aware that controversies in science are positive in that it allows researchers to shape the process of research (Field & Powell, 2001).

HOW TO GET THE RESEARCH ACCEPTED BY THE PUBLIC

How do applied psychologists gain the trust of the public? How do we educate them to understand psychological science and the data and research methods that we use? Those are the challenges that applied psychologist face. Basically, the message for the public, policymakers, and the media is that research is not perfect and not all research is created equal. Research methodologies are flawed, but they are equally flawed in the medical sciences, but the public trusts medical science more than psychological science, or so it seems, but we admit to no data to back up this perception. It needs to be recognized that when looking at the human condition there are no definitive answers or solutions. People do not live in vacuums and there are many factors, both externally and internally, that affect the results of psychological research studies. This is the understanding that the public needs to take into account. With that said, research has value and importance by educating those that affect policy and the general public to understand the research and the impacts that research has to society. To effect change, we need to play active roles in educating and disseminating research; the research will not make as strong an impact unless we apply it and do something with it. In this section, we talk about strategies to instill trust among the public for the research.

Dissemination of Research

Dissemination of research is key in being an applied psychologist. As in any relationship communication is a building block of creating trust with the public; applied psychologists must communicate to the public via dissemination of their research. As applied psychologists, *applied* being the key word, we need to disseminate research findings and derivative materials to ensure that the research is applied. Dissemination should take place in various forms of media that are accessible and available to others outside of academia and written free from academic jargon so that it is easily understandable to the general public. We already do well to publish in peer-reviewed academic journals and present findings to our peers at various meetings and conferences; however, dissemination goes beyond our academic circles if we seek to be true applied psychologists. Applied psychologists and other researchers/scientists alike would do better to inform the public by publishing and disseminating information outside of academic journals.

Most of the public will not read a journal article and, understandably so, because journal articles can be difficult to read for the lay person. A first-year graduate student in a different discipline read a psychological research journal article for the first time and was simply overwhelmed by the jargon, methodology, and statistics. She wondered how anyone could read a research article when they have never been taught to understand it. All the jargon, methodology, and statistics were like a foreign language to her. And indeed, to the general public this holds true. Journal articles are a foreign language to the public, why would they read a journal article any more than they would read a newspaper in a language other than their own. Journal articles, many of which are peer-reviewed, are designed and written for academic peers, not the general public.

Psychologists are not taught to write to the public, they are taught to write scientifically in American Psychological Association (APA) style. And that can be complicated for novices as well as some veterans. There are many graduate students from various disciplines (i.e., education and social work) who are also taught to write in APA style. Writing in APA style is a skill that we learn as we study to become applied psychologists. However, writing opinion/editorials, news release, or any type of written media to the public is not commonly included in the curriculum of scientists. So understandably, we struggle to adapt our writing styles to communicate to the public. Yet, it is an important skill we must exercise as a way of application of the research to the general community.

It is important that we disseminate research, yet, if we are to truly disseminate research it needs to go beyond the peer-reviewed academic journal articles. As applied psychologists we need to make a concerted effort to write for different forms of media. Publishing in newsletters that reach wider and diverse audiences, writing opinion/editorial pieces in national newspapers, contributing to national magazines that target particular audiences, writing press releases, and working with local legislators to get the information out are some ways that research can be disseminated to the wider public. These are avenues that reach the public.

Building Partnership With the Media. Research is often disseminated to the public through various media outlets. One way to improve trust of the public and appropriately disseminate research to the public is via the media. However, we know that oftentimes the media may distort or misrepresent research findings.

The public is primarily informed of research through television news, the radio, Internet, popular magazines, and discussions with friends and colleagues. However, the media often adds confusion and controversy to the research. Most reporting of research is superficial and sensationalistic. Many times the media misinterprets or misreports the findings of research. News headlines will imply causation from a correlational relationship, even when the research does not warrant findings of a causal nature. The media will generalize from people's personal experiences using anecdotes and stories. Or they may select one statistic from an entire study that fits the story that they are attempting to report. With the misrepresentation of data in the media, no wonder the public comes to mistrust the research. Because people may receive information on research from multiple sources, the interpretation of data may differ, adding to their confusion. Generally, the media is often not interested in on-going research; they want instant answers to hot topics. The more emotionally charged the issue, the more interested the media is because controversies sell newspapers, magazines, and on-air news programs. An informed, educated media source of unbiased information is greatly needed; research on those emotionally charged topics needs to be done and clearly disseminated to the public.

Consider the following headlines: "Day care causes kids to become bullies," "The day-care scare: Are nurseries turning toddlers into thugs?" Many social trends make the headlines and prompt people to take their lives into consideration. However, there is a problem with these social trends that make the headlines, oftentimes they are wrong. In April 2001, the National Institute of Child Health and Human Development (NICHD) released the results from their longitudinal child care study. This was one of the most comprehensive and complex studies of child care and the study had many positive findings. However, one single finding was a link between time spent in child care and behavior problems in 4-year olds. Despite the other positive findings, the media coverage centered on this particular finding, striking much controversy and ignoring the rest of the story (research). To this day, the controversy rings true as does the guilt and struggles of working parents.

Coverage, for instance, of the linkage between day care and bullying received a lot of attention, whereas the linkage between day care and verbal and cognitive achievement did not. More often than not, the research findings based on peer-reviewed data goes unreported. Instead, anecdotal or misinterpreted data is presented to the public. Thus, the importance in building relationships and communication with journalists is essential in building trust with the public. We need to ensure that the research that is reported takes into account the whole story and not just what is sensational or emotionally charged. We need to help journalists to understand the whole picture not just one small finding. We need to work with, assist, and build partnerships with journalists of print, television, radio, and film.

Collaborating with journalists, who are often the source of information to the public, is important. We need to work with and educate journalists in understanding the research so that it is reported to the public accurately and clearly.

One attempt to bridge communication and collaboration with researchers and journalists has been done by Boston University College of Communication and the Community, Families, and Work Program (CFWP) at the Brandeis University's Women's Studies Research Center. Together they hold an annual invitational Journalism–Work/Family Conference to serve as a catalyst for building relationships with journalists from print, TV, radio, video, and film. Journalists and researchers in work–family study are brought together to educate each other about research, how to report research to the public so that it is accurate, and to facilitate interaction between important researchers and interested journalists who want access to a steady stream of reliable and cutting-edge research findings.

Although not all applied psychologist may be involved in these types of events, applied psychologists can start to talk to local journalists in their areas, write opinion-editorials for local and national newspapers, and write press releases regarding important research. Applied psychologists need to take an active role with the dissemination of research to ensure that it is communicated clearly, accurately, and appropriately in the right context.

We know that the public likes stories and anecdotes, we also know that journalists will use anecdotes in the reporting. Applied psychologists need to take an active role in our relationships with journalists by anticipating this. We can assist them by providing qualitative along with quantitative data to provide richness and meaning to the numbers that people find so "scary." Qualitative data can help to bring life and meaning to the quantitative statistics and help bridge this fear and confusion of numbers. In this way we can attempt to ensure that the anecdotes and stories that are used in news articles and news reports are based on data.

Educating the Public

Who is to blame for this distrust and low regard for science and research? The researchers and scientists must take a large share of the blame. Researchers have not done a very good job of educating the public of the value of science and research or explaining its importance. The process of science is complex and can sometimes be confusing. Many people are genuinely interested in research, however, their knowledge of research and their comfort levels with research are low (Field & Powell, 2001).

Research should not be done in a vacuum. Beyond the research, applied psychologists need to be involved in helping the public to understand and trust the research. Trust is earned and not given by blind faith and we should not expect the public to trust research without educating and assisting them to understand research. If applied psychologists are to "alleviate human suffering and promote human health and happiness" (Hayes & Berens, 2003, p. 3), applied psychologists need to play an active role to use the research to inform the public and effect change.

Much of the research is getting out to the public; the rise of technology has assisted in making information more accessible to everyone via the World Wide Web. As research is being disseminated in many ways, we need to take more responsibility in educating the public on how to understand the importance of research and how it affects their lives.

Education is a necessary ingredient in improving the public's acceptance and respect for science and research. Rhodes (1997) suggests that to improve public understanding of science involves additional personal effort. As applied psychologists, we must take responsibility to nourish and develop youth's interest in science and research. We need to become engaged with elementary and high schools to develop new ways that will excite and bring interest to young people about science and research. Once the interest is built, understanding will follow. Education must begin early; by starting with the youth, this knowledge and understanding will transfer and transcend to adulthood and quite possibly future generations. This is done by introducing the importance and concepts of research and science to build appreciation and respect for research.

Science education needs to be continuous and extend beyond elementary and high school into college, regardless of major or concentration. It is important that we raise the scientific literacy of the citizenry at large. The education of nonscientists is just as important in college as the education of our science majors. The public can be taught to use research as a tool in their decision-making process. People truly want answers to society's questions; they want to know how to be good parents and what is best for their children.

In addition to learning about the concepts and importance of science and research, education should include distinguishing among the abundance of research. The process of science is complex and there are principles of science that the general public does not understand. It is important that we address these principles by educating the public. We need to teach them to think of research and science as a tool that can be applied to any empirical question. There is much research available on various important questions that society values. Learning to understand and decipher among the good and possibly bad research is important for the public. Use of critical thinking skills will assist the public in their understanding of research and help them to determine what research is trustworthy. Research is a tool that when used in conjunction with critical thinking skills can assist the public in answering the questions that are important to them using empirically based data.

Collaboration and Communication
With the Community

If we truly want the public to respect research, we need to practice give and take. Too often we as researchers take from various populations the data that we want, but more often than not we do not bring the results of the findings back to the people. Why should they care about research, when researchers often come into their schools and their neighborhoods to collect data and ask them to complete questionnaires and forms and then never hear from them again, and never learn what those research results show. To those people, research had nothing to offer them but more work and taking away some of their time.

As applied psychologists, we need to bring the research back into the community and collaborate with the community to apply the knowledge we have gained. For example, in the child-care setting, we know from research that quality is an essential component of "good" child care and does have implications for all areas of child development. Not all types of child care are created equal, thus applied psychologists have looked at how quality impacts children's developmental outcomes. In fact, the quality of the child-care center has been found to be positively related with preschool children's developmental outcomes. Moreover, quality of child care not only affects the developmental outcome of children from low income and at-risk backgrounds, but has positive effects for children of all backgrounds (Peisner-Feinberg & Burchinal, 1997). High-quality child care has been found to be related to fewer reports of problem behaviors, higher cognitive performance, higher language ability, and higher level of school readiness (Peisner-Feinberg & Burchinal, 1997).

Because we know that low-quality child care can have negative effects on child outcomes, the research on quality child care should be disseminated in ways that can be used by the community; whether it be the child-care community or the community at large (through community-based services). It is a give and take relationship that will allow the community to respect the research as well as be willing to participate in future research. In a case in which high-quality child care is related to more positive developmental outcomes, applied psychologists can communicate those findings and work with the community and providers to find avenues in which to improve the quality of lower quality centers.

It takes time and involvement to earn the trust of the public. We answer the questions and call ourselves applied psychologists; we need to become actively involve in the applied part of our identity/title. We have to be better at collaborating with the community to apply those solutions and effect change. No one can do it alone, but as a community of people with different expertise, we can work with those people in the public that will put into practice the research we do. It takes people of various disciplines and strengths to apply the solutions and help to improve and apply the research we work so hard to do.

CLOSING THOUGHTS

Gaining public trust for our research will be a continuous challenge for applied psychologists and all scientists. This chapter has outlined a few strategies to assist in the public's understanding and appreciation of research. Psychological science has been applied to answer pragmatic questions in contemporary society to inform policymakers and the public about a wide range of issues. The challenge is how we transform the research into messages and information that will be used by the public. We must actively use the strategies discussed to gain the public's trust and to effect change. Psychological research serves an important purpose and it is up to us psychologists to make sure that this purpose is achieved and that people are able to utilize our findings, and not be baffled by scary and confusing data.

As applied psychologists we must be responsible for the level of investment that others have in science. This is accomplished through dissemination, building relationships with the media, and through collaboration. The work we do is not done for the sake of research, but rather to gain information that will effect change and "make a difference" in the lives of children, families, the elderly, the poor, and all those around us.

REFERENCES

Aughinbaugh, A., & Gittleman, M. (2003, February). Maternal employment and adolescent risky behavior. *U.S. Bureau of Labor Statistics Working Paper 366*. Retrieved from http://www.bls.gov/ore/pdf/ec030030.pdf

Belsky, J. (1988). The "effects" of infant day care reconsidered. *Early Childhood Research Quarterly, 3*, 235–272.

Belsky, J., & Eggbeen, D. (1991). Early and extensive maternal employment and young children's socioemotional development: Children of the National Longitudinal Survey of Youth. *Journal of Marriage and Family, 53*, 1083–1110.

Brooks-Gunn, J., Han, W. J., & Waldfogel, J. (2002). Maternal employment and child cognitive outcomes in the first three years of life: The NICHD Study of Early Child Care. *Child Development, 73*(4), 1052–1072.

Field, H., & Powell, P. (2001). Public understanding of science vs. public understanding of research. *Public Understanding of Science, 10*(4), 421–426.

Friedman, S. L., Randolph, S., & Kochanoff, A. (2001). Childcare research at the dawn of a new millennium: Taking stock of what we know. In G. Brenner & A. Fogel (Eds.), *Blackwell handbook of infant development* (pp. 660–692). Malden, MA: Blackwell.

Greenberger, E., Goldberg, W. A., Crawford, T., & Granger, J. (1988). Beliefs about the consequences of maternal employment for children. *Psychology of Women Quarterly, 12,* 35–59.

Halpern, D. F. (1998). Teaching critical thinking for transfer across domains. *American Psychologist, 53*(4), 449–455.

Harvey, E. (1999). Short-term and long-term effects of early parental employment on children of the National Longitudinal Survey of Youth. *Developmental Psychology, 35,* 445–459.

Hayes, S. C., & Berens, N. M. (2003). Taking the scientific path: A road map for applied psychology students. In M. J. Prinstein & M. D. Patterson (Eds.), *The portable mentor: Expert guide to a successful career in psychology* (pp. 3–12). New York: Kluwer Academic/Plenum Publishers.

Makri-Botsari, E., & Makri, E. (2003). Maternal employment: Effects on her mental health and children's functional status. *Psychological Studies, 48,* 36–46.

NICHD Early Child Care Research Network. (2002). Early child care and children's development prior to school entry: Results from the NICHD study of early child care. *American Educational Research Journal, 39*(1), 133–164.

Peisner-Feinberg, E. S., & Burchinal, M. R. (1997). Relations between preschool children's childcare experiences and concurrent development: The Cost, Quality, and Outcomes Study. *Merrill-Palmer Quarterly, 43*(3), 451–477.

Rhodes, F. (1997, Fall). Science as a public trust. *Arts and Sciences, 18*(2). Retrieved from http://www.arts.cornell.edu/newsletr/spring97/science.htm

Silverstein, L. (1991). Transforming the debate about child care and maternal employment. *American Psychologist, 46*(10), 1025–1032.

Smolensky, E., & Gootman, J. A. (Eds.). (2003). *Working families and growing kids: Caring for children and adolescents.* Washington, DC: National Academic Press.

Vandell, D. L., & Ramanan, J. (1992). Effects of early and recent maternal employment on children from low-income families. *Child Development, 63,* 938–949.

Vander Ven, T., & Cullen, F. T. (2004). The impact of maternal employment on serious youth crime: Does the quality of working conditions matter? *Crime and Delinquency, 50*(2), 272–291.

Vander Ven, T. M., Cullen, F. T., Carrozza, M. A., & Wright, J. P. (2001). Home alone: The impact of maternal employment on delinquency. *Social Problems, 48*(2), 236–257.

Woodhead, M. (1988). When psychology informs public policy: The case of early childhood intervention. *American Psychologist, 43*(6), 443–454.

Youngblut, J. M., Brooten, D., Singer, L. T., Standing, T., Lee, H., & Rodgers, W. L. (2001). Effects of maternal employment and prematurity on child outcomes in single parent families. *Nursing Research, 50,* 346–355.

REWARDING CAREERS APPLYING
PSYCHOLOGICAL SCIENCE

9

Psychologists in the Forensic World

Deborah Davis
University of Nevada, Reno

Elizabeth F. Loftus
University of California, Irvine

On August 28, 1963 two young Manhattan "career girls" were brutally murdered in their apartment. A young junkie named Ricky Robles stole into the apartment in search of money to feed his addictions. Surprised by one girl, he attempted to rape her, only to be surprised again by her roommate as she returned home. Minutes later, Robles exited the apartment with only 30 dollars, leaving the mutilated bodies of the two girls tied up together on their bedroom floor.

No suspects were located for 7 months. Then, on April 14, 1964, Mrs. Minnie Edmonds was found murdered in an alleyway in Brooklyn, repeatedly stabbed and slashed in a manner reminiscent of the two "career girls." No suspect was identified until 9 days later, when a young Latino woman, Elba Borrero, was jumped from behind while walking home only one block from the location of the Edmonds murder. The man escaped. But Officer Isola located a suspect fitting the description of the attacker the next day. He presented the suspect to Elba Borrero, who positively identified him as her attacker. The young Black man, George Whitmore, Jr., soon began a 10-year journey through the New York justice system that not only exposed an ugly underside of New York city police detective misconduct and racist influence in the juries who judged Whitmore's case, but ultimately influenced the United States Supreme Court to offer greater protections to suspects deprived of their constitutional rights by police interrogators.

Police began the interrogation with the attack on Borrero, but soon turned to the Minnie Edmonds murder. Hours later, Whitmore had given detailed confessions to both crimes. But this was not to be the end of Whitmore's troubles. One detective thought he recognized a photo in Whitmore's pocket as Janice Wylie, one of the murdered career girls, and soon Whitmore was being interrogated about those killings as well. After more than 22 hours, he confessed to both murders, giving many details of the crimes that an innocent person could not know. There was only one problem—Robles, not Whitmore, was the killer. On the day of his arraignment Whitmore renounced his confession, saying it was obtained because police had beaten and coerced him. For the same reasons, he renounced his confessions in the other two cases.

Whitmore was soon convicted of the assault on Borrero. But even before this conviction, police had located and obtained a confession from the true murderer of the career girls, Ricky Robles. Whitmore's conviction for the Borrero mugging was reversed on appeal, when it was discovered that some trial jurors had made racist remarks during deliberations—and that violating judicial instructions, they discussed their knowledge of Whitmore's arrest in the career girls murders as one basis for their verdict for the Borrero case. Though it was now well known that Whitmore's confession in the career girls murder was false, and likely coerced, police resisted the idea that his confessions in the other cases might have been coerced and false as well. The D.A. elected to retry the Borrero case, and to take the Edmonds case to trial as well. But with a jury now exposed to widespread publicity on coercive police interrogations and the falsity of Whitmore's confession in the career girls case, the Edmonds trial ended in a hung jury.

Only a year later, the Supreme Court issued the well-known *Miranda* ruling stating that when a defendant is taken into custody he must be advised of his constitutional rights, and that statements made prior to this notification may not be used as evidence against him. Chief Justice Earl Warren wrote that courts must be aware of false and coerced confessions, and cited Whitmore as an obvious example of such coercion. Since the Miranda decision could be applied retroactively, Whitmore could no longer be tried for the murders, as no other evidence existed. Still, Whitmore was tried twice more for the Borrero mugging before it was finally thrown out for good, 10 years after Whitmore had first become a suspect (see account by Gado, 2002).

Thirty-one years later, on June 12, 1994, a new journey through the American justice system began for another Black man—Orenthal James Simpson. Simpson's ex-wife, Nicole, and her friend Ronald Goldman were found dead in front of her house, each with slashed throats and multiple stab wounds. OJ Simpson quickly became a suspect in the double murder, but this time substantial physical evidence led police to focus on Simpson. DNA analyses had apparently identified his blood at the crime scene, and the victims' blood in his car and on his clothing. One bloodsplattered glove was found at the crime scene, and its bloodsplattered mate appeared in Simpson's back yard. Bloody footprints at the murder scene seemed to match the brand and size of shoe owned by Simpson, and hairs found on Goldman's shirt and inside the knit cap found at the crime scene matched Simpson's hair, whereas hairs found on the glove at Simpson's house matched those of Goldman. Ample evidence documented Simpson's jealously of Nicole, many incidents of past physical abuse, and his threat to kill her if he found her with another man. No wonder police and many others believed the physical evidence clearly implicated OJ Simpson.

But Simpson's "dream team" of attorneys countered this evidence by putting the Los Angeles police department on trial for racism, corruption, and fabrication and mishandling of evidence. They presented this evidence to a jury including a large proportion of Black citizens, and their criticisms worked to achieve Simpson's acquittal. Such criticism was apparently less convincing to the predominantly White jurors who heard the lawsuit brought against Simpson by the relatives of the victims. The verdict in that case ordered Simpson to pay more than $32 million to their families.

The Whitmore and Simpson cases represent polar opposite outcomes for Black men in our justice system, and the two Simpson cases represented almost polar opposite outcomes for the same defendant in the criminal versus civil arena. How can psychology help us understand these and the many other criminal and civil cases that flood our courts each year?

Quite simply, human psychology is central to understanding every step of these cases, from causes of criminal behaviors or actions litigated in civil lawsuits, through investigation and adjudication of these cases, to post-verdict issues such as criminal rehabilitation, parole and postimprisonment programs, or long-term outcomes of parties to civil suits. Although the legal system was resistant to the involvement of researchers during its earlier history, the last 35 years have hosted a rapid expansion of the roles of psychologists at all levels.

At each level, psychologists actively conduct research investigating relevant issues, and then put this knowledge into practice. They provide information to legislators, businesses, police departments, and the courts with the goal of affecting such social policies as those involving crime control, police procedures, criminal rehabilitation, standards of safety in businesses, and many more—up to and including courtroom procedures and even the law itself. And they serve as expert witnesses and consultants providing evaluations of various sorts, and other assistance and advice to those at all levels of the system (for reviews of the roles of psychologists in the legal system, see Bartol & Bartol, 2004; Costanzo, 2004; Kuther, 2004; Wrightsman, 2001).

In the sections that follow, we explore the myriad roles of psychologists in the legal system, and discuss potential career paths available to psychol-

ogists interested in pursuing these applications. We first examine the role
of psychologists in shaping the law itself, and then review roles psychologists play in the operation of the legal system that applies and enforces
these laws.

"AMICUS CURIAE": PSYCHOLOGISTS AS ADVISERS TO THE COURTS

The role of psychologists with perhaps the most far-reaching consequences
is that of advising courts or legislators to help them determine what the law
should be. In the earlier history of our courts, judges were forced to rely on
their own intuitions and those of their advisors and the attorneys who argued before them as bases for logically deducing which of several proposed alternatives would represent the most effective law. This practice
has slowly been supplemented by scientific and other forms of professional
expert evidence. This more objective, science-based knowledge has allowed the courts as well as other lawmakers to shift away from logic/intu-
ition based to what might be called "evidence-based" decisions.

The "Legal Realism" movement, which began in earnest in the 1920s and
30s, essentially advocates "evidence-based" law. It thereby embraces the
role of social and other scientists in providing the evidence needed to initially choose laws that promote common societal good, as well as to evaluate these laws' actual effectiveness once put into practice (e.g., Llewellyn,
1931).

Relevant research findings are summarized and presented to the Courts
in the form of an "amicus curiae brief." This "friend of the court" brief is
provided by knowledgeable and interested parties with no direct involvement in the case at issue, and is designed to summarize and interpret existing knowledge that would help judges decide which ruling would represent
ideal social policy. Many issues confronting our courts are fundamentally
psychological, such as "Does capital punishment deter crime?" "How does
pornography affect attitudes or behavior?" "How are children affected by
being reared in gay households?" or "How does jury size affect jury decision making and verdict decisions?" Hence, it is not surprising that psychologists have provided the courts with amicus briefs addressing a variety of
behavioral issues.

Perhaps the most widely known case in which psychological testimony
was provided to the Courts was the 1954 case *Brown v. Board of Education*.
The historic ruling of the Court in that case challenged the "separate but
equal" doctrine, and abolished segregation in the nation's school systems.
The Court's ruling in the Brown case was the first to explicitly reference social science research as a basis of its ruling. Briefs submitted to the Su-

preme Court in support of abolishing segregation included a document signed by 32 prominent social scientists of the day entitled "The Effect of Segregation and the Consequences of Desegregation: A Social Science Statement."

Modern amicus briefs are often filed by the American Psychological Association, through its Committee on Legal Issues (COLI). They are typically written by a team of researchers, and are often reviewed by the APA before submission to the Court. This process is intended to ensure that information provided to the Court is as objective and accurate as possible. While there is a hope that the process is sufficiently neutral that the biases or agendas of involved individuals are avoided, many briefs have been highly controversial within the profession.

Exemplifying the team approach, the brief filed in the more recent case of *Kumho Tire Co. Ltd. V. Carmichael* (1999) addressed the issue of how jurors' opinions and decisions are affected by the testimony of expert witnesses. Do jurors simply adopt the expert's opinion, or do they instead carefully evaluate and give appropriate weight to the expert's testimony? What implications would this have for the conditions under which expert testimony on should or should not be admitted into evidence? The amicus brief filed in this case was authored by 18 social scientists, and summarized evidence from a number of scientific studies indicating that jurors do not simply adopt the opinions of expert witnesses uncritically (Vidmar et al., 2000).

The Brown and Kumho cases are only two of a host of cases for which the American Psychological Association (APA) has filed briefs. In fact, the APA maintains a Web site listing all amicus briefs filed by the organization, which can be found on the Internet at PsycLAW.org

Although amicus briefs sometimes influence judicial rulings, they are one of many factors—practical, political and others—that typically carry more weight than social science evidence. Courts sometimes simply discount scientific evidence in favor of their preferred rulings. Such was clearly the case in the 1986 Supreme Court ruling in *Lockhart v. McCree*. The defendant sought to overturn his death penalty conviction, arguing that a "death qualified" jury—one whose members agreed they could sentence a defendant to death if the evidence warranted—is inherently biased toward conviction, thereby violating the defendant's right to a fair trial. The brief summarized research indicating that the death qualification process excludes several classes of jurors (e.g., minorities, women, Jews, and liberals) and that *given exactly the same evidence* death qualified jurors were more likely to convict than those who were not death qualified. Hence, it suggested, death qualified juries do not include a representative cross section of the community, and are biased toward conviction, thereby violating the defendant's right to a fair and impartial jury of his peers. But faced with a country firmly favoring the death penalty, the Supreme Court simply could not accept these conclusions. Instead, it dismissed the results of the studies as irrelevant. Justice Rehnquist wrote the majority decision as follows: "We will assume for purposes of this opinion that the studies are both methodologically valid and adequate to establish that death-qualification in fact produces juries somewhat more 'conviction-prone' than non-death qualified juries. We hold, nonetheless, that the Constitution does not prohibit the states from death-qualifying juries in capital cases" (*Lockhart v. McCree*, 1986).

The Supreme Court was similarly unreceptive to findings showing the death penalty is disproportionately imposed upon Blacks (*McCleskey v. Kemp, 1987*). Despite clear evidence that, controlling for variables such as the severity of the crime or strength of evidence, Blacks are more likely to be sentenced to death than Whites, the Court acknowledged the disparity, but held that some unfairness is tolerable, since subjective judgment (hence some degree of bias) is an inescapable element of sentencing. The Court further held that to overturn the conviction of the appellant would require proof that jurors acted with "discriminatory purpose"—or, *intentional* bias. This requirement is more stringent than that necessary to demonstrate employment discrimination, pointing to the irony that a person denied housing or employment has more protection from discrimination than one on trial for his life (Ellsworth & Mauro, 1998, p.720).

It may be that Courts use amicus briefs in much the same way juries use expert testimony. That is, the Court may be genuinely influenced by social science findings when there is uncertainty among its members. But where the Court already has a clear preference, its members may find reason to disregard the findings when they conflict with preferred rulings, or use the amicus brief to justify preferred rulings when they coincide.

WHY DID THIS HAPPEN? PSYCHOLOGISTS WHO INVESTIGATE AND EXPLAIN CAUSALITY

Psychologists have investigated the social and psychological *causes* of many events litigated in our legal system. Causes of crime, for example, have been investigated by social scientists across several disciplines, including psychology. Some focus on societal causes such as poverty, social norms, or deterrent forces such as legal penalties for crime or the capabilities and size of law enforcement. Others focus on personal causes involving personality, racial hatred, family history, drug/alcohol abuse, or mental health. Often, explanations of crime are quite specific to the type of crime in question. Causes of adult rape, for example, tend to be different than those of robbery, serial murder, embezzlement, or child sexual abuse (see Bartol, 2002).

In fact, literature on psychological causes of crime offers insight into the murders in our example cases. For example, assuming for the sake of argument OJ Simpson did murder Nicole, what might have caused this behavior? His violent abuse, jealousy, stalking, and finally murder of his ex-wife may well have had been rooted (at least in part) in insecurity, specifically *anxious attachment style*, a pattern of personality formed during childhood as a result of specific dysfunctional caregiving behaviors of one's parents or primary caregivers (Bowlby, 1982). Although anxious attachment has not been specifically linked to spouse murder, research has established strong relationships between anxious attachment and physical/verbal partner abuse, enhanced jealousy, and stalking (e.g., Davis, Shaver & Vernon, 2003; Dutton, 1999; Fonagy, 1999). In addition, most women who are murdered by romantic partners have previously been abused by that partner, and are most likely to be murdered when they are leaving or have left their partner (see reviews by Bixenstein, 1999; Websdale, 1999 of causes of spousal homicide). Anxiously attached persons are particularly likely to abuse their partners and to react to threats to the relationship with anger and violence (Davis et al., 2003; Dutton, 1999), even murder.

Psychologists trying to explain Simpson's behavior might focus on aggressive behavior in his background. Simpson's background involved criminality and aggression, ranging from membership in a street gang the "Persian Warriors" as a teenager to involvement in what some view as a relatively violent sport of football. Hence, in circumstances where he had lost his wife, and where he was vigilant to the threat of her involvement with new lovers, Simpson's personality, along with a well-developed repertoire of violent behaviors rooted in a background encouraging violence, probably combined to facilitate or provoke the brutal murders.

As a young Black man, Robles—the true murderer of the career girls— may have likewise grown up poor, in a culture encouraging violence. But the likely proximate causes of his crime were poverty and drug addiction. Recall, he did not intend to commit murder. Instead, he entered the victims' apartment intending to find money to purchase drugs. Indeed, alcohol/drug use has been implicated in a variety of property and violent crimes, including rape (Bartol, 2002).

Psychologists also actively research causes of events involved in civil litigation. For example, *human factors* researchers investigate the interaction of humans with various mechanisms such as cars, aircraft, computers, manufacturing equipment, and much more, with the goal of understanding how things can be designed to facilitate performance and minimize accidents (see the *Handbook of Human Factors in Litigation* [2005] for reviews of various design issues involved in litigation). *Social or industrial* psychologists investigate the relationship of business policies and practices to behaviors involved in civil litigation: for example, the relationship of corporate policies on sexual harassment to the incidence of sexual harassment in the work-place; or the relationship of labor practices to discriminatory outcomes (such as inequality across race or gender in salary, promotion, etc.). Psychologists interested in language and communication might investigate failures in doctor–patient communication that result in treatment failures (and hence malpractice litigation). Across business, industry, and professional practices of all kinds psychologists do research to assess sources of error or misfortune, and to develop policies and procedures that will maximize productivity and eliminate unnecessary error.

Based on their research findings, psychologists advise lawmakers, manufacturers, and others regarding effective social policy (including laws, penalties for crime, etc.), ergonomic designs, communications skills, and a host of other policies and procedures expected to prevent crime or personal injuries litigated in the civil courts. They may do this as employees or as consultants who provide on-site consulting, continuing education seminars, relevant training, or other educational activities (or through the mechanism of amicus briefs described earlier).

When injuries do occur, through crime, professional malpractice, faulty designs, and so on, these same psychologists may serve as *expert witnesses* to testify as to their causes. In a criminal trial, a psychologist might be called to testify in the sentencing phase to provide *mitigating evidence* suggesting the person should be given a lesser sentence—arguing, for example, that a child abuser's crime was triggered by sexual abuse in his own childhood. Experts on *battered woman syndrome* might be called to explain to the jury why a woman would have reasonably viewed murder as the only available defense against what she perceived as imminent life-threatening danger from her husband (e.g., Walker, 1992, 1993). Similarly, expert testimony on *rape trauma syndrome* might be offered to explain why a rape victim would engage in behaviors that seem inconsistent with her claim of rape—such as failing to report the rape immediately, appearing to be emotionally composed rather than showing intense distress, having further contact with the rapist, or failures of memory regarding the rape—and to show that such behaviors are common among rape victims (e.g., Faigman, 1999). We recognize that the use of "syndrome" evidence is controversial. Some psychologists provide syndrome evidence in actual court cases, while other psychologists are often called in to provide opposing testimony.

For civil trials, the expert is likely to testify regarding departures from effective design or procedures, and how such departures could lead to the outcome in question. For example, experts on sexual harassment policies might testify to how inadequacies in a company's sexual harassment training/protections could have resulted in an employee being harassed (to support a finding of liability against the company). Or, a human factors design expert might testify as to how the defective design of an airplane cockpit could have led to perceptual failures of the pilot that caused a crash. This sort of testimony is what is known as *social framework testimony* (Monahan & Walker, 1988), presenting "general conclusions from social science research" in order to assist judges or jurors "in determining factual issues in a specific case" (p. 470).

PSYCHOLOGISTS AS ADVISORS TO LAW ENFORCEMENT

Psychologists work from within or outside police departments and correctional facilities to affect personnel selection and evaluation, or to develop and evaluate programs and procedures of various kinds. Some are full-time employees of police departments, and, in fact, there are two professional organizations for police psychologists, the Law Enforcement Behavioral Sciences Association (LEBSA), and a section of the American Psychological Association's Division 18 (Psychologists in Public Service) called the Police Psychology Subsection. However, many roles they play may also be performed by outside consulting psychologists.

One role is personnel selection. To screen applicants for law enforcement positions, psychologists may use written personality inventories, clinical interviews; and/or *situation tests* assessing responses in simulated situations designed to emulate those one would encounter on the job. Once police recruits are hired, psychologists participate in training programs as teachers or consultants. Teachers teach recruits as well as seasoned officers in such areas as cross-cultural awareness, communication skills, how to handle the mentally ill, working with victims of sexual assault, response to domestic violence calls, hostage negotiations, marital relationships, criminal psychology and profiling, stress management skills for coping with job related stresses, and organizational issues such as sexual harassment, racial discrimination, or employee substance abuse. Consultants perform any number of services for the police department, primarily acting as participant-observers in police procedures to detect sources of problems, developing effective training techniques and police procedures, and then evaluating their effectiveness. They may also provide clinical evaluations of officers, such as "fitness for duty" evaluations.

PSYCHOLOGISTS AS CRITICS OF POLICE PROCEDURES

Psychologists have also served as *unsolicited* advisors to police. As early as 1908, Hugo Munsterberg (regarded as the father of psychology and law) wrote extensively on two topics central to contemporary criticisms of police procedure: witness memory distortion, suggestibility and inaccuracy; and coercive interrogation practices and confession (Munsterberg, 1908). He pointed to frequently inaccurate eyewitness testimony, including misidentification of innocents as perpetrators of crime, and the possible role of police suggestion in facilitating such false identifications. He also wrote of the potential for coercive police interrogation practices to create false confessions, and interviewed suspects who had undergone long and coercive interrogations to test his theories regarding how to tell false memories or reports from true. Modern psychologists have responded to Munsterberg's call to arms with extensive study of these issues, and commitment to influence police practices that undermine the accuracy of witness reports, including those of suspects against themselves.

THE IMPACT OF POLICE PROCEDURES ON EYEWITNESS REPORTS

Beginning in the 1970s, research on eyewitness testimony and police procedures began in earnest. Major areas of concentration included effects of leading interviews on witness reports, and effects of suggestive police eyewitness identification procedures on witness perpetrator identification accuracy.

The "Misinformation Effect." In several studies, Loftus and her colleagues showed that even seemingly minor variations in interview questions affect reports of eyewitnesses. Witnesses in their studies were led to falsely remember seeing a yield rather than a stop sign, nonexistent broken glass and tape recorders, a white instead of a blue vehicle in a crime scene, incorrect colors of objects, curly rather than straight hair, and Minnie Mouse rather than Mickey Mouse. In other studies, Loftus and her colleagues showed that the language of questions can shape witness reports (see Loftus, 2002, 2003; Loftus & Palmer, 1974). These seminal findings ushered in many years of further research on biasing interviewing procedures (see Davis & Loftus, in press and other chapters in the upcoming *Handbook of Eyewitness Psychology*, in press for reviews of suggestive interviewing procedures in several specific witness contexts). Many of these later studies extended Loftus' findings to show how misleading questions can cause a person to develop false memories of much more dramatic incidents, including those involving the self as well as others, personally stressful as well as more mundane events, and long past as well as recent events. Generally, misleading interviews have been shown to lead people both to *add* things to their memories, as well as to *alter* memories of those things they did see (see Davis & Follette, 2001; Davis & Friedman, in press; Davis & Loftus, in press for review of a variety of distorting interview processes).

In response to accumulating evidence of the distorting effects of suggestive interviewing on witness accuracy, researchers began to develop interview procedures specifically designed to avoid suggestion. Among the most well-known of these is the *cognitive interview*, developed by Ronald Fisher and Ed Geiselman, which is designed to maximize both the *quantity* and *quality* (accuracy) of witness accounts (Fisher & Geiselman, 1992). In fact, some of this research and other key findings in the eyewitness area helped to shape the proposed procedures recommended in *Eyewitness Evidence: A Guide for Law Enforcement (hereafter Eyewitness Guide)* published by the U.S. Department of Justice (Technical Working Group, 1999). The aim of the *Eyewitness Guide* is to provide police with guidelines for interviewing and dealing with witnesses designed to minimize memory distortion and inaccuracy (see further details below).

Police Procedure and Eyewitness Identification Accuracy

Among the most disturbing results of biasing police procedures are the many proven cases of mistaken eyewitness identifications of innocent persons as perpetrators of crime. Investigations of the causes of wrongful convictions have uniformly found that mistaken eyewitness memory is the number one cause of wrongful conviction, playing a role in more than 80% of such cases (see Wells, Malpass, Lindsay, Fisher, Turtle, & Fulero, 2000 for review). The *Innocence Project* Web site now maintains a running tally of proven wrongful convictions, along with the various causes of the miscarriage of justice in each case (innocenceproject.org).

Faced in the late 1990s with growing evidence of the role of eyewitness misidentification in an ever increasing roster of proven wrongful convictions, Attorney General Janet Reno ordered the formation of a panel of psychologists, attorneys, and law enforcement personnel to develop national guidelines for the collection of eyewitness evidence. The panel began meeting in 1998, and by 1999 had produced a draft of the final guidelines now accessible on the Department of Justice Web site (see Wells et al., for an account of this process). The development and adoption of the Eyewitness Guide represents one of the most significant accomplishments of cognitive/social psychologists in impacting law enforcement. The process that began with Hugo Munsterberg in the early 1900s finally gained official acceptance by the United States Department of Justice at the close of the century. What led to this rather spectacular success?

During the 1970s, psychologists had provided relentlessly increasing evidence that eyewitness accuracy can be poor, particularly memories of people and events witnessed under poor "witnessing conditions" (such as brief exposure times, poor lighting, distracting conditions, obstructed views, stressful circumstances, and so on), or by witnesses with compromised "witnessing abilities" (such as drug or alcohol intoxication, or witnesses with impaired perceptual abilities, etc.); and moreover, that accuracy can be further compromised by biasing police interview and identification procedures (see reviews by Davis & Follette, 2001; Wells & Olson, 2003). Also during this period, psychologists were increasingly called as expert witnesses to explain to juries the potential for inaccuracy and the conditions under which accuracy is most likely to be impaired. (Loftus, 1986). This testimony was offered to help jurors evaluate the likely accuracy of witnesses in the cases they judged, and provided steady pressure on the justice system to avoid biasing eyewitness identification procedures.

Believing in the accuracy of their investigations and the guilt of their suspects, law enforcement personnel were generally resistant to testimony on witness memory inaccuracy, and tended to view psychologists as enemies who undermined efforts to incarcerate the guilty. If not for growing availability of DNA testing and its role in freeing the wrongfully convicted—largely by mistaken eyewitnesses—the *Eyewitness Guide* may never have come to pass. But the increasing tide of exonerations of the wrongfully convicted led not only to acknowledgment of the role of mistaken eyewitnesses in wrongful convictions, but also to the role of false confessions such as Whitmore's confessions to three separate heinous crimes (see below). In part, like false confessions, false witness statements are promoted by biasing interviewing procedures. However, a major role is also played by police eyewitness identification procedures.

Police might ask a witness to view a lineup to try to identify the perpetrator, only one of whom resembles the description the witness has given. In earlier times, for example, a witness who had described the perpetrator as Black might be asked to examine a lineup including only one Black person and five Whites. Even as recently as this spring, the first author served as an expert for a case where the perpetrator was described as having a large scar on his face. The lineup shown to witnesses included only one man with a scar. Witnesses have been shown to use a "relative judgment" strategy, whereby they often pick the lineup member *who most closely resembles* their memory of the perpetrator. Hence, a *biased lineup*, in which only one member resembles the witness's memory of the perpetrator has been shown to result in higher rates of false identifications of innocents (see review in Wells & Olsen, 2003).

The *Eyewitness Guide* provides guidelines for construction of fair lineups, including the admonition to select "foils" (nonsuspect members of the lineup) *all* of whom fit the witness's description. It also includes a number of other guidelines designed to reduce the suggestiveness of the lineup, and to ensure that the witness's choice is not influenced by comments or actions either of law enforcement personnel or other witnesses—as well as many other recommendations based on years of psychological research on how to maximize witness accuracy.

The Guide provides recommendations for conducting (in limited circumstances) "show-up" identification procedures, which are more suggestive than lineup procedures (see Wells & Olsen, 2003), and hence more likely to result in false identifications. In a show-up, police present the witness with one suspect alone, asking whether he or she is or is not the perpetrator of the crime. Whitmore became a suspect for the Borrero assault as a result of a show-up identification. Borrero and the officer who chased the suspect saw the attacker under what eyewitness experts would regard as poor witnessing conditions. The attack and chase took place at night under poor lighting, both saw the attacker's face briefly and at poor angles, the victim was frightened and under stress, and the attacker was Black, whereas Borerro was Hispanic and the policeman White. Research has shown that accuracy in identification of those of different races is lower than for those of one's own race (see Loftus & Doyle, 1997 for a review of cross-racial identification studies and other factors that psychologists have shown to impact eyewitness accuracy).

Although the attacker escaped, Officer Isola, who had chased the attacker the night before, searched the neighborhood for a suspect resembling the description of the attacker, apprehended Whitmore the next day and presented him to Borrero as the only suspect in the show-up identification. Whitmore became a suspect in the career girls and Minnie Edmonds murders because he had a picture of a White girl in his pocket that a police officer who had worked on the career girls murder mistakenly believed to be of one of the murdered girls. Whitmore spent 10 years in jail as the result of a double whammy of mistaken identifications.

Coerced Confessions

Once a suspect, Whitmore was further victimized by coercive police interrogations—another area of police procedures where psychologists' criticisms have led law enforcement to view them as "enemies of state." Whitmore was interrogated for many hours before confessing to the Edwards and career girls murders (more than 22 hours for the latter). His confessions contained many details of the murders and murder scenes an innocent person could not have known. Yet he was innocent, raising the question of what could have happened to lead him to not only falsely confess, but to include details he should not have known.

As with eyewitness identification procedures, social scientists have vigorously investigated police interrogation procedures and the manner in which they can produce false confessions such as those of Whitmore. Also, like mistaken eyewitness identifications, false confessions have played a causal role in the documented cases of proven wrongful convictions. As per recent Innocence Project data, more than 25% of the wrongfully convicted falsely confessed to the crimes. Even more surprising is the fact that false confessions appear to be more likely for more heinous crimes such as murder (Drizin & Leo, 2004). Perhaps in response to greater pressures to solve the more heinous crimes, police appear to deploy more coercive interrogation techniques against those suspected of such crimes. But what are these techniques?

Modern police departments are less likely to use overt physical attacks such as those Whitmore claimed to experience to elicit confessions. Instead, they use psychological techniques of persuasion to lead suspects to first waive their Miranda rights (Leo, 2001), and then to confess (see extensive reviews of these tactics by Davis & O'Donohue, 2004; Davis & Leo, in press; Gudjonnson, 2003; Kassin, 1997; Kassin & Gudjonnson, 2004; Ofshe & Leo, 1997). Some of these involve compromising mental capacity, so that suspects are more vulnerable to confusion and unable to clearly think and evaluate the information and demands of the police. Suspects are interrogated for long periods, sometimes beginning when they are already sleep deprived and under considerable stress. Sometimes these stresses, along with the pressures of the interrogation, lead suspects to confess just to escape what they find to be an intolerable situation. Suspects also falsely confess because they have been led to believe it is the best option open to them. Police are trained to lie and deceive suspects about the nature of evidence against them, the legal options open to them, and the likely consequences of their choices. They offer explicit or implicit threats of harsher punishment if the defendant refuses to confess and offers of leniency if he does. They lead suspects to believe there is overwhelming evidence of their guilt, that they are certain to be found guilty, and that the best way to achieve optimal outcomes is to confess. Essentially, they are led to believe confession is the wisest choice, regardless of guilt or innocence (see review in Davis & O'Donohue, 2004).

Suspects may sometimes be led by these same techniques to develop false memories of having committed the crime (Henkel & Coffman, 2004; Kassin, in press). This occurs when police first convince the person they *must have* committed the crime by confronting him with false evidence, and then use various imaging procedures to cause the person to actively imagine committing the crime. Many such procedures have been shown to result in false memories of having actually performed imagined events (e.g., see Davis & Follette, 2001; McNally, 2003 for a review). This is more likely to occur when the suspect has no clear memory of what he was doing at the time (e.g., due to intoxication), and when the suspect is unusually suggestible, often due to psychopathology, low intelligence, or youth (see Oberlander, Goldstein & Goldstein, 2003; Gudjonnson, 2003).

Enhanced suggestibility is a factor in false confessions not involving false memories as well. Suggestibility can lead the person to be more susceptible to police pressures of all kinds. Psychologists are asked to evaluate the suggestibility of the defendant (e.g., Gudjonnson, 2003), and whether he is "competent" to confess or waive Miranda rights (e.g., Oberlander, Goldstein & Goldstein, 2003). In fact, enhanced suggestibility may have played a role in Whitmore's false confessions. He was evaluated by psychiatrists prior to his trial for the career girls murder who found him sane and competent for trial, but possessed of below-average intelligence and poor verbal skills. Hence, it is unlikely that Whitmore was able to adequately understand and evaluate the options open to him, and to resist intense pressure from police authorities. But where did he get the details of the murders and crime scenes he should not have known?

Unfortunately, like many interrogations even today, Whitmore's interrogations were not recorded. However, we can safely assume that the detectives who interrogated Whitmore somehow fed him this information. In fact, one role served by experts today is to provide analyses of transcripts of interrogations leading to disputed confessions (where available) to show how evidence is *first* introduced into the interrogation. Did it come from the defendant or from his interrogators? It is crucial to show where apparently incriminating evidence such as that in Whitmore's confession has come from, since such details tend to cement the defendant's guilt in the minds of prosecutors, judges, and juries who later must evaluate the confession.

Confession experts serve three roles in the legal system. First, clinical psychologists might be asked to evaluate the suspect's mental status and capabilities to assess the possibility of enhanced suggestibility, inability to understand and evaluate the legal procedures and options, or resist interrogation pressures to waive Miranda rights and confess against self-interest. Second, the expert might be asked to testify in support of a motion to suppress the introduction of the defendant's confession into trial. Since *coerced* confessions are deemed inadmissible, the expert is asked to evaluate the coercive tactics of the interrogation in light of the ability of the defendant to resist coercive influences. Finally, if the confession is introduced in trial, the expert may testify to the jury to present evidence that false confessions do occur, to explain why a person might confess falsely and the way the police tactics work to cause them to do so, and to explain how the mental status of the defendant might have made him more susceptible to these tactics.

PSYCHOLOGISTS AND THE *PRODUCTION* OF EVIDENCE

Psychologists also play a central role in the investigation of issues and events litigated in our courts, and in doing so *produce* much of the evidence presented to judges and juries.

Case-Specific Research

In some cases, psychologists conduct research to answer questions specific to the case at hand. For example, for very high-profile cases, jury consultants often conduct a *change of venue survey*. Such cases often receive sufficient press coverage to widely influence opinions of the jury pool in the scheduled trial location. The survey is conducted to determine whether opinions of jury eligible residents in the scheduled trial location are significantly more developed and biased than those of residents in other locations. If so, the judge may move the trial to another location where, presumably, the jurors have been less influenced by media. This was done, for example, in the Oklahoma City Bombing case against Timothy McVeigh, whose trial was moved to Colorado, where change of venue research had shown the area to have been less saturated with media publicity on the bombing and the case against McVeigh, and where the jury pool showed less awareness of the evidence and presumption of guilt. Had Whitmore had the benefit of such research, he may not have been convicted in the first of his three trials for the Borrero assault. His conviction was eventually overturned as a result of trial jurors' awareness and discussion of the publicity over Whitmore's confession (not yet known to be false) to the career girls murders. But had he been tried by an unbiased jury uncontaminated by extensive unfavorable publicity, and perhaps been acquitted in the first trial, double jeopardy laws would not have allowed him to be retried for the same case, and he would surely have spent more than 7 years less in prison.

Psychologists are also asked to research questions specific to the central issue of the case to provide evidence in support of one party's position. Such research was conducted in support of a variety of trademark infringement cases (see Monahan & Walker, 1994, chap. 3). For example, one such project by the Maritz Company was conducted to support the Squirt Company's claim that a drink marketed by Seven-Up called "QUIRST" infringed their trademark for the drink called "SQUIRT." The Maritz Company demonstrated consumer confusion between the two drinks by showing that when asked about soft drinks they had just purchased 4.3% of customers who said they had just purchased SQUIRT had actually purchased QUIRST (as revealed when they were asked to show their purchase). The Court ruled that although 4.3% may seem small, is it not insignificant when considered in the context of total sales.

Forensic Tests and Interviews

Psychologists conduct a wide variety of tests and interviews introduced into proceedings ranging from pretrial motions to executions or parole hearings. Excellent discussions of the various instruments used for testing in the areas to be discussed below can be found in recently published texts and handbooks on forensic psychology (e.g., Goldstein & Weiner, 2003; Hess & Weiner, 1999; O'Donohue & Levinsky, 2004; Walker & Shapiro, 2003; Wrightsman, 2001).

Competency. An evaluation of competency may be conducted to determine whether a defendant is competent to plead guilty, stand trial, or be executed (i.e., "adjudicative competency"; see reviews by Mumley, Tillbrooke, & Grisso, 2003; Oberlander et al., 2003). Competence in these contexts refers to the person's ability to understand the nature and purpose of legal proceedings, and must be established at every stage of the criminal process, including reading of Miranda rights upon arrest, interrogation procedures, plea-bargaining involving guilty pleas, pretrial hearings, trial, sentencing hearings, and consummation of a death penalty. One or more established tests of competency may be combined with a clinical interview to determine competency. This may be done before trial or execution, but is often done after the fact to assess competency in circumstances where it is questioned after a procedure such as reading Miranda rights or interrogation of a suspect. In the latter case, the evaluation may be conducted to support a motion to suppress evidence obtained from an interrogation. Competency is also at issue in the civil arena, where psychologists provide evaluations of competency relevant to such issues as civil commitment, the elderly and control of their own affairs, or end of life decisions.

Insanity. The related concept of *insanity* may also be assessed by forensic psychologists, although insanity is a legal, rather than psychological, term. To complicate matters, several legal definitions or test criteria of insanity are used across the various state jurisdictions. The most recent American Law Institute (ALI) standard incorporates versions of all the elements of its predecessors, stating that "A person is not responsible for criminal conduct if at the time of the action, as a result of mental disease or defect, he lacks substantial capacity either to appreciate the criminality (wrongfulness) of his conduct or to conform his or her conduct to the requirements of the law" (American Law Institute, 1962, p. 401). Hence, the psychologist must evaluate the influence of the defendant's circumstances during the time period of the crime and as a result of the crime that might compromise cognitive capacity or ability to control one's behavior; as well as personal abilities and characteristics of the defendant. Had OJ Simpson been evaluated to support a plea of temporary insanity, for example, the forensic psychologist might have provided testimony supporting the claim that Simpson's pathologically insecure personality made him vulnerable to such jealousy and rage that he could not control his behavior when he saw

Nicole with Ron, and therefore was driven to kill the two victims by *irresistible impulse.*

Assessments of Dangerousness. Accurate assessment of an individual's propensity to behave violently is important in a variety of contexts. Within the legal system itself, this is most important when deciding whether to grant bail or parole or to commit a person to a mental institution against his or her will. In each of these contexts the potential for danger to others is central to the decision. Danger to oneself is also crucial to involuntary commitment to mental institutions. In some states, jurors must consider future dangerousness when deciding between the death penalty and life in prison. Psychologists are routinely employed by the legal system to aid in these decisions by providing assessments of dangerousness and risk of future violence.

Assessments of dangerousness can also become the basis of lawsuits filed by victims of violence across many contexts. In the landmark case of *Tarasoff v. Regents of the University of California*, UC Berkeley was held liable for the murder of Tara Tarasoff by a patient of their health center. The patient had expressed his desire to kill her in one of his sessions. Although the therapist warned the campus police, he did not warn Tarasoff. Upon her death, her parents sued and won a verdict against the university for negligence in failing to warn Tarasoff of the threat.

This duty to warn or otherwise protect persons against the violent actions of others is imposed across a variety of contexts. Businesses are obligated by law to provide reasonable protections to patrons against reasonably foreseeable dangers (including persons); airlines may be found liable for failures to detect and restrain those who later harm other passengers; school or industrial psychologists may be found liable for failure to detect dangerous propensities in employees or students who harm others; and parole boards and psychologists responsible for releasing mental patients may be held responsible for their later acts of violence.

For psychologists and others this sword can cut both ways. They can be sued by victims of violence for their role in allowing the perpetrator to remain free, or for failing to warn the victim of the risk that the perpetrator might commit such violence. But on the other hand, they can be sued by those incarcerated or institutionalized inappropriately, and hence suffer harm to reputations, careers or family life, and inappropriate deprivation of their liberty. Hence, across a variety of settings psychologists provide these crucial assessments of dangerousness, becoming vulnerable to lawsuits either from the targets of their assessments or from the victims of violence when errors of assessment are made in either direction.

Such assessments have been the focus of considerable controversy. Space limitations do not permit us to fully address this controversy. However, the central issues are:

1. Can such predictions be made with sufficient precision to ethically justify their use?
2. Can psychological assessments add anything to the prediction beyond what actuarial computations offer?
3. What role should clinical judgment play in such predictions?
4. What formal assessment instruments provide the most accurate predictions?
5. What levels of error are acceptable?

Unfortunately, psychologists are faced with such questions not only in their role as assessors of risk. They also serve as experts to evaluate, in hindsight, whether psychologists whose judgments turned out to be in error should be held liable. The expert must judge whether the assessor's judgment was reasonable in light of what he or she could or should have known, and whether he or she used appropriate assessment procedures to arrive at the original judgment. In light of the problems of assessment in this area, both roles are subject to controversy.

Assessing Victims' Damages. Psychologists are integral to civil trails, assessing the nature and extent of damage suffered by victims of physical injury or emotionally stressful injustices such as wrongful termination, sexual harassment, and others. To support or contradict victims' claims of such damages, psychologists perform a variety of assessments of cognitive and emotional conditions. Neuropsychologists or clinicians perform assessments of IQ and other indices of cognitive functioning to assess damage from head injuries, and offer testimony on emotional consequences such as depression, loss of self-esteem or initiative, posttraumatic stress disorder, or personality changes affecting professional or family life. Psychologists also test to detect *malingering,* or exaggeration or faking of disability. Malingering can be a problem, for example, when plaintiffs try to exaggerate their injuries to support larger monetary damage awards for their injuries, or when defendants might fake mental incompetence to avoid trial.

Child Custody Evaluations. Psychologists provide a wide range of assessments for divorce/child custody proceedings. Such evaluations tend to be dangerous and risky for psychologists, in that they involve high levels of stress, threats of litigation, risks of licensing board complaints, and even the risk of personal harm (Kirkland & Kirkland, 2001). They are also among the most difficult for psychologists, who are asked to determine the very difficult issue of what custody arrangement would be in the best interest of the child. This determination would seem to require ability to assess the relationships between all parties, the family systems in question, and a variety of special issues arising from allegations of substance abuse, domestic violence, physical or sexual abuse, or any combination of these problems. Some psychologists have questioned whether psychologists are equipped to make these judgments (Hagen, 1997), and often custody hearings are host to battles of opposing experts and their respective critics.

Imagine the complexity of evaluations performed in the Simpson custody battle with his dead ex-wife's family. In a stunning ruling for many observers, the Judge granted custody to Simpson, based in part on a court-ordered report by psychologist Jeffrey Lulow. Lulow felt that remaining with their grandparents would encourage the children to view their father as dangerous, uncaring, inadequate, or emotionally distant (quoted by Associated Press, 1997, p. 5A). Lulow concluded from testing Simpson as well as the Browns that Simpson's capacity for empathy was actually greater than that of the children's grandparents. The California appeals court later overturned this ruling, however, ordering the case back to trial under a new judge who would have to consider evidence regarding Simpson's guilt in murdering the children's mother.

Psychologists who perform assessments such as those in the Simpson case may make use of a variety of assessment instruments and clinical interviews with parents and children, siblings, and others considered relevant. However, a number of commonly used assessments have been criticized as lacking scientific support (e.g., Otto & Heilbrun, 2002), and psychologists who base their testimony on them have increasingly come under attack both by attorneys and the courts, as well as by other psychologists who doubt the validity of their methods and conclusions.

Child Victimization. Whether in the context of divorce or simply ongoing family life, psychologists may be called to evaluate issues surrounding child victimization. Like custody evaluations, child victimization evaluations have serious consequences for all concerned. The child may be removed by child protective services from the custody of one or both parents, and parents may face legal consequences such as criminal prosecution and imprisonment. Such evaluations also take place with regard to businesses (such as day-care centers), schools, or religious organizations whose employees are accused of acts of child victimization. Sometimes claims of abuse relate to ongoing or recent abuse, and sometimes they refer to abuse alleged to have taken place years in the past, as in recent scandals involving widespread child molestation among Catholic clergy. In this context psychologists entered one of the most controversial arenas of investigative interviewing in the discipline: that is, claims of child *sexual* abuse.

The late 20th century witnessed extraordinary escalation in claims of sexual abuse. Groups of young children in day-care centers across the nation began to claim they were abused by their caregivers, divorce related claims of sexual abuse soared, and adults began to "recover" memories of long-forgotten childhood sexual abuse. Faced with the need to evaluate these claims, parents, victims, and courts turned to clinical psychologists to perform the evaluations.

Clearly, legitimate cases of sexual abuse are not uncommon. But just as clearly, many false claims have ripped the lives of the accused, and even the alleged victims, asunder. The many preschool abuse cases reported in the 1980s—such as Kelly Michaels of the Wee Care Nursery School, the McMartin preschool in Los Angeles, the Little Rascals Day Care Center in North Carolina, and the Montessori School in Reno—resulted in imprisonment for some of the parties and/or disbanding of the schools. Childrens' claims were widely believed, even though they involved such wild and incredible allegations as forcing children to drink the employee's urine and eat her feces, raping children with knives, forks, and Lego blocks, tunneling underground to rob graves, hacking up corpses in front of children, setting children on fire (although no injuries were seen), murdering babies, mutilating animals, and being thrown to the sharks from boats.

Too late to save the lives and businesses of many of the accused, over time it became clear that most if not virtually all of these allegations were actually false, probably the result of coercive interviewing practices employed by psychologists and other investigators who were convinced before the interviews took place that the children had been abused (e.g., Garven, Wood, Malpass, & Shaw, 1998). The school abuse cases, along with the flurry of divorce-related accusations and investigations of sexual abuse spurred researchers to examine the way in which the process of investigating such claims—and in particular, the investigative interviews of police, psychologists, child protection agents, and others—might themselves influence the reports of the children and in some cases lead to false claims of abuse. This research has identified a number of suggestive interviewing practices that lead children to give false reports (Bruck & Ceci, 1999; Ceci & Bruck, 1993): for example, use of suggestive questions, implying that others have verified the abuse, use of positive and negative reinforcements such as praising or criticizing the child's responses, repeating a question until the expected response is obtained, inviting speculation (e.g., "Presuming your father did touch your penis, how would this have happened?"), and use of anatomically correct dolls that encourage children to use the dolls' genitals, whether they have actually been exposed to such behaviors in abusive contexts or not.

Likewise, a wave of cases involving "recovered" memories of childhood sexual abuse among adults spurred researchers to investigate how adults might come to develop false beliefs that they had been abused in childhood. As with the preschool cases, these adult claims of recovered memories of abuse often involved rather fantastic claims, such as abuse by not only parents, but multiple members of the community; and acts of "satanic ritual abuse," such as sexual abuse by members of the cult, ritual sacrifice of babies, and so on. And, as with the preschool cases, many such claims have since been proven false or at least cast into doubt (see Loftus & Ketcham, 1994; McNally, 2003; Ofshe & Waters, 1994 for many such accounts).

Attempting to understand how such dramatic false memories of abuse could be formed, the attention of researchers turned primarily to the role of therapists, their tendencies to *presume* that abuse has occurred even among patients who have no memories of abuse, to directly suggest that patients have been abused and to actively try to persuade their clients the abuse did take place, and the various techniques involved in *recovered memory therapy* that are employed to help clients "recover" repressed memories of abuse. These techniques include therapeutic procedures such as hypnosis, guided imagery, dream interpretation, and others that research has shown to lead to the creation of false memories (Brenneis, 1997; Loftus & Davis, in press; McConkey & Sheehan, 1995; McNally, 2003), and outside activities such as participation in "survivor groups," home writing assignments, and others that serve to maintain the thoughts of the person on the issue of abuse. Essentially these activities serve to convince the patient that abuse is a likely explanation of his or her problems, and to cause the patient to spend so much time thinking about and imagining the abuse that some of these images are eventually mistakenly perceived as memories.

Psychologists tend to be involved in both sides of cases of abuse that are litigated in the legal system. That is, they often perform the interviews or therapy in which abuse is reported, and later provide testimony in court supporting the child's or adult's claim of abuse. To counter these claims, psychologists with expertise in memory and social influence are called to critique the interviewing or therapeutic procedures that elicited potentially false claims or memories. Indeed, the conflict between the clinicians who uncover and treat abuse, and tend to see themselves as "victim advocates," and the research and clinical psychologists who study the potential of the clinician's interviewing procedures and therapeutic techniques to elicit false reports and false memories is one of the hottest areas of controversy in modern psychology (see Loftus & Davis, in press).

PSYCHOLOGISTS AS TRIAL CONSULTANTS

Among the most lucrative of professions in psychology and law is that of "trial consultant." Essentially, the role of trial consultants is one of advocacy, designed to help attorneys obtain the most favorable outcome for their cases. This is done in three major ways.

First, trial consultants may help the attorney to decide whether to take the risk of taking the case to trial. If the case is not sufficiently strong, it may be better to negotiate with the other side to settle the case out of court (as in civil lawsuits) or to plea bargain (as in criminal cases). If the case is to go to trial, the consultant may then offer two additional services—to help attorneys obtain the most favorable trial jury, and to help them plan the clearest and most persuasive presentation of their case. Although these advisory roles are sometimes undertaken without the benefit of *case specific* research, in most cases the trial consultant will conduct case specific jury research that provides the basis of his or her recommendations.

Jury Research Procedures

In most respects jury research is much like marketing research—only the product being "test marketed" is the trial team's side of the case. Essentially, the trial consultant presents a shortened version of the case to a group of "mock jurors" selected from the same population as jurors in the jurisdiction where the case is to be tried. Mock jurors' verdict decisions and reactions to such specifics as individual case issues, case parties, and specific case facts, evidence, and exhibits form the basis of a variety of crucial decisions for the trial team—ranging from whether to take the case to trial or try to settle it out of court, to jury selection preferences, to trial presentation strategy, including presentations of both attorneys and witnesses.

Jury research procedures vary in two general respects: whether the research is conducted via telephone survey versus in person, and the degree of elaboration of the case presentation. The full "trial simulation" form of jury research includes all central elements of the actual trial, and typically requires 1 to 2 full days. Mock jurors first fill out a "profiling" questionnaire, then read or watch the case presentation involving major trial elements (such as opening statements, witnesses for each side, judge's legal instructions, and closing arguments), fill out a "case reaction questionnaire" individually, deliberate to verdicts in groups of trial jury size, and finally, respond to specific questions targeting issues of interest to the trial attorney. Deliberations and responses to the specific questions are videotaped for later study, and used for evaluating one's case and planning trial strategy (see Davis, 1989 for review).

Uses of Jury Research

Case Risk Assessment. Often a major reason for doing jury research is to assess the likelihood of a favorable result in the event the case is taken to trial. Sometimes jury research will reveal that one's client's case is weak, suggesting that better outcomes might be obtained through out of court settlement or plea bargaining.

Trial Presentation Strategy. If the case does go to trial, perhaps the most important use of the jury research is to develop the most effective, persuasive presentation of the case. Jury research provides a literal gold mine of information that helps the trial team to improve the trial presentation. Essentially, the skilled trial consultant helps the attorney to plan a presentation designed to accomplish two main goals: to help jurors understand, process, and remember the trial presentation (particularly the client's side), and to make the presentation as persuasive as possible. This is done by making full use of the research findings of cognitive and social psychologists, which have identified strategies that generally enhance comprehension, memory, and persuasion; and personal presentation strategies that enhance likeability/credibility of attorneys and witnesses.

Research testing the "story model" of jury decision making (Pennington & Hastie, 1993) has shown that jurors tend to construct and adopt a "trial story" that explains what happened, why it happened, who is at fault, and so on. Hence, opening and closing arguments that offer a clear and comprehensive trial story which integrates and explains the evidence are more effective than those presented in other formats. Particularly for the defense, it is crucial to integrate a legal expository presentation with the trial story, which explains how to apply the law to the trial story (Spiecker & Worthington, 2003). Trial consultants use information from the mock jury to help the attorney develop a compelling trial story that incorporates themes that are compelling to jurors, and effectively relates the trial evidence to those themes and elements of the story.

The trial story must also be effectively tailored to the specific jurors who actually end up trying the case. The Simpson defense team's trial story based on racism, evidence tampering, and the invalidity of scientific evidence could only succeed when presented to jurors willing to believe that police would engage in such misconduct. To Black jurors, whose experiences have included racism and unjust treatment from all quarters of society, often including police, such a story could find credibility. But to White jurors, who rarely experience such racism and injustice, it would not. Indeed, although other things also varied between the civil and criminal Simpson trials, differences in the racial composition of the two Simpson juries are widely discussed as responsible for the acquittal in the criminal trial (where the jury included 9 Black jurors) versus the conviction in the civil trial (where the jury included only 1 Black (and 9 Whites)).

Once the trial story is selected, the consultant can also help the attorney present the story in the most comprehensible, memorable, and persuasive fashion. Comprehension, for example, is facilitated by very organized presentations and examinations of witnesses, by simplifying complex ideas and avoiding jargon, and by effective use of lists, charts, and other illustrative visual aids. Memory is enhanced by all the same things that enhance comprehension, as well as through use of interesting examples, by directly relating arguments to jurors' own concerns and experiences, use of verbally vivid language and catchy memorable phrases, such as Simpson's attorney Johnny Cochran's frequently repeated "If the glove doesn't fit, you must acquit!"

The credibility of the trial story is also enhanced through presentations of attorneys and witnesses. Hence, trial consultants make use of what is known about impression management and credibility to enhance the credibility of individual attorneys and witnesses (e.g., Boccaccini, 2002). Since attractive persons are generally perceived as more competent and likeable, the consultant may work with the person to improve appearance. A prosecution mock jury in the Simpson case didn't like prosecution attorney Marcia Clark's hairstyle, for example, and she changed it before trial. Demeanor might also require alteration to convey the desired impression, or, since specific phrasing of testimony may affect impressions of competence or honesty (e.g., O'Barr, 1982), consultants may help attorneys or witnesses use compelling wording. Finally, drawing on a growing body of research regarding how jurors reason about and assess monetary damages (e.g., Greene & Bornstein, 2003) or criminal penalties (e.g., Abwender & Hough, 2001), consultants also help the attorney to incorporate more effective damage presentations into closing arguments of civil trials, or sentencing arguments in the penalty phase of criminal trials.

Jury Selection Strategy

> *Never forget, almost every case has been won or lost when the jury is sworn.*
> —Clarence Darrow (Quoted by Strier, 1999, p. 93)

Trial attorneys widely regard jury selection as the most important, if not decisive phase of trial. True or not, attorneys and trial consultants devote considerable attention to jury selection (see Abbott & Batts, 1999; Davis & Follette, 2004 for reviews of jury consulting services). The two most common jury selection services are: to help the attorney develop *profiles* of jurors likely to be particularly favorable or unfavorable to the attorney's case, and to help the attorneys apply these profiles to the potential jurors from which the trial jury is selected.

During the jury selection phase of the trial, the attorney is confronted with a larger number of prospective jurors than will be seated on the trial jury. These jurors may have responded to pretrial questionnaires in advance of the courtroom process, as in the Simpson trial, and during jury selection they respond to questions posed by the judge and attorneys. Each attorney exerts a specific number of *preemptory challenges* that exclude targeted jurors. The goal is to strike jurors expected to be most biased *against one's side of the case.* Ideally, the remaining jurors will be those most fair and unbiased and well-suited to objectively hear the case. The consultant helps his or her client identify biased jurors and select them for challenge.

These recommendations are based in part on *profiles* developed in jury research. The *jury profiling questionnaire* given to mock jurors addresses demographic characteristics (such as age, race, gender, income, education), and attitudinal, personality, or experiential variables that might predict jurors case reactions. Responses to these questions are later analyzed to see which characteristics actually predict verdict, damage, or sentencing decisions. Profiles also reflect existing research documenting juror characteristics that tend to be associated with known biases in specific kinds of cases. For example, the personality variable "authoritarianism" is associated with antidefendant bias across a wide range of criminal cases (for a review, see Dillehay, 1999; also see Wrightsman, 2001 regarding other personality variables; and Wrightsman, Batson, & Edkins, 2004 for other measures of legally relevant attitudes). Armed with this profile and any information obtained about individual prospective jurors before trial (such as from the pretrial questionnaire if allowed), the consultant accompanies the attorney during the jury selection process, observing jurors as they respond to questions from the judge and attorneys. Based on these observations in open court and any other available information about individual jurors, the consultant offers recommendations about which jurors to exclude via preemptory challenge.

Like some other activities of forensic psychologists, the ethics and effectiveness of scientific jury selection have been challenged (see review by Kovera, Dickinson, & Cutler, 2003). Marcia Clark, for example, openly discussed her negative feelings about trial consultants in her book on the Simpson trial (Clark, 1997), saying she found the use of trial consultants by prosecutors unnecessary and unethical. Ironically, she dismissed trial consultant Don Vinson (among the most experienced consultants) on the second day of jury selection, and disregarded his recommendations (offered pro bono). The defense on the other hand, made full use of the services of Jo-Ellan Dimitrius throughout the entire process from pretrial jury research through the trial and verdict. The jury research of both consultants had shown that Black women were the group least likely to find Simpson guilty (three times more likely to acquit than even Black men; (Kressel & Kressel, 2002). But this finding directly contradicted Marcia Clark's own intuitions that women would be much more offended by Simpson's history of physical abuse of his ex-wife. Black women also tended to find Marcia Clark a pushy, "castrating bitch" (Bugliosi, 1996). Perhaps most importantly, Black men and women were found to be much more receptive to the defense trial story of police incompetence and corruption. Marcia Clark ignored these findings and went with her intuitions, whereas the defense team sought Black women and generally less educated jurors (who had been shown to be less impressed by DNA evidence). In the end, the trial jurors included 10 women, and 9 Blacks out of 12 jurors. Who is to say what role two sides' choices regarding trial consultants' recommendations may have played in the outcome?

CONCLUSIONS

The field of psychology–law offers interesting, exciting careers to young psychologists interested in applying psychology to important practical issues. Indeed, careers in psychology and law are among the fastest growing career opportunities. In order to facilitate such careers, some universities offer joint J.D./PhD programs providing graduates with degrees in both psychology and law (see Kuther, 2004 for review of training requirements and opportunities for consulting in the legal system). Our own years in the legal system have been fascinating and rewarding, stimulating and challenging, and at times frustrating and heartbreaking—but never boring. The legal world is a wonderful place to use psychological knowledge to affect real-world and very significant events. We recommend careers in psychology and law to those willing to face the challenges and heartbreaks of trying to change the world—or at least one life.

REFERENCES

Abbott, W. F., & Batts, J. (Eds.). (1999). *A handbook of jury research.* Philadelphia: ALA-ABA.

Abwender, D. A., & Hough, K. (2001). Interactive effects of characteristics of defendant and mock juror on U.S. participants' judgment and sentencing recommendations. *Journal of Social Psychology, 141,* 603–615.

American Law Institute. (1962). *Model penal code.* Washington, DC: American Law Institute.

Associated Press. (1997, March 17). Psychologist report offers insight to O. J. guardianship. *Lawrence Journal-World,* p. 5A.

Bartol, C. R. (2002). *Criminal behavior: A psychosocial approach* (3rd ed.). Englewood Cliffs, NJ: Prentice-Hall.

Bartol, C. R., & Bartol, A. M. (2004). *Psychology and the law: Theory, research and application.* Belmont, CA: Wadsworth.

Bixenstein, V. E. (1999). Spousal homicide. In H. V. Hall (Ed.), *Lethal violence: A sourcebook of fatal domestic, acquaintance and stranger violence* (pp. 231–257). New York: CRC Press.

Boccaccini, M. T. (2002). What do we really know about witness preparation? *Behavioral Sciences and the Law, 20,* 161–189.

Bowlby, J. (1982). *Attachment and loss: Vol. 1. Attachment* (2nd ed.). New York: Basic Books.

Brenneis, C. B. (1997). *Recovered memories of trauma.* Madison, CT: International Universities Press.

Brown v. Board of Education. (1954). 347 U.S. 483.

Bruck, M., & Ceci, S. J. (1999). The suggestibility of children's memory. *Annual Review of Psychology, 50,* 419–439.

Bugliosi, V. (1996). *Outrage: Five reasons why O. J. Simpson got away with murder.* New York: Island Books.

Ceci, S., & Bruck, M. (1993). Suggestibility of the child witness. *Psychological Bulletin, 113,* 403–439.

Clark, M. (1997). *Without a doubt.* New York: Viking Penguin.

Costanzo, M. (2004). *Psychology applied to law.* Belmont, CA: Wadsworth.

Davis, D. (1989). Flying with radar: Use of mock jury research to target critical issues and fine tune trial strategy. *Inter Alia: Journal of the State Bar of Nevada, 54.*

Davis, D., & Follette, W. C. (2001). Foibles of witness memory for traumatic/high profile events. *Journal of Air Law and Commerce, 66,* 1421–1549.

Davis, D., & Follette, W. C. (2004). Jurors CAN be selected: Noninformation, misinformation, and their strategic uses for jury selection. In W. T. O'Donohue & E. Levinsky (Eds.), *Handbook of forensic psychology* (pp. 781–805). New York: Academic Press.

Davis, D., & Friedman, R. D. (in press). Memory for conversation: The orphan child of witness memory researchers. In M. P. Toglia, J. D. Read, D. R. Ross, & R. C. L. Lindsay (Eds.), *Handbook of eyewitness psychology (Vol. 1): Memory for events.* Mahwah, NJ: Lawrence Erlbaum Associates.

Davis, D., & Leo, R. A. (in press). Strategies for prevention of false confessions. In M. Kebbell & G. Davies (Eds.), *Practical psychology for forensic investigations and prosecutions.* New York: Wiley.

Davis, D., & Loftus, E. F. (in press). Internal and external sources of distortion in adult witness memory. In M. P. Toglia, J. D. Read, D. R. Ross, & R. C. L. Lindsay (Eds.), *Handbook of eyewitness psychology (Vol. 1): Memory for events.* Mahwah, NJ: Lawrence Erlbaum Associates.

Davis, D., & O'Donohue, W. T. (2004). The road to perdition: Extreme influence tactics in the interrogation room. In W. T. O'Donohue & E. Levinsky (Eds.), *Handbook of forensic psychology* (pp. 897–996). New York: Academic Press.

Davis, D., Shaver, P. R., & Vernon, M. L. (2003). Physical, emotional and behavioral reactions to breaking up: The roles of gender, age and attachment style. *Personality of Social Psychology Bulletin, 29,* 871–884.

Dillehay, R. C. (1999). Authoritarianism and jurors. In W. F. Abbot & J. Batt (Eds.), *A handbook of jury research* (pp. 13:11–13:18). Philadelphia: ALA-ABA.

Drizin, S., & Leo, R. A. (2004). The problem of false confessions in the post-DNA world. *North Carolina Law Review, 82,* 891–1007.

Dutton, D. G. (1999). *The abusive personality.* New York: Guilford Press.

Ellsworth, P. C., & Mauro, R. (1998). Psychology and law. In D. T. Gilbert, S. T. Fiske, & G. Lindzey (Eds.), *The handbook of social psychology* (pp. 684–732). Boston: McGraw-Hill.

Faigman, D. L. (1999). *Legal alchemy: The use and misuse of science in the law.* New York: W. H. Freeman.

Fisher, R. P., & Geiselman, R. E. (1992). *Memory enhancing techniques for investigative interviewing: The cognitive interview.* Springfield, IL: Charles C. Thomas.

Fonagy, P.(1999). Male perpetrators of violence against women: An attachment theory perspective. *Journal of Applied Psychoanalytic Studies, 1,* 7–27.

Gado, M. (2002). The career girls murders. *Court TVs Crime Library.* http://www.crimelibrary.com/notorious_murders/not_guilty/career_girls/1.html

Garven, S., Wood, J. M., Malpass, R. S., & Shaw, J. S. (1998). More than suggestion: The effect of interviewing techniques from the McMartin Preschool case. *Journal of Applied Psychology, 83,* 347–359.

Goldstein, A. M., & Weiner, I. B. (Eds.). (2003). *Handbook of psychology: Vol. 11. Forensic psychology.* Hoboken, NJ: Wiley.

Greene, E., & Bornstein, B. H. (2003). *Determining damages: The psychology of jury awards.* Washington, DC: American Psychological Association.

Gudjonnson, G. H. (2003). *The psychology of interrogations and confessions: A handbook.* New York: Wiley.

Hagen, M. A. (1997). *Whores of the court.* New York: Regan Books/HarperCollins.

Henkel, L. A., & Coffman, K. J. (2004). Memory distortions in coerced false confessions: A source monitoring framework. *Applied Cognitive Psychology, 18,* 567–588.

Hess, A. K., & Weiner, I. B. (Eds.). (1999). *Handbook of forensic psychology* (2nd ed.). New York: Wiley.

Kassin, S. M. (1997). The psychology of confession evidence. *American Psychologist, 52,* 320–321.

Kassin, S. M. (in press). Internalized false confessions. In M. P. Toglia, J. D. Read, D. R. Ross, & R. C. L. Lindsay (Eds.), *Handbook of eyewitness psychology (Vol. 1): Memory for events.* Mahwah, NJ: Lawrence Erlbaum Associates.

Kassin, S. M., & Gudjonnson, G. H. (2004). The psychology of confessions: A review of the literature and issues. *Psychological Science in the Public Interest, 5,* 33–67.

Kirkland, K., & Kirkland, K. (2001). Frequency of child custody evaluations complaints and related disciplinary action: A survey of the association of state and provincial psychology boards. *Professional Psychology: Research and Practice, 32,* 171–174.

Kovera, M. T., Dickinson, J. J., & Cutler, B. L. (2003). Voir dire and jury selection. In A. M. Goldstein & I. B. Weiner (Eds.), *Handbook of psychology: Forensic psychology, Vol. 11* (pp. 161–175). New York: Wiley.

Kressel, N. J., & Kressel, D. R. (2002). *Stack and sway.* Boulder, CO: Westview Press.

Kumho Tire Co. Ltd. V. Carmichael. (1999). 526 U.S. 137.

Kuther, T. L. (2004). *Your career in psychology: Psychology and the law.* Toronto, Ontario: Wadsworth.

Leo, R. A. (2001). Questioning the relevance of Miranda in the twenty-first century. *The Michigan Law Review, 99,* 1000–1029.

Llewellyn, K. N. (1931). *The bramble bush.* Dobbs Ferry, NY: Oceana Press.

Lockhart v. McCree. (1986). 106 S. Ct. 1764.

Loftus, E. F. (1986). Ten years in the life of an expert witness. *Law and Human Behavior, 10,* 241–263.

Loftus, E. F. (2002). Memory faults and fixes. *Issues in science and technology (Publication of the National Academies of Science), 18*(4), 41–50.

Loftus, E. F. (2003). Make-believe memories. *American Psychologist, 58,* 864–873.

Loftus, E. F., & Davis, D. (in press). Recovered memories. *Annual Review of Clinical Psychology.*

Loftus, E. F., & Doyle, J. M. (1997). *Eyewitness testimony: Civil & criminal* (3rd ed.). Charlottesville, VA: Lexis Law Publishing.

Loftus, E. F., & Ketcham, K. (1994). *The myth of repressed memory: False memories and allegations of sexual abuse.* New York: St. Martin's/Griffin.

Loftus, E. F., & Palmer, J. C. (1974). Reconstruction of automobile destruction: An example of the interaction between language and memory. *Journal of Verbal Learning and Verbal Behavior, 13,* 585–589.

McCleskey v. Kemp. (1987). 107 S. Ct. 1756.

McConkey, K. M., & Sheehan, P. W. (1995). *Hypnosis, memory, and behavior in criminal investigation.* New York: Guilford Press.

McNally, R. J. (2003). *Remembering trauma.* Cambridge, MA: Belknap/Harvard University Press.

Monahan, J., & Walker, L. (1988). Social science research in law: A new paradigm. *American Psychologist, 43,* 465–472.

Monahan, J., & Walker, L. (1994). *Social science in law: Cases and materials.* Westbury, NY: The Foundation Press.

Mumley, D. L., Tillbrook, C. E., & Grisso, T. (2003). Five year research update (1996–2000): Evaluations for competence to stand trial (adjudicative competence). *Behavioral Sciences and the Law, 21,* 329–350.

Munsterberg, H. (1908). *On the witness stand: Essays on psychology and crime.* New York: The McClure Company.

O'Barr, W. M. (1982). *Linguistic evidence: Language, power, and strategy in the courtroom.* San Diego, CA: Academic Press.

Oberlander, L. B., Goldstein, N. E., & Goldstein, A. M. (2003). Competence to confess. In A. M. Goldstein & I. B. Weiner, (Eds.), *Handbook of psychology: Forensic psychology, Vol. 11* (pp. 335–357). New York: Wiley.

O'Donohue, W. T., & Levinsky, E. (Eds.). (2004). *Handbook of forensic psychology.* New York: Elsevier, Academic Press.

Ofshe, R. J., & Leo, R. A. (1997). The decision to confess falsely: Rational choice and irrational action. *Denver University Law Review, 74,* 979–1122.

Ofshe, R. J., & Waters, E. (1994). *Making monsters: False memories, psychotherapy, and sexual hysteria.* New York: Charles Scribner's.

Otto, R. K., & Heilbrun, K. (2002). The practice of forensic psychology: A look toward the future in light of the past. *American Psychologist, 57,* 5–18.

Pennington, N., & Hastie, R. (1993). The story model for juror decision-making. In R. Hastie (Ed.), *Inside the juror* (pp. 84–115). Cambridge, England: Cambridge University Press.

Spiecker, S. C., & Worthington, D. L. (2003). The influence of opening statement/closing argument organizational strategy on juror verdict and damage awards. *Law and Human Behavior, 27,* 437–456.

Strier, F. (1999). Whither trial consulting: Issues and projections. *Law and Human Behavior, 23,* 93–115.

Tarasoff, v. Regents of the University of California. 108 Cal. Rptr. 878 (Ct. App. 1973); reversed and remanded, 13 Cal. 3d 177 (1974); modified 17 Cal. 3d 425 (1976).

Technical Working Group for Eyewitness Evidence. (1999). *Eyewitness evidence: A guide for law enforcement.* Washington, DC: United States Department of Justice, Office of Justice Programs.

Vidmar, N., Lempert, R., Diamond, S., Hans, V., Landsman, S., MacCoun, R., Sanders, J., Hosch, H., Kassin, S., Galanter, M., Eisenberg, T., Daniels, S., Greene, E., Martin, J., Penrod, S., Richardson, J., Heuer, L., & Horowitz, I. (2000). Amicus Brief: Kumho Tire v. Carmichael. *Law and Human Behavior, 24,* 387–400.

Walker, L. E. A. (1992). Battered woman syndrome and self-defense. *Notre Dame Journal of Law, Ethics, and Public Policy, 6,* 321–334.

Walker, L. E. A. (1993). Battered women as defendants. In N. Z. Hilton (Ed.), *Legal responses to wife assault: Current trends and evaluation* (pp. 321–334). Thousand Oaks, CA: Sage.

Walker, L., & Shapiro, D. L. (2003). *Introduction to forensic psychology: Clinical and social psychological perspectives.* New York: Kluwer Academic.

Websdale, N. (1999). *Understanding domestic homicide.* Boston, MA: Northeastern University Press.

Wells, G. L., Malpass, R. S., Lindsay, R. C. L., Fisher, R. P., Turtle, J. W., & Fulero, S. M. (2000). From the lab to the police station: A successful application of eyewitness research. *American Psychologist, 55,* 581–598.

Wells, G. L., & Olson, E. (2003). Eyewitness identification. *Annual Review of Psychology, 54,* 277–295.

Wrightsman, L. W. (2001). *Forensic psychology.* Belmont, CA: Wadsworth.

Wrightsman, L. W., Batson, A. L., & Edkins, V. A. (2004). *Measures of legal attitudes.* Belmont, CA: Wadsworth.

10

Applying Psychology to Promote Health

Howard S. Friedman
University of California, Riverside

Ideas about close links between people's health and their thoughts, feelings, and behaviors date back thousands of years. For example, Biblical wisdom instructed that "A merry heart does good like a medicine" (Proverbs ch. 17, v. 22), and the ancient Greek medical approach of Hippocrates and his followers observed that the likelihood of disease could be affected by a person's work, nutrition, environment, and natural constitution. By the early 17th century, Shakespeare would invent the term "heart-ache" to capture the links between psychological distress and bodily pain (Hamlet, Act III, Sc. 1), and philosopher René Descartes was puzzling over relations between the mind (or soul) and the physical body. In all societies, in all times, certain individuals are designated to play the role of healer, treating patients using a wide variety of rituals, rites, and remedies (King, 1962). Yet age-old conceptions of distress, disease, behavior, and health were not amenable to scientific analysis until the emergence of psychology and modern biology in the late 19th century.

Unfortunately, once modern biology, modern psychology, and modern health care began to develop, specialization, politicization, and fragmentation separated out natural links between the biomedical and the sociobehavioral aspects of health. For example, surgeons used guilds, educational institutions, laws, and economic power to establish quality, standardization, and control in surgical care, but increasingly narrowed their approach to overall healing. Such fissures were compounded by structural divisions in societal approaches to health and well-being, such as separating internal medicine from psychiatry, psychiatry from psychology, and medicine from public health. Taken together, a number of such factors delayed the emergence of the scientific field called health psychology, which did not take formal shape until the late 1970s (Friedman & Adler, in press; Stone, Cohen, & Adler, 1979).

Today, health psychology is re-integrating social, psychological, cultural, and behavioral aspects with the more physiologic, biochemical, and medical aspects of health and well-being. As an academic discipline, health psychology involves the broadly construed scientific study of psychological processes related to health and health care. As a professional and policy-making field, health psychology uses the findings from basic psychological theory and peer-reviewed research to understand and encourage thoughts, feelings, and behaviors that promote health. Health psychology, building on many disciplines, provides novel pathways for the application of psychology to issues of health.

OVERVIEW OF RESEARCH

Psychological theory and research relevant to health promotion can be usefully divided into three domains. The first concerns the relations among thoughts, feelings, social relations and health. This domain might also be thought of as the relationship between mental and physical health. The second domain involves habits and behaviors that put one at risk or promote one's health. Many things that we do or fail to do have fairly direct links to illness. The third domain is made up of all the ways psychology can help improve medical care. This area includes issues at the level of individual practitioner–patient relations, and more broadly at the level of health care institutions. Although these three domains are often studied separately, in actuality the various aspects of health promotion and disease prevention are closely related, with many overlapping concepts, studies, and applications.

Mental and Physical Health

We are usually not surprised to hear that an aggressive, ultra-competitive businessman, who works as a vice president of sales in a large corporation, has had a heart attack. Similarly, we may worry about the health of a friend who is undergoing a nasty divorce or taking care of a very ill family member. That is, we tend to believe that the changes and challenges we face (which are termed *stressors*) and how we cope with the resulting stress and interpersonal relations will impact health. Indeed major areas of health psychology concern personality and health, coping with stress, and social relations and health.

Health psychologists sometimes pose the key question in this area as one of how psychological and environmental stress gets "under the skin." That is, the focus is on how emotions become neurotransmitters, how perceptions become biochemistries. But I prefer to phrase the question in the traditional way, as one of the interrelations of the mind and the body, or mental and physical health. With this broad approach, more complex (and realistic) links and causal models are especially likely to be considered. For example, it is important to recognize that early biological predispositions and early experiences play a role in the biological and psychological responses later in adulthood. Furthermore, mind and body influences are reciprocal processes.

As with the rest of modern psychology and biology, the foundational investigations in this area began in the 19th century. The work of French physiologist Claude Bernard (1880) focused attention on the stress on the body from emotional activation and made scientific the study of physiology and especially *homeostasis*. These ideas were refined by Walter Cannon, who discovered the relations among stress, the nervous system, and the endocrine system. Cannon (1932) proposed one of the most important concepts in health psychology, the so-called "wisdom of the body." After first studying the biology of digestion, Cannon went on to explore what causes our subjective feelings of a "knot in the stomach" when facing a stressful or fear-arousing situation. He documented that stress causes an increase in the blood sugar level, a large output of adrenaline (epinephrine), an increase in pulse rate, blood pressure, and respiration rate, and an increase in the amount of blood pumped to the skeletal muscles. Cannon called this the *fight-or-flight response*. Cannon explained how the body has the wisdom to exist in a changing social and environmental context in which homeostasis must be maintained, and foresaw that the study of psychophysiology should not ignore the larger issue of coping with environmental stress.

Subsequent research studied the physiological consequences of an ongoing response to threat (Selye, 1956). With sufficient chronic stress there would be disruption of metabolic and immune systems. Within modern neurobiology and psychoneuroimmunology, there is still ongoing debate about the extent to which stress phenomena mostly begin with a general weakening and vulnerability, or instead involve mostly disease-specific disruptions of a particular biological mechanism. In modern terms, there is analysis of how the body adapts to stress using *allostasis*—the ability to achieve stability through change (McEwen, 1998). The processes of allostasis use the autonomic nervous system, the hypothalamic-pituitary-adrenal axis, and the cardiovascular, metabolic, and immune systems to respond to challenge. In the short term, this can enhance functioning. However, when these systems are used frequently to help respond to a lot of stress, the body is damaged.

Psychological processes are critical here because a person's appraisal of the meaning of an event is key to determining if it will be experienced as stressful. An environmental event is not stressful if the individual appraises (interprets) it as manageable (Lazarus, 1966; Lazarus & Folkman, 1984; Taylor, 1998). For example, George Engel (1968, 1977) argued that a "giving up" response in the face of situations of loss may precede the development of various illnesses in individuals who have predispositions to the particular illnesses. Engel combined the environment (e.g., loss), the ability or inability to cope (e.g., giving up), and a set of common biological pathways (e.g., stress hormones) to various health problems.

As researchers overturned the assumption that the body's immune system acted autonomously (without input from the nervous system), the field called psychoneuroimmunology grew in prominence (Ader & Cohen, 1985; Kemeny, in press; Kemeny & Gruenewald, 2000). Psychoneuroimmunology studies how psychological factors affect immunity through the neuro-endocrine system. For example, the immune system can be classically conditioned; that is, the immune system can learn to respond to the environment and will communicate with the nervous system. Together, this research confirms the importance of integrating the biological, the psychological, and the social, both conceptually and empirically. The approach that emerged from the theorizing of Cannon, Selye, Engel, and others has come to be called the *biopsychosocial approach* to health.

Health Promoting Behavior

It is commonly estimated that at least half of all premature deaths in developed countries are directly linked to health-behavioral (lifestyle) factors. Such factors also cause tremendous morbidity (sickness). By far the most important of these is tobacco use. Other significant lifestyle behaviors include excessive alcohol consumption, driving while intoxicated, drug abuse, physical inactivity, poor nutrition (overeating, poor diet), and exposure to sexually transmitted diseases. On the other hand, it is well documented that people who stay fit, eat right, do not smoke, and so on are at significantly lower risk for disease and premature death (McGinnis & Foege, 1993; USDHHS, 2003).

These health promoting or health damaging behaviors are conceptually distinguished from contributors over which individuals seemingly have less control, namely their biological make-up (genes, hormones, physique, etc.) and their infection by noxious microbial agents (such as the influenza virus). Seemingly, you choose what to eat but not whether to inhale a virus. Note that it is implicitly being assumed that people can "decide" whether or not to engage in health damaging behavior, whereas having a disease-prone biological system or being infected by the flu is something we can do little about. Psychological research, however, makes it clear that behavior is more difficult and complicated than simply *deciding* to behave in a healthy or unhealthy manner. This is clear to anyone who has tried to quit smoking or drug abuse (and suffered various withdrawal symptoms); or someone who has made a New Year's resolution to lose weight (and has subsequently regained all the lost weight, as most people do); or someone in an intimate relationship who tries to resist sex drives; or someone who joins a health club and then cannot find sufficient time and energy for that daily workout. In other words, approaches to health promotion traditionally have assumed that people will be healthier once they are educated and convinced about health damaging behaviors, but health psychology has shown that health promotion is actually much more complex.

The Limits of Education. For example, consider the role of education. Common sense suggests that having understandable knowledge about healthy and unhealthy habits and behaviors will significantly improve one's health. This assumption underlies the very common recommendations and calls for "better education" as to health promotion. Unfortunately, education often does not work well, for a variety of reasons. What at first appears to be a series of simple decisions (such as eat right, don't smoke, play sports, avoid TV) turns out to be embedded in habits, peer groups, families, traditions, cultures, and other influences on human behavior.

Consider the case of sexually transmitted diseases (STDs). If a teenager is not sexually active, he or she will not contract an STD. If a teenager is sexually active but conscientiously and properly uses condoms, the risk of STD decreases dramatically. Yet despite the fact that most teenagers know about abstinence and about condoms, there are epidemics of sexually transmitted diseases. Health psychology research shows that targeted interventions that consider such variables as age, gender, skills, and culture can be more effective than general education, but even such focused interventions are not enough (DiClemente et al., 2004). Similarly, almost everyone in Western countries well knows that cigarette smoking is bad for one's health, but yet thousands start smoking every day and smoking remains the largest preventable cause of premature mortality! The issue of smoking is taken up again later in this chapter.

In addition to the basic health-behavioral lifestyle factors just described, there are many specific preventive behaviors that may be developed to prevent particular injuries or diseases. For example, new parents might begin using car seats (with special seat belts) for their infants. Light-skinned people living in sunny climates might be convinced to apply sunscreen (to prevent skin cancer). Measures designed to prevent illness from developing in the first place are termed *primary prevention*. These are distinguished from measures taken once a problem begins to develop, such as interventions to reduce high blood pressure; the latter are termed *secondary prevention* and are considered further in the following section on improving medical care. Here again, education can sometimes help somewhat with preventive behaviors, but dramatic effects require a deeper, more sophisticated, approach to healthy behavior (Friedman, 2002).

Many other things that individuals more or less choose to do might be considered health damaging behavior, although they are not usually considered in this light. For example, if you live in cities with high air pollution like Los Angeles or Houston, your risk of respiratory disease as well as premature death from cardiovascular disease rises. Similarly, if you move to (or do not move away from) high crime neighborhoods in high crime cities like Detroit, Washington, or New Orleans, your risk of being assaulted (and being killed) is much higher than average.

Public Health. It is well known that during the past 100 years or so, life expectancy in developed countries has dramatically increased. Many people wrongly believe however that this dramatic increase is mostly due to miracle drugs and miracle treatments like antibiotics and organ transplants (Ünal, Critchley, Fidan, & Capewell, 2005). Medical "miracle" treatments have indeed sometimes been developed, such as for serious infections, childhood leukemias, and cardiac arrhythmias, but these make a relatively minor contribution to overall health and longevity rates. Rather, the greatest gains have come from measures fittingly termed *public health*. As modern cities and suburbs developed, people obtained safe drinking water, better shelter, flush toilets, trash removal, and more whole (and safety inspected) nutritious food. (Ironically, note that this is right in line with what the ancient Greeks recommended two millennia ago.) On the individual level, hand washing and many other sanitary practices also increased, as people understood the transmission of infectious disease. Finally, vaccination against common but serious childhood infectious diseases reinforced these developing 20th-century trends. Together, these factors produced the dramatic decrease in the death rate from infectious disease (Grob, 1983; McKeown, 1976, 1979).

Understanding the importance of public health, which generally occurs outside the acute-care medical system, is very consequential for health psychology, because it reveals the tremendous importance of behavioral, social, and societal trends and the *relative* unimportance of high tech medicine to the health of the population. Still, it is clear that genetic damage, infection by pathogens, traumatic injury, and exposure to toxins (including pollution and radiation) can severely damage our bodily systems, beyond their ability to easily recover. Sometimes you are injured or sick and need to see a physician and thus enter the medical care system.

Improving Medical Care

Health care should be distinguished from *medical care*, although the two terms are often confused and used interchangeably. Health care, broadly speaking, involves all the things that individuals, families, groups, cultures, and societies do (or fail to do) that impact health. Medical care, in contrast, primarily involves those things done inside the medical care system, usually by physicians or nurses, and usually once one is getting sick or is at substantial risk of getting sick. So, for example, the majority of young adults in Western societies usually need little in the way of medical care. On the other hand, for these young adults to stay well, it is helpful if they live and behave in an environment that has clean air, no smoking, safe driving, little sexually transmitted disease, good nutrition, stable psychosocial relations, and so on. The distinction between health care and medical care is a vital one, on both conceptual and practical grounds, because the medical care system has neither the expertise nor the resources to address the full range of factors relevant to good health.

Within the medical care system, health psychology is making significant contributions to care, particularly in the areas of patient adherence with treatment, doctor–patient communication, adaptation to chronic illness, and the overall medical care environment.

Patient Adherence. Despite spending time, money, and considerable effort to seek medical care, most patients do not fully cooperate with the treatment prescribed by their doctors. This is the problem termed *patient adherence* (or *patient nonadherence*). If the practitioner views his role as a dominant, paternalistic one, the problem is sometimes termed one of *patient compliance*. If the practitioner views his or her role as an advisor on the medical care team, the problem is termed *patient noncooperation*. That is, many patients do not take their medications as prescribed, do not change their activities as instructed, do not return for follow up treatment, and much more.

Although the problem of patient adherence at first appears to be a simple and minor one, extensive research documents that it is a complex and extensive issue. One third or more of all patients do not adhere fully to their prescribed treatment; and depending on the individual, the doctor, the condition, and the treatment regimen, nonadherence rates of up to 80% can be observed (Dunbar-Jacob & Schlenk, 2001).

Various serious, wasteful, and dangerous outcomes result. Most simply, patients may not recover as expected. Sometimes, the condition can be exacerbated, as when a patient stops taking prescribed antibiotics prematurely and a more serious infection then takes hold. Obviously, tremendous medical resources are being wasted when a patient seeks and receives expert treatment but then does not follow through with the pill-taking, exercise, vaccination, dietary changes, or follow-up medical consultations prescribed. Furthermore, when the (nonadhering) patient remains sick, the physician may assume that the treatment is not working and so may increase dosages or add new treatments; or, the disease may then be misdiagnosed. Sociobehavioral scientists, including health psychologists and health sociologists, have investigated and explained this puzzling phenomenon, and have pointed to promising ways to remedy it.

Overall, the reasons for nonadherence can be as complex as human nature itself, but various specific influences can be isolated, studied, and addressed. Many times, patients do not fully understand the diagnosis, the prescription, or how to follow prescribed advice. Health illiteracy is an ongoing problem. Other times, there are financial or practical obstacles to following the medical regimen. For example, many patients cannot afford prescribed treatment (like expensive medications) or cannot leave work or take time out from taking care of their children or elderly parents (to exercise more or to see a specialist). Social and cultural matters can present significant obstacles to following treatments regimens, as when the treatment disrupts or goes against the expectations and traditions of one's family, religion, or subculture (DiMatteo, 2004; Roter & Hall, 1992).

Following doctors' orders may involve substantial changes in habits, recreation, or daily patterns of activity. Remembering to follow the treatment and being able to follow the treatment as prescribed may need the cooperation (assistance, encouragement) of one's spouse, one's boss, one's parent (for young children), one's friends, and so on, and such cooperation is often not fully forthcoming (Tucker, 2002). For example, it is very unlikely that a middle-aged working man with hypertension and incipient heart disease will directly and completely follow a doctor's orders to lose weight, eat much less salt and saturated fat, avoid stressful work, sleep 8 hours a day on a regular schedule, and conscientiously take expensive medications four times a day.

A final important reason for failures of patient adherence involves poor communication between practitioner and patient. This is considered next.

Doctor–Patient Communication. With expert knowledge of such topics as verbal and nonverbal communication, interviewing, and assessment, health psychologists are well-positioned to study and ameliorate some of the most common and stubborn problems in the medical care system. Faulty communication between health care practitioners and patients is dishearteningly common. Study after study shows that many patients do not fully understand what the doctor tells them, do not remember diagnoses and prescriptions, and often exit the clinic confused. Practitioners routinely fail to elicit important information from patients, speak in jargon, assume technical knowledge that the patient does not have, and have differing expectations than their patients.

It is usually not that patients are unintelligent or ignorant; patients can do well when the communication is optimal. However, here are just a few examples of unnecessary medical jargon: a "negative test result" is usually a good (positive) result; a "lesion" can mean any sore whatsoever; and the fancy diagnostic term *idiopathic* means the doctor does not know the cause of the disease or the reason for the condition.

Nonverbal communication—the use of facial expressions, voice tones, touch, and so on—is very important to frame or direct an interview or assessment. Furthermore, nonverbal communication generally conveys important information about feelings, pain, anxiety, embarrassment, trust, concern, and expectations. Yet some physicians look at the chart instead of at the patient, speak in a bored or hurried tone, are unskilled in reading patients' facial expressions and voice tones, and are insensitive to (and fail to observe) information that is being withheld due to embarrassment or fear. On the other hand, physicians who are good at verbal and nonverbal communication generally have more satisfied and better cared-for patients (Friedman, 1982).

A century ago, the prominent medical educator, Sir William Osler (1904), emphasized that a health care professional must listen carefully to the patient, for the patient may actually reveal the diagnosis. Fifty years later, pioneering sex researcher Alfred Kinsey used expert interviewing techniques to uncover a treasure trove of information about human sexuality that was previously unknown. With the proper communication in the optimal doctor–patient relationships, better diagnoses, treatments, and outcomes (in terms of both health and satisfaction) can result (Roter & Hall, 1992).

Adaptation to Chronic Illness. Today, even with serious diseases like heart disease, diabetes, and cancer, most people do not die soon after their illness is diagnosed. Rather, they face a crisis of adjustment to their new condition. In addition, they often will deal with a period of partial impairment and medical treatment that lasts for a long time. That is, they face adaptation to chronic illness. In fact, about half of the U.S. population has at least one chronic health condition such as arthritis, rheumatism, cancer, partial paralysis, cardiovascular disease, Parkinson's disease, depression, AIDS, multiple sclerosis, epilepsy, Alzheimer's, kidney disease, diabetes, asthma, or emphysema.

Health psychologists conduct research on and facilitate interventions for people and their families who are facing chronic illness. Some of these matters are emotional, as people may face anxiety, inadequacy, distress, or alienation. Other issues are more psychological, as successful adjustment often involves preserving a good self-image and a sense of control and effi-

cacy. Still other tasks are social, as a patient must preserve and alter relations with family, friends, and coworkers. Many diseases are stigmatizing in
some cultures or subcultures. Negative reactions by others may be due to
issues of fear, disfigurement, uncertainty, or just plain bias and prejudice.
For example, conditions that are more likely to be stigmatizing include cancer, AIDS, burns, gonorrhea, and various diseases of the brain (Alzheimer's,
stroke, epilepsy, etc.).

Much of the adaptation process is heavily influenced by the presence or
absence of the proper kinds of social support. Social support involves the
processes by which interpersonal relations promote psychological well-
being and protect people from declining health, particularly in the face of
stressful circumstances (Cohen, Gottlieb, & Underwood, 2000). Some support can be helpful, such as when a spouse or friend offers helpful information, reminders (such as to take medication), and unconditional friendship.
Illness support groups (of other people with the same disease) are also often very helpful. On the other hand, some social support can be harmful,
even when well-intentioned, such as when friends either ask too many unwanted questions or pretend that nothing has changed. Good adaptation
requires the structuring of proper social support, that is sensitive to the
particular context of the individual and the illness (Carver et al., 2000;
Revenson, 2001; Stanton & Revenson, in press). Often, people can come to
view their illness in a life-enhancing light and are not less happy than be-
forehand.

Health psychologists and other sociobehavioral scientists have also
been improving medical care by studying and integrating cultural factors. It
is well established that there is variation in the ways symptoms are noticed,
interpreted, and reported across cultures and subcultures (Adler & Stone,
1979; Zborowski, 1952; Zola, 1966). Interestingly, many conditions that are
considered diseases in the United States—ranging from depression to fatigue to hearing voices—are seen as normal or interpreted differently in different cultures (Foster & Anderson, 1978; Kleinman, 1986; Scheff, 1967).

The potential of psychology to improve the medical care environment
has a long but mixed history. Back in 1911, the psychologist Shepherd Ivory
Franz attended a conference on the integration of psychology and medicine
(Franz, 1912, 1913). Franz discussed such issues as the success of placebos,
in which sometimes beliefs are more powerful than the chemical action of
drugs. Yet placebo responses remain poorly understood. Today, almost a
century later, scientists are still calling for the integration of psychology
into medical training and practice. For example, a report from the Institute
of Medicine (Cuff & Vanselow, 2004) explicitly addresses the need for such a
behavioral science curriculum in medical training. Many of these topics are
within the scope of health psychology, including psychosocial contributions to chronic disease; psychosocial factors in pain; modification of

health-relevant behaviors; life-span developmental influences; communication skills; and social disparities in health and illness.

In sum, psychology can be applied to health promotion in three domains: the relations among thoughts, feelings, social relations and health; the behaviors that put one at risk for or promote health; and the various ways psychology can improve medical care, broadly construed. Although these three domains are often studied separately and seen as ancillary to medical care, these aspects of health are closely related to each other; all the pieces are necessary to create and achieve a valid and useful agenda for health promotion. Psychology offers the theories, the concepts, and the research tools to study and apply approaches to health promotion that are outside but complementary to the traditional biomedical approaches to medical care and disease.

HOW HEALTH PSYCHOLOGY RESEARCH CAN AFFECT SOCIETAL HEALTH

Although health psychologists often conduct basic research into fundamental processes relevant to health, it is clear that applications to improve health and prevent illness are never far from the process. Health psychologists generally move back and forth, and back and forth again, between clinical populations and general populations, and lab and field, and individual mechanisms and societal phenomena. Indeed a great strength of the discipline of health psychology involves the multiple levels of study and analysis. This back and forth movement to applications also yields mutual scientific dividends, as results in the laboratory inform approaches in the field, and observations in the field in turn inform the research to be done in the laboratory. Health psychology makes it straightforward to follow exhortations of influential psychologists like Kurt Lewin (1951) and Gordon Allport (1954) to move back and forth between the lab and the field, and between theory and data.

Although it is often assumed that illness can be conquered one disease at a time, or one risk factor at a time, or using one intervention at a time, health is more complicated than that. In other words, it is often assumed, incorrectly, that we need some health psychology to help people lose weight, other health psychology to help people quit smoking, and still other health psychology to promote exercise and friendship and so on and so on. It is often further assumed that we need some health psychology to study heart disease and some health psychology to study cancer, and some other health psychology to study diabetes. It is true that acquiring an in-depth understanding of each problem and condition can be helpful in ameliorating particularly stubborn problems in each of these areas, but it is also true that there are general principles that help health promotion across a wide range of risks, conditions, and diseases (Friedman, 2000, 2003). A good, comprehensive example of the workings of health psychology to promote health concerns the matter of individual differences in health and disease.

Self-Healing Personalities. Who gets sick and who stays well? One of the most fascinating questions in the application of psychology to promote health concerns the issue of what I have termed *disease-prone personalities* and *self-healing personalities* (Friedman 1991/2000, 1998; Friedman & Booth-Kewley, 1987; Friedman & VandenBos, 1992).

For many years, researchers have been studying health psychology disease by disease. For example, some research concerns the effects of emotional states on arthritis and asthma. Other attention focuses on anxiety and stress effects on headaches and ulcers. The Menningers (1936), pioneering and influential psychiatrists, noted that very aggressive and ambitious men seemed prone to heart disease; this and the work of the cardiologists Rosenman and Friedman (Rosenman et al., 1964) on Type A Behavior set off hundreds of studies of psychology and coronary heart disease. How can we make sense of all this? Integrative statistical analyses, called meta-analyses, combine the results of various studies. The results reveal associations between various psychological disturbances (like chronic anger or anxiety or depression) and various diseases (Booth-Kewley & Friedman, 1987; Friedman & Booth-Kewley, 1987; Miller, Smith, Turner, Guijarro, & Hallett, 1996; Smith & Gallo, 2001). In other words, it is not the case that anxiety is related only to ulcers and repression exclusively to asthma. Rather, there is increasing evidence for a generic "disease-prone personality." This line of thinking is confirmed by behavioral and nutritional research that shows that eating fruits and vegetables is not only good for heart health but it also is protective against cancer, helps boost immune responses and so on. Similarly, physical activity is helpful in preventing or slowing the progression of a variety of diseases.

Looking at the other side of the coin, we can uncover people who have psychosocial and behavioral patterns and life pathways that tend to maintain their health. The "Self-healing personality" refers to a healing emotional style involving a match between the individual and the environment, which maintains a physiological and psychosocial homeostasis, and through which good mental health promotes good physical health (Friedman, 1991/2000). Self-healing, emotionally balanced people may be calm and conscientious but are also often responsive, energetic, curious, secure, and constructive. Self-healing personalities have better odds of a longer, healthier life.

Contrary to some common wisdom, a self-healing style does not involve a lack of challenge; many self-healing individuals enthusiastically embrace challenge and are found in socially valued careers. Interestingly, self-healing personalities are often similar to the mentally healthy orientations, involving efficacy and commitment, that have been described by humanistic and clinical psychologists (Antonovsky, 1979; Bandura, 1997; Csikszentmihalyi, 1991; Maddi & Kobasa, 1984). They are often people one likes to be around, consistent with the tie between mental and physical health.

This importance of individual biopsychosocial patterns to health and longevity across long periods of time is well-illustrated by a longitudinal study involving bright California schoolchildren—856 boys and 672 girls—who were born around the year 1910. They were intensively studied on their psychosocial and intellectual development, and then followed throughout adulthood. For the past dozen years, my students, collaborators, and I have been gathering their death certificates, coding their dates and causes of death, and constructing new psychosocial indexes to predict their life pathways to health and longevity (Friedman et al., 1995). A striking finding is that childhood social dependability or "conscientiousness" is predictive of longevity. Children, especially boys, who were rated as prudent, conscientious, truthful, and free from vanity (four separate ratings, which were averaged) live significantly longer throughout the life span. They are about 30% less likely to die in any given year. Personality does indeed predict longevity.

This finding that personality predicts survival across the life span raises many fascinating questions concerning causal mechanisms. Why are conscientious, dependable children who live to adulthood more likely to reach old age than their less conscientious peers? The protective effect of conscientiousness is partly but not primarily due to a reduction in the risk of injury. Although there is some tendency for the unconscientious to be more likely to die a violent death, conscientiousness is also protective against early death from cardiovascular disease and cancer. Furthermore, analysis of unhealthy behaviors such as smoking and drinking shows them to be somewhat relevant as explanatory mechanisms, but a significant effect of conscientiousness remains after controlling for drinking and for smoking and other aspects of personality. In other words, a person who was conscientious as a child is less likely to suffer an early death from injury, and less likely to engage in unhealthy habits, but also stays healthier and lives longer for other reasons as well. In short, a conscientious, dependable personality, in stable psychosocial environments, is a key predictor and may be a central underlying causal factor. This is likely because certain people wind up with healthy habits and behaviors, a balanced socioemotional and psychophysiological style, supportive social interactions, and environments conducive to good health. What are the implications for intervention? Let us consider the case of smoking.

Cigarette Smoking. A particularly good example of how health psychology can help address these complex issues of health promotion (despite their complexity) concerns cigarette smoking in the United States. Over the past four or five decades, since the dangers of smoking were first publicized in the Surgeon General's report of 1964, the percentage of men who smoke cigarettes has declined markedly, by over 50%. But the decline has been gradual, and it has leveled off with about one fourth of men still smoking. If education were the key to promoting health, then most men would have stopped smoking within a decade (by 1975 or so, once the government reports were fully disseminated); none would smoke today since everyone has heard or read of its dangers. In fact, many men did stop smoking soon after 1964 but many more did not, and many young people subsequently took up smoking.

A full accounting of the very substantial but imperfect diminution in smoking cannot be given, but it is very informative to consider the following factors in light of our discussion thus far; all of these factors have been found to play some important role. First, education obviously plays a part, but education is often not a powerful intervention by itself. Second, social pressures by friends and family are very important; many people quit smoking or refrain from smoking because of urgings by their friends or because they identify with a group that does not smoke. Third, taxes, laws, and other government regulations play a role; as tobacco taxes go up and smoking in public is restricted, smoking rates go down. Fourth, advertising plays a part, as antismoking messages are displayed and cigarette advertising is constrained. Fifth, doctors' advice and warnings to their patients can function well in some cases. Sixth, biological elements can be addressed for those people who develop an addiction, such as by prescribing nicotine patches, or nicotine gum, or meditation and exercise. Seventh, efforts can be fruitfully directed at improving the overall mental health of people at high-risk points in their lives, such as the teenage years; it is often the poorly adjusted or immature or abused teenager who turns to unhealthy pathways. Eighth, social environments such as clubs, schools, workplaces, recreational settings, and so on can gradually change; as the general milieu becomes more antismoking, smoking rates fall off more rapidly. In the 1970s, smoking was common throughout most workplaces (including universities), but norms and restrictions gradually changed. All these factors in turn feed related influences (Glantz et al., 1996; Koven, 1996; Turner, Mermelstein, & Flay, 2004; United States Office on Smoking and Health, 1986, 1994; USDHHS, 2003). Note, however, that there will still be many people who, for a variety of as-yet unknown biopsychosocial reasons will continue to engage in health damaging behaviors.

In short, health psychology can be effective in moving people and society away from unhealthy behaviors and toward a self-healing personality, but simple concepts and narrow or isolated efforts are usually insufficient. Overall, we have reason to be optimistic, knowing that our theories and techniques work in many individual cases and are quite effective over time at the societal level. But we also see that we still have a lot to learn and understand.

CAREERS IN HEALTH PSYCHOLOGY

As I have explained, many different forces influence health; so it is not surprising that health psychologists are employed in many different positions. Accomplishment in all of these positions is facilitated by a sophisticated knowledge of the theories and methods of psychology, and an equally sophisticated understanding of the nature of health and disease.

Basic research on health psychology's concepts, methods, and interventions is based in universities. Professors and associated researchers in academic health psychology usually work in psychology departments or in medical schools, where they develop the theories, methods, and analyses that form the basis of the discipline. Health psychology professors may be trained in or specialize in a variety of subfields of psychology, including social psychology, developmental psychology, physiological psychology, and clinical psychology. For example, a developmental health psychologist might study the development of eating patterns during adolescence. Of course, many key approaches are interdisciplinary. For example, my lifespan longitudinal study of the longevity and causes of death of the bright California schoolchildren drew upon: personality expertise to assess individual differences, social expertise to examine social support, developmental expertise to examine pathways, epidemiological expertise to include sociodemographic variables, and medical expertise to code cause of death (Friedman et al., 1995; Tucker et al., 1997). Some universities have programs that combine elements of all of these subfields into more unified health psychology graduate programs, but interdisciplinary collaboration is often equally effective.

Often, clinical health psychologists work directly with individuals facing the challenges of pain or illness. Sometimes, these are clinical psychologists in private practice helping someone with a chronic condition (like chronic fatigue syndrome). But such individual efforts have been limited because health insurance traditionally has been oriented to paying for socalled medical "disorders" (like heart disease or schizophrenia) rather than paying for efforts to help a patient cope with disease or change behavior. So it has been easier for clinical health psychologists to work with patient populations in hospital settings, where the problem is acute. For example, the clinical health psychologist might work on pain control, rehabilitation, or disease-related depression. Increasingly, health psychologists in medical settings serve as consultants to physicians or to researchers of specific clinical phenomena.

In many countries, it is up to the government to promote health in the broad population. Traditionally, governments have focused on clean water, nutritious food, sanitation, childhood inoculations, and control of vectors (rats, mosquitoes). Then, in developed countries, governments turned increasing attention to matters of unsafe driving, violence, and drug addiction and abuse. Most recently, governments have increasingly recognized the societal problems of tobacco, alcohol, obesity, inactivity, and stress. Health psychologists concerned with such matters of health promotion thus often work in government agencies. These may range from county health agencies, which focus on such matters on sexually transmitted diseases or child nutrition; to national public health centers like the Centers for Disease Control and Prevention (CDC), which attempts to promote healthy behaviors and foster safe and healthful environments on a national scale, such as by discouraging smoking and monitoring epidemics.

With limits on what both individual doctors and governments can do, there is increasing presence of health psychology in nonprofit, nongovernmental health organizations. For example, health psychology is relevant in family planning, with such groups as Planned Parenthood. Similarly, there are many AIDS foundations, working to prevent HIV infection and help those infected. On an international level, there are agencies such the World Health Organization (WHO), which is the United Nations specialized agency for health. Note that level of education required for these positions depends on the job. For example, clinic or field workers in an HIV prevention program might have bachelors' degrees, while program supervisors may have masters' degrees, and those designing and researching the programs would have doctoral degrees.

As businesses and other private companies recognize the importance of health promotion to their workforce, health psychologists take up business positions. These might be in occupational safety, employee health promotion, or managing and financing health plans. Finally, of course, some people with training in health psychology go on to obtain further education and employment in the medical field, such as in nursing, occupational therapy, or medical practice. In all of these positions, the most important training involves a rigorous preparation in the relevant concepts and the relevant science, as well familiarity with the specific phenomenon of interest.

CONCLUSIONS

Although psychology has plenty of recommendations to help health promotion efforts, the more significant contribution comes at a deeper level. Our understanding of what it means to be healthy and of how best to stay healthy involves a number of implicit assumptions about health and well-being. Traditional health care generally gives too little attention to the psychological, social, behavioral, and societal aspects of staying healthy and recovering from illness. It turns out that emotions, motivations, habits, cultural beliefs, environments, expectations, and interpersonal relations are key elements of health. The real value of health psychology is in making explicit and then rigorously testing traditional and expanded notions about health and health promotion. Health psychology is not about the "art of medicine"; rather, it is about a science of the art of medicine, and a science of the nature of health (Friedman, 2002).

Because of the many levels of health psychology, health psychologists work in many different settings. Some have careers in academic health psychology (in universities), where they develop the theories, methods, and analyses that underpin the discipline. Others work as clinical health psychologists helping individuals facing the challenges of pain or illness. Still others work in medical schools and hospitals, serving as consultants to physicians and to researchers of specific clinical phenomena.

Health psychologists focused on health promotion often work in government agencies, such as county health agencies, or national public health centers. Or you might find them in nonprofit health organizations, such as in family planning or AIDS amelioration groups, or in world health agencies. Other health psychologists can be found in business related positions, such as in occupational safety, work-site consultation, employee health promotion, or health economics. Success in all of these positions requires a deep knowledge of psychology and its methods, matched by an equally sophisticated understanding of the nature of health.

ACKNOWLEDGMENT

This work was supported by grant AG08825 from the National Institute on Aging. The views expressed herein are those of the author and not those of the NIA.

REFERENCES

Ader, R., & Cohen, N. (1985). CNS-immune system interaction: Conditioning phenomena. *The Behavioral and Brain Sciences, 8*, 379–394.

Adler, N. E., & Stone, G. C. (1979). Social science perspectives on the health system. In G. C. Stone, F. Cohen, & N. E. Adler (Eds.), *Health psychology—A handbook* (pp. 19–46). San Francisco: Jossey-Bass.

Allport, G. W. (1954). *The nature of prejudice.* Cambridge, MA: Addison-Wesley.

Antonovsky, A. (1979). *Health, stress and coping.* San Francisco: Jossey-Bass.

Bandura, A. (1997). *Self-efficacy: The exercise of control.* New York: Freeman.

Bernard, C. (1880). *Leçons de pathologie expérimentale et leçons sur les propriétés de la moelle épinière.* Paris: Librarie J.-B. Baillière et fils.

Booth-Kewley, S., & Friedman, H. S. (1987). Psychological predictors of heart disease: A quantitative review. *Psychological Bulletin, 101,* 343–362.

Cannon, W. B. (1932). *Wisdom of the body.* New York: W. W. Norton.

Carver, C. S., Harris, S. D., Lehman, J. M., Durel, L. A., Antoni, M. H., Spencer, S. M., & Pozo-Kaderman, C. (2000). How important is the perception of personal control? Studies of early stage breast cancer patients. *Personality and Social Psychology Bulletin, 26,* 139–149.

Cohen, S., Gottlieb, S. L., & Underwood, L. G. (2000). Social relationships and health. In S. Cohen, L. G. Underwood, & B. H. Gottlieb (Eds.), *Social support measurement and intervention* (pp. 3–25). New York: Oxford University Press.

Cuff, P. A., & Vanselow, N. (2004). *Improving medical education: Enhancing the behavioral and social science content of medical school education.* Washington, DC: National Academies Press.

Csikszentmihalyi, M. (1991). *Flow: The psychology of optimal experience.* New York: HarperCollins.

DiClemente, R. J., Wingood, G. M., Harrington, K. F., Lang, D. L., Davies, S. L., Hook, E. W. III, Oh, M. K., Crosby, R. A., Hertzberg, V. S., Gordon, A. B., Hardin, J. W., Parker, S., & Robillard, A. (2004). Efficacy of an HIV prevention intervention for African American adolescent girls: A randomized controlled trial. *Journal of the American Medical Association, 292*(2), 171–179.

DiMatteo, M. R. (2004). Social support and patient adherence to medical treatment: A meta-analysis. *Health Psychology, 23*(2), 207–218.

Dunbar-Jacob, J., & Schlenk, E. (2001). Patient adherence to treatment regimen. In A. Baum, T. A. Revenson, & J. E. Singer (Eds.), *Handbook of health psychology* (pp. 571–580). Mahwah, NJ: Lawrence Erlbaum Associates.

Engel, G. L. (1968). A life setting conducive to illness: The giving up-given up complex. *Bulletin of the Menninger Clinic, 32,* 355–365.

Engel, G. L. (1977). The need for a new medical model: A challenge for biomedicine. *Science, 196,* 129–136.

Foster, G. M., & Anderson, B. G. (1978). *Medical anthropology.* New York: Wiley.

Franz, S. I. (1912). The present status of psychology in medical education and practice. *Journal of the American Medical Association, 58,* 909–911.

Franz, S. I. (1913). On psychology and medical education. *Science, 38,* 555–566.

Friedman, H. S. (1982). Nonverbal communication in medical interaction. In H. S. Friedman & M. DiMatteo (Eds.), *Interpersonal issues in health care.* New York: Academic Press.

Friedman, H. S. (1991/2000). *Self-healing personality: Why some people achieve health and others succumb to illness.* New York: Henry Holt, re-published by www.iuniverse.com

Friedman, H. S. (1998). Self-healing personalities. In H. S. Friedman (Editor-in-chief), *Encyclopedia of mental health* (Vol. 3, pp. 453–459). San Diego: Academic Press.

Friedman, H. S. (2000). Long-term relations of personality and health: Dynamisms, mechanisms, tropisms. *Journal of Personality, 68,* 1089–1108.

Friedman, H. S. (2002). *Health psychology* (2nd ed.). Upper Saddle River, NJ: Prentice-Hall.

Friedman, H. S. (2003). Healthy life-style across the life-span: The heck with the Surgeon General! In J. Suls & K. Wallston (Eds.), *Social psychological foundations of health and illness* (pp. 3–21). Boston: Blackwell.

Friedman, H. S., & Adler, N. E. (in press). The history and background of health psychology. In H. S. Friedman & R. C. Silver (Eds.), *Foundations of health psychology.* New York: Oxford University Press.

Friedman, H. S., & Booth-Kewley, S. (1987). The "disease-prone personality": A meta-analytic view of the construct. *American Psychologist, 42,* 539–555.

Friedman, H. S., Tucker, J. S., Schwartz, J. E., Tomlinson-Keasey, C., Martin, L. R., Wingard, D. L., & Criqui, M. H. (1995). Psychosocial and behavioral predictors of longevity: The aging and death of the "Termites." *American Psychologist, 50,* 69–78.

Friedman, H. S., & VandenBos, G. (1992). Disease-prone and self-healing personalities. *Hospital and Community Psychiatry: A Journal of the American Psychiatric Association, 43*, 1177–1179.

Glantz, S. A., Slade, J., Bero, L. A., Hanauer, P., & Barnes, D. E. (1996). *The cigarette papers.* Berkeley: University of California Press.

Grob, G. N. (1983). *Mental illness and American society, 1875–1940.* Princeton, NJ: Princeton University Press.

Kemeny, M. E. (in press). Psychoneuroimmunology. In H. S. Friedman & R. C. Silver (Eds.), *Foundations of health psychology.* New York: Oxford University Press.

Kemeny, M. E., & Gruenewald, T. L. (2000). Affect, cognition, the immune system and health. In E. A. Mayer & C. B. Saper (Eds.), *The biological basis for mind body interactions* (1st ed., Vol. 122, pp. 291–308). New York: Elsevier Science.

King, S. H. (1962). *Perceptions of illness and medical practice.* New York: Russell Sage Foundation.

Kleinman, A. (1986). *Social origins of distress and disease: Depression, neurasthenia, and pain in modern China.* New Haven, CT: Yale University Press.

Koven, E. L. (1996). *Smoking: The story behind the haze.* New York: Nova Science Publishers.

Lazarus, R. S. (1966). *Psychological stress and the coping process.* New York: McGraw-Hill.

Lazarus, R. S., & Folkman, S. (1984). *Stress, appraisal, and coping.* New York: Springer.

Lewin, K. (1951). *Field theory in social science: Selected theoretical papers.* New York: Harper & Row.

Maddi, S. R., & Kobasa, S. C. (1984). *The hardy executive: Health under stress.* Homewood, IL: Dow Jones-Irwin.

McEwen, B. S. (1998). Stress, adaptation and disease: Allostasis and allostatic load. *Annals of the New York Academy of Sciences, 840*, 33–44.

McGinnis, M., & Foege, W. (1993). Actual causes of death in the United States. *Journal of the American Medical Association, 270*, 2207–2212.

McKeown, T. (1976). *The modern rise of population.* London, England: Edward Arnold.

McKeown, T. (1979). *The role of medicine.* Princeton, NJ: Princeton University Press.

Menninger, K. A., & Menninger, W. C. (1936). Psychoanalytic observations in cardiac disorders. *American Heart Journal, 11*, 1–21.

Miller, T. Q., Smith, T. W., Turner, C. W., Guijarro, M. L., & Hallett, A. J. (1996). A meta-analytic review of research on hostility and physical health. *Psychological Bulletin, 119*, 322–348.

Osler, W. (1904). *The master-word in medicine. Aequanimitas and with other addresses to medical students, nurses, and practitioners of medicine* (pp. 369–371). London: H. K. Lewis.

Revenson, T. A. (2001). Chronic illness adjustment. In J. Worrell (Ed.), *Encyclopedia of women and gender, Vol. 1* (pp. 245–256). San Diego: Academic Press.

Rosenman, R. H., Friedman, M., Straus, R., Wurm, M., Kositcheck, R., Hahn, W., & Werthesson, N. (1964). A predictive study of coronary disease. The western collaborative group study. *Journal of the American Medical Association, 189*, 103–110.

Roter, D. L., & Hall, J. A. (1992). *Doctors talking with patients/patients talking with doctors: Improving communication in medical visits.* Westport, CT: Auburn House.

Scheff, T. J. (Ed.). (1967). *Mental illness and social processes.* New York: Harper & Row.

Selye, H. (1956). *The stress of life.* New York: McGraw-Hill.

Smith, T. W., & Gallo, L. C. (2001). Personality traits as risk factors for physical illness. In A. Baum, T. A. Revenson, & J. E. Singer (Eds.), *Handbook of health psychology* (pp. 139–174). Mahwah, NJ: Lawrence Erlbaum Associates.

Stanton, A. L., & Revenson, T. A. (in press). Progress and promise in research on adjustment to chronic disease. In H. S. Friedman & R. C. Silver (Eds.), *Foundations of health psychology.* New York: Oxford University Press.

Stone, G. C. F., Cohen, F., & Adler, N. E. (Eds.). (1979). *Health psychology—A handbook.* San Francisco: Jossey-Bass.

Taylor, S. E. (1998). Positive illusions. In H. S. Friedman (Ed.), *Encyclopedia of mental health* (Vol. 3, pp. 199–208). San Diego: Academic Press.

Tucker, J. S. (2002). Health-related social control within older adults' relationships. *Journals of Gerontology Series B: Psychological Sciences and Social Sciences, 57,* 387–395.

Tucker, J. S., Friedman, H. S., Schwartz, J. E., Criqui, M. H., Tomlinson-Keasey, C., Wingard, D. L., & Martin, L. R. (1997). Parental divorce: Effects on individual behavior and longevity. *Journal of Personality and Social Psychology, 73,* 381–391.

Turner, L., Mermelstein, R., & Flay, B. (2004). Individual and contextual influences on adolescent smoking. *Annuals of the New York Academy of Sciences, 1021,* 175–197.

Ünal, B., Critchley, J. A., Fidan, D., & Capewell, S. (2005). Life-years gained from modern cardiological treatments and population risk factor changes in England and Wales, 1981–2000. *American Journal of Public Health, 95,* 103–108.

USDHHS (United States Department of Health and Human Services). (2003). *Prevention makes common "cents."* Washington, DC: USDHHS.

U.S. Office on Smoking and Health. (1986). *Smoking and health, a national status report: A report to Congress.* Rockville, MD: U.S. Dept. of Health and Human Services, Public Health Service, Centers for Disease Control, Center for Health Promotion and Education.

U.S. Office on Smoking and Health. (1994). *Preventing tobacco use among young people: A report of the Surgeon General.* Atlanta, GA: U.S. Department of Health and Human Services, Public Health Service, Centers for Disease Control and Prevention, National Center for Chronic Disease Prevention and Health Promotion.

Zborowski, M. (1952). Cultural components in responses to pain. *Journal of Social Issues, 8,* 16–30.

Zola, I. K. (1966). Culture and symptoms: An analysis of patients presenting complaints. *American Sociological Review, 31,* 615–630.

11

Cognitive Psychology: Applications and Careers

Kathy Pezdek
Claremont Graduate University

Kenneth A. Deffenbacher
University of Nebraska at Omaha

Shirley Lam
Claremont Graduate University

Robert R. Hoffman
Institute for Human and Machine Cognition

Psychological research is often conceptualized as being either basic research or applied research. Basic psychological research, usually laboratory based, is conducted to gain a scientific understanding of human behavior, often primarily for the purpose of advancing relevant theories. Applied psychological research is conducted for some additional reasons: to gain a scientific understanding of human behaviors that occur in work and everyday life, or to solve practical problems encountered in daily pursuits. In this chapter, historical and current trends in cognitive psychology research are presented to demonstrate the rich tradition of applied research in this specific field of psychological research.

Cognitive psychology is the study of human intelligence and how it works. This includes the study of thinking, reasoning, problem solving, decision making, memory, language, perception, and attention. Cognitive psychology research is well known for its strong theoretical base. Whether inductively (theory is derived from data) or deductively (the theory comes first and the empirical test follows), cognitive psychology research is strongly linked to theory. However, it is an oversimplification to categorize cognitive psychology as basic research, from which few applications have been derived. Furthermore, it is a fact that many cognitive psychologists work in industry, educational settings, and the private sector (e.g., human factors consulting firms). From psychology's early days to the present, there has been an interest in applications. The first President of the American Psychological Association (APA), G. Stanley Hall, conducted applied research, especially on topics in human development. Few realize that he was also the founder of the APA journal, *Journal of Applied Psychology* in 1917. The rich history of research in applied cognitive psychology is reviewed in more detail by Hoffman and Deffenbacher (1992).

The primary purpose of this chapter is to dispel the myth that cognitive psychology research is primarily basic research that has little applicability to real-world problems. This chapter briefly focuses on five domains of applied cognitive psychology. Each of these is a domain in which there is a rich history of research and in which a significant number of cognitive psychologists are currently employed outside of academia. The domains to be discussed are forensic psychology, marketing and advertising, education, the military, and human factors. Within each domain, a brief history of cognitive psychology research on this topic is discussed, some of the current work on this topic is presented, and examples of careers in this field are provided.

FORENSIC APPLICATIONS OF COGNITIVE PSYCHOLOGY

There are numerous forensic applications of cognitive psychology. In this chapter we focus on two of these, eyewitness identification and deception detection.

Eyewitness Identification

One of the most prominent psychologists prior to World War I was Hugo Munsterberg. Munsterberg received a PhD in physiology under Wilhelm Wundt, the founder of psychology as a science, and then obtained an M.D. degree. William James recruited Munsterberg to Harvard where in 1908, they established the Division of Applied Psychology. There he was engaged in research in many areas of applied psychology including advertising, film criticism, and legal psychology. Today, Munsterberg is especially well remembered for his work on psychology and law. In his book, *On the Witness Stand* (Munsterberg, 1908), he presented research demonstrating the unreliability of eyewitness perception and memory and argued that scientific psychology had much to offer the legal community.

Attorneys and legal scholars were outraged with Munsterberg's suggestion that legal decisions should in any way be influenced by psychological research. Moore (1907), for example wrote, "Among the legal profession it is familiar learning that experiments are valuable only when the conditions are fairly identical with those attending the occurrence under investigation. . . . Imagine him (Munsterberg) butting in with his so-called scientific experiments to appraise the testimony of a witness" (p. 127). There was a deep-rooted tension between legal procedures and scientific methods, and attorneys and judges were not keen on changing their procedures. In fact, the records of American courts indicate that psychological research was not cited, nor did psychologists provide expert witness testimony, until the 1950s (Loh, 1981), and even then it was on topics of mental disorders, pretrial publicity, and civil rights, not on the veracity of eyewitness memory.

Today, the legal community has a somewhat more favorable view of psychological research in general, and specifically, of research on eyewitness memory. There are several reasons for this change. First, it is now clear that the information on eyewitness memory provided in expert testimony has "general acceptance"[1] among psychologists (Kassin, Tubb, Hosch, & Memon, 2001). The consensus within the field of psychology regarding the standards of scientific proof has aided in the acceptance of this research in legal contexts. Second, it is now well established that errors in eyewitness identification are responsible for more cases of wrongful conviction than all other causes combined (Wells et al., 2000). Third, although police and the judicial system have no control over the personal and situation-specific factors connected to a crime, they can control the manner in which eyewitness memory is tested, whether by interview or lineup. Researchers have determined that some methods of assessing witness memory are likely to promote incomplete or inaccurate recall or false identifications of innocent suspects (Wells et al., 2000). The quality and quantity of their research has been such that the U.S. Department of Justice has issued a set of national guidelines for the collection of eyewitness evidence in criminal cases (Technical Working Group for Eyewitness Evidence, 1999). Applied cognitive psychology research provided the scientific basis for the content of these guidelines, and some of the researchers actually participated in writing them.

Finally, sufficient reliable evidence has accumulated in the past 30 years that we now have a much clearer understanding of how the personal and situation-specific variables operate on memory with respect to crime (Cutler & Penrod, 1995). These variables include the duration of time the witness had

---

[1]According to the Frye test, scientific evidence can be presented in court by an expert witness only if it is "sufficiently established to have gained general acceptance in the particular field in which it belongs" (*Frye v. United States*, 1923, p. 1014).

to view the perpetrator, the amount of time between the occurrence of the crime and the testing of the witnesses' memory, the level of stress experienced by the witness during the encoding of his or her memories of the crime, and whether the witness and perpetrator were of different races.

As a consequence of the explosion of eyewitness memory research, it has become common for eyewitness memory researchers to testify as expert witnesses. In fact, in the frequently cited decision of *People v. McDonald*, 1984, the Court wrote,

> When an eyewitness identification of the defendant is a key element of the prosecution's case but is not substantially corroborated by evidence giving it independent reliability, and the defendant offers qualified expert testimony on specific psychological factors shown by the record that could have affected the accuracy of the identification but are not likely to be fully known to or understood by the jury, it will ordinarily be error to exclude that testimony. (p. 254)

An expert witness is an individual with special knowledge or expertise who can assist jurors in evaluating the facts of a case. Expert witnesses are usually retained by one side—either the defense or the prosecution. Most cognitive psychologists who testify as eyewitness expert witnesses do so as consultants, as have the first two authors of this chapter; they have an academic position and qualify as expert witnesses based on their publication record. Eyewitness experts are permitted to testify about general factors that are known to affect the accuracy of eyewitness evidence; they are not ordinarily permitted to testify about the facts in the specific case in which they are testifying, or the memory ability of specific eyewitnesses. This is to prevent the expert witness from "invading the province of the jury," a legal cliché that refers to taking over the role of the jury in determining the outcome of any trial.

Detecting Deception

Throughout history people have sought effective ways to detect deception. During the Middle Ages, Germans used excruciating torture techniques to elicit confessions from the accused, but then, ironically, had priests and clerics witness the confessions to determine if they were true confessions or not. False confessions were punishable by death; true confessions were not. The success of these early deception detection techniques will never be known. The scientific quest for behavioral indicators of deceit has become more rigorous in the past few decades (see DePaulo et al., 2003, for a review of this work). This may be due in part to an upsurge of highly publicized cases involving inaccurate assessment of truth and deception. For example, in the Central Park jogger case, five young men (aged 14–16) confessed to assaulting and raping a jogger. According to Kassin (2002), who reviewed videotaped confessions, the young men appeared truthful and their narratives were particularly compelling because they were detailed and seemingly the product of personal experience. The young men were convicted and sent to prison based on this confession evidence alone. Thirteen years later, someone else confessed to the crime. DNA evidence subsequently proved the young men innocent; they had been coerced into falsely confessing by police investigators' leading techniques. (See Kassin, 1997, for a discussion of the psychology research on false confessions.) Are there cues that effectively differentiate between descriptions of true and false events—even self-incriminating confessions?

Deception detection is a "hot topic" in applied cognitive psychology now because although there exist three classes of forensic techniques for detecting deception, the empirical support for each of these is mixed. There is clearly room here for additional research and the development of more valid forensic techniques for detecting deception.

The first forensic tool for detecting deception is the polygraph. The assumption underlying the use of the polygraph is that compared to truthtellers, liars will show differential patterns of specific physiological reactions. However, a number of researchers have questioned the scientific support for the correlation between deception and physiological reactions (Iacono, 2001; Lykken, 1998). According to these critics, physiological reactions shown in a polygraph test can also be the result of an innocent person's anxiety about being the subject of an investigation. A blue ribbon panel appointed by the National Research Council recently reviewed the scientific evidence on the polygraph and concluded that the polygraph is not a valid technique for detecting deception (CRSEP, 2002).

The second forensic tool for detecting deception involves observing people's nonverbal behaviors—gestures, eye contact, smiling, facial musculature movement, and blinking—while they describe events. It has been proposed that whereas verbal behavior is not automatically processed, nonverbal behavior is automatically processed. As such, nonverbal behaviors associated with lying should be more difficult to mediate cognitively, and thus should be more revealing of deception. In two recent reviews of the psychological research on detecting deception, DePaulo et al. (2003) and Vrij (2000) reported that a number of nonverbal behaviors can be effective in detecting deception. However, there is a great deal of inconsistency in findings among these studies, and it appears, for example, that many nonverbal behaviors may be effective in identifying lies only when the lies are more difficult to tell.

In the 1950s the Supreme Court of Germany ruled that credibility assessment must be conducted in all contested cases of child sexual abuse and expert testimony on the findings must be provided to the court (Undeutsch,

1989). This served as a serious call to action for forensic psychologists. The third deception detection approach, the Criterion-Based Content Analysis (CBCA), followed from this call. The CBCA, was developed in Germany in the 1950s by Udo Undeutsch (see Undeutsch, 1989). It is an important deception detection technique because it is reported to be the most widely used veracity assessment technique worldwide (Vrij, Akehurst, Soukara, & Bull, 2002). The main assumption of this approach is that narratives of deceptive accounts differ qualitatively from those of truth-tellers; they will include, for example, more details, more superfluous details, and more contextual embedding. Although empirical tests of the validity of this content analysis technique have not been impressive (Lamb et al., 1997; Pezdek et al., 2004; Vrij, 2005), some of the features in this technique have proven to be effective discriminating between true and deliberately fabricated accounts. Of interest for cognitive psychologists is that fact that the most discriminating features are those that tap memory processes and cognitive characteristics that have also been effective in discriminating between real versus imagined event memories (Johnson, Foley, Suengas, & Raye, 1988).

Detecting deception is a practical real-world problem. Clearly there is a need to develop tools to detect deception more effectively, and cognitive psychologists are ideally suited for this task. Whether those who work on deception detection are employed by police departments, government agencies such as the FBI, or universities, cognitive psychology research will eventually make a significant contribution to solving this practical problem.

COGNITIVE PSYCHOLOGY APPLIED TO MARKETING AND ADVERTISING

Since the early 1900s, psychologists have successfully promoted the applicability of their research to business consumers. The psychology of advertising can be traced to the turn of the century, when H. S. Gale lectured at the University of Minnesota and demonstrated principles of perception and attention using advertisements (Gale, 1900). Around that same time, Walter Dill Scott took up the psychology of advertising while at Northwestern University. The field of advertising was experiencing a period of rapid growth and an increasing number of advertisers came to believe that psychology could help them influence people's thoughts and behaviors. In 1901, Scott was asked by an advertising executive to present some lectures to business groups on advertising and public speaking. These talks were published in advertising magazines as well as in a series of six articles in *Psychological Bulletin* published between 1911 and 1916, and in his two early books (Scott, 1903, 1907). Later, Scott (1910) broadened his area of study and published a more general book on the psychology of business.

Munsterberg's applied interests also included the psychology of advertising. In his book *Business Psychology*, Munsterberg bridged a gap between psychological science and the business world, explaining that "really to understand mental conditions in business means to understand the structure and function of the mind" (Munsterberg, 1917, p. 25). He addressed topics such as the "prevailing prejudice against applied psychology," and also discussed theories of perception, memory and attention and their application to business.[2]

Since the early 20th century, many market researchers and advertisers have embraced the methods, concepts, and theories from cognitive psychology. The fields of marketing and advertising—really interdisciplinary fields—have benefited a great deal from the inclusion of cognitive psychology research. The application of cognitive psychology to survey methodology is just one area that has strongly influenced market research. A prime example is Sudman, Bradburn, and Schwarz's book, *Thinking About Answers: The Application of Cognitive Process to Survey Methodology* (1996), which provides guidelines for producing better survey instruments by understanding the factors that influence respondents' answers.

Through the application of cognitive research, market researchers have developed procedures for how to conceptualize, design, and implement surveys that increase the ease with which respondents answer questions. Survey designers need to take into account such factors as the order of questions, context effects, and the specificity of a question. For example, instead of asking demographic information (e.g., age, ethnicity, and income) at the beginning of a survey, it may serve well to ask these personal questions later on, after the respondent feels invested and is more likely to complete the survey and less likely to leave questions blank. The field of marketing has adapted tools and techniques from cognitive psychology in other areas as well, such as in the development of interviewing methods (Bradburn & Sudman, 1979), questionnaire design (Schuman & Presser, 1981), and protocol analysis (Ericsson & Simon, 1993).

The study of consumers' unconscious processes has been a hot topic in marketing and advertising research. Although consumers engage in decisive, conscious processing of information in advertisements, unconscious information processing occurs as well. The research on unconscious processing is grounded in the empirical literature on implicit learning and memory (Krishnan & Trappey, 1999). Researchers in this area assess how consumer behavior is affected by the information that is processed without awareness (Bargh, 2002).

With the publication of Vance Packard's (1957) best selling book, *The Hidden Persuaders*, Americans became intrigued with the notion that they were

---

[2]For a complete review of psychology of marketing and advertising leading up to the 1940s, see Poffenberger (1942).

pervasively being influenced by subliminal stimuli. A conspiracy theory even emerged that movie theatres were using subliminal messages presented on the screen as an advertising ploy to drive up profits at concession stands. Later, self-help tapes were sold with the promise that you could stop a bad habit just by listening to a tape while you slept. However, cognitive researchers have debunked this urban legend of subliminal brainwashing. Studies experimenting with display times, auditory messages, and nonsense versus "real" subliminal messages revealed that subliminal perceptual effects were minimal, if present at all (Moore, 1982).

There are many examples of cognitive psychologists who have conducted basic research and are now turning their attention to applied problems in marketing and advertising. For example, Richard Harris, a leader in the area of basic psycholinguistic research on memory and comprehension of metaphor, has also conducted research on people's memory for advertising (Harris, Dubitsky, Perch, Ellerman, & Larson, 1980; Harris, Trusty, Bechtold, & Wasinger, 1989). This research assessed people's ability to remember whether statements from advertisements were merely implied or explicitly asserted. Results suggest that people generally do not remember whether an advertisement asserted a statement concerning a product's performance (e.g., Tylenol *stops* headaches) or merely implied this claim (e.g., Tylenol *helps reduce* headaches). Also, memory for advertisements may change over time, generally from remembering a weak implied claim to believing that the product will perform much better than was actually stated.

It has also been useful for cognitive psychologists to take an information-processing approach to considering how viewers process marketing and advertising information. For example, it is important to know how to attract and maintain viewers' attention, how much information viewers are able to process in a specific period of time, and how to communicate information so that it is likely to be remembered over time. According to James Bettman's information-processing model of consumer choice (Bettman, 1979), consumer choice results directly from a consumer's motivations, information acquisition, and processing capacity.

One application of the information-processing approach is found in research concerning consumers' processing of brand information. Richardson, Dick, and Jain (1994) examined consumer loyalty to national brands over store brands despite product similarity and higher prices for national brands. To evaluate brand loyalty, the researchers compared participants' responses to national brand and store brand products in terms of their extrinsic characteristics (e.g., price, packaging, brand name—attributes that are not physically a part of the product) and intrinsic characteristics (e.g., ingredients—attributes that are physically a part of the product). They reported that consumers chiefly processed extrinsic rather than intrinsic product information.

In addition to market and advertising research concentrating on increasing consumption, the principles of marketing and advertising have also been applied to promoting prosocial causes and marketing health and social programs. For example, researchers have examined how media can be used to favorably change society's attitudes toward gays and lesbians (Riggle, Ellis, & Crawford, 1996). It was reported that viewing videos depicting events surrounding a gay protagonist can have positive impact on participants' attitudes toward homosexuals in general. Similarly, Crano and his colleagues (cf. Dawson, Burgoon, & Crano, 2003) have implemented an effective media program to inform school-age children about AIDS prevention. Crano has also evaluated the effectiveness of the television advertisements used in the National Youth Anti-Drug Campaign launched by the 1998 White House Office of National Drug Control Policy. Many federal agencies, such as the National Institute on Drug Abuse (NIDA), the Food and Drug Administration (FDA) and the Centers for Disease Control and Prevention (CDC) employ cognitive psychologists as part of market research and advertising teams to promote a variety of programs. The media interventions described by Albert Bandura in chapter 3 in this volume are also relevant examples of how marketing and advertising research can be productively applied to improve the condition of people.

EDUCATIONAL APPLICATIONS OF COGNITIVE PSYCHOLOGY

Some of the earliest research in applied psychology involved educational applications. Ebbinghaus (1885), well known for his seminal memory experiments, was also interested in the development of intelligence and school psychology. Along these lines he conducted experiments on the memorization of poetry, then a common classroom task (Hoffman, Bringmann, Bamberg, & Klein, 1987).

It is interesting to note that the APA journal, *Journal of Educational Psychology*, was founded in 1916, one year prior to the founding of the *Journal of Applied Psychology*. In its first year, the *Journal of Educational Psychology* published a lively symposium on "Mentality Tests" (1916). The contrasting views of Alfred Binet and Robert M. Yerkes were published as part of this symposium. Alfred Binet and Theophile Simon (1905a, 1905b) worked for the French Ministry of Public Instruction and developed mental tests for school children. They introduced the concept of "mental age," the precursor of the construct, intelligence. G. Stanley Hall is well known as a founding figure in developmental psychology in North America. His book, *Educational Problems* (1911), provides a two-volume discussion of a wide range of educational topics to which he felt psychology could contribute.

Cognitive psychology naturally lends itself to numerous applications in education. Today, research on teaching mathematics and reading stand out as domains where cognitive psychology research has advanced educational practice. Many cognitive psychologists are working on these domains in both academic and applied settings.

Mathematics Instruction

Two facts have become clear to researchers and educators who study mathematics instruction in the United States. First, the basic level of mathematics achievement in this country has declined over recent decades. And second, mathematics achievement of Japanese and Chinese students far exceeds that of U.S. students. Harold Stevenson and James Stigler with their colleagues (Stevenson et al., 1985) administered mathematics tests to first and fifth graders in 120 classrooms in Taipei (Taiwan), Sendai (Japan), and the Minneapolis (U.S.) metropolitan areas. The tests required computation and problem-solving skill. They found that the highest-scoring classrooms in the United States obtained an average score lower that that of the lowest-scoring Japanese classroom and all but one of the 20 classrooms in Taipei. These findings compelled Stevenson and Stigler (1992) to investigate the cultural differences and features of classroom instruction that might account for these trends. Their research teams systematically observed classrooms in each of these three countries. They identified classroom differences associated with cognitive processing advantages for the Asian students. These include, for example, the finding that Asian lessons are more coherent, they are more likely to be motivated by a practical problem, and lessons are oriented toward problem solving rather than rote learning.

Looking at mathematical achievement at the level of the individual, educators have increasingly realized that mathematics achievement can be remedied by understanding the cognitive processes underlying mathematical thinking. For example, Resnick (1984) demonstrated that novices who make mistakes do not do so at random. Every mathematical problem solver has a mental model for how to solve a specific type of problem, and they use this mental model in deriving a solution. A novice problem solver is likely to have an incorrect or imperfect mental model that they apply to solve a problem (Chi, Feltovich, & Glaser, 1981). By analyzing the types of mathematical errors made by students, one can understand the nature of the mental model they are utilizing, diagnose their cognitive processing errors, and then remediate their procedural solutions. Much of the cognitive research on mathematics is of this type. John Seely Brown and Richard Burton, working in the 1970s at Bolt Beranek and Newman, developed the earliest diagnostic models for debugging students' procedural errors in basic mathematics (Brown & Burton, 1978). In terms of considering sources of funding available for applied cognitive research, it is interesting to note that their research was funded both by the Army Research Institute and the Navy Personnel Research and Development Center.

Reading

Teaching and learning reading is another educational domain in which there has been a substantial contribution by cognitive psychologists. Reading is a paradox. For adults who read well, reading is an apparently effortless activity. However, for many children, learning to read is a difficult and very effortful process. Reading with an alphabetic writing system such as ours involves learning letter-to-sound and letter-to-meaning correspondences. And although an alphabetic writing system is economical, learning to read English is difficult because the phonemes in English can be represented in multiple ways; each vowel sound is not coded with a unique symbol. For example, the vowel sound in *bat* is about the same as that in *laugh*. In American English, there are more than a dozen vowel sounds but only five vowel letters (*a, e, i, o,* and *u*). Thus, each vowel letter can be pronounced multiple ways.

Learning to read involves cognitive, linguistic, and social skills that develop from early childhood. The most important of these is a child's language competence. Most of the language skills prerequisite to reading develop prior to preschool. For example, knowledge of grammar develops rapidly and the basic syntactic structures of language are learned by age 2 (Bloom, Barss, Nicol, & Conway, 1994).

Two approaches have been taken by cognitive psychologists researching the process of learning to read—stage theories and nonstage incremental theories. There are a number of stage theories of reading, each specifying sequential steps involved in learning to read (e.g., see Gough & Juel, 1991). Each stage theory of reading begins with a visual association stage, in which a child learns the association between the visual features of letter sequences and sounds. The last stage of reading involves associating strings of words to their sounds and meanings. Alternatively, recent incremental theories propose that reading involves many types of knowledge that are gradually acquired (see Perfetti, 1992). According to incremental reading theories, what appear to be stages or qualitative shifts in reading strategies result not from progressive stages, but from changes in the complexity and quantity of the information acquired.

There are important implications for teaching reading from the cognitive research on this topic. The major instructional methods that have traditionally been used to teach reading have been *whole-word* and *phonics* instruction. The cognitive research clearly suggests a disadvantage for the *whole-word* approach, and this has been confirmed by assessments of reading instruction programs (Foorman, Francis, Fletcher, Schatschneider, & Mehta, 1998). A more recent approach to teaching reading is called *whole-language* instruction. The *whole-language* approach involves teaching language meanings that focus on language experiences of the child. For example, the child dictates short stories that are transcribed and is then taught to read the stories. This approach has been adopted in numerous school districts throughout the United States. Although *whole-language* instruction helps to make reading fun and meaningful for children, the research clearly suggests that children become more skilled independent readers if they are also taught alphabetic and phonemic principles (Rayner, Foorman, Perfetti, Pesetsky, & Seidenberg (2001).

Many cognitive psychologists work in educational settings. The most common opportunity for such applied work is doing program evaluation research for school districts. Most large school districts and all State Departments of Education employ researchers to do program and outcome evaluations, for example, as educational research analysts for district initiatives and to evaluate school reform programs for underperforming schools. Cognitive psychologists are especially well trained for such positions. Cognitive psychologists also work for companies such as Educational Testing Service and other companies that produce educational materials. Finally, many cognitive psychologists conduct research on educational issues in academic and applied research settings. This research is often funded by the traditional funding sources such as the U.S. Department of Education, as well as by the research divisions of the branches of the armed services.

APPLICATIONS OF COGNITIVE PSYCHOLOGY TO THE MILITARY

The entry of the United States into World War I in 1917 prompted major undertakings on the part of psychologists. Psychologists helped solve some of the practical problems created by a sudden and massive mobilization of the armed forces and their adoption of new technology such as airplanes and submarine hydrophones (sonar). One of the most notable successes in applying psychology to the needs of the military was the development of a means for testing the mental abilities (intelligence) of approximately 1,700,000 recruits by war's end.

The U.S. Army needed a means to select and evaluate recruits in the armed forces. In particular they wanted to be able to identify individuals with mental deficiencies, to classify them by their intelligence level, and to select those for special training (officers, for instance). In the interests of efficiency, they wanted a group test, one that was easy to administer and score. Given that 40% of recruits at the time were illiterate and many were not fluent in English, an intelligence test that could be administered to them was needed, as well. A committee headed by noted comparative psychologist Robert M. Yerkes, with the help of Lewis Terman, the developer of the Stanford–Binet intelligence test, Edward Thorndike, the well-known learning theorist, and others, quickly developed the Army Alpha group intelligence test for literate persons and the Army Beta test for illiterates and those who spoke another language (Yoakum & Yerkes, 1920).

Psychologists applied their human research and evaluation skills to a number of other military applications during World War I. Many of these applications related to developing means of proper selection and training people for specific military jobs, particularly flight training. Other applications had to do with assessing the performance of military personnel under adverse environmental conditions, for instance, the effects of fatigue and oxygen deprivation on aviators. The success of wartime research and development by psychologists not only gave birth to military psychology as a discipline in American psychology but also helped to spur an increased postwar interest in applying psychological knowledge and techniques more generally (Hoffman & Deffenbacher, 1992).

The entry of the United States into World War II in 1941 produced yet another burst of application of psychological science to military needs. More than 2,000 psychologists contributed to the war effort. Applications of cognitive psychology included continuation of the work begun in World War I concerning the effects of environmental factors on human performance and the selection and training of persons for special duties such as aviator or radar operator. However, the research on selection and training soon revealed many cases of soldiers' misuse of or improper training to use equipment. These results were a contributing factor to psychologists becoming involved in the analysis of human errors, the preparation of training and operating manuals, and the design of radar and sonar consoles, gun sights, aircraft instrument panels, communication systems, and much more.

Born in World War I, military psychology certainly matured in World War II. For present purposes, the principal new development was the emergence of an understanding of the importance of the fit of human and machine: "Probably the most important contribution of the psychologists of World War II was to demonstrate that the man-machine, rather than the machine alone, is the fundamental fighting unit" (Bray, 1948, p. 224). Indeed, this demonstration helped set the research agenda for much postwar industrial as well as military research involving the application of cognitive psychology. The method for much research of this sort became one of analyzing training procedures and errors produced in human–machine interaction. The goal was to develop training guidelines and machine design standards that would enable humans to optimize their performance in terms of efficiency and safety, by having the workplace environment fit well with human needs and capabilities. As we see in the next section of this chapter, this goal became the definition of a new field of psychology that emerged in the years following World War II, a field referred to in North America as "engineering psychology," "human factors engineering," and "ergonomics."

The major areas of application of psychology to the military include personnel selection and classification, training, human factors, leadership and team effectiveness, clinical diagnosis and treatment, survey research, and the study of environmental stressors (Gal & Mangelsdorff, 1991). Hence, these areas involve all the major disciplines in psychology, including industrial/organizational, clinical, cognitive, and social psychology. Our focus is on the areas of application to which cognitive psychology has made and will continue to make the greatest contributions—training, human factors, and environmental stressors.

Applications to Military Training

Today, as since World War I, an obvious emphasis for the military has been to develop more effective means to train personnel, particularly to ensure the maximum level of operational readiness. Among the principal applications for research by cognitive psychologists are training for basic skills (reading and mathematics, for example), military skills such as infantry and seamanship, technical skills (electronics, foreign languages, for instance), and special skills such as flight training. Most recently, research on team training and training for situational awareness is receiving special emphasis. In the process of conducting research to solve the practical problems related to training, cognitive psychologists borrow as needed from the established base of research and theory in cognitive psychology but likewise contribute to this base. They do so by refining existing models and developing new models of cognitive and information processing as a result of cognitive task analysis and research they conduct in task ecologies in which military personnel must operate. For instance, efforts to test and refine existing knowledge and to develop new knowledge are occurring for applied cognitive psychologists who seek to understand the nature of training task requirements and the design of instructional systems, how to assess training performance through criterion-referenced procedures, and how to enhance training through the use of technology such as simulators and computer-based training (e.g., Cuevas, Fiore, Bowers, & Salas, in press).

Human Factors Research in the Military

From the time of World War II, there has been considerable research emphasis on changing equipment design to enhance human performance (Hoffman & Deffenbacher, 1992). More recently, researchers have also sought to improve human performance by seeking ways to reduce operator workload (through the use of job aids, for instance) as well as ways to reduce the potentially negative impact of acute stress such as that elicited in combat. Use of artificial intelligence to enhance human decision making has also been receiving increased attention by researchers (Gal & Mangelsdorff, 1991).

Though the military views the study of environmental stressors as a distinct area of research emphasis, we view application of cognitive psychology to such study as simply another use of human factors psychology. Research is conducted to improve the mutual fit of personnel and equipment under adverse operational conditions (Gal & Mangelsdorff, 1991). These conditions include sustained operations without sleep, operating under environmental extremes such as noise, heat, cold, or high altitude, operating with vehicles that produce high acceleration, vibration, motion sickness, or stress, and operating under hazardous atmospheric conditions (toxic fumes, radiological, chemical, or biological warfare).

Employment Opportunities

Work settings for cognitive psychologists researching military applications are quite diverse. Many researchers in this area are university faculty with research grants or contracts from a branch of the Department of Defense or they are employed either as uniformed or civilian psychologists by a military research laboratory. There are many such laboratories, each employing from several persons to hundreds. Alternatively, some cognitive psychologists working on military applications are employed by private sector contractors, working either in the contractor's laboratory or onsite at a military laboratory. Applied cognitive psychologists also work at military bases and schools performing research related to the training function. Regardless of employer, applied cognitive psychologists who can help in the creation of decision-making architectures for cognitively complex tasks and who know how to do cognitive task analysis are much in demand; this sort of applied research is often referred to as cognitive engineering.

COGNITIVE PSYCHOLOGY AND HUMAN FACTORS ENGINEERING

Though we earlier indicated that the birth of human factors psychology as an identifiable field occurred in the years after World War II, human factors research by other names was being conducted a century ago. Hoffman and Deffenbacher (1992) have reviewed a number of these studies. Consider just some of the research sponsored by the railroad industry, for instance. Perhaps the most famous of these studies was that conducted by Bryan and

Harter (1897), a study concerning the learning of Morse code. Morse code is a system for communicating on radio waves using patterns of dashes and dots as alphabetic signals. Hugo Munsterberg (1913) developed a number of laboratory "tasks in miniature," based on analyses of the tasks performed by railway motormen under emergency conditions, particularly analyses of decisions made. Finally, George Stratton (1909), an early cognitive psychologist who founded the psychology department at the University of California, studied the rapid perceptual judgments made by locomotive engineers. His research not only included laboratory studies with special apparatus but also nocturnal field studies and observations made from trains.

A much more recent example of research related to the issue of safety in the transportation industry is a fascinating analysis of how the application of cognitive psychology can help reduce the problem of collisions between trains and vehicles at railroad grade crossings (Leibowitz, 1985). The problem is a serious one, for there are approximately 650 fatalities per year from 7,000 railroad collisions occurring annually, a relatively large number, considering there are about 27,000 locomotives in operation.

Certainly motorists have considerable advance warning, either by an active warning system or a passive one involving a crossbuck sign and perhaps warnings painted on the pavement. Trains are required to sound their horns on approach to a crossing and to activate their headlights even during daylight; they are also required to travel at slower speeds within more urban areas. Locomotives are large, roughly 3 m wide by 4.5 m high. Despite such warnings and adequate visibility, however, drivers often choose to cross the track in front of an approaching train, certainly a risky decision. On a flat grade, without attached rail cars, a locomotive traveling 48 km/hr (30 mph) requires about 185 m to come to a stop, after emergency brakes are applied. If its speed is greater or it is pulling a load, the stopping distance will be proportionately greater.

Why do motorists make such risky decisions? For one thing, we are often an impatient lot, a tendency that is exaggerated at railroad crossings, for we never know how long we might be delayed at an intersection if we decide to stop and wait for the train to pass. Second, most of the time we can safely ignore the official warnings. Whenever we make the decision to cross and do so safely, that behavior is reinforced, thereby increasing our self-confidence in our judgment and the probability that we shall make the same decision again. Further increasing the probability of taking the risky decision is that on a particular day the probability of injury or death for a given person is extremely low. Additionally, perceived risk of a collision with a train is likely reduced even further by our experience of the low frequency of encountering trains at certain crossings.

Inasmuch as nearly 80% of all grade crossings in the United States only have crossbuck signs as a warning, many drivers must make their crossing decision based on their estimate of the safe time interval (Leibowitz, 1985). Clearly, sensory and perceptual cues as to the distance and speed of an oncoming train are critical to these drivers' safe time estimates. Two sorts of cues identified by cognitive psychologists interested in perception would appear to be most relevant here. The most important of these imparts a systematic bias in the direction of underestimating the speed of the approaching train and therefore overestimating the amount of time available for a safe crossing. This phenomenon is referred to as the illusion of velocity and size (Leibowitz, 1985). For actually equal velocities, the larger of two objects will be seen to be moving more slowly. The onrushing locomotive is actually traveling much faster than it appears.

The second perceptual cue pertains to the fact that if two objects are moving in straight lines at constant velocities and are on a collision course, their relative positions remain constant in the visual field. As a result, the most accurate cue to the velocity of the oncoming train, in this case, is the rate of increase in the size of the expansion pattern on the driver's retina. This rate of growth in the size of the visual angle created by the image of the train is not linear. For a train at a distance at which a driver's decision is usually made, the rate of growth of the expansion pattern is relatively low; as the distance decreases from there, the expansion pattern grows at a rapidly accelerating rate, ordinarily a signal of imminent collision (Leibowitz, 1985). Unfortunately, the automobile driver who has made the decision to go ahead and attempt a crossing is no longer observing this rapidly growing expansion pattern on his or her retina and misses information that might otherwise lead to a decision to stop and wait for the train to pass.

Clearly separating highways and railways by means of overpasses or bridges is not economically feasible in most cases. Therefore driver education programs that make clear the nature of the various factors that bias railway crossing decisions would appear to be the best bet. It might also be possible, of course, to increase the perceived velocity of large objects such as locomotives by means of special markings or lights placed on them.

Of course, human factors psychologists are concerned with much more than safety issues involving transportation, the workplace, and home use of certain products. A number of them have published descriptions of the sorts of work they have been doing; these accounts have been published on a regular basis for the past several years in *Psychological Science Agenda*, the newsletter of the Science Directorate of the American Psychological Association. Some of these psychologists have been concerned with human-centered approaches to the design of instruments and controls for the aircraft cockpit, for space vehicles, for aircraft control centers, for ships, and for various land vehicles. Others have been concerned with development of both partial-task and full-scale simulations to improve communications, training, and team resource management. A substantial number of human factors psychologists are involved with human–computer interaction (HCI) and information technology applications. Some of those working on HCI applications design graphic and multimedia human–computer interfaces and interactive voice response systems for telecommunications companies. Others working on HCI applications are employed by companies that produce computer hardware and/or software. Here, for example, a human factors psychologist might apply cognitive psychology research to explain flaws in the design of the software for a user interface or she might be concerned with exploring attention and perception questions for users who need or desire to navigate 3-D virtual environments.

Regardless of the particular application of cognitive psychology, human factors psychologists find employment opportunities with all sorts of employers, including government (especially federal), not-for-profit institutions, consulting firms, private industry, and universities. For instance, federal government opportunities exist in the Department of Defense, Department of Transportation, Federal Aviation Administration, National Aviation and Space Administration, National Institute for Occupational Safety and Health, and the Nuclear Regulatory Commission, among others.

CONCLUSIONS

Cognitive psychologists have made substantial contributions to solving applied problems in a wide range of domains. As with most applied projects, cognitive psychologists working in industry, educational settings, and the private sector tend to work in interdisciplinary teams. For example, cognitive psychologists working in the field of human factors are likely to be working with engineers and industrial designers. Cognitive psychologists working in forensic settings are likely to be working with criminologists and sociologists. Those working in market research and advertising companies are likely to be working with social psychologists and individuals with business training. In addition to mastering cognitive psychology, individuals seeking careers in applied settings would do well to study related fields to familiarize themselves with the content and methods that their future colleagues are likely to be employing.

It is also advisable for those seeking applied careers to seek internship opportunities as part of their training. Internship experience will not only help make a more competitive resume, it will also help individuals decide what types of work settings they are more likely to enjoy and be productive in. It is encouraging to know, however, that cognitive psychologists have a toe-hold in many applied domains, and given the short history of the field of cognitive psychology, this trend is only likely to increase into the future.

REFERENCES

Bargh, J. A. (2002). Losing consciousness: Automatic influences on consumer judgment, behavior, and motivation. *Journal of Consumer Research, 29,* 280–285.

Bettman, J. R. (1979). *An information processing theory of consumer choice.* Reading, MA: Addison-Wesley.

Binet, A., & Simon, T. (1905a). Applications des methods nouvelles au diagnostic du niveau intellectuel chez des enfants normaux et anormaux d'hospice et d'ecole primaire. *Anee Psychologique, 11,* 245–366.

Binet, A., & Simon T. (1905b). Methodes nouvelles pour la diagnostic du niveau intellectuel des anormaux. *Anee Psychologique, 11,* 191–244.

Bloom, P. S., Barss, A., Nicol, J., & Conway, L. (1994). Children's knowledge of binding and coreference: Evidence from spontaneous speech. *Language, 70,* 53–71.

Bradburn, N. M., & Sudman, S. (1979). *Improving interview method and questionnaire design.* San Francisco, CA: Jossey-Bass.

Bray, C. W. (1948). *Psychology and military proficiency.* Princeton, NJ: Princeton University Press.

Brown, J. S., & Burton, R. R. (1978). Diagnostic models for procedural bugs in basic mathematical skills. *Cognitive Science, 2,* 155–192.

Bryan, W. L., & Harter, N. (1897). Studies in the physiology and psychology of the telegraphic language. *Psychological Review, 4,* 27–53.

Chi, M. T. H., Feltovich, P. J., & Glaser, R. (1981). Categorization and representations of physics problems by experts and novices. *Cognitive Science, 5,* 121–152.

Committee to Review the Scientific Evidence on the Polygraph (2002). *The Polygraph and Lie Detection.* Washington, DC: National Academy Press.

Cuevas, H. M., Fiore, S. M., Bowers, C. A., & Salas, E. (2004). Fostering constructive cognitive and metacognitive activity in computer-based complex task training environments. *Computers in Human Behavior, 20,* 225–241.

Cutler, B. L., & Penrod, S. D. (1995). *Mistaken identification: The eyewitness, psychology, and the law.* New York: Cambridge University Press.

Dawson, E. J., Burgoon, M., & Crano, W. D. (2003). Parents' and their children's beliefs and knowledge of HIV/AIDS in a multicultural Hispanic/Anglo population. In L. K. Fuller (Ed.), *Media-mediated AIDS* (pp. 175–202). Cresskill, NJ: Hampton Press.

DePaulo, B. M., Lindsay, J. J., Malone, B., Muhlenbruck, L., Charlton, K., & Cooper, H. (2003). Cues to deception. *Psychological Bulletin, 129,* 74–118.

Ebbinghaus, H. (1885). *Memory: A contribution to experimental psychology* (trans. by H. A. Ruger & C. E. Bussenues, 1913). New York: Teachers College, Columbia University.

Ericsson, K. A., & Simon, H. A. (1993). *Protocol analysis: Verbal reports as data.* Cambridge, MA: MIT Press.

Foorman, B. R., Francis, D. J., Fletcher, J. M., Schatschneider, D., & Mehta, P. (1998). The role of instruction in learning to read: Preventing reading failure in at-risk children. *Journal of Educational Psychology, 90,* 37–55.

Frye v. United States. (1923). 293 F. 1013 (D.C. Cir.).

Gale, H. S. (Ed.). (1900). *Psychological studies.* Minneapolis, MN: H. S. Gale.

Gal, R., & Mangelsdorff, A. D. (Eds.). (1991). *Handbook of military psychology.* New York: Wiley.

Gough, P. B., & Juel, C. (1991). The first stages of word recognition. In L. Rieben & C. A. Perfetti (Eds.), *Learning to read: Basic research and its implications* (pp. 47–56). Hillsdale, NJ: Lawrence Erlbaum Associates.

Hall, G. S. (1911). *Educational problems.* New York: Appleton.

Harris, R. J., Dubitsky, T. M., Perch, K. L. Ellerman, C. S., & Larson, M. W. (1980). Remember implied advertising claims as facts: Extensions to the "real world." *Bulletin of the Psychonomic Society, 16,* 317–320.

Harris, R. J., Trusty, M. L., Bechtold, J. I., & Wasinger, L. (1989). Memory for implied versus directly stated advertising claims. *Psychology & Marketing, 6,* 87–96.

Hoffman, R. R., Bringmann, W., Bamberg, M., & Klein, R. M. (1987). Some historical observations on Ebbinghaus. In D. S. Gorfein & R. R. Hoffman (Eds.), *Memory and learning: The Ebbinghaus centennial conference* (pp. 57–76). Hillsdale, NJ: Lawrence Erlbaum Associates.

Hoffman, R. R., & Deffenbacher, K. A. (1992). A brief history of applied cognitive psychology. *Applied Cognitive Psychology, 6,* 1–48.

Iacono, W. G. (2001). Forensic 'lie detection': Procedures without scientific basis. *Journal of Forensic Psychology Practice, 1,* 75–86.

Johnson, M. K., Foley, M. A., Suengas, A. G., & Raye, C. L. (1988). Phenomenal characteristics of memories for perceived and imagined autobiographical events. *Journal of Experimental Psychology: General, 177,* 371–376.

Kassin, S. M. (1997). The psychology of confession evidence: *American Psychologist, 52,* 221–233.

Kassin, S. M. (2002). False confessions and the jogger case. *The New York Times,* November 1, *Op-Ed.*

Kassin, S. M., Tubb, V. A., Hosch, H. M., & Memon, A. (2001). On the "general acceptance" of eyewitness testimony research. *American Psychologist, 56,* 405–416.

Krishnan, H. S., & Trappey, C. V. (1999). Nonconscious memory processes in marketing: A historical perspective and future directions. *Psychology & Marketing, 16,* 451–457.

Lamb, M. E., Sternberg, K. J., Esplin, P. W., Hershkowitz, I., Orbach, Y., & Hovav, M. (1997). Criteria-based content analysis: A field validation study. *Child Abuse & Neglect, 21,* 255–264.

Leibowitz, H. W. (1985). Grade crossing accidents and human factors engineering. *American Scientist, 73,* 558–562.

Loh, W. D. (1981). Psychological research: Past and present. *Michigan Law Review, 79,* 659–707.

Lykken, D. T. (1998). *A tremor in the blood: Uses and abuses of the lie detector.* New York: Plenum Press.

Mentality tests. (1916). *Journal of Educational Psychology, 7,* 163–166, 229–240, 278–286, 348–360, 427–433.

Moore, C. (1907). Yellow psychology. *Law Notes, 11,* 125–127.

Moore, T. E. (1982). Subliminal advertising: What you see is what you get. *Journal of Marketing, 46,* 38–47.

Munsterberg, H. (1908). *On the witness stand: Essays on psychology and crime.* Garden City, NY: Doubleday.

Munsterberg, H. (1913). *Psychology and industrial efficiency.* Boston, MA: Houghton Mifflin.

Munsterberg, H. (1917). *Business psychology.* Chicago, IL: La Salle Extension University.

Packard, V. (1957). *The hidden persuaders.* New York: Random House.

People v. McDonald. (1984). 37 Cal.3d 351, 690 P.2d 709, 716, 208 Cal.Rptr. 236, 245.

Perfetti, C. A. (1992). The representation problem in reading acquisition. In P. B. Gough, L. C. Ehri, & R. Treiman (Eds.), *Reading acquisition* (pp. 145–174). Hillsdale, NJ: Lawrence Erlbaum Associates.

Pezdek, K., Morrow, A., Blandon-Gitlin, I., Goodman, G. S., Quas, J. A., Saywitz, K. J., Bidrose, S., Pipe, M.-E., Rogers, M., & Brodie, L. (2004). Detecting deception in children: Event familiarity affects criterion-based content analysis ratings. *Journal of Applied Psychology, 89,* 119–126.

Poffenberger, A. T. (1942). *Principles of applied psychology.* New York: Appleton-Century-Crofts.

Rayner, K., Foorman, B. R., Perfetti, C. A., Pesetsky, D., & Seidenberg, M. S. (2001). How psychological science informs the teaching of reading. *Psychological Science in the Public Interest, 2,* 31–74.

Resnick, L. B. (1984). Beyond error analysis: The role of understanding in elementary school arithmetic. In H. N. Cheek (Ed.), *Diagnostic and prescriptive mathematics: Issues, ideas and in-*

sights (1984 Research Monograph, pp. 2–14). Kent, OH: Research Council for Diagnosis and Prescriptive Mathematics Research.

Richardson, P. S., Dick, A. S., & Jain, A. K. (1994). Extrinsic and intrinsic cue effects on perceptions of store brand quality. *Journal of Marketing, 58*, 28–36.

Riggle, E. D. B., Ellis, A. L., & Crawford, A. M. (1996). The impact of "media contact" on attitudes toward gay men. *Journal of Homosexuality, 31*, 55–69.

Schuman, H., & Presser, S. (1981). *Questions and answers in attitude surveys*. New York: Academic Press.

Scott, W. D. (1903). *Psychology of advertising*. Boston, MA: Small & Maynard.

Scott, W. D. (1907). *The psychology of public speaking*. New York: Noble & Noble.

Scott, W. D. (1910). *Increasing human efficiency in business*. New York: Macmillian.

Stevenson, H. W., & Stigler, J. W. (1992). *The learning gap: Why our schools are failing and what we can learn from Japanese and Chinese education*. New York: Touchstone.

Stevenson, H. W. Stigler, J. W., Lee, S-Y, Lucker, G. W., Kitamura, S., & Hsu, C-C (1985). Cognitive performance and academic achievement of Japanese, Chinese, and American children. *Child Development, 56*, 718–734.

Stratton, G. M. (1909). Some experiments on the perception of the movement, color, and direction of lights, with special reference to railway signaling. *Psychological Review Monograph Supplements, 10*(40), 85–104.

Sudman, S., Bradburn, N. M., & Schwarz, N. (1996). *Thinking about answers: The application of cognitive process to survey methodology*. San Francisco, CA: Jossey-Bass.

Technical Working Group for Eyewitness Evidence. (1999). *Eyewitness evidence: A guide for law enforcement* [Booklet]. Washington, DC: United States Department of Justice, Office of Justice Programs.

Undeutsch, U. (1989). The development of statement reality analysis. In J. C. Yuille (Ed.), *Credibility assessment* (pp. 101–120). Dordrecht, The Netherlands: Kluwer.

Vrij, A. (2000). *Detecting lies and deceit: The psychology of lying and the implications for professional practice*. New York: Wiley.

Vrij, A. (2005). Criteria-Based Content Analysis: A qualitative review of the first 37 studies. *Psychology, Public Policy, and Law, 11*, 3–41.

Vrij, A., Akehurst, L., Soukara, S., & Bull, R. (2002). Will the truth come out? The effect of deception, age, status, coaching, and social skills on CBCA scores. *Law and Human Behavior, 26*, 261–283.

Wells, G. L., Malpass, R. S., Lindsay, R. C. L., Fisher, R. P., Turtle, J. W., & Fulero, S. M. (2000). From the lab to the police station: A successful application of eyewitness research. *American Psychologist, 55*, 581–598.

Yoakum, C. S., & Yerkes, R. M. (1920). *Army mental tests*. New York: Holt.

12

Emerging Career Opportunities in the Transdiscipline of Evaluation Science

Stewart I. Donaldson
Christina A. Christie
Claremont Graduate University

The discipline and profession of psychology have blossomed, and master's and doctoral level psychologists seem to be enjoying many new career opportunities. For example, the American Psychological Association now boosts more than 50 separate divisions with members working on a diverse range of topics such as: addictions; adult development; advertising; aging; child, youth, and family services; conflict resolution; criminal justice; ethnic minorities; human resources; law and psychology; lesbian, gay, and bisexual issues; media; police and public safety; and social policy issues among others. As noted in chapter 1, now more than ever before, psychological scientists or those trained in research psychology at the graduate level are choosing to apply psychological science and to chart new territories within nonacademic careers. The purpose of this chapter is to describe a growing, socially meaningful, and potentially lucrative career niche for those interested in applying psychology—the transdisciplinary profession of evaluation science.

THE TRANSDISCIPLINE OF EVALUATION SCIENCE

Globalization

Rossi (1990) declared that evaluation science is "alive and flourishing, constituting the most exciting career a young social scientist may embark upon" (p. 7). Even Rossi probably did not anticipate, or could have imagined, how pervasive, productive, and global in scope the field of evaluation would become in the decade following his observation. Today, societies all around the globe are embracing the values of accountability and professionalism, and organizations of all shapes and sizes are commissioning professional evaluations at an increasing rate in an effort to promote human welfare and achievement (Donaldson & Scriven, 2003).

One indicator of the emergence and globalization of evaluation practice is the number of psychologists and other professionals now participating as members of organized evaluation associations and societies. In 1990, there were approximately five major evaluation professional associations, whereas today there are more than 50 worldwide (Mertens, 2003, 2005; Russon, 2004). For example, Table 12.1 lists a sample of organizations that illustrate this new professional networking and development activity. Maybe more importantly, an international alliance has been formed to link these professional organizations in an effort to share knowledge about how to improve the practice of evaluating a wide range of programs, policies, projects, communities, organizations, products, personnel, and to promote social betterment worldwide (Russon, 2004).

Evaluation as a Profession

> Evaluation is a profession composed of persons with varying interests, potentially encompassing but not limited to the evaluation of programs, products, personnel, policy, performance, proposals, technology, research, theory, and even of evaluation itself. (American Evaluation Association, 2004)

Why have psychologists (and other professionals) become involved in evaluation practice and evaluation societies at an unprecedented rate in the past decade? One way to begin to gain insight about this question is to examine the discourse and activities that occur within these professional networks. Brief descriptions of four of the largest and most well-established professional associations are provided below for this purpose.

The *American Evaluation Association* (AEA) is an international professional association of evaluators devoted to the application and exploration of program evaluation, personnel evaluation, technology, and many other forms of evaluation. Evaluation involves assessing the strengths and weaknesses of programs, policies, personnel, products, and organizations to improve their effectiveness. AEA has approximately 3,700 members representing all 50 U.S. states as well as more than 50 foreign countries. AEA's mission is to: improve evaluation practices and methods, increase evaluation use, promote evaluation as a profession, and support the contribution of evaluation to the generation of theory and knowledge about effective human action.

TABLE 12.1
Sample of Professional Evaluation Organizations

- African Evaluation Association
- American Evaluation Association
- Association Comorienne de Suivi et Evaluation
- Associazione Italiana de Valuatazione
- Australasian Evaluation Society
- Bangladesh Evaluation Forum
- Botswana Evaluation Association
- Brazilian M&E Network
- Burundi Evaluation Network
- Canadian Evaluation Society
- Central American Evaluation Association
- Danish Evaluation Society
- Deutsche Gesellschaft fur Evaluation
- Egyptian Evaluation Association
- Eritrea Evaluation Network
- Ethiopian Evaluation Association
- European Evaluation Society
- Finnish Evaluation Society
- Ghana Evaluators Association
- Ghana Evaluation Network
- International Program Evaluation Network (Russia/NIS)
- Israeli Association for Program Evaluation
- Japanese Evaluation Association
- Kenya Evaluation Association
- Korean Evaluation Association
- La Societe Francaise de l'Evaluation
- Malawi M&E Network
- Malaysian Evaluation Society
- Namibia Monitoring Evaluation and Research Network
- Nepal M&E Forum
- Nigerian Evaluation Association
- Programme for Strengthening the Regional Capacity for Evaluation of Rural Poverty Alleviation Projects in Latin America and the Caribbean (PREVAL)
- Reseau Malgache de Suivi et Evaluation
- Reseau Nigerien de Suivi et Evaluation
- Reseau Ruandais de Suivi et Evaluation
- Societe Quebecoise d'Evaluation de Programme
- Societe Wallonne de l'Evaluation et de la Prospective
- South African Evaluation Network
- Spanish Public Policy Evaluation Society
- Sri Lanka Evaluation Association
- Swiss Evaluation Society
- Thailand Evaluation Network
- Ugandan Evaluation Association
- UK Evaluation Society
- Utvarderarna (Sweden)
- Zambia Evaluation Association
- Zimbabwe Evaluation Society

The *Canadian Evaluation Society* (CES) is dedicated to the advancement of evaluation theory and practice. CES has approximately 1,800 members who are involved with the betterment of programs and services through the use of evaluation. In the field of evaluation, CES promotes leadership, knowledge, advocacy, and professional development.

The primary goal of the *European Evaluation Society* (EES) is to promote theory, practice, and utilization of high quality evaluation especially, but not exclusively, within the European countries. This goal is obtained by bringing together academics and practitioners from all over Europe and from any professional sector, thus creating a forum where all participants can benefit from the co-operation and bridge building. The society was founded in The Hague in 1994. The first official board was elected in autumn 1995 and started its work in January 1996. EES now supports a membership of approximately 1,000.

The *Australasian Evaluation Society* (AES) is a professional organization for people involved in evaluation. Evaluation is used in a range of professions. The AES has more than 650 members involved in all aspects of evaluation and performance measurement. Members include evaluation practitioners, managers, teachers and students from all levels of government, educational institutions, research agencies, community organizations, businesses, and interested individuals. Members meet regularly through Regional Groups in major cities in Australia and New Zealand. AES aims to improve the theory, practice and use of evaluation through (a) establishing and promoting ethics and standards in evaluation practice, (b) providing a forum for the discussion of ideas including society publications, seminars, and conferences, (c) linking members who have similar evaluation interests, (d) providing education and training in matters related to evaluation, and (e) acting as an advocate for evaluation in Australasia.

One pattern to note in the earlier descriptions is that psychologists share many of the same values and interests as those expressed in the mission statements of the evaluation associations and societies. For example, the American Psychological Association's *Ethical Principles of Psychologists and Code of Conduct* emphasizes that psychologists should strive to be socially responsible to the community and society in which they work and live, be concerned for other's welfare, show respect for people's rights and dignity, strictly adhere to scientific standards related to systematic inquiry, and to vigorously adhere to professional ethics and standards as they apply their expertise toward efforts to improve human welfare (American Psychological Association, 2002). Psychologists are particularly well suited to specialize in evaluating programs, policies, personnel, and the like. For example, many social, health, community, and organizational programs and interventions are developed based on psychological theory, principles, and research (Donaldson, 2003). Furthermore, psychologists have pioneered and developed many of the contemporary methods used to conduct systematic inquiry in evaluation and applied research (e.g., Campbell, 1978; Cronbach, 1982; Graham & Donaldson, 1993; Lipsey & Wilson, 1993; Shadish, Cook, & Campbell, 2002). Those trained in psychology typically bring important substantive knowledge about the phenomena under investigation, very strong critical thinking skills, and a solid methodological foundation and tool kit to the evaluation table.

However, as the field of evaluation has grown and evolved, psychologists have sought to improve their effectiveness in this area by acquiring specific knowledge about evaluation theory, practice, and research (Alkin & Christie, 2004; Donaldson & Lipsey, in press; Donaldson & Scriven, 2003). Evaluation-specific knowledge and skills can dramatically enhance the already strong research and inquiry foundation that is typically built in psychological science education and training. In addition, internship and professional experiences pursuing ideas and gaining knowledge outside of disciplinary boundaries, coupled with working along side of professionals trained in other disciplines in efforts to promote human welfare, is part of the uniqueness and thrill commonly reported by psychologists practicing evaluation science.

Why a Transdiscipline?

Scriven (2003) provided a transdisciplinary vision for the future of evaluation science:

> I hope and expect that the essential nature of evaluation itself will crystallize in our minds into a clear and essentially universal recognition of it as a discipline, a discipline with a clear definition, subject matter, logical structure, and multiple fields of application. In particular, it will, I think, become recognized as one of the elite group of disciplines, which I call transdisciplines. These disciplines are notable because they supply essential tools for other disciplines, while retaining an autonomous structure and research effort of their own. (p. 19)

He further argued that traditional departments in the applied social sciences, including psychology, have an opportunity to enrich their programs and reap important benefits if they infuse transdisciplinary evaluation curricula and experiences into their existing training efforts.

> Applied social science will divide into the progressive, evaluation-enriched school, and the conservative, evaluation-impaired school. The evaluation-enriched group ... will become the winner in nearly all bids for grants and contracts aimed at separating solutions from non-solutions of social and educational problems. The evaluation-impaired branch, following in the tracks of

typical applied social science departments today, will gradually wither on the vine, with its aging adherents exchanging stories about the good old days. (pp. 19–20)

Evaluation science has the practical quality of providing tools for and enhancing other disciplines, as well as improving the effectiveness of professionals from a variety of fields. For example, basic psychological research and theory often suggests ways to develop human action in the form of programs or policies to improve some aspect of the human condition. The evaluation of these efforts often serves as an empirical test of the accuracy of psychological principles and theories. That is, it is one thing to demonstrate cause and effect relationships in controlled or research-like conditions; it is a different challenge to demonstrate that these principles can be put into effective action in society. Evaluation science can enhance the discipline of psychology by sorting out which psychological principles and findings are effective for preventing or ameliorating human problems in real-world settings.

Evaluation science can also help professionals such as various types of leaders, managers, administrators, educators, policymakers, researchers, philanthropists, service providers, and the like make better decisions and become more effective. Evaluation science can be thought of as a turbo charger, or a powerful enhancement, of professional training across numerous subareas of psychology. For example, social psychologists can use evaluation to help develop programs and policies based on social psychological principles. Developmental psychologists can use evaluation science to enhance developmentally appropriate services and education in efforts to promote healthful human development. Health psychologists use evaluation to determine the effectiveness of a wide range of prevention and health promotion efforts. Industrial and organizational psychologists use evaluation to select and develop the careers of employees, as well as to design and evaluate a wide range of organizational programs, policies, and problems. In short, training and skills in evaluation science promises to improve the ability of psychologists to be effective at applying psychological science across many domains.

At the same time evaluation science is being used to enhance other disciplines, and to develop cumulative knowledge about interventions designed to prevent and solve psychological, social, and educational problems (e.g., see Lipsey & Wilson, 1993), it is developing a unique knowledge base and research effort of its own—focused on how best to practice evaluation science. For example, in recent years there have been significant advances in understanding the range of approaches and theories for conducting evaluations (Alkin, 2004; Donaldson & Scriven, 2003), how closely evaluation theory reflects actual practice (Alkin & Christie, 2005; Christie, 2003; Fitzpatrick, 2004), research about the best ways to ensure the productive use of evaluation findings (Henry & Mark, 2003), strategies for overcoming excessive evaluation anxiety (Donaldson, Gooler, & Scriven, 2002), improving the relationships between evaluators and stakeholders (Donaldson, 2001), and the development of standards of practice (e.g., Joint Committee on Standards for Education Evaluation, 1994) and guiding principles (e.g., American Evaluation Association, 2004). This core of knowledge about evaluation practice itself is being used to inform and improve the growing number of common applications of professional evaluation science (i.e., program evaluation, policy evaluation, personnel evaluation, organizational evaluation, and so forth).

We believe the outlook for those with psychology degrees, seeking to apply psychological knowledge and evaluation science toward improving human functioning, will remain bright in the years ahead. In addition, we predict that many new opportunities will emerge for those trained in psychology whom can also apply evaluation science. Although we now have evidence of a wide range of career paths that involve using psychology and evaluation science, due to space constraints here, we focus our subsequent discussion on career opportunities in probably the most common application of evaluation science today—program evaluation. This discussion first provides a brief overview of the links between psychology and program evaluation, distinguishes applied research from program evaluation, and provides examples of common work settings where psychologists are now using evaluation science to better the human condition.

EVALUATION CAREER OPPORTUNITIES FOR PSYCHOLOGISTS

Psychology is a discipline in which human behavior and the dynamics that explain why people act in particular ways is of great concern. Evaluation science, on the other hand, generates information for decision making, often answering the bottom-line question, "Does it work?" The *it* being, in this case, a program. Follow-up questions to this basic question, frequently asked by those evaluating are, "Why does it work?" "For whom does it work best?" "Under what conditions does it work?" "How do we make it work better?" Evaluators provide program stakeholders (e.g., program directors, funding agencies, staff, and clients, as well as the public at large) with defensible answers to these important questions. When we consider the large number of programs designed to modify human behavior (for examples, cf. Donaldson & Scriven, 2003; Lipsey & Wilson, 1993), the link between psychology and evaluation science becomes noteworthy. Hence, the link between evaluators and psychologists becomes far less disparate.

Evaluation is the tool used to determine, "What makes a good program good?" Professional evaluators often perceive themselves as service providers, offering assistance to stakeholders in examining program effectiveness (i.e., the impact of programs on clients). Results from evaluations often identify a program's strengths and areas of needed improvement (Rossi, Lipsey, & Freeman, 2004). This information is typically presented to key program stakeholders (usually program developers, directors, and managers) and is then used to revise or perhaps redesign the program so that others can be better served. Evaluators serve the public good, and shape social, educational, and psychological services by helping organizations establish which programs work best and why (Cronbach et al., 1980).

Evaluation: Different From Research

Evaluation is the process of systematically gathering information for program improvement and decision making. Evaluators employ the same methodological tools used by researchers such as study designs, and data collection and analysis techniques. However the two processes differ in important ways: the origin of study question(s) and the purpose for which study information is gathered (Fitzpatrick, Sanders, & Worthen, 2003). Regarding study questions, evaluation questions are typically elicited from program stakeholders, whereas research questions originate from a researcher or research team. That is, researchers hypothesize about phenomena, and then develop research studies to answer his or her question. Regarding study findings, evaluation generates information for program improvement and decision making; that is, evaluation is decision oriented and is intended for utilization by individuals seeking the information. Conversely, research is conclusion oriented. By and large, researchers generate hypotheses about phenomena with the purpose of producing information that can be generalized across context, people, and time, whereas evaluators typically serve an identified group of stakeholders (e.g., program staff) with the goal of providing information that will be useful for making decisions about specific programs within a relatively defined timeframe.

The distinctions between evaluation and research have implications when considering career opportunities. Psychological researchers typically work in university settings or "think tanks," particularity those conducting independent research. Researchers generally develop a focused program of study and pursue questions that build on previous research. Alternatively, evaluators generally work in program settings, in either an internal or external capacity. Internal evaluators are typically employed full-time by a particular program or an organization that runs multiple programs while external evaluators are hired as consultants and frequently evaluate several programs (for different organizations) simultaneously. Although evaluators often develop an area of expertise (e.g., early childhood education, health behavior, organizational development), it is not typical for evaluators, particularly external evaluators, to develop a program of study that spawns from previous study findings due to the nature of stakeholder driven inquiry, which dictates the evaluation process.

Evaluators who study smaller programs may work alone. In such cases, the evaluator meets with stakeholders to determine the evaluation focus, designs the study, identifies or develops data collection tools, collects and analyzes data, and prepares a final report and presentation of study results. It is not uncommon for each phase of the evaluation to require regular engagement with program stakeholders. In some instances, the evaluator may request that program stakeholders assist with data collection or interpretation, or with other stages of the evaluation process. Larger programs and evaluations usually require that evaluators work with a team. The team often consists of a project director who oversees the day-to-day activities of the evaluation, data collectors, and perhaps data analysts. Project directors are typically required to have a solid background in evaluation science and perhaps even the topic being evaluated. Therefore, it is quite common that project directors have either a master's or doctoral degree, whereas data collectors have at least a bachelor's degree and are often part-time employees who are also full-time students. Similar to the project director, a data analyst will often have a masters or doctoral degree. Large evaluation projects may also have additional staff, which assumes roles that help facilitate successful evaluation planning and implementation. For example, large multisite evaluations might hire a project liaison to serve as the bridge between the evaluation team and the program staff at each site. A project liaison is typically someone who is familiar with the communities where the evaluation is being conducted. A participant recruitment coordinator or a data collection coordinator may also be hired to oversee those critical aspects of the study.

Where Do Evaluators Work?

Evaluation is conducted in almost all areas of psychology, including, but not limited to: social, developmental, cognitive, health, educational, clinical, counseling, community, and industrial/organizational psychology. Training in evaluation provides psychologists with an opportunity to serve and work with people and programs (which, in many settings, are designed to promote human and social betterment) in a role other than that of a clinician.[1] Thus, a professional trained in both psychology and evaluation will encoun-

---

[1]That is not to say that clinical skills are not important when conducting evaluation. In fact, many of the skills necessary for effective counseling, such as group facilitation, active listening, and reflection, are especially valuable when working with program stakeholders. Imagine the

ter a multiplicity of career opportunities in an array of settings. There are five broad program settings in which the evaluator with psychology training often works: nonprofit, education, health care, government, and corporate. Each setting presents exciting and challenging evaluation opportunities for psychologists. Although each employment opportunity is discussed generally below, it is important to note that psychologists have the potential to work in each of the five settings. It should also be mentioned that many psychologists that conduct evaluation do not limit their practice to working in just one setting but rather work in a variety of settings.

Nonprofit Organizations. Nonprofit charitable foundations and social service agencies frequently commission professional evaluations. Charitable foundations largely fund programs that are designed to promote human and social betterment. For example, the Packard Foundation is a philanthropic organization that provides grants to nonprofit organizations in the areas of conservation and science, population, children, families, and communities (see http://www.packard.org). Because foundations are in the business of granting money, these organizations are often concerned with assessing the extent to which the programs they fund are meeting their stated goals. As a result, psychologists may be hired by the foundation to evaluate programs they are supporting. Thus, the evaluator's primary relationship is with the foundation rather than the funded programs. Foundations often use evaluators to evaluate program initiatives, that is, to study a specific program's implementation in different contexts. In addition to conducting their own internal evaluations, foundations often provide programs with funds earmarked specifically for evaluation. In this case, the funded program is responsible for hiring an evaluator to conduct the evaluation. There are also occasions where foundations (as well as other organizations that fund initiatives) hire an initiative evaluator in addition to providing programs with funding for a local evaluation.

Social service evaluations focus on a range of programs, from child abuse prevention to vocational training for former gang members, to pregnancy prevention, and are often community based and target disenfranchised populations. External evaluators conduct most of the evaluation work at these organizations and are often supported by grants that have funding allocated specifically for evaluation. Social service agencies are facing increased competition for financial support and, as a result, are under increased pressure to provide evidence of program effectiveness. Therefore, evaluation is becoming standard practice for most grant-funded programs, regardless of the funding source.

---

evaluator working with a group of stakeholders with disparate views on which aspects of a program should be studied. Clinical and counseling skills are particularly useful when negotiating with the group, attempting to get group members to see one another's perspectives, or developing consensus.

Evaluation practice has become prevalent enough that larger social service agencies now have evaluators on staff (or even an evaluation department) to oversee the agency's evaluation activities. The presence of an internal evaluator does not, however, preclude agencies from hiring external evaluators who may work with the internal evaluators on a specific evaluation, or conduct an evaluation independent of the internal evaluator.

In the nonprofit setting, the ultimate goal of evaluation is to promote social change. As such, participation of program staff and other important stakeholders in the evaluation process increases the likelihood that evaluation findings will be used for ongoing program improvement (Cousins & Earl, 1995). This participatory approach highlights the tendency of many in the nonprofit setting to view evaluation as an activity that stretches beyond accountably reporting to one that provides meaningful information that can be used to design and deliver more effective programs. Thus, psychologists interested in positively impacting programs and policies designed to eradicate social problems and inequities, prevent adverse behaviors, and promote community well-being may consider and thrive in a career as an evaluation scientist in the nonprofit setting.

Educational Settings. In the educational setting, evaluation is often used to assess performance programs and services in order to determine their effectiveness, efficiency, and equity. Individual schools and school districts document the progress and performance of educational goals and objectives through evaluation science. As in the nonprofit setting, educational evaluation studies are often funded by grants and are intended to provide critical information to policymakers and program planners (see http://www.ed.gov/offices/OUS/PES/ index.html).

The majority of educational evaluation takes place in traditional school settings (i.e., K–12 schools and higher education). School-based educational programs focus on academic development and achievement and are supported primarily by federal, state, and local funding. Therefore, educational programs are commonly evaluated. At the federal and state level, the U.S. and state departments of education support a great number of studies investigating the impact of educational programs. Evaluators work directly for federal and state offices of education as internal evaluators, or may be hired as external consultants. When hiring external evaluators, a competitive grant process is followed; that is, a request for proposals (RFP) is disseminated, to which any qualified evaluator can respond. There are firms, non- and for-profit, large and small that focus exclusively on conducting educational evaluation.

Local school districts often employ full-time staff to conduct evaluations of their programs. Large school districts, such as Los Angeles Unified School District, may have an entire office (in some cases employing 50 or more people) dedicated to evaluation. Additionally, local districts, including those with an internal evaluation staff may hire external evaluators to study their programs and policies. At the local district level, evaluation is often used to provide information to the school board, district, school administrators, and teachers, with the goal of improving program performance. Evaluation is generally used formatively, meaning that the information generated from program evaluations is used to improve programs on an ongoing basis. Summative evaluations may also be conducted from which schools are able to determine, for example, which reading curriculum has the greatest impact on student literacy scores. Hence, summative evaluation conducted in the school setting is an "endpoint" evaluation of a particular program that has specific and expected outcomes.

Educational evaluators conduct studies that focus on the various aspects of schooling, which include educational policy, programs focusing on school administration, teachers, and students. For example, evaluations are conducted to determine the impact of systemic change initiatives, such as school reform policies that allow districts to open charter schools. Educational evaluations also study the effects of policy and program changes designed to strengthen school administrations, such as the impact of introducing additional assistant principals to large high schools. Evaluation helps to determine the effectiveness of teacher professional development and other programs designed to improve teaching and learning. And, of course, educational evaluators study the impact of programs on students.

Student programs in the educational setting focus on both the academic and social enhancement of children. For example, an evaluator might study programs targeting students with special needs, such as an innovative behavior modification program for children with autism. An evaluation may also help determine the effects of programs designed to increase student achievement, such as a new science program. Educational evaluators, particularly those with a background in psychology, have recently been asked to study programs designed to assist teachers in understanding how to best serve children with psychological disorders, such as depression, attention deficit disorder, and bipolar disorder.

Heath-Care Settings. Hospitals and other health-care facilities such as outpatient clinics also spend a great deal of resources evaluating programs and performance. Much of this work is done internally, and some by external consultants. Some evaluations in this setting are supported by grant funds, whereas others are supported directly by the organization or facility. Those conducting evaluations in the health-care settings work to develop and monitor benchmarks, and improve program performance.

Hospitals are similar to other large organizations in that they use evaluation to systematically measure performance outcomes (summative). This evaluative information is then used to strengthen accountability and program performance. In the medical setting, accountability is often concerned with cost and compliance. That is, evaluation is used to monitor spending, the capacity for the number of patient visits and procedures conducted, and the extent to which clinicians and other personnel are adhering to facility regulations. Such regulations may range from the handling of bio-hazardous materials to maintaining accurate medical records.

Evaluation is also used formatively in the health-care setting, to improve performance. Here, individual performance, as well as overall program performance, is examined. Thus, the performance of individual practitioners, such as doctors and nurses is sometimes evaluated on a continual basis. Evaluators may observe that a particular clinician has an excess of patients with reoccurring illnesses. The evaluator or a clinical or administrative supervisor would then attempt to identify a cause, and the clinician would be advised accordingly. Additionally, the performance of clinical groups (e.g., pediatric oncology critical care nursing teams) can also be evaluated in this manner.

An array of programs implemented within the health-care setting are evaluated as a means to enhance performance and increase efficiency as well as the efficacy of the health-care services. These include administrative programs, such as new scheduling plans, as well as clinical programs, such as bereavement groups and yoga programs for cancer patients.

Government Settings. Almost all areas of government—city, county, state, and federal—sponsor programs that include funding for evaluation. The federal government, however, has several agencies that regularly sponsor evaluation, and is therefore the focus of this section. These federal agencies include, but are not limited to, the Government Accountability Office (GAO), the independent evaluation arm of congress, the National Institutes of Health (NIH), Mental Health (NIMH), Drug Abuse (NIDA), the Centers for Disease Control (CDC), and the National Science Foundation (NSF). Evaluators studying government programs work either directly for the government agency, or are contracted externally through a competitive bidding process (like that described in the educational setting).

Psychologists conducting evaluations for federal government agencies are often studying demonstration or other innovative programs and policies. These programs are often evaluated to test their effectiveness, and to determine the components and conditions under which programs are likely to be successful. A wide range of programs are sponsored by the government, for example an evaluator at NIMH may be studying the latest behavioral intervention designed to reduce HIV infection, while an evaluator at the GAO may be assessing the impact of recent changes to the welfare to work program. Results from these studies are often used to shape policy or to guide the wider dissemination of a program. These evaluations are aimed at making difficult decisions as to whether touted programs should be implemented on a grand scale or not at all.

Corporate Settings. In this setting, psychologists use evaluation science to select, train, and develop employees, including various types of managers, executives, and leaders. They also use it extensively to manage change efforts, and to *develop and evaluate* a wide range of organizational development interventions in areas such as:

- Team Building
- Conflict Resolution
- Downsizing and Reengineering
- Quality Circles
- Total Quality Management
- Job Enrichment
- Self-Managed Work Teams
- Goal Setting
- Career Planning and Development
- Mentoring and Coaching
- Work and Family Balance
- Workforce Diversity
- Corporate Health Promotion and Employee Wellness
- Stress Management
- Organizational Learning, Culture, & Strategic Change

(see Cummings & Worley, 2001; Donaldson & Bligh, chap. 14, this volume). Consequently, corporate evaluation science (Donaldson, forthcoming) is becoming one of the most powerful tools in the industrial/organizational psychologist's repertoire. For a variety of reasons, many evaluations conducted in corporate settings are not published or made public. Thus, it tends to be more difficult to synthesize and develop cumulative knowledge about corporate programs and applications of evaluation science. Nonetheless, evaluation has become an important corporate activity upon which many financial, strategic, and human resource decisions are made.

As with the other domains discussed, evaluators in the corporate setting are hired to work both internally, as staff on the corporate payroll (typically in large organizations), and as external evaluators and consultants. Evaluators often work with management and human resource professionals, and corporate evaluations are conducted at all levels, from the line and staff levels to the executive leadership and board levels. Although improving performance and profitability is often a primary goal of corporate evaluation science, psychologists almost always include the human component in their evaluation work. That is, they focus their evaluation work on simultaneously improving employee well-being, quality of work life, organizational effectiveness, and the bottom line. Successful evaluators in the corporate setting often report that corporate evaluation science is more lucrative than some of the other applications discussed earlier, and that they are more often required to sign confidentiality agreements and refrain from publishing or disseminating evaluation findings while working in this setting.

We have tried to provide a realistic account of some of the settings where psychology and evaluation science are now being applied to promote human welfare and achievement. It is important to emphasize that there are a vast array of applications within the five settings we described, as well as many other settings where evaluation science is being used, and will likely be used more in the near future. Consequently, the career opportunities for psychologists interested in improving human potential and society at-large through evaluation science are vast. Training in psychology with a strong foundation, co-concentration, minor or certificate in evaluation science, presents a professional with a lifetime of stimulating, rewarding, and profitable career opportunities shaping social, educational, psychological and organizational policies, programs and services.

CONCLUSION

The globalization and accelerating demand for professional evaluations to improve programs, personnel, projects, policies, communities, organizations and the like, are creating new opportunities for psychologists. Master's and doctoral level professionals interested in applying the science of psychology have the potential to thrive in careers that enable them to work within, and benefit from, the emerging transdiscipline of evaluation science. Careers that involve the application of both psychological and evaluation science to improve the human condition are personally meaningful and fulfilling, socially important, intellectually challenging and stimulating, and most often enable one to earn a respectable and decent living. Of course, the setting one chooses to apply psychology and evaluation science most directly affects the latter, with corporate evaluation science often providing very lucrative career paths. But ultimately, the real payoff to society over time will be if the number of psychologists applying the science of psychology and evaluation to prevent and ameliorate human problems continues to keep pace with the dramatic growth in this area we have witnessed in the past decade.

REFERENCES

Alkin, M. C. (2004). *Evaluation roots.* Thousand Oaks, CA: Sage.

Alkin, M. C., & Christie, C. A. (2004). An evaluation theory tree. In M. C. Alkin (Ed.), *Evaluation roots* (pp. 12–66). Thousand Oaks, CA: Sage.

Alkin, M. C., & Christie, C. A. (Eds.). (2005). Theorists' models in action [Special issue]. *New Directions for Evaluation, 106.*

American Evaluation Association. (2004, July). Guiding principles for evaluators. Retrieved February 24, 2004, from http://www.eval.org

American Psychology Association. (2002). Ethical principles of psychologists and code of conduct. *American Psychologist, 57*(12), 1060–1073.

Campbell, D. T. (1978). *Qualitative knowing in action research.* In M. Brenner & P. Marsh (Eds.), The social contexts of methods (pp. 184–209). London: Croom Helm.

Christie, C. A. (2003). The practice-theory relationship in evaluation. *New Directions for Evaluation, 97,* 7–35.

Cronbach, L. J. (1982). *Designing evaluations of educational and social programs.* San Francisco, CA: Jossey-Bass.

Cronbach, L. J., Ambron, S. R., Dornbusch, S. M., Hess, R. D., Hornik, R. C., Phillips, D. C., Walker, D. F., & Weiner, S. S. (1980). *Toward reform of program evaluation.* San Francisco: Jossey Bass.

Cousins, J. B., & Earl, L. M. (1995). The case for participatory evaluation: Theory, research, practice. In J. B. Cousins & L. M. Earl (Eds.), *Participatory evaluation in education* (pp. 3–18). Great Britain: Bargess Science Press.

Cummings, T. G., & Worley, C. G. (2001). *Organization development and change.* Cincinnati, OH: South Western College Publishing.

Donaldson, S. I. (2001). Overcoming our negative reputation: Evaluation becomes known as a helping profession. *American Journal of Evaluation, 22,* 355–361.

Donaldson, S. I. (2003). Theory-driven program evaluation in the new millennium. In S. I. Donaldson & M. Scriven (Eds.), *Evaluating social programs and problems: Visions for the new millennium* (pp. 111–142). Mahwah, NJ: Lawrence Erlbaum Associates.

Donaldson, S. I. (forthcoming). *Program theory-driven evaluation science: Strategies and applications.* Mahwah, NJ: Lawrence Erlbaum Associates.

Donaldson, S. I., Gooler, L. E., & Scriven, M. (2002). Strategies for managing evaluation anxiety: Toward a psychology of program evaluation. *American Journal of Evaluation, 23*(3), 261–273.

Donaldson, S. I., & Lipsey, M. W. (in press). Roles for theory in contemporary evaluation practice: Developing practical knowledge. In I. Shaw, J. Greene, & M. Mark (Eds.), *Handbook of evaluation.* London: Sage.

Donaldson, S. I., & Scriven, M. (2003). *Evaluating social programs and problems: Visions for the new millennium.* Mahwah, NJ: Lawrence Erlbaum Associates.

Fitzpatrick, J. (2004). Exemplars as case studies: Reflections on the links between theory, practice, and context. *American Journal of Evaluation, 25*(4), 541–559.

Fitzpatrick, J. L., Sanders, J. R., & Worthen, B. R. (2003). *Program evaluation: Alternative approaches and practical guidelines* (3rd ed.). Boston, MA: Allyn & Bacon.

Graham, J. W., & Donaldson, S. I. (1993). Evaluating interventions with differential attrition: The importance of nonresponse mechanisms and use of follow up data. *Journal of Applied Psychology, 78,* 119–128.

Henry, G., & Mark, M. (2003). Toward an agenda for research on evaluation. *New Directions for Evaluation, 97,* 53–56.

Joint Committee on Standards for Education Evaluation. (1994). *The program evaluation standards: How to assess evaluations of educational programs.* Thousand, Oaks, CA: Sage.

Lipsey, M. W., & Wilson, D. B. (1993). The efficacy of psychological, educational, and behavioral treatment: Confirmation from meta-analysis. *American Psychologist, 48,* 1181–1209.

Mertens, D. M. (2003). The inclusive view of evaluation: Visions for the new millennium. In S. I. Donaldson & M. Scriven (Eds.), *Evaluating social programs and problems: Visions for the new millennium* (pp. 91–108). Mahwah, NJ: Lawrence Erlbaum Associates.

Mertens, D. M. (2005). The inauguration of the International Organization for Cooperation in Evaluation. *American Journal of Evaluation, 26*(1), 124–130.

Patton, M. Q. (1997). *Utilization-focused evaluation: A new century text* (3rd ed.). Thousand Oaks, CA: Sage.

Rossi, P. (1990). Forward. In H. T. Chen (Ed.), *Theory-driven evaluations*. Newbury Park, CA: Sage.

Rossi, P. H., Lipsey, M. W., & Freeman, H. E. (2004). *Evaluation: A systematic approach* (7th ed.). Thousand Oaks, CA: Sage.

Russon, C. (2004). A decade of international trends in evaluation. *The Evaluation Exchange, IX*(4).

Scriven, M. (2003). Evaluation in the new millennium: The transdisciplinary vision. In S. I. Donaldson & M. Scriven (Eds.), *Evaluating social programs and problems: Visions for the new millennium* (pp. 19–42). Mahwah, NJ: Lawrence Erlbaum Associates.

Shadish, W. R., Cook, T. D., & Campbell, D. T. (2002). *Experimental and quasi-experimental designs for generalized causal inference*. Boston, MA: Houghton Mifflin.

13

Social Psychology:
Applications and Careers

William D. Crano
Claremont Graduate University

Can we solve the problems of racial and ethnic intolerance that plague our country?

Can we predict and control the factors responsible for violence toward women?

Can advertisements on the mass media keep young adolescents from abusing drugs?

Can we foster more ecologically responsible behavior in our citizenry?

Can we simulate the actions of nations to determine their likely responses to threats or reinforcements?

Is a 50% divorce rate an inevitability in this country?

How, in a pluralistic democracy, can minorities make their positions salient?

What causes people to act altruistically, to help others in need, often at their own personal expense?

Questions of these kinds occupy the thoughts of many of us. For social psychologists, such questions dominate not only their thoughts, but also their work. Many of the issues with which social psychologists contend are in one way or another relevant to important social issues. Most social psychologists consider it fortunate that the fundamental substance of their field is so inherently interesting and pertinent to the major concerns of

daily social life.[1] In this chapter, we review some of the activities of professional social psychologists in their attempts to answer questions of the
type presented here. This presentation illustrates the broad range of problems and issues that occupy the attention of many professional social psychologists. As may be inferred readily from the questions that began this
chapter, these problems and issues are not trivial; they are part of the fundamental social fabric of our way of life.

BASIC OR APPLIED RESEARCH—OR BOTH?

To begin our deliberation on applied social psychology, we must revisit the
early days of this discipline, because the founders of the field established
the blueprint that has guided social psychology's development over the
past century. Let us begin our story with the great Kurt Lewin, whom
Oskamp (1991) described as "the most influential single figure in shaping
modern social psychology" (p. 202). In one of his most famous aphorisms,
Lewin declared that there was "nothing so practical as a good theory"
(Lewin, 1964).[2] This declaration from one of the founding fathers of the field,
and which most social psychologists accept as an article of faith, points to
the duality of our concerns and approaches. In his maxim, Lewin was responding to the tension that existed in social psychology between basic research and the applications of basic findings to that amorphous place
called "the field"—in short, to society. As will be shown, this tension exists
even today, though the cleavage between the two orientations is much less
pronounced than in Lewin's time, when there was a clear and strong tension between proponents of the basic and applied approaches and orientations. It is obvious that Lewin did not see this tug of war as appropriate or
profitable. He developed an approach known as action theory, whose goal
was the production of *actionable knowledge*—that is, knowledge that could
be put to direct use in the context in which it was discovered (Argyris, 1993;
Reason & Bradbury, 2001). Through his action theory approach, Lewin was
saying to the proponents of applied research that theory building and the
enlargement of the knowledge base of psychology were essential, practical,
and necessary. Simultaneously, he was reminding basic researchers that
their work should have real practical application, and that they must be
sensitive to the potential of their work to contribute to the enhancement of

---

[1]They often do not reflect on the opposite side of the coin, that they also are unlucky because the problems with which they must contend are so intractable.

[2]His other famous dictum was that he was "autocratic in his insistence on democracy." This
insistence is understandable. Like many of the founders of the field, Lewin was a Jew who was
forced to flee Nazi Germany near the beginning of the Second World War. He repaid his adopted
country with research he designed to maintain wartime morale in America.

society. Without the mutual interplay of both, he felt, the full potential of the science would not be realized.

To foster his action theory position, Lewin advocated "action research," which focused on practical problems and often, ideally, was undertaken in the context in which the problems were found, rather than in the more conventional laboratory setting. The issues he confronted were thorny—racial and ethnic prejudice, wartime morale, democratic versus autocratic leadership—and his results were not always completely definitive. However, his general approach to understanding, which involved tackling problems that really mattered, and studying them in the context in which they occurred, was new and influential. It may have taken a while, but it is safe to say that today's social psychology has recognized the wisdom of Lewin's approach to knowledge generation and eventual understanding. Many of us now realize that the generalizability of our theories into the rough and tumble world of practical reality is facilitated when the research on which the theory is based is undertaken in the field.

This is not to argue that all of social psychology is focused on practical, vital, socially relevant problems that affect our day-to-day lives. There is no arguing that much of social psychology, perhaps the majority of social psychological research, is characterized by the study of basic, fundamental phenomena, which may or may not be immediately relevant to practical concerns. Partly for historic reasons, which saw the field focusing more on individual processes, actions, and actors, and less on group and intergroup phenomena, social psychology seemed in the 1960s to begin to veer away from applications, and toward more basic, laboratory science, where the principal research methods involved the randomized experiment, conducted in the pristine and sometimes sterile environment of the psychological laboratory (McGuire, 1973). There is much to recommend this approach, but not to the exclusion of all other approaches (Campbell & Stanley, 1963). Today, renewed interest in social psychology in quasi-experimental designs, and in intergroup and intragroup phenomena, now sees the pendulum swinging toward applications (Shadish, Cook, & Campbell, 2002).

What has caused the pendulum to swing can be traced to a host of factors, not the least of which is society's demand for a return on its investment. Social science is expensive, and it often is supported by public funds. The public naturally and reasonably expects something tangible in return for its investments. The bulk of social psychologists have responded to this reasonable demand, and the field is richer for it, theoretically, methodologically, and statistically. As a result of this movement, today's social research is more grounded in real issues, consistent with Lewin's action approach of more than 70 years ago, it is more applied, and it is more relevant to the needs of society. At the same time, its theories are more realistic and more testable, and in consequence, may be supported (or disconfirmed) with greater certainty. Moreover, contemporary theories generally are more likely than before to be tested in contexts that involve more than randomized experimental designs. As our theories have evolved and enlarged as a result of the more even interplay of theory and practice, so too have our methods and the venues in which we apply them. All of these developments have resulted in accelerated progress.

Even so, perhaps despite this progress, there remain differences in emphasis in basic and applied research. For fundamental researchers, application of the knowledge they have gained in their basic research often, though not always, is a secondary consideration. The focus of basic social psychology is to identify principles that govern human beliefs and actions, and how others affect, and are affected by, those beliefs and actions (Allport, 1985). Whether or not these principles are (or ever will be) applicable to real problems often is *considered* by basic social psychologists, it is on their radarscopes, but it does not drive their work. Their emphasis is on discovery and understanding of causal relationships and the factors that affect them. Making use of this knowledge is not a central goal, but it certainly can occur, and when it does, most are pleased.

In addition to the constrained focus of the purely basic social psychologist in terms of applicability, the context of their work also may be relatively particularistic. Social psychologists concerned principally with basic phenomena generally, though not always, conduct their research in the tightly controlled context of the experimental laboratory. The analysis of variance, or some variant thereof, is the statistical method of choice, and differences that come about on some theoretically implicated variable often are considered in terms of their statistical, and not practical, significance. This constriction of method and statistic sometimes makes it difficult to explore complex practical or applied problems that do not lend themselves to the germ-free confines of the experimental laboratory.

At the other end of the social psychological spectrum are those whose work is concerned with the generalization and application of their laboratory-oriented cousins' hard-won basic insights to questions of social importance. These researchers find their rewards in attacking obdurate social problems—drug abuse, unsafe sex, smoking, organ donation, and so on.[3] They seek to glean ideas that have some utility in their applied work from fundamental researchers and theorists. Applied research, by its very nature, often is not undertaken in the laboratory, nor is its central goal the generation of new knowledge (though this certainly can occur). Rather, the

---

[3]Obviously, not all applied research is directed toward *important* social issues. Using social psychological research on persuasion to sell more soap or tires or bubblegum is not necessarily of great social relevance.

insights of the social psychological laboratory are brought into the field—the workplace, the political arena, the salesroom—where problems and difficulties of making proper conclusions are magnified owing to the lack of control over the research context (relative to that of the laboratory).

It is perhaps for this reason that social psychology places such a premium on proper research methods and research design. Concern with the appropriate design of research operations is characteristic of most fields of psychology. But in social psychology, given its double life in the laboratory and the field, solution to problems of research design is widely recognized as essential. This concern has had important and positive consequences. Along with creating many new and different methodological and analytic research procedures, methodologists concerned with social psychological inquiry are not above borrowing techniques from fields as far afield as political science, anthropology, economics, sociology, and mathematical statistics. This creative use of other people's methodologies has enriched the field considerably.

A REAL SPLIT?

The dichotomy between basic and applied research in social psychology presented here has been starkly drawn, principally for illustrative purposes. In fact, most social psychologists recognize that there is no necessary incompatibility between applied and basic social research. Lewin was right. Each orientation motivates and nourishes the other. Although some social psychologists focus all of their efforts on fundamental discovery, whereas others are concerned solely with the application of theory-based information gleaned from the pristine confines of the social psychological laboratory, most social psychologists do both types of research. Even those whose principal allegiance is to applied field research often find themselves testing theory and creating basic, fundamental, knowledge. Often, they will do so outside the experimental laboratory, but the venue for research is less important than its goals, and the quality of the research designed to reach them. By the same token, even social psychologists concerned with the most fundamental processes often are drawn to applied work because the nature and promise of their work cries out for application. So, where does the distinction lie?

Crano and Brewer (2002) located the (sometimes) division of basic and applied research in social psychology primarily in terms of their immediacy of payback:

Essentially, the difference between the two (basic and applied approaches) lies in whether relatively long-term or short-term gains are expected from the outcomes of the research. The *applied* label refers to those research efforts that are directed toward affecting a particular phenomenon in some preconceived way (e.g., which of several advertising campaigns will produce the greater number of product sales; which serum formula will terminate the symptoms of skin cancer most effectively; which remedial program will reduce illiteracy in the urban ghetto). Because the goals of applied research are relatively concrete, feedback on the effectiveness of any experimental manipulation is immediate. For *basic* research, on the other hand, the goal of each research project is to contribute to that ephemeral universe of knowledge, or, in somewhat more specific terms, to add to the accumulative pattern of data that will ultimately determine the survival value of alternative theoretical interpretations of the phenomena under investigation (e.g., *which* theory of consumer motivation; *which* etiology of skin cancer; *which* explanation of the nature of mass illiteracy). In this (basic research) enterprise, the value of any particular research contribution can only be judged from a historical perspective. (pp. 24–25)

ALTERNATION

Many social psychologists appear to agree that work in both applied and basic research is proper, and their work alternates between these venues, to a greater or lesser extent. The alternation of research efforts between laboratory and field, applied and basic, is as it should be. One of psychology's great research methodologists, Donald Campbell, observed that research progress is best viewed as a cyclical process, in which ideas developed in the laboratory are taken to the field, where they are invariably shown to be less than completely adequate (Campbell, 1969; Campbell & Stanley, 1963). The information gleaned from failed (or less than completely successful) applications is brought back to the laboratory, where field-based insights are used to enrich and instruct future basic research. Basic research enriched by field studies gradually inches its way toward clarity and understanding. Consistent with Lewin's action theory approach, Campbell's recommended cyclical process produces research and understanding that is grounded in the actual problems experienced, and in the social context in which they occur. As a result, with this approach, the findings generated in the laboratory are more readily applicable to those problems.

As has been discussed, the boundary between basic and applied research in social psychology is not impermeable. Both types of research are necessary. Both types of research contribute to knowledge and practice. And both types are well represented in social psychology. In the following pages, we consider how basic and applied research contributes to our understanding of some important social phenomena. Given the mission of this volume, we focus primary attention on applications. But it is fair to say that without the underpinnings made available by basic research, there would be little to apply, just as it is fair to say that without insights provided by applied work, our basic research would be considerably more primitive and less socially relevant than it is.

AREAS OF APPLICATION

Earlier in this chapter, we alluded to a widely acknowledged definition of social psychology that was provided by yet another founding member of social psychology, Gordon Allport. In his view, social psychology is the discipline that focuses on "the social nature of the individual person," and uses scientific methods "to understand and explain how the thought, feeling, and behavior of individuals are influenced by the actual, imagined, or implied presence of others" (Allport, 1985, p. 3).

There are a number of important features of this definition that deserve mention. First, Allport distinguishes social psychology from the other social sciences (political science, sociology, cultural anthropology) by its stress on the individual person. Our sister social sciences generally are much more systems oriented, that is, they are concerned not so much with individual actors, but with large groups—nations, cultures, societies.

Next, Allport insists on the use of the scientific method, which involves logic, consensus regarding the proper and allowable investigative techniques to be employed, and data-checking feedback to verify the validity of hypotheses or expectations. He argued that for a scientist, it is not enough to postulate, speculate, or pontificate; rather, the discipline imposed by logic *and* empirical, data based confirmation or disconfirmation of expectations is necessary to support a position scientifically. This insistence on the scientific method separates the field from other approaches in which authority, faith, voodoo or other forms of mumbo jumbo are used to establish truth. To this day, a strong bias toward the scientific method continues in social psychology, and helps maintain its vitality and contribution to understanding social life. It is unfortunate that this same observation cannot be made unflinchingly and unequivocally when describing some of its sister disciplines.

The final feature of Allport's definition of social psychology that deserves close scrutiny is his emphasis on the thoughts, feelings, and behavior of individuals, and how they are influenced by others (whether present or absent, real or imagined). This emphasis on thoughts, feelings, and behavior, and the ways in which they may be influenced, brings us to a consideration of the three central pillars of social psychology: attitudes, group and intergroup phenomena, and interpersonal relations. Social psychology is a burgeoning enterprise, but most of its work can be captured within the framework of these three broad concerns. We consider in turn each of these fundamental building blocks of the science of social psychology, and along the way demonstrate the interplay of basic and applied research devoted to their study.

Attitudes, groups, and interpersonal relations—the subareas from which applied social psychologists take their inspiration and direction, are quite diverse. Research interest in each is intense, and the research devoted to each sphere of endeavor is expanding exponentially. On the pages that follow, some of the diversity and intensity will become apparent, along with a picture of the potential of the field to contribute to the solution of vexing social problems. Obviously, given the accelerating rate of research, it is next to impossible to present all that is there, but the examples offered will provide a picture of the enterprise.

ATTITUDES

The study of attitudes (or beliefs, values, and opinions) is one of the defining features of social psychology, whether applied or basic. In fact, research on attitudes has been a central preoccupation of social psychology from the earliest days of the field (Crano, 2000). Social psychologists are interested in attitudes because we believe they are associated with behavior or action, in short, with how people act. Because predicting how a person will behave under varying contextual and interpersonal conditions is a primary goal of all of psychology, the relevance of attitudes to social psychology is obvious.

We could locate the beginnings of the field's preoccupation with attitudes at any of a number of points in the mists of ancient prehistory. We might start, as Allport suggested we might (but later rejected), with some of the great thinkers of the past—Plato, Aristotle, Hobbes, Comte, Hegel, and so on. A more productive and realistic starting point, however, is to be found in the decades between the two World Wars. After World War I, the United States and the world were in a state of flux. The great depression, the rise of Nazism, race riots, the spread of communism, all of these major social upheavals required explanation, and social psychology, in its scientific infancy, was asked to contribute to the needed and necessary knowledge base. During and after World War II, citizens again were faced with massive problems and dislocations. Maintaining troop and homeland morale during the nation's most dangerous war, the evolving nuclear thereat, coming to grips with the reality of genocide, the cold war, the movement of women into the workforce, all required insights into important questions that could not be ignored. Social psychology again was asked to step forward, and in many ways, the manner in which it did has shaped the face of the field, and of the more global society in which the science is embedded.

Social psychology was fortunate that a number of young researchers trained in the scientific method and, though their work in the War, experienced in the practical utilization of social psychological principles, were coming home to take their places in the major educational institutions of the country. These men, some of whom had fled the Nazi regime, had honed their skills on important, sometimes life-and-death questions. They had learned what worked and what did not in attempting to mobilize troops and citizens in a war of survival. Now they were coming home. Of these returnees, one of the central social psychological contributors to the development of the field was Carl Iver Hovland, a young man who trained at Northwestern and Yale between the two World Wars. Hovland's particular genius resided in his ability to integrate the insights and empirical observations of his co-workers into a coherent whole, which could be used as a basis for understanding and later decision making. William McGuire (1996) commented that Hovland "could attend a symposium of papers that seemed to have little in common and, if called on to summarize them, seemed able on the spot to abstract out their unifying themes and show that the papers converged in interesting and complex ways to produce a coherent picture" (p. 49). This is a rare talent, and it is no wonder that Hovland was rightly honored for his many contributions during his lifetime.

During the Second World War, Hovland was tasked with determining how our propaganda films affected troop morale and effectiveness, and how they could be improved. He needed not just to know whether or not a persuasive pitch worked, but how it worked, or why it failed to do so. Hovland returned to Yale after the war intent on systematizing the insights he had developed in his important and very applied work as analyst and creator of propaganda. His subsequent research on attitudes set the tone of research for decades of work in social psychology in the United States. In the Yale Communication and Attitude Change Program, which he founded, Hovland assembled one of the most formidable casts of researchers that social psychology has ever witnessed. Some of the products of that early work (e.g., Hovland, Janis, & Kelley, 1957; Sherif & Hovland, 1961), which were produced nearly a half century ago, still ring true and still stimulate thought and further research. The Yale group, for example, studied the characteristics of an information source that makes it more or less credible to an audience, and the features of messages that make them more or less persuasive. The ways in which emotion, specifically fear, affect people's tendencies to accept or reject a recommendation was a central focus, as was the association of personality factors in facilitating or retarding persuasion. Social psychology still is wrestling with these issues, and current theories of attitude formation and change owe much to Hovland's seminal insights.

A powerful linkage between basic and applied social science in Hovland's research program was inevitable, given the nature of the work being undertaken, and ways in which the intellectual questions had come about. As a result, Hovland's crew could not help but be interested in problems that had a practical as well as a fundamental side. Their studies accomplished two central goals. They led to an ever evolving and increasingly refined conceptualization of the factors involved in persuasion (or propaganda, or social influence—the terms often are used more or less synonymously). And, they provided practitioners with techniques that were readily exportable to the field.

Partly as a consequence of the pioneering efforts of Hovland and his systematic program of research, we now have a burgeoning industry devoted to the marketing of everything from Levis to Ivory Snow to drug prevention. Principles of attitude change, whose origins and development can be traced to Hovland's laboratory at Yale, are now used and misused to market an infinite variety of goods and services, many of which are not particularly good, nor particularly serviceable. The marketing or advertising industry makes wide use of individuals with social psychological training. Thus, those seeking a career in marketing, advertising, and their allied fields would do well to study social psychology, as this discipline is concerned precisely with the kinds of knowledge that people in these fields should have mastered.

On the more prosocial side of the ledger, we should consider social marketing, which also has become an important enterprise in this country. Social marketing typically involves the use of mass media to promote programs that are designed to aid the health and well-being of the target audience. The anti-drug ads that appear periodically on TV are good examples of this form of marketing (see Crano & Burgoon, 2002, for a discussion of this program). The billboards on the street offering free AIDS testing and advice about the best ways of avoiding HIV infection, too, are examples of social marketing. The social marketing movement has been part of the social landscape at least for the past half century. Such efforts often are supported by governmental agencies attempting to intervene in problems afflicting the health of the community. In the case of HIV/AIDS or drug abuse, the community is the entire country. Accordingly, many millions are invested in programs, publicly and privately supported, to facilitate prosocial goals. Opportunities to contribute to this kind of work are available in both the public and the private sector. Training in the social psychology of persuasion or attitude change provides a useful background for securing such opportunities.

Of course, marketing in the private sector in the service of product sales supplies an ever-greater set of opportunities, and is considerably more lucrative than public sector work, owing to the massive investment businesses make to ensure their products are viewed sympathetically. Clearly, some might find greater intrinsic value in selling drug prevention than a particular brand of shaving cream, but in both cases, social psychological theory and research has much to offer.

GROUPS

Another area in which applied research on attitudes is becoming increasingly evident is concerned with research on stereotyping and discrimination. These social ills have been with the country since before its birth, with the dawn of slavery in the northern hemisphere. Social psychologists have made strong efforts to help alleviate injustices of this type. More than a half century ago, for example, Allport (1954) analyzed the nature of prejudice, and made recommendations for its reduction. Later research by social psychologists into the nature of cooperation and independence (e.g., Aronson, 2000; Aronson & Patnoe, 1997), hate (Sternberg, 2005), the effects of personal contact on interracial harmony (Pettigrew & Tropp, 2000; van Dick et al., 2004), the impact of negative teacher expectancies on the achievement of young school children (Rosenthal & Jacobson, 1968), the depredations of segregation on children's performance and self-image (e.g., Miller & Brewer, 1984), and the harmful effects of stereotyping on academic achievement (Davies, Spencer, & Steele, 2005; Sackett, Hardison, & Cullen, 2004) are evidence of the field's continuing concern with this critically important social problem. Theories and research devised to understand and attenuate racism are a common feature of social psychological research, and as it progresses, our understanding of these destructive tendencies and actions grows (see Dovidio, Glick, & Rudman, 2005; Gaertner & Dovidio, 2000; Stephan & Stephan, 1996).

Not all movements in group psychology are concerned with negative factors like stereotyping and discrimination. Traditionally in the United States, volunteerism has played a vital role in the well-being of many members of the society, and these prosocial activities, too, have come under the scrutiny of social psychology. Volunteers in schools, churches, hospitals, and hospices keep the wheels of everyday life rolling. Most children's sports teams would be impossible without strong community support in the form of volunteering parents; most of our most cherished philanthropic organizations could not survive without the generous humanitarian efforts of volunteers. Who are these people, and why do they act as they do? Questions of this sort have fascinated social psychologists, and recent research has been conducted in search of reasons behind these altruistic behaviors (e.g., Omoto & Snyder, 2002; Snyder, Omoto, & Lindsay, 2004). For example, in their social psychological analysis of volunteerism, Omoto and Snyder suggest that there are costs involved in the altruistic giving of time and energy for the good of others. At times, the stigma attached to the focus of the volunteer's efforts is transferred to the helpers themselves. Nonetheless, volunteers persist, and their selfless actions provide examples of the best that society can do.

At a very broad level of group analysis is the study of social identities, and the manner which these identities help shape our relations with the groups to which we belong, or with which we compete (e.g., Hogg, 2003; Tajfel & Turner, 1986). The general idea behind this theory is that the groups with which we identify help us determine who we are—they are, in other words, part of our self-identity. The theory has been expanded to understand such diverse features as leadership (Hogg, 2001), collective action (Sturmer & Simon, 2004), riots, and crowd behavior (Reicher, 2000). Studying large-scale social movements of this type from a social psychological perspective provides insights into group and crowd processes that are not available in other disciplines.

A perhaps unexpected role of applied social psychologists may be found in the study of jury selection and jury behavior. Whereas our previous consideration of the social psychology of groups was concerned with intergroup relations, the study of the inner workings in groups, with within- or *intra*-group relations, also has captured the attention of many social psychologists. One example of such a focus is in the social psychological analysis of the courtroom, specifically with the dynamics of jury decision making. In terms of this specific substantive focus, social psychology appears to share some similarity with the work of cognitive psychologists (e.g., see the work discussed by Pezdek et al., chap. 11, this volume). However, the orientation of these two groups of scholars is quite different. Social psychologists involved in jury research typically conceptualize the jury as a small group. As such, the jury is prone to the same relational issues and problems as any other small group. For example, social psychologists long have been fascinated with processes of conformity and independence. Why do some people always bend to the power of the majority, and what does the majority bring to bear when attempting to enforce compliance (Cialdini & Goldstein, 2004; MacDonald, Nail, & Levy, 2004)? Similarly, the impact of minority factions on majority persuasion and decision making has attracted considerable attention (Crano & Chen, 1998; Gardikiotis, Martin, & Hewstone, 2004; Kerr, 2001). Work by Davis and his colleagues has been concerned with the malleability of individual jurors when the bulk of their peers share a view contrary to theirs (e.g., Tindale, Nadler, Krebel, & Davis, 2004). We have discovered much about the nature of juries by applying what we know about small groups in general. It should come as no surprise that many researchers have migrated to the jury room (e.g., see Nemeth, 1977, 2001; Witte & Davis, 1996). Students interested in working in jury selection or in studying jury behavior would do well to study social psychology. Although not all social psychology programs offer training in "psych and law," many do, and they can be sorted out through the social psychology network, an invaluable site for anyone wishing to learn more about the field (see www.socialpsychology.org).

INTERPERSONAL RELATIONS

Another area of applied psychology in which social psychologists have made important applied contributions is in the study of interpersonal relations. This term refers to the host of factors that affect the ways in which people relate to one another, be they lovers, competitors, or strangers meeting for the first time. We have long been concerned with the acquaintance process (Newcomb, 1961, 1978), adult attachment (Berscheid, Snyder, & Omoto, 2004; Rholes & Simpson, 2004), and the transition from liking to loving relationships (Hendrick & Hendrick, 1992). Those interested in personnel development or human resources development, in hiring, or in management, have found studies of interpersonal relationships invaluable. Although specific training in these areas is generally required, the background knowledge provided by the study of interpersonal relations is fundamental to this work.

The fundamental focus of social psychology is directed to important social issues. From its inception, the field has been grounded in the ongoing problems of the society. Training in this field prepares students for a wide range of professions, all of which may serve the society at large. Of course, there are many other routes to socially relevant professions, but historically, social psychology has been a fine training ground for these professions, and recent movements in the field toward a more applied orientation suggest that this will continue to be so. The work with which the field is preoccupied is interesting, diverse, and important, and training in the field allows the possibility that one may make important contributions. This chapter was developed to illustrate some of these possibilities, and to facilitate the interested reader's exploration of a fruitful and rewarding career.

REFERENCES

Allport, G. (1954). *The nature of prejudice*. Reading, MA: Addison-Wesley.

Allport, G. (1985). The historical background of social psychology. In G. Lindzey & E. Aronson (Eds.), *The handbook of social psychology* (3rd ed., Vol. 1, pp. 1–46). New York: Random House.

Argyris, C. (1993). *Knowledge for action*. San Francisco: Jossey-Bass.

Aronson, E. (2000). *Nobody left to hate: Teaching compassion after Columbine*. New York: W. H. Freeman.

Aronson, E., & Patnoe, S. (1997). *The jigsaw classroom: Building cooperation in the classroom* (2nd ed.). New York: Addison Wesley Longman.

Berscheid, E., Snyder, M., & Omoto, A. M. (2004). Measuring closeness: The Relationship Closeness Inventory (RCI) revisited. In D. J. Mashek & A. P. Aron (Eds.), *Handbook of closeness and intimacy* (pp. 81–101). Mahwah, NJ: Lawrence Erlbaum Associates.

Campbell, D. T. (1969). Reforms as experiments. *American Psychologist, 24*, 409–429.

Campbell, D. T., & Stanley, J. C. (1963). Experimental and quasi-experimental designs for research on teaching. In N. L. Gage (Ed.), *Handbook of research on teaching* (pp. 171–246). Chicago: Rand-McNally. Reprinted as *Experimental and quasi-experimental designs for research.* Chicago: Rand-McNally, 1966.

Cialdini, R. B., & Goldstein, N. J. (2004). Social influence: Compliance and conformity. *Annual Review of Psychology, 55*, 591–621.

Crano, W. D. (2000). Milestones in the psychological analysis of social influence. *Group Dynamics: Theory, Research, and Practice, 4*, 68–80.

Crano, W. D., & Brewer, M. B. (2002). *Principles and methods of social research.* Mahwah, NJ: Lawrence Erlbaum Associates.

Crano, W. D., & Burgoon, M. (2002). *Mass media and drug prevention: Classic and contemporary theories and research.* Mahwah, NJ: Lawrence Erlbaum Associates.

Crano, W. D., & Chen, X. (1998). The leniency contract and persistence of majority and minority influence. *Journal of Personality and Social Psychology, 74*, 1437–1450.

Davies, P. G., Spencer, S. J., & Steele, C. M. (2005). Clearing the air: Identity safety moderates the effects of stereotype threat on women's leadership aspirations. *Journal of Personality and Social Psychology, 88*, 276–287.

Dovidio, J. F., Glick, P. G., & Rudman, L. (Eds.). (2005). *On the nature of prejudice: Fifty years after Allport.* Malden, MA: Blackwell.

Gaertner, S. L., & Dovidio, J. F. (2000). *Reducing intergroup bias: The Common Ingroup Identity Model.* Philadelphia, PA: Psychology Press.

Gardikiotis, A., Martin, R., & Hewstone, M. (2004). The representation of majorities and minorities in the British press: A content analytic approach. *European Journal of Social Psychology, 34*, 637–646.

Hendrick, S. S., & Hendrick, C. (1992). *Liking, loving and relating* (2nd ed.). Belmont, CA: Brooks/Cole.

Hogg, M. A. (2001). A social identity theory of leadership. *Personality and Social Psychology Review, 5*, 184–200.

Hogg, M. A. (2003). Intergroup relations. In J. Delamater (Ed.), *Handbook of social psychology. Handbooks of sociology and social research* (pp. 479–501). New York: Kluwer Academic/Plenum Publishers.

Hovland, C. I., Janis, I. L., & Kelley, H. H. (1957). *Communication and persuasion.* New Haven, CT: Yale University Press.

Kerr, N. (2001). Is it what one says of how one says it? Style vs. substance from an SDS perspective. In C. K. W. De Dreu & N. K. De Vries (Eds.), *Group consensus and minority influence: Implications for innovation* (pp. 201–228). Malden, MA: Blackwell.

Lewin, K. (1964). Field theory and the phase space. In D. Cartwright (Ed.), *Field theory in social science: Selected theoretical papers by Kurt Lewin* (p. 169). New York: Harper & Row.

MacDonald, G., Nail, P. R., & Levy, D. A. (2004). Expanding the scope of the social response context model. *Basic and Applied Social Psychology, 26*, 77–92.

McGuire, W. J. (1973). The yin and yang of progress in social psychology: Seven koan. *Journal of Personality and Social Psychology, 26*, 446–456.

McGuire, W. J. (1996). The Yale communication and attitude-change program in the 1950s. In E. E. Dennis & E. Wartella (Eds.), *American communication research: The remembered history* (pp. 39–59). Mahwah, NJ: Lawrence Erlbaum Associates.

Miller, N., & Brewer, M. B. (Eds.). (1984). *Groups in contact: The psychology of desegregation.* Orlando, FL: Academic Press.

Nemeth, C. J. (1977). Interactions between jurors as a function of majority vs. unanimity decision rules. *Journal of Applied Social Psychology, 7*, 38–56.

Nemeth, C. J. (2001). Dissent, diversity, and juries. In F. Butera & G. Mugny (Eds.), *Social influence in social reality: Promoting individual and social change* (pp. 23–32). Ashland, OH: Hogrefe & Huber.

Newcomb, T. M. (1961). *The acquaintance process.* Oxford, England: Holt, Rinehart, & Winston.

Omoto, A. M., & Snyder, M. (2002). Considerations of community: The context and process of volunteerism. *American Behavioral Scientist, 45*, 846–867.

Oskamp, S. (1991). *Attitudes and opinions* (2nd ed.). Englewood Cliffs, NJ: Prentice-Hall.

Pettigrew, T. F., & Tropp, L. R. (2000). Does intergroup contact reduce prejudice: Recent meta-analytic findings. In S. Oskamp (Ed.), *Reducing prejudice and discrimination: The Claremont Symposium on applied social psychology* (pp. 93–114). Mahwah, NJ: Lawrence Erlbaum Associates.

Reason, P., & Bradbury, H. (2001). *Handbook of action research.* London: Sage.

Rholes, W. S., & Simpson, J. A. (2004). *Adult attachment: Theory, research, and clinical implications.* New York: Guilford.

Rosenthal, R., & Jacobson, L. (1968). *Pygmalion in the classroom.* New York: Holt, Rinehart, & Winston.

Reicher, S. (2000). Crowd behavior. In A. E. Kazdin (Ed.), *Encyclopedia of psychology, Vol. 2* (pp. 374–377). Washington, DC: American Psychological Association.

Sackett, P. R., Hardison, C. M., & Cullen, M. J. (2004). On interpreting stereotype threat as accounting for African American–White differences on cognitive tests. *American Psychologist, 59*, 7–13.

Shadish, W. R., Cook, T. D., & Campbell, D. T. (2002). *Experimental and quasi-experimental designs for generalized causal inference.* Boston: Houghton Mifflin.

Sherif, M., & Hovland, C. I. (1961). *Social judgment theory.* New Haven, CT: Yale University Press.

Snyder, M., Omoto, A. M., & Lindsay, J. J. (2004). Sacrificing time and effort for the good of others: The benefits and costs of volunteerism. In A. G. Miller (Ed.), *The social psychology of good and evil* (pp. 444–468). New York: Guilford Press.

Stephan, W. G., & Stephan, C. W. (1996). *Intergroup relations.* Boulder, CO: Westview Press.

Sternberg, R. J. (2005). *The psychology of hate.* Washington, DC: American Psychological Association.

Sturmer, S., & Simon, B. (2004). Collective action: Towards a dual-pathway model. In W. Stroebe & M. Hewstone (Eds.), *European review of social psychology, Vol. 15* (pp. 59–99). Hove, England: Psychology Press/Taylor & Francis.

Tajfel, H., & Turner, J. C. (1986). The social identity theory of intergroup behavior. In S. Worchel & W. G. Austin (Eds.), *Psychology of intergroup relations* (2nd ed., pp. 7–24). Chicago: Nelson-Hall.

Tindale, R. S., Nadler, J., Krebel, A., & Davis, J. H. (2004). Procedural mechanisms and jury behavior. In M. B. Brewer & M. Hewstone (Eds.), *Applied social psychology. Perspectives on social psychology* (pp. 136–164). Malden, MA: Blackwell.

van Dick, R., Wagner, U., Pettigrew, T. F., Christ, O., Wolf, C., Petzel, T., Castro, V. S., & Jackson, J. S. (2004). Role of perceived importance in intergroup contact. *Journal of Personality and Social Psychology, 87*, 211–227.

Witte, E. H., & Davis, J. H. (1996). *Understanding group behavior, Vol. 1: Consensual action by small groups.* Mahwah, NJ: Lawrence Erlbaum Associates.

14

Rewarding Careers Applying Positive Psychological Science to Improve Quality of Work Life and Organizational Effectiveness

Stewart I. Donaldson
Michelle C. Bligh
Claremont Graduate University

A hallmark of modern societies is the centrality of work and work-related activities (e.g., preparation for work and careers). Most adults are expected to spend the majority of their waking hours engaged in work- or career-focused endeavors into the foreseeable future (Donaldson, Gooler, & Weiss, 1998). A large body of research now suggests that work and careers are of primary importance, both socially and personally, for individuals across the globe. For example, the nature of one's work often imposes a schedule and structure on one's life, establishes patterns of social interaction, dictates economic status and well-being, provides others with a means of judging one's status and personal worth, and consequently becomes a major determinant of healthful adjustment and overall quality of life (Donaldson & Weiss, 1998). These conditions present psychologists with an array of settings to use psychological science to promote human welfare.

As was discussed in chapter 1, international and national associations of psychologists have made the improvement of work and work life a top priority in recent years. For example, the Work and Organizational Psychology Division of the International Association of Applied Psychologists spearheads activities to enhance the collaborations between those who, in different countries, devote themselves to scientific study in the field of work and organizational psychology (see International Association of Applied Psychology, 2005). Productivity in the workplace is one of the broad areas where psychological science desires to make substantial contributions as part of the American Psychological Society (APS) endorsed national research agenda, "The Human Capital Initiative" (American Psychological Society, 2004). Furthermore, Division 14 of the American Psychological Association now has more than 6,000 members dedicated to applying psychology in the workplace (Society of Industrial and Organizational Psychology, 2005a). Favorable career opportunities and salaries promise to attract many more psychology majors in the coming years to pursue careers that involve applying psychology to improve the world of work (see Fennell, 2002).

THEORY, RESEARCH, AND APPLICATION

Behavioral scientists have a long history and impressive track record of using psychological science to improve quality of work life, human performance and productivity, and organizational effectiveness. From Frederick Taylor's early efforts developing principles for maximizing human efficiency at work, to Elton Mayo's research at the Western Electric Company illustrating the impact of social factors at work, to the selection and training of Army recruits during World Wars I and II, to the group dynamics, team building, and organization development work of Kurt Lewin, the relevance of applying psychological principles and research to improve quality of work life and organizational effectiveness has been well established (see Cummings & Worley, 2005; Landy & Conte, 2005; Riggio, 2003).

As the field has evolved and matured, the list of topics and pressing research questions has expanded beyond easy summation. A common framework that can be used to begin to understand psychological issues at work is to examine theory, empirical research, and applications across pressing and popular topics facing workers and work organizations in the 21st century. Behavioral scientists typically build theories of organizational behavior based on systematic research findings (utilizing both quantitative and qualitative research) and on grounded observations of various types of work and organizational behavior. Theories supported by sound empirical research are often applied to the development of programs, policies, or change interventions. These organizational development interventions frequently focus on the dual purposes of improving the quality of work life and organizational effectiveness (Cummings & Worley, 2005; Donaldson, 2004). Theory-driven and research-based human resource and organizational improvement efforts can be evaluated using state-of-the-art evaluation science approaches, and evaluation findings can be used to continually improve and institutionalize these positive change efforts. Evaluation findings can also be used to confirm, reject, or refine theories of organizational behavior. One of the most important goals of the applied psychological scientist in the 21st century will be to further our understanding of how best to maximize the intersection of worker well-being and organizational effectiveness.

APPLYING POSITIVE PSYCHOLOGICAL SCIENCE

There has been considerable discussion and emphasis placed on positive psychology and positive applications of psychological science in recent years (Aspinwall & Staudinger, 2003; Carr, 2004; Compton, 2005; Kauffman & Scoular, 2004; Nakamura & Csikszentmihalyi, 2003; Seligman, 2003; Seligman & Csikszentmihalyi, 2003). The basic thrust of this new theme is to encourage psychological scientists to increase the number of research efforts, interventions, and programs directed at enhancing human well-being and optimal functioning. The main idea is to expand the knowledge base about developing positive human strengths to complement the strong tradition of problem or deficit-based psychological science.

The recent move within psychology toward increasing the amount of research in areas of understanding human strengths and optimal human functioning has many predecessors and comrades. For example, models of occupational health promotion and wellness have similar foci. In the areas of workplace health promotion and wellness, there is a wealth of research and interventions focused on moving workers up the Illness-to-Wellness Continuum shown in Fig. 14.1 toward optimal human functioning (see Donaldson, Gooler, & Weiss, 1998). That is, research and interventions in these areas focus on moving workers from the neutral point of the absence of illness toward optimal physical and mental health, as opposed to moving those who are showing signs or symptoms of illness toward the neutral point (a traditional objective of clinical and counseling psychology). Research in other areas such as enhancing developmental assets (Lerner, 2003), protective factors (Hawkins, Van Horn, & Arthur, 2004; Werner, 2000), resiliency and hardiness (Friedman, chap. 10, this volume), positive models of organizational development and scholarship (Cummings & Worley, 2005; Cameron, Dutton, & Quinn, 2003), the search for best practices (Chapman, 2004; Geringer, Frayne, & Milliman, 2002; Harris, 2005), new positive measurement tools (Lopez & Snyder, 2003) and research methods such as appreciative inquiry (Cooperrider & Avital, 2004; Preskill & Coghlan, 2003) and the success case method (Brinkerhoff, 2003) all represent examples of shifts away from traditional problem- or deficit-based conceptual frameworks, to strength-based or optimal functioning conceptual orientations.

Applied psychological scientists who focus on work issues are well positioned to frame organizational issues and research in a positive or appreciative manner (Cameron, Dutton, & Quinn, 2003; Cooperrider, Whitney, & Stavros, 2003; Preskill & Catsambas, in press), thus realizing some of the

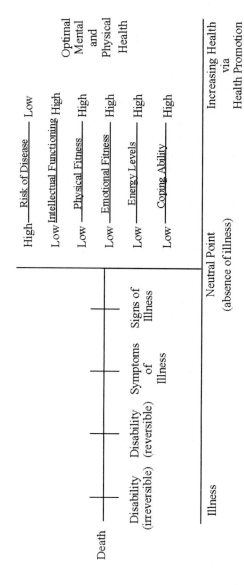

FIG. 14.1. The Illness-to-Wellness Continuum. *Note.* From *Occupational Health Promotion: Health Behavior in the Workplace* (p. 7), by G. S. Everly and R. L. Feldman, 1984, New York: John Wiley. Reprinted with permission.

fruits and potential of applied positive psychology (Aspinwall & Staudinger, 2003; Seligman & Csikszentmihalyi, 2000). For example, applied psychologists commonly work on topics focused on enhancing human potential and organizational success such as best ways to:

- Maximize person–job–organization fit and optimal functioning through rigorous selection, socialization, and training programs;
- Build optimal team performance;
- Develop organizational leaders;
- Provide effective mentoring and coaching;
- Support career development and planning;
- Foster and capitalize on diversity and cross-cultural relationships;
- Optimize work and family balance;
- Create healthful work environments through comprehensive wellness programs;
- Promote organizational learning and continuous improvement;
- Inspire and facilitate positive organization development and strategic change.

Although the vast majority of applied psychological science focused on work has traditionally occurred in corporate or for-profit business settings, an exciting trend in recent years has been the rapid expansion of organizational development and applications of positive psychological science toward improving not-for-profit, human service, educational, government, health care, and community-based organizations (Cummings & Worley, 2005; Donaldson, 2004). For example, not-for-profit human service organizations such as schools, universities, health promotion and counseling clinics, and organizations that specialize in personal and career development, often set as their mission and purpose to enhance the well-being and optimal functioning of their clients. That is, organizational effectiveness in these organizations is often defined and measured by the extent to which these organizations successfully improve and promote optimal human functioning. In fact, Hansfeld (1983) proposed a typology that conceptualized these processes as "people changing technologies" aimed at altering the personal attributes of people in order to improve their well-being and functioning. Applied psychological scientists have an important role to play in designing and evaluating the success of people changing technologies, and in developing and creating effective human service organizations more broadly.

Globalization, new models and concepts of management and leadership (see Bligh & Meindl, 2004), and advances in information technology are also creating new opportunities for positive applied psychological science (Donaldson & Weiss, 1998). For example, research efforts to understand how to best enhance and benefit from workforce diversity, cross-cultural collaboration and communication, new models of leadership development, and new work arrangements such as telecommuting and virtual teams are underway (e.g., see Igbaria & Tan, 1998; Pearce & Congor, 2003; Riggio & Orr, 2004; Sternberg, 2003). These efforts are typically focused on how best to maximize human well-being and performance in global and virtual workplaces. Careers that involve improving work life, job performance, and organizational effectiveness are likely to provide many opportunities in the years ahead for increasing the application of applied positive psychological science toward promoting human welfare across the globe.

TRAINING OPPORTUNITIES

As presented in chapter 1, the discipline and profession of applied psychology has matured in a way that has provided a wide range of training options for the next generation of psychological scientists. Although there are many possible paths to becoming equipped to contribute in this area, psychology master's and doctoral programs that provide training and concentrated study in organizational behavior, human resource and organizational development, industrial/organizational psychology, applied social psychology, and applied research methods and evaluation provide some of the best options for undergraduate psychology majors. Programs in these areas often emphasize and provide a range of coursework and practical experience geared toward building critical areas of competence for applying positive psychology in work or organizational settings.

For example, Table 14.1 provides a sample of the types of competencies that applied psychology training programs often strive to develop in preparing psychological scientists to work in organizational settings. These areas of competency ensure that applied psychological scientists have a strong background and understanding of the history and recent developments in the discipline and profession of psychology, very strong evaluation, critical thinking, and systematic inquiry skills, professional skills essential for working in a range of organizational settings, and both a breadth and depth of content knowledge in key domains. Various clusters of these competencies are typically developed at both the master's and doctoral levels through formal coursework, supervised research and experience, independent readings/study, internships and on-the-job training, professional development workshops, modeling, mentoring, and coaching (see Society of Industrial and Organizational Psychology, 2005b). As noted in chapter 1, the American Psychological Association provides a list of graduate pro-

TABLE 14.1
Areas of Competence to Be Developed in Applied Psychological
Scientists Preparing to Work in Organizational Settings

Foundations

History and Systems of Psychology
Fields of Psychology (including new developments in positive psychology)
Organizational Theory: Micro to Macro
Human Resource and Organizational Development: Theory & Research
Basic Research Methods
Statistical Methods/Data Analysis
Applied Research Methods & Evaluation Science: Qualitative & Quantitative
  Criterion Theory and Development
  Personnel Evaluation
    Personnel Recruitment, Selection, and Placement
    Performance Appraisal and Feedback
  Program Evaluation
    Human Resource Development: Theory, Program Design, and Evaluation
    Organization Development: Theory, Program Design, and Evaluation
Ethical, Legal, and Professional Contexts of Applied Psychology
Consulting and Business Skills

Some Key Topic Areas

Career Development
Health and Stress in Organizations
Leadership and Management
Small Group Theory and Team Processes
Work Motivation
Judgment and Decision Making
Human Performance/Human Factors
Individual Assessment
Individual Differences
Job Evaluation and Compensation
Job/Task Analysis and Classification
Attitude Theory, Measurement, and Change
Consumer Behavior

Note. Expanded version of American Psychological Association Division 14 Graduate
Training Guidelines (Society of Industrial and Organizational Psychology, 2005b).

grams that offer training in applied psychological science on its Web site
(American Psychological Association, 2005a).

CAREER OPPORTUNITIES

Options for psychological scientists who develop concentrations in organizational behavior, industrial/organizational psychology, applied social psychology, human resource management, and organizational development

promise to remain very favorable during the next decade (Donaldson & Berger, chap. 1, this volume). Expertise in these areas typically provides professionals great career flexibility, the ability to seek diverse jobs and experiences, upward mobility, and the opportunities to work for multiple organizations in various locations across a career. For example, with these specializations one often has the ability to work in one or more of the following occupations across a career:

1. Internal Organizational Researcher, Consultant, or Educator
2. External Organizational Researcher, Consultant, or Educator
3. Founder and/or Leader of an Organization
4. College or University Professor or Administrator
5. Research Scientist

Although the range of specific job titles for applied psychological scientists in these areas has grown dramatically in recent years and is beyond simple classification and description (see American Psychological Association, 2005b; Donaldson & Berger, chap. 1, this volume), Table 14.2 provides a sample of common job titles for psychologists specializing in improving quality of work life and organizational effectiveness. The development and application of positive psychological science to build better organizations and to promote worker well-being and performance are common themes that can be used to describe many of the day-to-day work activities that holders of these jobs typically engage in.

TABLE 14.2
Sample Job Titles of Applied Psychologists Specializing
in Quality of Work Life and Organizational Effectiveness

Professor of Psychology, Management, Organizational Behavior, and Industrial Relations
Research Scientist
Research Psychologist

Corporate Vice President, Director, Manager, Staff Member of

Organizational Development, Organizational Effectiveness, Management Development, Human Resources Research, Employee Relations, Training and Development, and Leadership Development

---

President, Vice President, Director of

Private research, consulting companies, and organizations of various types including not-for-profit, human service, educational, government, health care, and community-based organizations

---

Note. Modified version of American Psychological Association Division 14 Sample Job Titles Document (Society of Industrial and Organizational Psychology, 2005c).

Detailed descriptions of the numerous job and career opportunities that now exist for applied psychological scientists specializing in improving quality of work life and organizational effectiveness are beyond the scope of this chapter. However, in an effort to provide readers with a somewhat realistic account of what it would be like to work in some of the most common occupations today, brief descriptions of the jobs of Human Resource Recruiter or Headhunter, Director of Organizational Development, Executive Coach and Leadership Development Expert, Occupational Health Psychologist, External Change Management Consultant, and Human Factors Psychologist are provided next. These brief career summaries illustrate the broad range of research methodologies, statistical tools, and theoretical content that applied psychologists draw on when faced with new and complex organizational issues. This sampling of careers highlights the varied paths and opportunities available to do interesting work, continually develop new skills, and experience the way positive psychology is applied in the "real world" across a broad range of settings.

Human Resource Recruiter or Headhunter

Most people are all too familiar with the traditional job-hunting strategy, which includes perfecting your resume, scouring the want-ads, mailing out cover letters and resumes, and networking with friends and colleagues to get that important first phone call or interview. Increasingly, both organizations and employees are circumventing this traditional process. Instead, companies are saving time and energy by drawing on the skills of professional headhunters and recruiters. These skilled professionals apply psychological methods of psychometrics, testing, and evaluation to find the best qualified candidates and to match them to positions in which they are likely to thrive and excel.

Headhunters are generously compensated for their ability to consistently pick the right person for the right job, and their success is not due to luck, intuition, or a "shotgun" approach in which candidates with varied skills are targeted. The success of headhunters, and their ability make the perfect match again and again, is directly linked to their thorough training in principles of applied psychology. A good headhunter has a tremendous edge, as he or she combines the science of selection with extensive organizational research. This approach leads to a thorough understanding of the hiring organization's culture, strategy, structure, leadership, and characteristics of the job itself. Unfortunately, this type of diligence, or a thorough understanding of both the individual and the organization, is typically lacking on both sides of the traditional job-hunting and selection process.

The headhunter starts with a job analysis to develop a detailed understanding of both the immediate functions of the position as well as the con-

textual environment in which job duties take place. Understanding technical aspects of the position, key aspects of the business, and the vocabulary
of the industry helps to identify prospective candidates and give them a realistic job preview regarding what to expect from a position. Headhunters
often conduct in-depth, face-to-face interviews and focus groups with members of the organization's management and work teams. The goal of these
interactions is to understand key dimensions of the organization's structure, management style, working environment, and business strategy.
Based on this information, the headhunter specifically defines the position's scope of responsibility and identifies required Knowledge, Skills, and
Abilities (or KSAs; American Educational Research Association, American
Psychological Association, & National Council on Measurement in Education, 1999). He or she subsequently compiles and communicates this information back to the organization for additional feedback.

To identify the most qualified candidates, headhunters rely on the science of psychological measurement and assessment to obtain an in-depth
profile of each client's personality characteristics, preferences, behavioral
competencies, and other dimensions of person–organization fit. In addition,
individual interviews are conducted with each client in order to assess experiences, preferences, skills, and integrity. To facilitate the interviewing
process, the headhunter submits summary reports or a "short list" to the
organization covering the final candidates' track records, history, core
traits and values, and an assessment of their potential for overall "fit" with
the organization. Finally, many headhunters assist both parties in conducting the final negotiations concerning compensation, benefits, and other job
characteristics as an impartial, objective outsider. The relationship is not
terminated there, as headhunters often maintain consistent communication
with the placed candidate and his or her manager to identify potential difficulties and facilitate their resolution throughout the adjustment process.
The ultimate goal of the Human Resource Recruiter or Headhunter is to
maximize person–job–organization fit, optimal functioning, and well-being
through rigorous evaluation and selection procedures.

Director, Organizational Development

One of the most difficult problems organizations face is fostering and managing change. Only a small proportion of change efforts actually succeed, a
fact that has led to an entire industry of "fad" change models but also provides unique opportunities to psychologists trained in the area of Organizational Development (OD). An OD Director's work focuses primarily on the
alignment of various interrelated organizational systems. Any large-scale
change effort creates "ripple effects" that impact nearly every aspect of the

organization. For example, human resource systems, including selection processes, job design, rewards and compensation, performance appraisals, and training and development must align with and support desired changes. Less obvious, but no less important, are the changes required in other systems. For example, financial management systems may also need modification through the realignment of budgeting and resource allocation processes to free up needed resources. Management Information Systems (MIS) often need to be modified or redesigned to measure and track new practices and allow access to relevant data. Organizational structure and design may also be altered: Layers of management may be increased or reduced and organizational roles often change. As an OD Director, responsibilities include coordinating with change agents in each of these systems in order to foster alignment among all of these interacting elements of the organization.

An Organizational Development Director may draw on psychological models such as Lewin's force field analysis (Cummings & Worley, 2005; Lewin, 1951) to guide the organization through the change process. A force field analysis involves identifying both internal and external driving forces for change (i.e., a leader's vision, interdepartmental conflict, a changing customer base, competitive pressures, or new product development) as well as restraining forces (i.e., managerial resistance to loss of control, skepticism based on prior failures of change initiatives, or staffing shortages that prevent extensive training). This analysis allows the OD Director to further identify which driving forces may be strengthened, as well as which restraining forces may be eliminated, diminished, or counteracted. Overall, if it appears that driving forces are strong enough to move back restraining forces, the change effort may be feasible and worth pursuing. The next step is the development of a detailed change plan, including implementation tactics designed to move the relevant forces.

OD Directors spend a great deal of their time applying the science of psychology at the individual, team, departmental, and organizational levels of analysis. Job responsibilities are dynamic and multifaceted. Other sample project assignments may include designing and implementing system-wide assessments targeting topics such as organizational culture, climate, or job satisfaction. OD Directors also lead their teams through the process of compiling survey results, defining areas for longitudinal improvement tailored to the organization, and developing a communication plan in order to disseminate the results to multiple audiences. This communication strategy may include creating executive presentations for top management, facilitating town hall meetings with various employee groups, monitoring the content of the company's Web site, and designing monthly newsletters and external press releases.

Executive Coaching and Leadership Development

Executive coaching is a relatively new leadership development intervention that has become an increasingly popular way for organizations to develop their existing leadership capital. Realizing that good leadership is critical to achieving and maintaining high levels of performance, organizations spend billions of dollars annually to internally train and develop their leaders. In an increasingly dynamic and complex global economy, leaders need to be proficient in an ever-larger set of skills, including collaboration, teambuilding, strategy formulation and implementation, communication to a wide variety of stakeholders, and cognitive skills such as problem definition, solution generation, and problem solving. Executives are often promoted into leadership positions based on their superior technical skills, yet success in higher levels of management requires a completely different skill set and leadership style. All too frequently, leaders are given little training or guidance in how to make this transformation. As a result, organizations are increasingly hiring executive coaches, who are generously compensated to help executives develop the skills that are predictive of success at higher levels.

Executive coaching is broadly defined as a one-to-one counseling relationship between the professionally trained coach and a leader. The primary purpose of the relationship may vary, but generally centers around improved organizational performance, leadership development, the improvement of top management team performance, as well as promoting the optimal functioning and well-being of the leader. Executive coaches draw on a range of psychological methods in their work, which is a developmental process that frequently includes on-going phases of assessment, feedback, planning, implementation, and follow-up. Assessments include a wide variety of psychological measurements, including personality and behavioral competencies, hypothetical decision-making scenarios, "stretch" exercises, interviews, and 360° feedback involving peers, teammates, and subordinates. Planning of specific interventions, based on data gathered during this initial assessment phase, is usually a collaborative effort between the executive and coach. Together, the two parties agree on a detailed implementation strategy, which may take place over months or even years, with scheduled follow-ups to assess the executive's progress and to make interim modifications if necessary.

More broadly, psychologists assist organizations in a wide variety of leadership development functions, with formal titles in the areas of Training and Development, Leadership Development, and Managerial Effectiveness. This type of leadership development often includes larger groups of leaders at all levels of the organization and encompasses many activities, including skill building, performance enhancement, career development, and individualized coaching for a manager's change strategy. Tasks may also entail program development to assess current managerial competencies within the organization and identify key internal and external talent needed to achieve a high performing leadership team. In addition, using research on managerial traits and skills as a guide, leadership development may require tailoring existing measures of managerial competencies to the unique culture and context of the organization and the industry. Tools may include questionnaires, interviews, focus groups, and 360° performance assessments, which allow the creation of personalized feedback to each manager, and specially designed surveys to target and track specific competencies by organizational level and department. The results, compiled by work site, can be used to develop a longitudinal leadership development program, where managers are brought together to hear prominent leadership speakers, further assess their own strengths and weaknesses as leaders over time, and develop detailed individualized leadership goals for further development between meetings.

Occupational Health Psychologist

Current demographic and sociological trends have fostered the growth of another emerging area that draws on positive applied psychological science—Occupational Health Psychology (OHP). The National Institute for Occupational Safety and Health (NIOSH) defines OHP as a field concerned with "the application of psychology to improving the quality of work life and to protecting and promoting the safety, health, and well-being of workers" (National Institute for Occupational Safety and Health, 2005). Today's organizations are increasingly comprised of older, more diverse populations, who spend a much longer portion of their lives in the workforce. At the same time, the structure of work itself, and the dimensions of compensation that make work attractive, have undergone significant changes. Improvements in public health, sanitation, and advances in microbiology, together with changes in population demographics and lifestyle, have also contributed to fundamental changes in the workforce. Taken together, these trends have dramatically altered traditional views of workplace health and safety, and have generated a new area of psychology that specifically focuses on ways to maximize worker wellness and productivity.

The major health risks that the American workforce faces have shifted markedly over the last century, from viral and bacterial epidemics to chronic degenerative diseases (e.g., coronary heart disease, cancer). Many current health risks are closely associated with lifestyle factors such as dietary habits, physical activity, and exposure to environmental toxins and stressors. Moreover, the threat of accidents in the workplace can be directly linked to psychological issues such as stress, fatigue, and compliance with safety initiatives. Underlying all of these threats to worker wellness and productivity is the important role of prevention as an effective organizational intervention.

Spanning the areas of clinical psychology, human factors psychology (see below), and industrial and organizational psychology, OHP addresses issues of prevention and intervention through research on a wide range of issues that are broadly associated with health and wellness in the workplace. Specific topics include workplace environment assessments, equal employment opportunities and affirmative action issues, job analyses and training needs assessments, workplace violence, assessment and management of organizational stress, mental health in the workplace, and organizational risk factors for illness. In addition, research in the field examines issues concerning how changing organizational structures and processes influence the health and well-being of workers and their families, and interactions among the work environment, the individual, and work–life balance are frequently addressed. For example, an OHP might study the relationship among occupational stress, safety, and demographic and sociological variables (e.g., race/ethnicity, gender, age, sources of social support). OHPs also work to develop and implement programs to enhance safe work behaviors and prevent or reduce the risk of occupational illness and injury. Using their training in research methods, statistics, and epidemiology, OHPs may also evaluate the social and economic costs of occupational illness and injury, and provide recommendations for how to alter employees' perceptions of health risks and adherence to safety regulations through communication and training.

External Change Management Consultant

As an independent change management consultant, training in applied psychological science opens up opportunities to work with companies in critical transitional periods, such as immediately following a corporate merger or acquisition (M&A). Organizations confront a wide variety of issues, including a changing corporate identity, communication difficulties, human resource problems, and intergroup conflicts in the aftermath of a merger. As a result, organizations often utilize external consultants to guide them through the difficult and potentially painful process of postmerger integration. A background in applied psychological science provides the change management consultant with a theoretical framework for understanding and managing the complicated process of bringing together groups from very different organizations and businesses. Outcomes such as lowered trust, commitment, satisfaction, and productivity, as well as increased absenteeism, turnover, and attitudinal problems, can be mitigated through the application of a broad range of theories in work and organizational psychology.

Prior to the M&A, change management consultants meet with top executives and human resource leaders of both companies, focusing specifically on ways to manage the large-scale integration of one or more organizations and the resulting implications for employees. Transformation initiatives often entail multiple stages of strategy development, interim or transition management, how to align various stakeholders (i.e., employees, stockholders, customers, and vendors) around the new structure and strategy, and training and communication.

Change management consultants draw on various aspects of their psychological training in order to leverage processes of measurement, empowerment, and integration. Involving other people in a change effort is critical, as it helps foster ownership of the change effort among all employees, not just top management. Often, the difference between success and failure in an organizational restructuring may be largely attributed to how many people are integrally involved in its planning and implementation. One of the best ways to give people a sense of ownership is to involve them directly at each stage of the change process. Psychological measurement (including interviews, focus groups, and employee and customer surveys) can therefore be utilized effectively as a change tool, helping the consultant to identify areas of resistance, communicate current priorities, and monitor changes longitudinally.

Data collection and analysis skills provide a number of additional benefits throughout the change process. Quantitative data and/or qualitative open-ended questions and interview content help provide evidence that change is needed to employees who are "on the fence." In addition, results of data collection can help to clarify the purpose and direction of the change effort, by forcing people to consider its specific impact on their work in unambiguous terms. In addition, measurement is a form of communication—it informs people what the organization values and considers most important. Tracking the effectiveness of a restructuring effort communicates to employees that it is important, provides a way to judge how well it is being implemented, and may suggest needed modifications in its design. In turn, this information can be used to identify areas of training and education in order to foster effective leadership prior to, during, and after a merger or consolidation.

Human Factors Psychologist

Human Factors Psychology, or Engineering Psychology as it was once called, is the study of the ways in which employees interact with technological systems. Technology is increasingly a widely prevalent, taken-for-granted characteristic of today's organizations, and employees interact with a wide variety of technological systems, ranging from computer systems, simulations, and complex transportation systems, to hand tools, assembly lines, and systems that monitor nuclear power plants. Human factors psychology applies basic research to both address and prevent existing technological problems, in order to design technological systems that are effective, comfortable, safe, and minimize human error. Through an understanding of the cognitive, social, and physical capabilities and limitations of employees, and by directly applying this knowledge in the design process, psychologists can develop systems that are specifically tailored to employee and organizational characteristics.

Human factors psychology draws on the basic principles of ergonomics, an area of study that focuses on how to design equipment for the workplace that maximizes productivity through minimizing operator discomfort, fatigue, and stress. Through the combination of ergonomic principles and a systems perspective, human factors psychologists work to develop effective interfaces between employees and technology. In order to design the most efficient and productive system possible, psychologists must have a detailed understanding of where the technology will be used, how it will be used, and what other systems it will influence and be influenced by. Therefore, professionals in human factors draw on a broad range of psychological principles, including perceptual processes, cognitive functioning, socioemotional well-being, as well as the physical actions involved in dealing with equipment across varying contexts. Technological implementation often has unanticipated and unintended consequences, which can be minimized with a thorough understanding of employees' needs and the organizational context and systems that surround the technology and its use.

Human factors psychologists often spend a great deal of time learning to understand which groups are most likely to use a product, and what characteristics of the group might influence the way the product is used. For example, products used in stressful contexts such as hospital emergency rooms may be more prone to user error, so a product may need to be modified or designed with additional safeguards in order to take user variations into account. In addition, human factors psychologists may conduct detailed analyses of a complicated task, breaking a longer process into smaller pieces in order to understand how characteristics of each stage of the task might influence product design.

After a product makes it through the preliminary design stage, human factors psychologists often spend time in applied settings to observe employees using the technology and interview them about their experiences. Through watching employees from different user profiles interact with the technology in real-world settings, the psychologist can begin to systematically track potential problems with the design both within and across different organizational contexts. Potential ergonomic difficulties, ease of use, confusion concerning certain aspects of the product or how it fits into a larger task, and sources of resistance can all be identified and explored. Using focus group techniques, human factors psychologists may also bring a group of employees together who interact around the technology, in order to identify coordination issues, common usage problems, and sources of confusion or communication problems concerning how the new technology was designed. This data collection may lead to modifications in the technology to bring actual usage patterns into alignment with the product's design.

CONCLUSION

Work and careers will continue to be among the most consuming and rewarding dimensions of our lives in the 21st century. Applications of positive psychological science now offer great promise for enhancing quality of work life and organizational effectiveness across a wide range of diverse work and organizational settings. Career opportunities as change agents promoting human welfare are plentiful and rapidly expanding. They are also among the most intellectually challenging, personally rewarding, and financially lucrative careers now available to applied psychologists. It is our hope that this chapter has opened up new vistas for you, and possibly inspired you to consider seeking a career niche that allows you to contribute to efforts to promote optimal human functioning and organizational effectiveness in the evolving workplaces of tomorrow.

REFERENCES

American Educational Research Association, American Psychological Association, & National Council on Measurement in Education. (1999). *Standards for educational and psychological testing.* Washington, DC: AERA Publications.

American Psychological Association. (2005a). *Non-academic careers for scientific psychologists: Graduate program in applied psychology.* Retrieved March 8, 2005, from http://www.apa.org/science/nonacad-grad.html

American Psychological Association. (2005b). *Non-academic careers for scientific psychologists: Interesting careers in psychology.* Retrieved March 8, 2005, from http://www.apa.org/science/nonacad_careers.html

American Psychological Society. (2004). Why study psychology? *Observer, 17*(4), 31–35.

Aspinwall, L. G., & Staudinger, U. M. (2003). *A psychology of human strengths: Fundamental questions and future directions for a positive psychology.* Washington, DC: American Psychological Association.

Bligh, M. C., & Meindl, J. R. (2004). The cultural ecology of leadership: An analysis of popular leadership books. In D. M. Messick & R. M. Kramer (Eds.), *The psychology of leadership: New perspectives and research* (pp. 11–52). Mahwah, NJ: Lawrence Erlbaum Associates.

Brinkerhoff, R. O. (2003). *The success case method: Find out quickly what's working and what's not.* San Francisco: Berrett Koehler.

Cameron, K., Dutton, J. E., & Quinn, R. E. (Eds.). (2003). *Positive organizational scholarship: Foundations of a new discipline.* San Francisco: Berrett-Koehler Publishers.

Carr, A. (2004). *Positive psychology: The science of happiness and human strengths.* New York: Brunner-Routledge.

Chapman, L. S. (2004). Expert opinions on "best practices" in worksite health promotion. *American Journal of Health Promotion, 18*(6), 1–6.

Compton, W. C. (2005). *An introduction to positive psychology.* Belmont, CA: Wadsworth.

Cooperrider, D. L., & Avital, M. (Eds.). (2004). *Constructive discourse and human organization: Advances in appreciative inquiry* (Vol. 1). Oxford, England: Elsevier Science.

Cooperrider, D. L., Whitney, L. W., & Stavros, J. (2003). *Appreciative inquiry handbook: The first in a series of AI workbooks for leaders of change.* Bedford Heights, OH: Lakeshore Communications, Inc.

Csikszentmihalyi, M. (2003). *Good business: Flow, leadership and the making of meaning.* New York: Viking.

Cummings, T. G., & Worley, C. G. (2005). *Organization development and change* (8th ed.). Mason, OH: South-Western College Publishing.

Donaldson, S. I. (2004). Using professional evaluation to improve the effectiveness of nonprofit organizations. In R. E. Riggio & S. Smith Orr (Eds.), *Improving leadership in nonprofit organizations* (pp. 234–251). San Francisco, CA: Jossey-Bass.

Donaldson, S. I., Gooler, L. E., & Weiss, R. (1998). Promoting health and well-being through work: Science and practice. In X. B. Arriaga & S. Oskamp (Eds.), *Addressing community problems: Research and intervention* (pp. 160–194). Newbury Park: Sage.

Donaldson, S. I., & Weiss, R. (1998). Health, well-being, and organizational effectiveness in the virtual workplace. In M. Igbaria & M. Tan (Eds.), *The virtual workplace* (pp. 24–44). Harrisburg, PA: Idea Group Publishing.

Everly, G. S., & Feldman, R. L. (1984). *Occupational health promotion: Health behavior in the workplace.* New York: Wiley.

Fennell, K. (2002). *Where are new psychologists going? Employment, debt, and salary data.* Presentation at the Annual Convention of the Midwestern Psychological Association, Chicago, Illinois.

Geringer, M. J., Frayne, C. A., & Milliman, J. F. (2002). In search of "best practices" in international human resource management: Research design and methodology. *Human Resource Management, 41*(1), 5–30.

Hansfeld, Y. (1983). *Human service organizations.* Upper Saddle River, NJ: Prentice-Hall.

Harris, S. (2005). *Best practices of award-winning elementary school principals.* Thousand Oaks, CA: Corwin Press.

Hawkins, D. J., Van Horn, L. M., & Arthur, M. W. (2004). Community variation in risk and protective factors and substance use outcomes. *Prevention Science, 5*(4), 213–220.

Igbaria, M., & Tan, M. (2004). *The virtual workplace.* Harrisburg, PA: Idea Group Publishing.

International Association of Applied Psychology. (2005). Retrieved May 31, 2005, from http://www.iaapsy.org

Kauffman, C., & Scoular, A. (2004). Toward a positive psychology of executive coaching. In P. A. Linley & S. Joseph (Eds.), *Positive psychology in practice* (pp. 287–302). New York: Wiley.

Landy, F. J., & Conte, J. M. (2005). *Work in the 21st century: An introduction to industrial and organizational psychology.* Boston, MA: McGraw-Hill.

Lerner, R. M. (2003). Developmental assets and asset-building communities: A view of the issues. In R. M. Lerner & P. L. Benson (Eds.), *Developmental assets and asset-building communities: Im-*

plications for research, policy, and practice (pp. 3–18). New York: Kluwer Academic/Plenum Publishers.

Lewin, K. (1951). *Field theory in social science.* New York: Harper & Row.

Lopez, S. J., & Snyder, C. R. (Eds.). (2003). *Positive psychological assessment: A handbook of models and measures.* Washington, DC: American Psychological Association.

Nakamura, J., & Csikszentmihalyi, M. (2003). The motivational sources of creativity as viewed from a paradigm of positive psychology. In L. G. Aspinwall & U. M. Staudinger (Eds.), *A psychology of human strengths: Fundamental questions and future directions for a positive psychology* (pp. 257–269). Washington, DC: American Psychological Association.

National Institute for Occupational Safety and Health. (2005). *Occupational health psychology.* Retrieved May 31, 2005, from http://www.cdc.gov/niosh/ohp.html

Pearce, C. L., & Conger, J. A. (Eds.). (2003). *Shared leadership: Reframing the hows and whys of leadership.* Thousand Oaks, CA: Sage.

Preskill, H., & Catsambas, T. (in press). *Reframing evaluation through appreciative practices.* Newbury Park: Sage.

Preskill, H., & Coghlan, A. (2003). *Evaluation and appreciative inquiry: New directions for evaluation, Vol. 100.* San Francisco: Jossey-Bass.

Riggio, R. E. (2003). *Introduction to industrial/organizational psychology* (4th ed.). Upper Saddle River, NJ: Prentice-Hall.

Riggio, R. E., & Orr, S. S. (2004). *Improving leadership in nonprofit organizations.* San Francisco, CA: Jossey-Bass.

Seligman, M. (2003). *Authentic happiness: Using the new positive psychology to realize your potential for lasting fulfillment.* New York: Free Press.

Seligman, M., & Csikszentmihalyi, M. (2000). Positive psychology: An introduction. *American Psychologist, 55*(1), 5–14.

Society of Industrial and Organizational Psychology. (2005a). *SIOP mission statement.* Retrieved May 31, 2005, from http://www.siop.org/siophoshin.htm

Society of Industrial and Organizational Psychology. (2005b). *SIOP guidelines for education and training at the doctoral level in industrial-organizational psychology.* Retrieved May 31, 2005, from http://www.siop.org/PhDGuidelines98.html

Society of Industrial and Organizational Psychology. (2005c). *Building better organizations: Industrial-organizational psychology in the workplace.* Retrieved May 31, 2005, from http://www.siop.org/visibilitybrochure/memberbrochure.htm

Sternberg, R. J. (2003). WICS: A model of leadership in organizations. *Academy of Management Learning and Education, 2*(4), 386–401.

Werner, E. E. (2000). Protective factors and individual resilience. In J. P. Shonkoff & S. J. Meisels (Eds.), *Handbook of early childhood intervention* (pp. 115–132). New York: Cambridge University Press.

15

Preparing for a Rewarding Career Applying the Science of Psychology

Dale E. Berger
Claremont Graduate University

The field of psychology is experiencing a quiet revolution. As shown in chapter 1, the number of PhDs granted annually has more than doubled and the number of Master's degrees has tripled since the 1970s. The growth in careers outside of academia and clinical/counseling has been especially striking, as graduates with training in the science of psychology have established their value in an ever widening array of new settings.

In this chapter we hear applied psychologists provide their own perspectives on their training and career development. Drawing on these and other sources, we consider how graduate psychology programs can facilitate successful applied careers for current and future students, and we offer suggestions for students who wish to prepare for an applied career. An important lesson is that there is a wide variety of exciting new careers for which no discipline can prepare people better than psychology. Yet, we can be even more effective as a discipline if we learn from the experience of psychologists who have already established successful careers in applied areas.

EXAMPLES OF APPLIED CAREERS

How do students prepare for an applied career in psychology and how do they find jobs? For questions like this, it is best to go directly to people who have done it. I asked a variety of psychologists who are working in applied settings to tell me about their career paths. I asked what they thought they might do when they were students, what influenced their choices, how they found their first jobs, what they do in their current position, and what advice they have for students and for faculty. I received a flood of information describing a wide range of experiences. Common threads woven through these experiences allow us to draw general lessons, both for students who wish to enter applied careers and for faculty who wish to help their students with appropriate preparation for these careers. Following are excerpts from some of these accounts.

Katie Fallin, PhD
(Developmental Psychology)
Research Analyst, First 5 LA

First 5 LA is the Los Angeles County Proposition 10 commission. Proposition 10 established a tax of 50 cents-per-pack on tobacco products, which generates approximately $700 million a year to be invested in the healthy development of California's children from prenatal to age 5. Most of the money is distributed to the counties on the basis of population, to be spent with local needs and priorities in mind. Thus, Los Angeles County receives about $200 million each year to allocate wisely in support of children.

Katie says, "In my position as a research analyst, I provide background research and data support to inform the planning and implementation of our funding initiatives; I design and manage contracts with independent research organizations who conduct large-scale, longitudinal evaluations of our funded initiatives; I work closely with outside partners on research projects funded by First 5 LA; and I work with organizations who have received our programmatic grants to assist them with their program evaluations."

Katie goes on to say, "My career path has been one of opportunity and instinct rather than planning ahead. In college I had a vague notion that I wanted to do something having to do with improving the lives of young children but I didn't know how I would accomplish that. I knew that an academic career was not for me because it felt too far removed from children's lives—I think I felt a need to have a more direct impact. Clinical work, on the other hand, felt too 'close'—I knew that I would have a difficult time working directly with children who had clinical issues. Applied psychology offered the right balance."

"Throughout my graduate career I held a part-time research assistant position conducting lab-based research looking at preschoolers' understanding of emotions and emotion regulation. Through this position I learned basic research methods; I presented at conferences, wrote and published articles."

Earlier Katie worked as a nanny for 3 years, she worked in a child-care center as an undergraduate, and in graduate school she worked as a program coordinator for a summer jobs program for high potential, low opportunity teenagers. She goes on to say, "Despite my research and work experiences, I felt as though I didn't have a full understanding of the relationship of research to public policy. In order to fill this gap in my training, I took a 3-month crash course in public policy at the federal level. Through this experience I became more interested in evaluation and intervention research on a large scale."

Katie's advice for current students who are thinking about an applied career is to gain breadth of knowledge and experiences. She says, "Both academic and applied career paths require a strong grounding in research principles, methods, statistics, and psychological science. However, an applied career can require greater breadth of knowledge and experience across a variety of topics and domains than an academic career. For example, in my current position I have worked on projects dealing with child abuse and neglect, early literacy, parent support and assistance, child health and nutrition, breastfeeding, health insurance, child-care quality, as well as program evaluation, nonprofit management, capacity building, and community strengthening."

By following her interests and developing her skills as a scientifically trained developmental psychologist, Katie was well prepared for this position, even though it did not even exist while she was a student.

Douglas Kent, PhD
(Social Psychology)
National Planning and Accountability Leader,
Planning and Accountability Unit,
United States Department of Agriculture

This story began when, as a graduate student, Doug helped a friend with data analysis on a small project for the Westminster Police Department in Orange County, California. The department, facing a problem with new Vietnamese gangs, had initiated efforts to dismantle these gangs. Doug found this fascinating, and took the opportunity to conduct a rigorous evaluation of this program as his required internship experience. The police found Doug's report to be so useful that they asked him to evaluate their domestic violence program. He wrote successful grant proposals to support the creation of a new Office of Research and Planning, which he ran within the police department. With funding from the U.S. Justice Department and state sources, Doug employed four researchers and several interviewers to talk with gang members so he could design a program to debunk what members perceived as gang benefits.

His advice is to take the initiative and create job opportunities: "The best job opportunities are often those that one creates for oneself." Doug has since moved on to his position in Washington, D.C., but the Office of Research and Planning continues to thrive in the Westminster Police Department, currently managed by another psychology graduate student, Julia Jim.

Virtually every police department would benefit from an Office of Research and Planning, even if they do not realize it yet. A psychologist with appropriate scientific training can be the best person to direct this type of office.

Julia Jim, M.A.
(Social Psychology)
Director of Research and Planning,
Westminster Police Department

Julia says, "The department relies on my knowledge of survey research and other research methodology to collect much needed public opinion data and police performance data, and to help interpret these data. I am also responsible for evaluating a grant program on domestic violence. All findings and information are provided to police management and used to make informed decisions. It is rewarding to see my work have such a direct impact on practice so quickly." Julia's advice to students is "Trust your abilities and follow your passions."

Julia is working on her dissertation, planning to use data on actual interactions of police with people arrested for traffic violations. These data will have greater validity than ratings from college sophomores on hypothetical scenarios. Basic research sometimes can best be conducted in applied settings.

Lisa Meredith, PhD
(Social Psychology)
Senior Behavioral Scientist, RAND Corporation

Lisa conducts research on health provider attitudes and behaviors, mental health services, the doctor–patient relationship, and psychological factors in health and health behavior. She has also worked in many other areas including environmental risk perception, psychological consequences of terrorism, smoking cessation, racial/ethnic disparities in health care, and military quality of life. She says "One of the wonderful aspects about working in a nonprofit research organization like RAND is the opportunity to apply my skills as a human behavior expert across a number of different contexts, content areas, and to work with a diverse team of colleagues from both my own and other disciplinary backgrounds."

Even as an undergraduate, Lisa knew that she wanted a career in psychology doing research applied to solving real-world problems of public policy. RAND was a perfect setting for her, and she began her career there as a Research Assistant after she earned her Masters in General Experimental Psychology. She continued to move up through the ranks at RAND as she worked on her PhD in Applied Social Psychology.

Lisa says, "The coursework that I found most useful for my career includes everything I learned about the scientific method, which I find is an advantage that other social scientists do not share with us. I also benefited from learning a variety of different analytic methods. The ability to combine a theoretically driven foundation to a practical problem is what I have found to be most valuable in my day-to-day life."

Lisa condensed her advice to students into a single word: "perseverance." She says, "if you have a sense of what you want to do later in life, then it might take a while to get there and seem a bit challenging, but stick with it. In my experience, even when I deviated slightly from tradition, it always worked out smashingly when 'I did it my way.' Of course, that is not to say that teamwork is unimportant but I believe that everyone should follow his or her convictions."

Robert Lunn, PhD
(Cognitive Psychology)
Senior Researcher,
Owner of his own research consulting firm

Bob entered graduate school with strong statistics, systems training, and computer programming skills, and he sought graduate training in cognitive psychology to enhance these skills. He says, "However, somewhere in my graduate program my focus changed from methodology to science. In practice, being a scientist means using an inherent curiosity, recognizing that something is not consistent with the current explanation, integrating available data with known scientific principles, asking appropriate questions, and converting findings into results that are easily understood." Bob's dissertation on text induced visual fatigue won the James McKeen Cattell award for the outstanding dissertation in psychology in the United States that year.

His first job after graduate school was senior statistician at the consulting firm of JD Power and Associates, where he was promoted to executive director of survey research operations, with responsibility for hundreds of employees. He recently left that position to run his own consulting business.

Bob indicated that all critical events in his career involved people who took time to work with him. He said that without that help and encouragement, he would probably still be a computer programmer. His key advice to students is "Find your mentors; don't expect them to find you. You cannot overestimate the importance of this task. Along these lines, selecting a mentor is a two-way street. Just because you select someone, don't expect them to reciprocate automatically. You grow into a mentoring relationship. It is up to you to earn their respect."

Other advice is to build your skills, and be positioned to take advantage of opportunities. "The key is to be in the right place with the broadest set of job skills. When opportunity knocks, you have to be ready to answer the door." Other advice from Bob is "Take a lot of methodology courses, and keep your notes. You never know when you will be using them again!"

He observed "I think the distinction between 'applied' and 'basic' science is mostly irrelevant because the fundamental product of any scientific endeavor is enhanced understanding. Knowledge does not care about its pedigree."

"To me, the primary distinguishing feature concerning the study of psychology is its cross disciplinary flexibility. Psychologists work with equal ease across different knowledge domains for at least two reasons. They are taught to think as scientists and they receive significant training in research and statistical skills."

A final point from Bob is intriguing: "Future psychology training needs to include a strong emphasis in systems analysis. Systems analysis provides a means of studying and simulating complex systems, orders of magnitude more complex than classical statistical methods are designed to handle. Concepts such as 'feedback loops,' 'lags,' 'system memory,' and 'reservoirs' need to be incorporated into the psychologist's way of thinking. Current psychology training overemphasizes methods based on linear associations. Unfortunately, the world is not linear."

Patricia Winter, PhD
(Social Psychology)
Research Social Scientist, USDA Forest Service

Patricia's research addresses recreation patterns in the public forests (especially those linked to ethnic and racial diversity); communication regarding natural resources; attitudes, values, behaviors and conflicts linked to natural resources; and the social and recreation-related aspects of fire management. Her official duties include all aspects of planning and conducting research, including face-to-face interviews, on-site observations, on-site surveys, archival analysis and synthesis, lab experiments, quasi-experiments in a field setting, mailed surveys, focus groups, and telephone interviews. For example, renovation of a picnic area was guided by her documentation of special needs and desires of different ethnic groups who used the area. Another study drew on persuasion research to guide experiments on the effectiveness of different wording on signs. On a broader scale, she led a socioeconomic assessment of 26 counties in California to provide the four southern California national forests with extensive demographic, historical, environmental, social, and projection information to be used for their forest plan revisions.

Patricia noted that she was not even aware of research opportunities with the Forest Service while she was a graduate student. However, she worked as a researcher in a rehabilitation hospital and taught environmental and social psychology part-time, her special areas of interest. This combination of applied research experience and intimate knowledge of relevant content areas prepared her well for her current career.

Patricia cautioned that there is not just one path to an applied career. Rather, students should seek a wide range of experience in applied settings. She especially recommended developing writing skills, taking statistics and research methods courses, and gaining publication experience. Grant writing is likely to be a useful skill in most applied settings. Networking with faculty and fellow students is important; connections are likely to be useful in the future. However, students and faculty need to understand that an advanced degree is not enough; graduates still must prove their value by applying their knowledge and skills effectively. Work experience in applied settings helps students develop their understanding of how they can contribute most successfully.

Justin Menkes, PhD
(Organizational Psychology)
Organizational Consultant

Justin says: "I have a terrific job, and I've never been happier. I started a company with my former boss. We specialize in executive assessment and work with companies going through mergers and acquisitions, or doing succession planning—so far we've worked with DuPont, Hewlett Packard, and Interbrew. Every day I apply the skills I learned in graduate school—statistics, research skills, evaluation tools."

"As an undergraduate, I had no single professional interest, so I tried everything (this is what I would recommend to others unsure of their path—try everything and talk to everyone. Find out what they are doing, why they do it, and see if you can relate to their choices). My undergraduate major was political science. I graduated and went to work for a congresswoman writing policy. I realized politics was not my future so I tried theater (acting and writing), and teaching. I finally took a counseling position and decided to get my masters in psychology. During my masters I took business courses and realized that psychology in business was an area of special interest to me. When I finished I found a job with a management consulting firm. After 6 months I knew I'd found an interesting niche, and left to get my doctorate. I worked professionally throughout my schooling—but not just for the obvious financial need. I found that the professional experiences profoundly enriched my education. My consulting work slowed my school progress, delaying my graduation by a year or two. But it was worth it. I graduated with an immediate ability to make a living doing what I love."

"A strong foundation in psychology is essential. In graduate school, I constantly revisited the question: 'How does this theory or topic help us be better practitioners confronting the problems of today's business environment?' " He emphasizes, "Essential skills are writing, methodology, and critical thinking."

"My undergraduate program taught me writing skills. My graduate statistics and methods courses gave me tools to build and analyze assessment methodologies. Evaluation courses taught me how to think critically. Organizational behavior courses gave me a broad knowledge of topics in the field, and lessons learned from past research. This is the stuff I use every day."

Heather Brown, PhD
(Social Psychology)
Director of Institutional Research,
Cypress College, California

Heather is a social psychologist with strong interests in education. Among her responsibilities, she is asked to design and direct studies to measure institutional effectiveness, facilitate strategic planning, and respond to state and national organizations and agencies. Importantly, she is asked to anticipate the information, research, and evaluation needs of the college, and recommend research projects based on those needs.

She says, "General skills I use frequently include communicating research in written and oral form to technical and lay audiences, critical thinking skills and problem-solving skills, knowing not to take data at face value, how to examine data from multiple views until you have confidence in the interpretation; and sound research methods, especially in program evaluation and survey research."

She also mentions, "Knowledge of database structures, relationships, and content are very helpful in discussions with IT programmers and front-line staff, who input the data." Heather noted that her teaching experience is important, because it gives her greater credibility with faculty, and a better understanding of the context of her research.

Heather says that as an undergraduate and even as a graduate student, she did not have clear career plans. She assumed she would teach college. About half-way through her doctoral program, she took a part-time position as a Research Analyst in the Research and Planning Department of a local community college. She says, "In retrospect, what I thought then would probably be only a one-year detour turned out to be a key fork in the road for my career path. The IR field has regional, state, and national associations, publications, and resources, which are very helpful to people who are new to the field. Although I didn't know it when I started down the path, there are many career options available to people with IR skills and experience: Director, Dean, Vice President ... even some college presidents began their career in IR. Others may step away from responsibilities on campus to take consulting roles, or to work at state, regional, or national levels in postsecondary education."

Sara Simon, PhD
(Cognitive Psychology)
Project Director,
Integrated Substance Abuse Programs, UCLA

Sara is a cognitive psychologist. She says, "I run clinical trials for testing medications, do training for people in the substance abuse field, and work on imaging studies and international projects with the World Health Organization and for the State Department. The clinical trials are primarily for testing drugs that are thought to affect cognition. My initial involvement always is developing outcome measures, but my major effort is making sure that data collection is done properly and is well-documented. The training and work on projects involves explaining to counselors, health-care workers, and clinicians what cognitive deficits are common with different substances of abuse, and what that means in the context of treatment."

"The skills that I use are mainly research skills. Any of the programs that I run or evaluate are based on asking the right question, collecting data that will answer it, careful documentation, and statistics. I also use my knowledge of cognition. Of particular value is the ability to create a test, particularly a cognitive test that will provide the data needed."

"As an undergraduate, or even a graduate student, I definitely did not expect to work in an applied setting. My heart was set on being an academic.

However, after my post doc when I had a chance either to work in a small liberal arts college or work on a research project using brain imaging, I chose the research project. From there I followed one project and another until I found that I had more data on cognition in methamphetamine abusers than anyone else in the country. While this may no longer be the case, I have been able to use my knowledge to become part of a lot of very interesting projects."

"The upside of applied research is that you really make a difference. Working in clinics, even on cognitive projects, I talk to counselors about ways to mediate cognitive deficits and they immediately try them. I discuss ways to compensate for cognitive problems with substance abusers. The findings from my studies are being used by treatment providers all over the world because people I work with who do training have made it part of their courses."

"The downside is that I am always scrambling for money. The one skill that I didn't learn that would have been of value is grant writing. Almost all applied settings seem to get grant money of one sort or another and it would be a useful skill to emphasize."

Robert Huebner, PhD
(Social Psychology)
Deputy Director, Division of Treatment
and Recovery Research at the National Institute
on Alcohol Abuse and Alcoholism

Bob describes his job and career path as follows. "The FY 2004 budget for the Institute is about $450 million, of which about $112 million is devoted to behavioral research on treatment interventions. The focus of work in my division is treatment and services research. We work with researchers in the field to develop ideas for research studies, help them navigate the grant application process, and monitor grants after awards have been made. More importantly, we synthesize what is known in a particular area and provide guidance to the field on gaps in research knowledge and where we should be going. Our national perspective on what's happening in the field facilitates this endeavor."

"Before joining NIAAA, I was a social science analyst in the Program Evaluation and Methodology Division at the U.S. General Accounting Office (GAO). There I was the project manager on a study on homelessness in the

U.S. requested by the Senate Labor and Human Resources Committee. My training in applied social psychology prepared me well for the research world in Washington, D.C. Especially helpful were my courses in evaluation research, statistics, and survey research. My internship experience was instrumental in learning what can and cannot be done in terms of research in real-world practice settings. I think the biggest thing I took away from Claremont was the idea that you could create opportunities in human service settings. We basically did that at my internship site and I did that again when I moved to the NIAAA from the GAO. It was my suggestion to a project officer at NIAAA that an evaluation be done of a new national demonstration program for the homeless. This suggestion led to a job offer from NIAAA to do just that."

Mariam Manley, PhD
(Social Psychology)
President, PRES Associates (consultants)

Until recently, Mariam was Principal Evaluator for McREL (Mid-Continent Research for Education and Learning). She now has her own consulting organization for which a recent project involved evaluating all Title I and Vocational Programs for the State of Wyoming.

Mariam says, "I regularly conduct literature reviews to identify potential measures and methods for studies that I conduct. I regularly use logic modeling techniques, research design, survey design, do instrument development, and qualitative research methods such as focus groups, interviewing, site visits, and so forth. I'm constantly running univariate and multivariate statistical analyses. As the principal investigator on most of my studies, I am responsible for supervising project staff, research assistants and other less senior staff in data collection, project management, and so forth. Interpersonal skills are perhaps some of the most critical in my line of work, in knowing how to work with clients, how to communicate with them in a meaningful non-academic manner, and how to sometimes facilitate rather tricky political situations. I also regularly serve as a co-investigator with other researchers and so the ability to work jointly and collaboratively is essential."

"Probably though, the most useful skills are my report writing and presentation skills. While I can easily find and hire people who can run high-level statistical analyses, people who can do high-level statistical analysis

AND present such results to laypeople are essential and very difficult to find. What really gets my interest is working in applied settings where I can directly see the relevance of my work. The work is never boring—there are always new projects, and I am always learning."

Maura Harrington, MBA, PhD
(Organizational Psychology)
Director of Consulting Services
and Senior Researcher,
Lodestar Management/Research, Inc.

Maura is responsible for effective development and delivery of external consulting services in her organization, she is a project manager, and she serves as internal expert consultant for specialized tasks, such as client relations, management assistance, theoretical grounding, and data analysis. To broaden her knowledge base and increase her credentials in the business environment, Maura earned an MBA degree as she was working on her PhD program.

Skills that Maura identifies as especially important for her work are the design of research and evaluation, project management, and consulting and communication. Maura says, "What interested me about applied research, particularly in organizations, was the opportunity to use data to identify problems and create solutions that improve the functioning and effectiveness of organizations. I am almost zealous empowering organizations to make data-informed decisions, in turn, effect positive change for all stakeholders."

Vivian Nagy, PhD
(Social Psychology)
Organizational Research Department,
Kaiser Permanente

After earning her PhD in Social Psychology, Vivian worked for the Veterans Administration doing basic health-care research. She found her Kaiser Permanente position through networking with friends as she was seeking a research position in which she could see how the work she did makes a difference in people's lives.

Vivian says, "My job entails collecting data to help managers make decisions or make improvements. Typical projects I work on are patient satisfaction surveys for hospitals and clinics, employee opinion surveys, program evaluation, and 360-degree feedback surveys for leadership development."

"My graduate training did not prepare me completely for the applied work I do at Kaiser Permanente. From graduate school I learned the standard statistics, experimental designs, and how to write up research for publication. All of this background is important, and in my work it is assumed that I know how to do all of this."

"However, other functions that are just as important in my work are:

- to understand what information a manager needs and why;
- develop a research project that will not only meet those needs and but can be easily understood and explained by people without a research background;
- deliver results to managers that clearly indicates next steps for them.

In addition to the fundamental research skills that are taught in graduate psychology, the skills I would emphasize for a position in applied psychology are organizational skills and consulting skills—listening, influence, negotiation, communication, strategic thinking, teamwork, change management, and leadership."

Jeffrey Mercer, PhD
(Social Psychology)
Senior Research Manager,
Microsoft Corporation

Jeff entered graduate school with a strong interest in social responsibility and a deep distrust of established organizations, especially large corporations—he was, and is, something of a modern day Hippie. He was teaching part time when a colleague asked him for help on a consulting project with Toyota Motor Sales. One thing led to another, and Jeff soon was working full time in the strategic research and planning department at Toyota's U.S. headquarters of automotive consumerism—identifying who wants what and why.

In describing his work with Toyota, Jeff says, "When conceptually framing a study, I rely heavily on my theoretical knowledge of social psychology—applying what I know about information processing, attitude formation and change, individual differences, etc. Having a breadth of knowledge and skills is really necessary to be effective in the applied setting. A large portion of my time is spent analyzing data and creating presentations of the findings (in PowerPoint) to management. I constantly work to communicate the results in a way that is meaningful and does not overwhelm or lose the audience—this is a very difficult task.

"I enjoy the work I do far greater than I would have ever imagined. I have been able to create for myself a position that is intellectually stimulating, allows me great freedom, prestige and influence, and compensates me fairly well. My company also supports my development as a research psychologist—sending me to training courses and research conferences. But this was not my knowledge of Corporate America as a graduate student, and Corporate America was the last place I ever thought I would end up."

Jeff collected data for his dissertation within a research project on corporate responsibility that he managed for Toyota. The project included a very large national survey and many focus groups from around the United States. His findings, which include data on the importance of environmental responsibility, were quickly used to guide corporate policy. Recently, Jeff has taken a new position as Senior Research Manager with Microsoft.

LESSONS LEARNED

Let us consider what we can learn from this wide range of experiences. First, we should note that there are thousands of scientifically trained psychologists working in nonacademic settings, and almost any science-based graduate psychology program can find comparable cases. For example, the series "Why study psychology?" in the American Psychological Society's Observer features career path vignettes from a wide range of leading psychology researchers (e.g., APS, Why Study Psychology?, 2004). The American Psychological Association's Science Directorate has published a series of columns on "Interesting Careers" in the monthly issue of *Psychological Science Agenda*, available online at http://www.apa.org/science/psa/psacover.html. Compilations of stories from psychologists employed in many different settings can be found at http://www.apa.org/science/nonacad_careers.html and at http://www.apa.org/monitor/feb01/careerpath.html. Although each person's experience is unique, there are common threads, and both students and faculty can gain beneficial insights from these experiences.

Beginning with lessons for students, the strongest message is to follow your own personal passions. Several professionals noted that it really is true that you can get people to pay you for doing things you want to do; some warned against staying in situations that are uncomfortable, and urged students to be willing to take chances to follow their interests.

It is critical to build skills to support your ability to contribute. You are creating a flexible tool kit, a jack knife that you will be able to use in unforeseen ways. Foremost among these skills is solid grounding in the scientific method and research skills. Core training in the scientific method is fundamental to success for many. Several professionals noted that their special contribution often was asking "How do you know?" or "Show me the data!" in combination with the ability to identify what needs to be learned, to provide the means to obtain relevant information, to analyze and interpret data, and explain findings to decision makers and other stakeholders. Applying the scientific method in field settings is not easy—this is 'hard' science in ways that physics and chemistry are not—but psychologists with appropriate scientific training are uniquely qualified to deal with messy situations. The ability to engage the question "How do you know?" can be critical to success.

Content knowledge includes knowledge of previous research, methodology, and theoretical frameworks in an area of expertise. In applied work, it is often necessary to have content knowledge in more than one area. Breadth is critical, with the ability to develop depth quickly where it is needed. This may imply taking courses outside of psychology. Often creativity is little more than translating an idea from a different area into a new application. Students need to seek exposure to other fields and new ideas.

Communication skills are often a weak link, especially the ability to translate sophisticated statistical and theoretical findings into language that is useful to people who have not had scientific training. Presenting your work at professional conferences is good practice, but it is also good to practice presenting your work to nonacademic audiences. Can you explain your research to your Grandmother or your Aunt Amy?

Field experience is crucial for many reasons. It is important to establish real credibility in your field. If you will be working with teachers, then you should spend time in classrooms, take courses in education, and gain teaching experience. If you will be consulting in business, get some business experience, take courses in management, and participate in networking opportunities. Familiarity with the context and broader system is essential—what are the practical and political constraints, what are the special resources and opportunities? Outsiders are often viewed with skepticism, and it is necessary to demonstrate your value and establish credibility. Conducting research on an applied topic is much easier if you are working from the inside.

Finally, be flexible. Virtually every career history has key turning points where opportunities appeared and career paths changed. Many expressed some surprise along with delight at their good fortune. Of course, good fortune is more likely to come to someone who prepares for it and is proactive. New positions can be developed in many organizations that don't yet know that they need a research psychologist. Do your homework, and be ready with solutions for other people's problems.

Faculty and administrators of psychology programs can also learn important lessons from the experiences of psychology alumni in applied careers. First, consider what we generally do well. Most importantly, we do provide solid grounding in the scientific method. This is fundamental to the success of many of our graduates. The scientific method provides a means to address the question "How do you know?" in messy situations. I believe this is a key advantage we have over our sister disciplines.

Working within the scientific method develops critical thinking skills. An ability to work with logic, formal methods, and theoretical frameworks give psychologists another special advantage.

Training in design and analysis provides the formal tools necessary to implement the scientific method and support critical thinking. Our courses in research design and statistics are often supplemented with advanced quantitative and qualitative methodology courses, giving psychology students an opportunity to assemble a rich methodological toolkit.

Graduate programs generally do a good job teaching scientific writing. Most graduate students have a well-worn *APA Publication Manual*, with writing skills honed in papers, theses, dissertations, and other research projects.

Yet, there are things that graduate psychology programs can do better to prepare our graduates for applied careers. First, it is useful for students to be exposed to disciplines other than psychology. We don't have all of the answers. Other disciplines such as education, management, economics, sociology, and political science are concerned with many of the same issues that concern us. Our graduates will be working with people from these disciplines, and it is important to have an understanding of their knowledge, theories, methodology, and vocabulary. Applied problems are often best approached from several directions at once, using transdisciplinary thinking. Psychology has no monopoly on productive approaches.

The applied world often is more complex than the world of the laboratory. Interactions are rampant; there are feedback loops, political constraints, resource limitations, time imperatives, personnel issues, complex histories, discontinuities, and crises. We generally don't do a good job of preparing graduates for nonlinear systems.

We cannot prepare all graduates to be clones of ourselves. We should do a better job facilitating connections with mentors and experience in applied settings. It is important to note that many applied jobs require experience, information, and skills that faculty may not have. Ways need to be found for students to gain relevant supervised experience from qualified professionals in applied settings. Many well-placed experienced people are willing and even eager mentors for our students, and we need to support those relationships.

We do not always do a good job preparing graduates to communicate complex findings in lay terms, either written or oral. Many professionals indicated that practical communication is a key skill that they developed outside of academia, and that it is a weakness they see in new graduates.

Both students and faculty need a tolerance for ambiguity. It is often the case that no one knows exactly what sort of career a student will develop. A job may not even exist while the student is preparing for it. As we have seen, there are many rewarding career paths in diverse settings for applied psychologists. However, positions for applied psychologists generally are not advertised as such. Organizations often fail to recognize that an applied psychologist is the best person to fulfill a need. Careful career planning and preparation is necessary to assure that psychologists are competitive for their target positions.

ONE APPROACH TO PREPARING STUDENTS TO APPLY THE SCIENCE OF PSYCHOLOGY

How can we provide better preparation for psychology graduates to enter applied fields? I'd like to tell you about one approach. This began in the late 1960s when the Executive Officer for APA, Arthur Brayfield, developed a vision of applying the science of psychology to the public interest. The goal was to improve social conditions through increasing our knowledge of how things really work and disseminating that knowledge to people who can use it to influence policy. With this premise, he established a graduate program in "Public Affairs" Psychology at Claremont Graduate University in Southern California (Brayfield, 1976).

I draw on the Claremont experience because I know it well. I came to Claremont in 1970, and I had the opportunity to chair the graduate psychology program for more than 12 years. My colleagues and I have learned a lot about preparing psychologists for careers in applied settings, and I would like to share some of our experience with you.

Portfolio System. A key feature of our PhD program is a portfolio system for building and documenting appropriate skills and experiences. Preparation of a portfolio can be viewed as planned resume-building. Prior to taking oral exams and beginning a dissertation, each student is required to complete an individualized portfolio of products that focus on career building. Depending on the interests and goals of the student, the portfolio may include items such as publishable research, technical reports, grant proposals, or courses in other disciplines. Every portfolio includes mentored work experience, either working in an applied setting or teaching. Every portfolio also includes a literature review that synthesizes knowledge around a selected issue, which ordinarily will be the basis for a dissertation. Finally, every portfolio includes at least two research tools, such as survey methods, qualitative methods, special computer applications, applied data analysis, or evaluation. Upon completion of the graduate program, the student will have the knowledge, skills, and experience that are needed to compete successfully for desirable employment opportunities. The portfolio process assures that students take a proactive role in preparing themselves for their target career.

Methodology. When we ask our alumni what aspect of their graduate work at Claremont they have found to be most useful on the job, many say that methodological training served them especially well. We offer a wide range of methodology courses beyond the required sequence of statistics and research methods courses. Most students take additional methodology such as program evaluation, qualitative research methods, meta analysis, survey methods, factor analysis, structural equations modeling, multilevel modeling, or multivariate topics. We expect the hallmark of our alumni to be a thorough grounding in methods of inquiry—question framing, research methods, analysis, and presentation.

Research Experience. We aim to have doctoral students involved in research throughout their graduate career. During the first year in the program each student participates in directed research with a faculty member. This often involves working with faculty and a group of students on a project initiated by the faculty. Each student is required to complete an empirical master's thesis, and most complete several additional research projects prior to beginning work on the dissertation. Our students have an average of two conference papers and one professional publication on their resume when they complete the PhD program. This experience pays off when students enter the job market. The great majority of our alumni are in positions where they conduct research themselves or supervise research efforts of others.

Much of the research conducted by students and faculty in our program addresses applied topics or issues motivated by applied questions. This does not mean that the work is atheoretical or limited to a specific problem in a specific setting. Quite to the contrary, applied work is usually driven by a need for a better understanding of the underlying mechanisms that are involved in a problem, and applied research contributes importantly to theory development.

Field Experience. All students are required to complete at least one semester of supervised field work in a setting similar to where they would like to work when they complete the program. They also participate in a seminar where students share experiences, thereby broadening and generalizing their practical experience base. Students who intend to teach are required to gain teaching experience and participate in a graduate seminar on teaching.

Organizations are often willing to pay a student or a small group of students for a specific project. It is not unusual for an internship placement to turn into a permanent job, sometimes a position that the organization didn't realize they needed until they saw what the intern could do for them. We require that a qualified person in the workplace serve as a supervisor/mentor for each student intern to assure that the student gains appropriate experience. The faculty member responsible for the field placement seminar keeps in contact with the field supervisor to monitor the placement.

The list of the benefits of work experience is long, for the students and for the program. Students gain a wealth of informal knowledge about how the work actually gets done. From organizational policies and procedures to office politics, there is practical knowledge that cannot be gained in the classroom. The financial benefits of paid fieldwork can be critically important; many students need to support themselves and perhaps a family. Professional contacts with people and organizations can pay off with employment opportunities. Students with contacts in the field are much more effective at finding and securing rewarding jobs on their own initiative. Students often draw on resources of their workplace to further their own research agenda. With planning and luck, a student may find an issue of interest to the organization that also is suitable for dissertation research or for a portfolio item.

Fieldwork can provide a reality check. Students sometimes discover that a target career is not as attractive as it appeared from the outside. The fieldwork experience allows students to discover a poor fit early enough to be able to make adjustments in their graduate curriculum. Field experience affords students a new, more mature perspective on their graduate studies. Reflection on applied issues can provide ideas for research, and motivation for completing the graduate program. On the other hand, some students discover that they do not need to complete a PhD to attain their personal goals.

The experience that students accumulate in field placements benefits the faculty and other students in the program as well. Discussions in graduate seminars are enriched, and experienced students become informational resources for other students. Our network of working students and alumni particularly benefits students seeking internships and employment.

Students. Most students attracted to a graduate program in applied psychology are likely to have a background in psychology, but some will come from fields such as sociology, nursing, education, management, and information science. About half of the students in our program have been out of school for several years, raising a family or working outside the home. Many sought an applied psychology program because they want to make a contribution to society.

Faculty. In an applied psychology program faculty need to strike a balance between what it takes to advance in their own academic careers and what it takes to help students develop nonacademic careers. Faculty must be involved with students in research and other activities that are unlikely to make important additions to the faculty member's vitae, and at the same time conduct and publish research needed to be tenured and promoted in their college or university.

It is often the case that faculty are more interested in theoretical and conceptual aspects of a problem, while students are more interested in applied aspects. This difference in orientation can sometimes be frustrating for both faculty and students. It helps if faculty recognize that they are not necessarily training their students to be like themselves, but rather they are training students to be effective in the applied workplace. On the other side, it helps if students appreciate the importance of seeking a conceptual understanding that transcends the specifics of even messy situations. The person who knows "how" may always have a job, but the person who knows "why" will be their boss.

Finally, we have learned that applied psychology is intrinsically rewarding for both students and faculty who wish to have a positive impact on society. Most of the problems we face are problems of behavior—how we behave toward each other, our environment, and ourselves. It is gratifying to be able to use special knowledge and skills to engage these problems productively.

CONCLUSION

Psychologists bring special abilities to applied settings, often based on training in the scientific method and the natural connections of psychology to many applied issues. Psychologists are able to use principled methods to separate science from pseudoscience, knowledge from opinion. Over the past generation, psychologists have become remarkably successful at securing a wide range of influential positions where they are able to contribute productively to improving the human condition. Yet, as a discipline we have not always embraced the applied side of psychology. We can do better. With more flexibility and planning, we can be more effective with training and placement. We have a large number of students eager to enter the field, and many more new opportunities can be created if we are proactive. As the world continues to change around us, the success of psychology depends on adapting to this change and capitalizing on opportunities. The opportunities for psychology have never been better; indeed the need has never been greater for scientifically trained psychologists to apply those skills in socially constructive ways.

REFERENCES

American Psychological Association (2001). The career path less traveled. *Monitor on Psychology, 32*(2). Retrieved February 1, 2005, from http://www.apa.org/monitor/feb01/careerpath.html

American Psychological Association. (2004). *Non-academic careers for scientific psychologists: Interesting careers in psychology.* Retrieved February 1, 2005, from http://www.apa.org/science/nonacad_careers.html

American Psychological Association. (2004). *Psychological science agenda.* Retrieved August 17, 2004, from http://www.apa.org/science/psa/psacover.html

American Psychological Society. (2004). Why study psychology? *Observer, 17*(4), 31–35.

Brayfield, A. H. (1976). How to create a new profession: Issues and answers. *American Psychologist, 31*, 200–205.

About the Contributors

Albert Bandura is David Starr Jordan Professor of Social Sciences in Psychology at Stanford University. He is a proponent of social cognitive theory. In this theory, self-development, adaptation, and change are the products of a reciprocal interplay between personal, behavioral, and environmental influences. His book, *Social Foundations of Thought and Action: A Social Cognitive Theory*, provides the conceptual framework and analyzes the large body of knowledge bearing on this theory. His most recent book, *Self-Efficacy: The Exercise of Control*, assigns a central role to people's beliefs in their efficacy in regulating their styles of thinking, motivation, emotional well-being, and accomplishments. He was elected to the presidency of the American Psychological Association, Western Psychological Association, honorary presidency of the Canadian Psychological Association, and to the American Academy of Arts and Sciences and to the Institute of Medicine of the National Academy of Sciences.

Dale E. Berger is Professor of Psychology at Claremont Graduate University. He teaches required statistics courses for psychology graduate students, advanced courses in statistics and data analysis, and the psychology of thinking. His research interests include drinking and driving, and he consults on applied research methods and data analysis. He and his students have developed an Internet site in support of teaching statistics (http://wise.cgu.edu), featuring tutorials with interactive statistics applets. Throughout his career at Claremont, including twelve years as department chair and Dean, he has been a passionate advocate for using the tools and knowledge of social science to address social issues. Professor Berger was recipient of the Western Psychological Association (WPA) Outstanding Teaching Award in 1997 and he served as WPA President 2002–2003.

Michelle C. Bligh is an assistant professor in the School of Behavioral and Organizational Sciences at Claremont Graduate University. Her research interests include charismatic leadership, organizational culture, interpersonal trust, and political and executive leadership. Her recent work has appeared in *The Leadership Quarterly, Journal of Applied Psychology, Leadership, Employee Relations,* and *The Psychology of Leadership: New Perspectives and Research.* Through her work at the Kravis Leadership Institute and the Center for International Leadership, she has helped local and state law enforcement, consulting firms, healthcare organizations, and real estate firms to assess and improve organizational culture, change management, and leadership development.

Christina A. Christie is an assistant professor, Director of the Master's of Arts Program in Applied Psychology and Evaluation, and Associate Director of the Institute of Organizational and Program Evaluation Research in the School of Behavioral and Organizational Sciences at Claremont Graduate University. Her research interests focus on investigating the relationship between evaluation theory and practice and issues related to the development of descriptive theories of evaluation. She has received funding from a variety of sources to evaluate social programs targeting high-risk and underrepresented populations. Dr. Christie co-founded the Southern California Evaluation Association, a local affiliate of the American Evaluation Association and is the former Chair of the Theories of Evaluation Division of the American Evaluation Association. In 2004, Dr. Christie received the American Evaluation Association's Marcia Guttentag Early Career Achievement Award.

William D. Crano is Professor of Psychology at Claremont Graduate University. He received his A.B. from Princeton, and his M.S. and PhD from Northwestern. He has served on the faculties of Michigan State, Texas A&M, and the University of Arizona. He was Program Director in Social Psychology for the National Science Foundation, and served as Liaison Scientist for the Office of Naval Research, London, as a NATO Senior Scientist, and was a Fulbright Senior Research Fellow. He founded the Center for Evaluation and Assessment at Michigan State, and directed the Public Policy Resources Laboratory of Texas A&M. Crano's research is currently funded by the National Institute on Drug Abuse. Crano has written 10 books, which have been translated into three languages, more than 30 book chapters, and more than 200 scholarly articles and scientific presentations. He is the past president of the Society for Experimental Social Psychology, and is a Fellow of the American Psychological Association, the American Psychological Society, and the Society for Personality and Social Psychology. He serves on the Community Influences on Health Behavior review panel for the National Institutes of Health, and has served on the editorial boards of three journals in social psychology and communication.

Deborah Davis received her PhD in social psychology from Ohio State University. She has since taught at Southern Illinois University, Georgia State University, and the University of Nevada, where she has been since 1978. Dr. Davis is also President of *Sierra Trial and Opinion Consultants*, a firm that specializes in trial consulting services such as jury selection, mock juries, witness preparation and others. Dr. Davis has also published on several topics in psychology and law, including witness memory, coerced confessions, issues of sexual consent, and empirical approaches to evidentiary ruling; topics on which she has served as an expert witness in both criminal and civil trials.

Kenneth A. Deffenbacher is currently Regents' Professor and Chair of the Department of Psychology at the University of Nebraska at Omaha. For the past 30 years, his research interests have centered on two related topics, basic research concerning perception and memory for the human face and an area of applied cognitive psychology, where he has been concerned with variables affecting eyewitness perception and memory, particularly the effects of heightened stress, exposure to mugshots, and the relation of expressed confidence of eyewitnesses to their identification accuracy.

Stewart I. Donaldson is Professor and Chair of Psychology, Director of the Institute of Organizational and Program Evaluation Research, and Dean of the School of Behavioral and Organizational Sciences, Claremont Graduate University. Dean Donaldson continues to develop and lead one of the most extensive and rigorous graduate programs in applied psychology. He has taught numerous university courses, professional development workshops, and has mentored and coached more than 100 applied psychology graduate students and working professionals during the past decade. Dean Donaldson has also provided organizational consulting, applied research, or program evaluation services to more than 100 different organizations. He has been Principal Investigator on more than 20 extramural grants/contracts to support applied psychology research and scholarship. This represents more than $3,500,000 of extramural funding that he has secured to support applied psychology graduate students, colleagues, and research programs. Dr. Donaldson has published a wide range of peer-reviewed articles and chapters on applied psychology topics. His recent books include *Evaluating Social Programs and Problems: Visions for the New Millennium* (Erlbaum, 2003; with Michael Scriven), *Applied Psychology: New Frontiers and Rewarding Careers* (Erlbaum, 2006; this volume with Dale E. Berger and Kathy Pezdek), and a forthcoming book on *Program Theory-Driven Evaluation Science: Strategies and Applications.* He has been honored with Early Career Achievement Awards from the Western Psychological Association and the American Evaluation Association.

Howard S. Friedman is Distinguished Professor of Psychology at the University of California, Riverside. He directs a large project on health and longevity across the life-span, funded by the National Institutes on Health. Professor Friedman is author of more than 100 influential scientific articles and chapters in leading books and journals and was named a "most-cited psychologist." He has written textbooks on *Health Psychology* (Prentice Hall, 2002) and *Personality* (Allyn & Bacon, 2006) and has edited several scholarly volumes in health psychology. He also wrote the comprehensive trade analysis entitled *The Self-Healing Personality: Why Some People Achieve Health and Others Succumb to Illness* (1991/2000), and he served as Editor-in-chief of the award-winning *Encyclopedia of Mental Health* (Academic Press). Dr. Friedman is a thrice-elected Fellow of the American Psychological Association (in Personality and Social Psychology, Health Psychology, and in Media Psychology) and an elected Fellow of the American Association for the Advancement of Science and the Society of Behavioral Medicine. Professor Friedman has received the *Distinguished Teaching Award* from the University of California, Riverside, and the Western Psychological Association's *Outstanding Teaching Award.* Friedman is a magna cum laude graduate of Yale University and was a National Science Foundation Graduate Fellow at Harvard University, where he received his doctoral degree.

Patricia M. Greenfield received her PhD from Harvard University and is currently Professor of Psychology at UCLA, where she is a member of the developmental group and directs the Children's Digital Media Center. Her central theoretical and research interest is in the relationship between culture and human development. She is a past recipient of the American Association for the Advancement of Science Award for Behavioral Science Research, and has received teaching awards from UCLA and the American Psychological Association. She has held fellowships at the Bunting Institute, Radcliffe College, the School of American Research, Santa Fe, and the Center for Advanced Study in the Behavioral Sciences, Stanford. Her books include *Mind and Media: The Effects of Television, Video Games, and Computers* (Harvard, 1984), which has been translated into nine languages. In the 1990s she coedited (with R. R. Cocking) *Interacting with Video* (Elsevier, 1996) and

Cross-Cultural Roots of Minority Child Development (Erlbaum, 1994). She has done field research on child development, social change, and weaving apprenticeship in Chiapas, Mexico since 1969. This cumulative work is presented in a new book entitled *Weaving Generations Together* (SAR Press, 2004). A project in Los Angeles investigates how cultural values influence relationships on multiethnic high school sports teams. Another project entitled "Bridging Cultures" utilizes research on cross-cultural value conflict between Latino immigrant parents and the schools as the basis for teacher and parent training.

Diane F. Halpern is Professor of Psychology and Director of the Berger Institute for Work, Family, and Children at Claremont McKenna College. She has won many awards for her teaching and research, including the 2002 Outstanding Professor Award from the Western Psychological Association, the 1999 American Psychological Foundation Award for Distinguished Teaching and the Outstanding Alumna Award from the University of Cincinnati. She is the author of more than 350 journal articles and book chapters and several books including *Thought and Knowledge: An Introduction to Critical Thinking* (4th ed., 2003), and *Sex Differences in Cognitive Abilities* (3rd ed., 2000). Her most recent effort is co-edited with Susan Murphy, entitled *From Work–Family Balance to Work–Family Interaction: Changing the Metaphor* (2004). Diane has served as president of the Western Psychological Association, the Society for the Teaching of Psychology, and the Division of General Psychology of the American Psychological Association. Currently, she is Past-President of the American Psychological Association.

Robert R. Hoffman is a Senior Research Scientist at the State of Florida Institute for Human and Machine Cognition and also an Adjunct Instructor at the Department of Psychology of the University of West Florida in Pensacola. He received his B.A. (1972), M.A. (1974) and PhD (1976) in Experimental Psychology at the University of Cincinnati. He was a Postdoctoral Associate at the Center for Research on Human Learning of the University of Minnesota (James J. Jenkins, Sponsor) and following that was on the faculty of the Institute for Advanced Psychological Studies and the Department of Psychology at Adelphi University on Long Island. He joined the Institute for Human and Machine Cognition in 1999. He is a Fulbright Scholar, a McMicken Scholar, an Honorary Fellow of the British Library, and a Fellow of the American Psychological Society. He has received awards for outstanding teaching and scholarship and grants from a variety of sources. He serves on editorial boards of a number of journals and has edited or co-edited seven scholarly volumes and four Special Sections (or issues) of technical journals. His research has garnered him a designation as one of the pioneers of Expertise Studies. Hoffman has been recognized on an international level in at least five disciplines—remote sensing, meteorology, experimental psychology, human factors, and artificial intelligence. Within psycholinguistics, he has made pioneering contributions, having founded the journal *Metaphor & Symbol*, and having written extensively on the theory of analogy. That work bridged to the field of artificial intelligence, where he has also contributed extensively to the emerging notions of Human-Centered Computing. In the area of human factors he has made special contributions on the methodology of knowledge elicitation, workstation and display design for environmental science, and is currently helping to forge the Theory of Complex Cognitive Systems.

Shirley Lam is a PhD student at Claremont Graduate University where she studies applied cognitive psychology. Specializing in the study of memory and suggestibility, her research has primarily focused on eyewitness memory and autobiographical memory. She also works as a research analyst at IAG Research, where she has worked on projects assessing the effectiveness of television advertisements. Other research interests include marketing research, information processing of advertisements, statistics and research methodology. In addition, Shirley is an outdoor sports enthusiast and enjoys spending much of her free time traveling to different countries to mountaineer, rock climb, and kayak.

Elizabeth F. Loftus is Distinguished Professor at the University of California, Irvine. She holds positions in the Department of Psychology & Social Behavior and the Department of Criminology, Law & Society. She received her PhD from Stanford University. Since then she has published 20 books and more than 400 scientific articles and chapters. She is past president of the American Psychological Society, and was twice elected president of the Western Psychological Association. She has five honorary doctorates for her research on memory. She was recently elected a member of the National Academy of Sciences and the Royal Society of Edinburgh (Scotland's National Academy).

Stuart Oskamp earned his PhD at Stanford and is Professor Emeritus of Psychology at Claremont Graduate University. His main research interests are in the areas of attitudes and attitude change, environmentally responsible behavior such as recycling and energy conservation, intergroup relations, and social issues and public policy. His books include *Attitudes and Opinions* (2005), *Applied Social Psychology* (1998), and *Social Psychology: An Applied Perspective* (2000). He has been elected president of the American Psychological Association Division of Population and Environmental Psychology and the Society for the Psychological Study of Social Issues, and he has served as editor of the *Journal of Social Issues* and the *Applied Social Psychology Annual* and is the founding editor of the *Claremont Symposium* series of volumes.

Kathy Pezdek is Professor of Psychology at Claremont Graduate University where she has served on the faculty and directed the PhD program in Applied Cognitive Psychology since 1981. She is a cognitive psychologist specializing in the study of visual memory. Dr. Pezdek's extensive research has focused on the study of eyewitness memory, autobiographical memory and memory for real world scenes. She is a Fellow of the American Psychological Society, has served as the editor of the journal, *Applied Cognitive Psychology*, and serves on the editorial board of numerous journals spanning cognitive psychology, developmental psychology, and psychology and law. Dr. Pezdek frequently testifies as an expert witness in the area of eyewitness identification.

Robert Rosenthal received his A.B. (1953) and PhD (1956) in psychology from UCLA and is a diplomate in Clinical Psychology. From 1957 to 1962 he taught at the University of North Dakota where he was director of the PhD program in clinical psychology. From 1962 to 1999 he was at Harvard University where he was first a lecturer on Clinical Psychology (1962 to 1967), Professor of Social Psychology (1967 to 1995), Chair of the Department of Psychology (1992 to 1995), and Edgar Pierce Professor of Psychology (1995 to 1999). Since 1999 he has been Distinguished Professor at the University of California at Riverside and Edgar Pierce Professor of Psychology, Emeritus, Harvard University. Professor Rosenthal's research has centered for nearly 50 years on the role of the self-fulfilling prophecy in everyday life and in laboratory situations. For more than 40 years he has been studying the role of nonverbal communication in (a) the mediation of interpersonal expectancy effects and in (b) the relationship between members of small work groups and small social groups. He also has strong interests in sources of artifact in behavioral research and in various quantitative procedures. In the realm of data analysis, his special interests are in experimental design and analysis, contrast analysis, and meta-analysis. His most recent books and articles are about these areas of data analysis and about the nature of nonverbal communication in teacher–student, doctor–patient, manager–employee, judge–jury, and psychotherapist–client interaction. He is Co-Chair of the Task Force on Statistical Inference of the American Psychological Association. He has lectured across the world and received numerous honors and awards. Professor Rosenthal is the author or co-author of some 400 articles in the journals and books of his field and is the author, co-author, editor, or co-editor of 25 books.

P. Wesley Schultz is Professor of Psychology at California State University, San Marcos. His research interests are in applied social psychology, particularly in the area of sustainable behavior. Recent books include *Social Psychology: An Applied Perspective* (Prentice-Hall, 2000), *Psychology of Sustainable Development* (Kluwer, 2002), and *Attitudes and Opinions* (Erlbaum, 2005). His current work focuses on social norms, and the importance of social norms in fostering sustainable behavior. He has worked on projects for a variety of organizations, including the Environmental Protection Agency, National Institutes of Health, U.S. Department of Justice, and the California Integrated Waste Management Board.

Stanley Sue is University Distinguished Professor of Psychology and Asian American Studies at the University of California, Davis. He received a B.S. degree from the University of Oregon (1966) and the PhD degree in psychology from UCLA (1971). From 1981 to 1996, he was a Professor of Psychology at UCLA, where he was also Associate Dean of the Graduate Division. From 1971 to 1981, he was Assistant and Associate Professor of Psychology at the University of Washington. He also served as Director of the National Research Center on Asian American Mental Health, an NIMH-funded research center, from 1988 to 2001, and was Director of the Asian American Studies Program from 1996 to 2001 at UC Davis. His research has been devoted to the study of the adjustment of, and delivery of mental health services to, culturally diverse groups. His work documented the difficulties that ethnic minority groups experience in receiving adequate mental health services and offered directions for providing culturally-appropriate forms of treatment. In recognition of his work in this area, Dr. Sue has received a number of awards including most recently the 2003 APA Distinguished Contributions to Applied Research Award; 2003 Stanley Sue Award, Society of Clinical Psychology (APA Division 12); and 2005 Lifetime Achievement Award, California Psychological Association.

Sherylle J. Tan is a developmental psychologist and the associate director of the Berger Institute for Work, Family, and Children at Claremont McKenna College. Dr. Tan received her bachelor's degree in psychology from the University of California, Irvine and completed her master's and PhD in psychology with an emphasis in applied developmental psychology at Claremont Graduate University. Since arriving at the Berger Institute, she co-created and coordinated *Take a Kid to College Day*, which is now in its second year, and manages and coordinates the Institute's research projects. Prior to coming to the Berger Institute, Dr. Tan was the Evaluation Specialist for the Los Angeles Child Guidance Clinic. She was the primary evaluator for two early intervention, preschool-based mental health programs funded by First 5 LA (Proposition 10 Commission): the award-winning Building Block program and the Stepping Up to School Readiness program. She has also worked as a consultant for several nonprofit agencies.

Philip G. Zimbardo is internationally recognized as the 'voice and face of contemporary psychology' through his widely seen PBS-TV series, *Discovering Psychology*, his media appearances, best-selling trade books on shyness, and his classic research, *The Stanford Prison Experiment*. Zimbardo has been a Stanford University professor since 1968, having taught previously at Yale, NYU, and Columbia University. He is now an Emeritus Professor, having retired two years ago, but hired back the next day, part time, to teach a unique course, *Exploring Human Nature: A Life-Changing Experience*. He has been given numerous awards and honors as an educator, researcher, writer, and service to the profession. Among his more than 350 professional publications and 50 books is the oldest current textbook in psychology, *Psychology and Life*, now in its 17th edition. His current research interests are in the domain of experimental social psychology, with a scattered emphasis on: social influence, mind control, cults, violence, terrorism, evil, torture, hypnosis, time perspective, the normal bases of madness, shyness, political psychology, and perceptual biases. Earlier research centered around equally diverse domains, from exploratory, sexual and drug behavior in albino male rats, to social affiliation in college students, dissonance, persuasion and attitude change, police confession techniques, and some others. Noted for his personal and professional efforts to actually 'give psychology away to the public', Zimbardo has also been a social-political activist, challenging the Government's wars in Vietnam and Iraq, as well as the American Correctional System. Although disliking administrative tasks, Zimbardo managed to be President of the Western Psychological Association, twice, President of the American Psychological Association, and is currently the newly elected Chair of the Council of Scientific Society Presidents (CSSP) representing 63 scientific, math and technical associations with 1.5 million members.

Author Index

Subject Index